THE U.S. LEGAL SYSTEM

MAGILL'S CHOICE

THE U.S. LEGAL SYSTEM

Volume 1

Acquittal–Jurisdiction

Edited by
Timothy L. Hall
University of Mississippi Law School

SALEM PRESS, INC.
Pasadena, California   Hackensack, New Jersey

Parts of this publication previously appeared in *American Justice* (1996), *Magill's Legal Guide* (1999), and *Encyclopedia of the U.S. Supreme Court* (2000), all copyrighted by Salem Press, Inc. New material has been added.

Library of Congress Cataloging-in-Publication Data
The U.S. legal system / editor, Timothy L. Hall.
  p. cm. — (Magill's choice)
Includes bibliographical references and indexes.
  ISBN 1-58765-189-0 (set : alk. paper) — ISBN 1-58765-190-4 (v. 1 : alk. paper) — ISBN 1-58765-191-2 (v. 2 : alk. paper)
  1. Law—United States—Popular works. 2. Justice, Administration of—United States—Popular works.   I. Title: US legal system. II. Title: United States legal system.   III. Hall, Timothy L., 1955- IV. Series
  KF387.U15 2004
  349.73—dc22

                                                      2003027174

First Printing

PRINTED IN THE UNITED STATES OF AMERICA

CONTENTS

CONTENTS

Publisher's Note

The U.S. Legal System surveys legal terminology, procedures, and structures of the United States in articles that emphasize basic legal concepts and offer practical guidance to how the federal and state legal systems work. It focuses on the mechanics, officials, and institutions of the system, rather than on the substance of specific laws and court cases. Its articles examine such subjects as the training, practices, and ethics of attorneys and law firms; the organization, procedures, and workings of the various kinds of courts; the selection, work, and ethics of judges; the responsibilities of other court officers, such as bailiffs, clerks, and reporters; the selection and use of juries; types of laws; and types of law enforcement bodies—from city police to U.S. marshals. Many articles in the set cover basic legal concepts, such as double jeopardy, due process, and reasonable doubt. All this information is covered in the 256 essays and 5 appendices of *The U.S. Legal System.*

Within these volumes, readers will find answers to questions such as these:

- Through what procedures do arrested persons go?
- What are the ethical responsibilities of attorneys?
- How are the federal and state judicial systems connected?
- How are judges selected?
- What do "Miranda rights" mean to an arrested person?
- What is meant by *habeas corpus*?
- How are plea bargains arranged?
- How does the adversary system affect the way court cases are tried?
- How does the juvenile justice system differ from the adult criminal justice system?
- What procedures are involved in appealing court verdicts?
- What is meant by "jury nullification"?
- What does "precedent" have to do with case law?
- What is the difference between hearsay and nonhearsay evidence?
- What makes Louisiana's legal system unique among the fifty states?

The legal system affects citizens and residents of the United States in ways big and small. From buying and selling property to purchasing insurance to paying parking tickets and receiving Social Security payments, persons of all walks of life must contend with and, sometimes, challenge the legal workings of American society. Legal terms and expressions that may at first glance seem foreign often describe the most common legal practices in which millions engage. Torts, negligence, and breaches of contract, for example, are offenses defined by and handled under civil law. Crimes such as robbery, assault and battery, and murder are handled under criminal law and are dealt with by the criminal justice system. *The U.S. Legal System* covers both kinds of law.

Designed to be easy to use, this alphabetically arranged two-volume set contains 256 essays, which range in length from 250 to 3,000 words. Its highlights include 50 articles on such subjects as types of attorneys and attorney practices and conduct; more than 35 articles on courts and judges; more than 75 articles on judicial procedural matters, ranging from "Acquittal" to "Witnesses"; more than 30 articles on constitutional issues, categories of law, and law codes, ranging from "Administrative law" to "United States Code"; 11 articles on types of law-enforcement officers and agencies; 20 articles on aspects of arrest and arraignment; 20 articles on sentencing and punishment; 6 articles on military law; and additional articles on other legal matters.

Organization of Essays

Every essay begins with a concise definition of the subject at hand. The main body of each essay develops its subject, placing it within the context of the legal system as a whole and supplying historical background and case examples to illustrate points. Essays on procedural matters, such as "Arrest" and "Summon," trace each step of the procedures. Fifty textual sidebars, tables, and charts supplement the information in the essays themselves.

All essays conclude with lists of alphabetically arranged cross-references to related topics that are the subjects of other articles in the set. Essays of more than one thousand words in length contain Suggested Readings sections that direct readers to up-to-date books and articles on the subject.

Appendices and Indexes

Appendices at the end of the second volume include an extensive bibliography, a glossary of basic legal terminology keyed to the essays in the set, a list of state bar associations, an annotated list of legal resources, and an annotated list of legal-assistance organizations. The last three appendices contain contact information and addresses for the organizations; this information includes the addresses of more than 150 Web sites that were valid in late 2003. Following the appendices are an index to essay topics by category, an index to court cases, and a detailed subject index. The Categorized Index lists all the essay topics, with starting page numbers, under 33 topical headings, ranging alphabetically from "Arrest, Arraignment, and Indictment" through "Verdicts." Most articles are listed under more than one category heading.

In sum, then, *The U.S. Legal System* offers four tools for finding articles on specific subjects:

- Alphabetical arrangement of topics
- Cross-references within articles
- Categorized Index
- Subject Index

Most of the articles in *The U.S. Legal System* were originally published in *Magill's Legal Guide* (1999), with the rest coming from Salem's award-winning *American Justice* (1996) and *Encyclopedia of the U.S. Supreme Court* (2000) sets. All these articles have been carefully reviewed and updated as necessary. All the bibliographies have been extensively updated.

The editors of Salem Press wish, once again, to thank the nearly one hundred scholars who wrote the essays used in this project. We are especially grateful to Professor Timothy L. Hall, of the University of Mississippi Law School, for serving as the project's Editor.

CONTRIBUTORS

William Allison
University of Saint Francis

Earl R. Andresen
University of Texas at Arlington

W. Dene Eddings Andrews
Indiana State University

John Andrulis
Western New England College

Mary Welek Atwell
Radford University

Thomas E. Baker
New Mexico State University

Michael L. Barrett
Ashland University

Paul Bateman
Southwestern University School of Law

Patricia A. Behlar
Pittsburg State University

Bernard W. Bell
Rutgers Law School, Newark

Sara C. Benesh
University of New Orleans

Alvin K. Benson
Brigham Young University

Joseph M. Bessette
Claremont Mackenna College

Steve D. Boilard
Independent Scholar

Michael W. Bowers
University of Nevada, Las Vegas

Fred Buchstein
John Carroll University

Michael H. Burchett
Limestone College

Ann Burnett
North Dakota State University

William H. Burnside
John Brown University

Maxwell O. Chibundu
University of Maryland School of Law

Thomas Clarkin
University of Texas

Douglas Clouatre
Kennesaw State University

William H. Coogan
University of Southern Maine

Edward R. Crowther
Adams State College

Rebecca Davis
Georgia Southern University

Robert N. Davis
University of Mississippi Law School

Thomas E. DeWolfe
Hampden-Sydney College

Steven J. Dunker
Northeastern State University

William V. Dunlap
*Quinnipiac University School
of Law*

C. Randall Eastep
Brevard Community College

Loring D. Emery
Independent Scholar

John Fliter
Kansas State University

Michael F. Flynn
*Nova Southeastern University Law
School*

Phyllis B. Gerstenfeld
*California State University,
Stanislaus*

Marc Goldstein
Independent Scholar

J. Kirkland Grant
Touro College School of Law

Michael Haas
University of Hawaii at Manoa

Timothy L. Hall
*University of Mississippi Law
School*

J. Denny Haythorn
Whittier Law School

Murray Henner
Hofstra University

Steve Hewitt
University of Saskatchewan

Arthur D. Hlavaty
Independent Scholar

Kenneth M. Holland
University of Memphis

John C. Hughes
Saint Michael's College

Robert Jacobs
Central Washington University

Dwight Jensen
Marshall University

Ronald Kahn
Oberlin College

Marshall R. King
Maryville University at St. Louis

Theodore P. Kovaleff
Independent Scholar

Michele Leavitt
North Shore Community College

Thomas T. Lewis
Mount Senario College

Michael A. Livingston
Rutgers-Camden School of Law

William Shepard McAninch
*University of South Carolina School
of Law*

Dana P. McDermott
Independent Scholar

Bruce E. May
University of South Dakota

Linda Mealey
College of St. Benedict

Diane P. Michelfelder
Utah State University

Fred H. Miller
University of Oklahoma College of Law

Mark C. Miller
Clark University

William V. Moore
College of Charleston

Charles H. O'Brien
Western Illinois University

Erin Gwen Palmer
Independent Scholar

Gordon A. Parker
University of Michigan, Dearborn

Bruce G. Peabody
University of Texas at Austin

Oliver B. Pollak
University of Nebraska at Omaha

Christina Polsenberg
Michigan State University

William L. Reinshagen
Independent Scholar

Thomas J. Roach
Purdue University, Calumet

Stephen F. Rohde
Independent Scholar

John Alan Ross
Eastern Washington University

Paul F. Rothstein
Georgetown University School of Law

Joseph R. Rudolph, Jr.
Towson State University

Michael L. Rustad
Suffolk University Law School

Kurt M. Saunders
California State University, Northridge

Rose Secrest
Independent Scholar

Elizabeth Algren Shaw
Kitchen, Deery & Barnhouse

R. Baird Shuman
University of Illinois at Urbana-Champaign

David M. Siegel
New England School of Law

Donald C. Simmons, Jr.
Mississippi Humanities Council

Christopher E. Smith
Michigan State University

Roger Smith
Independent Scholar

David R. Sobel
Provosty, Sadler & deLaunay

Susan A. Stussy
Neosho County Community College

William A. Taggart
New Mexico State University

Leslie V. Tischauser
Prairie State College

David Trevino
Ohio Northern University

Dean Van Bibber
Fairmont State College

William T. Walker
Chestnut Hill College

Annita Marie Ward
Salem-Teikyo University

Marcia J. Weiss
Point Park College

Richard L. Wilson
*University of Tennessee at
    Chattanooga*

INTRODUCTION

Law in the United States is an elaborate, interconnected system of rights and responsibilities. There are laws to tell us what we may do and what we may not. There are also law enforcement agents charged with seeing that we do not ignore the demands of law. Legal rules and procedures also exist to respond to the almost endless variety of disputes in which individuals find themselves with other people, with large institutions such as corporations, and with the law itself. Particular servants of the legal system, such as courts and judges, devote countless hours to the management and resolution of these disputes. Citizens, however, even though frequently affected by law, may be unaware of the law's presence in particular aspects of their lives. Even when they encounter the law in some tangible sense, they may only be aware of a small part of the larger legal system. *The U.S. Legal System* is designed to provide a broader context for understanding how the web of laws, legal procedures, and legal actors affects our lives.

In referring to a "system" of law, however, one must be cautious. Law—in spite of its apparent formality—is often a patchwork affair. It springs from sources as varied as the United States Congress, state legislatures, and local city councils, and its creation may be prompted by concerns variously momentous or trivial. In the spring of 2003, for example, while federal lawmakers debated whether the president of the United States had misrepresented the grounds for waging war against Iraq over the previous year, five Georgia legislators proposed a law that would make it a crime for a restaurant in the state not to serve sweet tea. This latter proposal, no doubt intended as an act of levity, nevertheless highlights the reality that American law can address a spectrum of subjects virtually as wide as the interests of the men and women who create it.

During the twentieth century, American law witnessed explosive growth, as lawmakers at every level seized on the possibilities of legal rules and processes to address the problems of contemporary American life. Consequently, today, scarcely any aspect of life escapes the law's gaze. Legal regulations superintend matters as varied as how the food we eat is prepared, what kind of education we should receive, and how our final remains should be interred. The law requires us to seek permission before we drive a car, put up a fence, sell a glass of wine in a restaurant, or fish for trout in a stream. Laws superintend both the amount of pollution that a factory may inflict upon the environment and, at least in many localities, whether we may burn the leaves of autumn in our backyards. High and low, the law finds its objects. Law makers at every level of government in the United States create each year enormous numbers of legal rules, and scarcely have these rules taken their places in law books before new rules appear to supplement or replace them.

Laws, once created, must be enforced and interpreted. Here, again, those who seek to find some grand scheme of organization in American law are destined to be discouraged. No single law enforcement agency has responsibility for enforcing all laws in the United States. The traffic cop and the game warden, the Federal Bureau of Investigation or Secret Service agent and the state highway patrol officer—all these labor to see particular portions of the law enforced. None of them have carte blanche to arrest every law breaker. Frequently their efforts at law enforcement overlap and sometimes even conflict. These various law enforcement personnel respond to different superiors and have different spheres of authority. Similarly, no single court—not even the United States Supreme Court—has responsibility for interpreting all laws. The Supreme Court, for example, interprets federal laws, treaties, and other legal regulations, as well as the U.S. Constitution, but consciously avoids making definitive pronouncements concerning the meaning of state and local laws. These latter have their own interpreters, and the interpreters do not invariably speak with a single voice. A corporation, for example, that does business in many states, will often find itself subject to different legal requirements in each state, and different interpretations by different courts of even requirements that appear the same.

Thus, talk of a single, all-encompassing legal "system" is liable to be seriously misleading, conjuring up images of coordination when there is often something more like cacophony. If American law were a house, it would be many roomed, with different architects constantly planning new additions without significant coordination among themselves and a multitude of construction contractors busily expanding floor space without a single set of plans. The great American jurist, Oliver Wendell Holmes, once noted that "the law of the law has not been logic, but experience," and this dictum applies with equal force to the U.S. legal system. It is not a creature of logic but of life, and a host of living experiences that have given it its present shape. In fact, it might even be more appropriate to speak of American legal "systems," to emphasize the multiple creators, interpreters, and enforcers of law in the United States, and the frequently disorderly character of the legal order they attempt to create and sustain.

It is possible, however, to overstate law's haphazardness. The Congress and the local city council generally act with awareness of each other, and the law's many interpreters follow common guidelines in trying to make sense of legal complexities. Furthermore, the agent of the Federal Bureau of Investigations and the highway patrol officer for the state of Alabama may wear or carry different badges, but law enforcement work in all its various incarnations has common features and—especially by virtue of the U.S. Constitution—common limits. Consequently, the community of those who make and interpret and enforce law in the United States is quite broad, but its fellow-laborers are not strangers to one another, and the products of their respective labors share many family resemblances.

Relying on the similar features of legal rules and procedures in a variety of contexts, *The U.S. Legal System* provides an introduction for lay readers to law in the United States. It centers attention especially on the everyday life of the law and the kinds of legal matters most likely to be encountered by readers. Moreover, the articles in *The U.S. Legal System* devote primary attention to descriptions of the how the law works, rather than on what the law commands in a particular area. In the main, the articles presented here focus more on law's processes than its substance, more on its players than its principles. Readers may not discover here a list of prohibited drugs ("controlled substances"), for example. But they will learn what happens to the individual arrested for drug possession. They may not find detailed guidelines for ethical behavior by attorneys, but they will be able to locate a general discussion about how lawyers charge clients for the work they perform.

Legal procedures thus take a central place in the articles that follow. What happens in the course of an arbitration or an arraignment or an appeal? Where does one turn to lodge a complaint against an attorney who has behaved improperly? What can citizens do to reverse the effect of a court decision they believe to have been wrongly rendered? These and many other questions about the law's processes will find answers in the pages that follow. Readers will find information here about a variety of courts and other legal institutions that influence and seek to manage the life of the law. Without, perhaps, finding an answer to every legal question, they will find a resource for discovering the way that law operates in this country.

For those readers seeking, then, insight into the law's working, *The U.S. Legal System* will be a valuable resource. Yet, the law is not some abstract force, operating apart from the actions of human agents. Law in the United States is not just a matter of rules and regulations, but of people and jobs. The law has a face—many faces, in fact—and this reference volume is intended in part to picture these faces.

A vast assortment of individuals tend to legal affairs in the United States, since the law is a major employer in this country. Millions of Americans labor to create, enforce, and sometimes frustrate the operation of law. Even if we were to take the advice of the character from William Shakespeare's play, *Henry VI, Part II* (1590-1591), and "kill all the lawyers," the law would still do a brisk business and would employ innumerable agents to carry out its work. Charles Dickens observed in his novel *Bleak House* (1852-1853) that the one great principle of English law was to "make business for itself," and at least some observers would be happy to apply this judgment to American law. From the legislator in the state capitol who votes for the passage of a bill, the traffic cop who writes a speeding ticket, and the lawyer who looks for a technicality to get a client off, the law as a field of occupation has an almost insatiable appetite for new workers. Its apprenticeships are many and varied: police academies, law schools, and court reporting institutes, for example. All these tributaries, and hundreds of others, feed the demands of the legal system for employees, and no book about the American legal system would be complete if it did not introduce readers to the many human faces of the law: law enforcement personnel, judges, lawyers, and court reporters being just a few of the legal laborers described in the pages that follow.

Those citizens who are not law's officers and agents are frequently its objects, since law touches the lives of individuals in myriad respects. Those who encounter the law frequently feel powerless, as though they have fallen into the path of some juggernaut and can neither turn it aside nor escape its relentless operation. *The U.S. Legal System* is intended to combat this sense of powerlessness by helping readers understand the operation of the law as it affects their lives. It aims to answer at least some of the questions that ordinary citizens are likely to face as they encounter the legal system. Of course, the answers to these questions are not intended to replace the advice of an attorney when individuals face particular legal problems. These problems generally turn on specific circumstances that require the expertise of a lawyer to evaluate, and so readers should not neglect to seek the advice of an attorney when they have specific legal difficulties. Nevertheless, *The U.S. Legal System* may help individuals recognize when they have a problem requiring professional consultation and help them, as well, to prepare for the consultation itself by becoming more aware of the kinds of issues their problem may raise.

In compiling the articles that follow, Salem Press has solicited the expertise of many scholars across the country. The law is too vast an enterprise to be comprehended in its details by a single mind, and no single author—certainly not the present editor—can hope to equal the combined knowledge represented among the many contributors to *The U.S. Legal System*. Along with Dr. R. Kent Rasmussen, the project editor for this series of volumes, I have attempted to assemble a series of articles that will thoroughly introduce readers to the many aspects of the legal system in America. In addition, the editors have labored to see that the information presented is in its most current form—no small effort since the one unchanging feature of law in the United States is that it relentlessly changes. The result, I hope, is a collection of reference articles that will be useful to all those readers seeking some guidance in understanding the vast enterprise that is the United States legal system.

—*Timothy L. Hall*
University of Mississippi Law School

The U.S. Legal System

ACQUITTAL

Legal and formal certification of the innocence of a defendant who has been charged with a crime

An acquittal automatically follows a determination through legal process that a defendant is innocent of the charged crimes for which he or she has been tried. An acquittal can result when the jury finds a defendant not guilty, when a judge determines that there is insufficient evidence in a case, or by dismissal of indictments by the court. Once an accused person has been acquitted of crimes, that person may not be lawfully prosecuted a second time for the same crime. If such prosecution were to take place, it would place the defendant in double jeopardy of losing life, liberty, or property, which is in violation of common law and of the U.S. Constitution and state constitutions.

Typically, protection against double jeopardy extends to any prosecution associated with the same act or acts. For example, if an individual has been acquitted of a charge of using a weapon to commit murder, the defendant cannot be retried for any assault committed on the alleged victim. However, when a trial is terminated because of a procedural defect, the defendant is not protected by the rule against double jeopardy. Thus, the defendant can be prosecuted again on the same charge or on related charges. In most states, no degree of procedural error on the part of the state can justify acquittal of a suspect whose conviction is sure based on the evidence. In addition, no evidence can be excluded for reasons of procedural error provided that the procedural error does not affect the confidence that can be safely vested in the evidence.

A motion for a judgment of acquittal can be made prior to submission of the case to the jury, at the close of all the evidence presented before the jury, or after the jury has been discharged. If the evidence is insufficient to produce a conviction, the defendant or the court may request a judgment for acquittal before the case is turned over to the jury. If a motion for judgment of acquittal is made at the close of all the evidence, the court can choose to reserve a decision on the motion, submit the case to the jury, and decide on the acquittal either before or after the jury returns a verdict. After the jury returns a verdict of guilty or is discharged

without having returned a verdict, a motion for judgment of acquittal may be made or renewed within a specified time frame
(usually fourteen days) after the jury is discharged. In order to
make a motion for judgment of acquittal after the jury has rendered its verdict, it is not necessary that a motion was made prior
to the submission of the case to the jury.

—Alvin K. Benson

See also Appeal; Damages; Defendants; Directed verdicts; Dismissal; Double jeopardy; Jury nullification; Reasonable doubt;
Trials; Verdicts.

ADMINISTRATIVE LAW

Body of law that deals with the powers and procedures of adminis
trative agencies; it includes judicial review of agency actions

Administrative agencies implement and interpret government
policies at the federal and state levels. Agencies are granted these
responsibilities by the legislative branch of government. These
agencies have the power of discretionary authority when implementing laws made by the legislature. The executive branch of
government also maintains control over administrative agencies
by its authority to set budget priorities for programs and through
executive appointment of agency directors.

In order for administrative agencies to implement policy successfully, they must have discretion and enforcement authority.
Without the power of enforcement, an agency cannot perform its
mission. Administrative agencies fulfill their policy implementation obligations by adjudication, rule making, and other similar
functions. The concept of administrative law developed from several sources, including both constitutional law and common law
(law that is accepted although generally unwritten). Agencies
promulgate policy through policy initiatives which they develop
themselves. The rules and regulations enforced by agencies are
created to control the functions and activities of private citizens
and companies that operate within the jurisdiction assigned to
each agency.

Enforcement of these rules and regulations is also carried out by the agencies. Violations of administrative law, either by individuals or by companies, are dealt with by the agency responsible for the law. Agencies can impose fines and sanctions, deny benefits, and perform inspections or audits to ensure compliance. The aggrieved party can seek redress for agency actions through an agency hearing or through the judicial process with the courts. During an agency hearing, an aggrieved party can retain legal counsel and is entitled to fair and impartial due process throughout the proceedings. These hearings are similar to regular court hearings in that careful documentation, pleading, rulings, objections, evidence, and the verdict are all recorded in the event the case is appealed to the judicial system.

Administrative law is intended to guard against abuses of agency power and thereby to provide justice for society at large as well as for individual participants in the case at issue. The three major areas of administrative law are rule making, adjudication, and judicial review. Each of these areas continues to define the direction and authority of administrative law. The ability to combine management, legal, and political considerations is critical in resolving problem areas in administrative law.

See also Attorney types; Attorneys, United States; Attorneys general, state; Defendants; Legislative counsel; Paralegals.

ADVERSARY SYSTEM

System in which individual parties play the leading role in discovering and presenting evidence at trials, what has come to be known as the adversary system has predominated in the United States but criticisms of the way it works have been mounting

In contrast to many European systems, the American legal system has often been described as adversarial rather than inquisitorial in nature. In inquisitorial systems, judges play an active role in investigating the truth of matters and in rendering decisions accordingly. In adversarial, or adversary, systems, however, judges play a role more like a referee at a sporting event in which the parties are the athletes.

Adversary Versus Inquisitorial Systems

An adversary system implicitly trusts that parties with opposing interests are motivated to discover and present all of the facts relevant to the dispute. Indeed, it is generally in the parties' best interest to do so. A system of adversarial justice therefore places chief responsibility on the parties to gather the facts supporting their cases and to present these facts at trial. In most cases, parties interview witnesses in advance, in search of those favorable to their causes. Although judges—and in some jurisdictions, even jurors—may question witnesses, parties choose which witnesses testify; they also conduct the main questioning of these witnesses. If a case requires expert testimony, the parties pay for, prepare, and call as witnesses experts who support their positions. In cases involving juries, judges in the adversary system mainly ensure that the fight between two parties remains fair. The jury decides a verdict based on the evidence presented by the competing parties. In cases without juries, judges add to their refereeing duties the work of pronouncing winners and losers. It is expected that they will do so impartially, after the parties have presented to them all relevant evidence.

In contrast with an adversary system, an inquisitorial system places on judges the chief role in discovering and developing evidence in a case. Parties to a matter may disclose to a court relevant evidence, such as documents and witnesses with knowledge of pertinent facts. Judges, however, call and question witnesses. Parties are allowed to question the witnesses at trial, along with the questioning conducted by the judge, but are generally not allowed to interview witnesses in advance of their appearance at a trial. Instead of receiving testimony from expert witnesses paid by the parties, inquisitorial systems tend to rely upon experts chosen by the court, often from nationally recognized panels of specialists in particular areas.

Modifications of the Adversary System

Although the American system of justice remains adversarial in important respects, it has increasingly adopted practices more consistent with inquisitorial systems. In part, this transformation stems from recurring criticisms of the adversary system: for example, that zealous advocates conceal or distort the truth to advance the causes of their own clients. Modern discovery rules, which require parties in both civil and criminal cases to provide each other with information about cases in advance of trial, have attempted to abolish "trial by surprise" or "trial by ambush." Additionally, modern legal ethics rules prevent attorneys from permitting their clients and witnesses to lie in court. "Rambo litigation tactics," the modern nickname for unfair litigation practices by lawyers bent on winning at all costs, face increasing scrutiny. Lawyers who engage in such practices are increasingly likely to be punished by courts. Furthermore, judges in some matters, especially family law matters and those involving especially complex issues, increasingly take active roles in managing the preparation of cases for trial and in encouraging parties to settle their disputes.

These changes have not, however, subdued other criticisms of the adversary system. In particular, critics maintain that the system's reliance on professional advocates (lawyers) who vary in ability and motivation threatens the quest for truth and the likelihood that cases will yield just results. Since most of the preparation and presentation of cases lies within the hands of advocates, these critics maintain, inequality in their abilities or motivations will inevitably distort the capacity of courts to discover the truth. Similarly, parties with differing economic assets may have differing abilities to investigate their claims and support them by proof. These criticisms have continued to produce suggestions that the American legal system be redirected toward procedures relying less on the skill of advocates or the wealth of parties, and more on courts committed to an active role in discovering the truth.

Adversarial Ethics

A corollary of the adversary system is its reliance upon lawyers who play the role of advocates for the interests of their clients. Questions arise about what ethical rules should bind these advocates. For example, should they be given leave to pursue any ends necessary to help their clients to prevail without being held responsible for those ends, or should they be held morally accountable for the objectives of their clients and be severely constrained in the means by which they pursue these objectives? The American legal profession, basically committed to the adversary system of justice, has nevertheless attempted to moderate adversarial zeal in some respects. For example, modern principles of legal ethics stipulate that a lawyer's representation of a client does not necessarily mean the lawyer endorses the client's aims. Nevertheless, the same principles prohibit lawyers from helping clients pursue fraudulent or illegal objectives.

Rules of legal ethics also require lawyers to maintain their clients' secrets in many cases, even when such secrets involve matters the lawyers themselves might find morally objectionable. However, these rules provide exceptions to the normal principles of confidentiality when sufficiently important interests are at stake. For example, in most jurisdictions lawyers cannot remain silent when they know their clients or witnesses have committed perjury in court. Furthermore, in most jurisdictions lawyers who know their clients are poised to commit crimes that may seriously injure or kill other persons are permitted to disclose this information when it is necessary to prevent the crimes. Additionally, courts have increasingly placed limits on excessive zealousness in the pursuit of a client's cause. Modern procedural and ethical rules prohibit litigation tactics designed simply to harass opponents or delay proceedings. Such rules attempt to tame at least some of the adversary character of the adversary system.

—Timothy L. Hall

Suggested Readings

General treatments of American law containing discussions of the adversary system include Lawrence M. Friedman's *American Law: An Introduction* (rev. ed. New York: W. W. Norton, 1998), Robert A. Kagan's *Adversarial Legalism: The American Way of Law* (Cambridge, Mass.: Harvard University Press, 2001), and Jay M. Feinman's *Law 101: Everything You Need to Know About the American Legal System* (New York: Oxford University Press, 2000). The adversary system is defended in Stephan Landsman's *The Adversary System: A Description and Defense* (Washington, D.C.: American Enterprise Institute, 1984) and is criticized in Marvin E. Frankel's *Partisan Justice* (New York: Hill and Wang, 1980). A more balanced approach is Jay Tidmarsh's *Complex Litigation and the Adversary System* (New York: Foundation Press, 1998). The late twentieth century saw many thoughtful inquiries concerning the role of lawyers as advocates of their clients' causes. The most vigorous champion of an aggressively partisan role for lawyers has probably been Monroe Freedom, who stated his position forcefully in *Lawyers' Ethics in an Adversary System* (Indianapolis: Bobbs-Merrill, 1975). Charles Fried made a similar case in "The Lawyer as Friend: The Moral Foundations of the Lawyer-Client Relation," in *Yale Law Journal* 85 (1976). For an investigation of whether lawyers practicing within the adversary system can be morally praiseworthy, see the essays in *The Good Lawyer: Lawyers' Roles and Lawyers' Ethics*, edited by David Luban (Totowa, N.J.: Rowman & Allanheld, 1983).

See also Attorney confidentiality; Cross-examination; Discovery; Effective counsel; Evidence, rules of; Judges; Juries; Lawsuits; Officers of the court; Perjury; Public interest law; Trials; Verdicts; Witnesses.

ADVISORY OPINIONS

Judicial decisions issued about hypothetical cases, usually at the request of a legislative or executive branch of government to determine the constitutionality of proposed legislation

Advisory opinions allow legislatures and executive officials to determine issues of constitutionality before proposed legislation is enacted. Although these opinions are commonly issued by some state and many foreign courts, the U.S. Supreme Court stated that the federal courts will rule only on actual controversies and not on hypothetical issues.

The prohibition on advisory opinions from U.S. federal courts dates from very early in U.S. history. On July 18, 1793, President George Washington sought an advisory opinion from the Supreme Court regarding the interpretation of the 1778 Franco-American Treaty. On August 8, 1793, the justices of the Court wrote a letter to formally decline to provide the requested advice, citing separation of powers concerns. Chief Justice John Jay stated that the justices were "judges of a court in the last resort" and should refuse to issue opinions except as a result of normal litigation undertaken by real parties in an actual conflict.

The first chief justice of the United States, John Jay, could never have imagined how important the role of the Supreme Court in American government and society would become. (Collection of the Supreme Court of the United States)

This ruling reinforced the independence of the federal courts and reaffirmed the attorney general's role as legal adviser to the president. However, this prohibition does not apply to the states, and some state constitutions do allow the state courts to issue advisory opinions.

—*Mark C. Miller*

See also Attorney general of the United States; Judges; Judicial review; Opinions; Reporters, Supreme Court; Standing.

AFFIDAVITS

Sworn statements given voluntarily and witnessed by authorized persons that are used in court proceedings that do not involve cross-examination

The medieval word from which the term "affidavit" is derived means "he who has made an oath." This meaning has changed little through the years. Affidavits, commonly used in courtroom proceedings throughout much of the world, are written statements given voluntarily and sworn before magistrates or other persons recognized by the courts, often notary publics.

Such statements must be signed by affiants attesting to the veracity of their statements in the presence of a person authorized to administer the oath. Such people must also sign the affidavits they administer. They usually affix their official seals to such documents as well. Both parties must be present at the signing to assure the authenticity of the signatures.

Affidavits are used only in situations that do not require cross-examination, inasmuch as parties employing these documents usually are not present in court during hearings and other such procedures.

The crucial difference between affidavits and depositions is that although depositions are taken outside the courtroom much as affidavits are, the person being deposed is cross-examined during the deposition, which is then put in final form to be signed and witnessed in the same manner as affidavits. Affidavits are often used to itemize losses in civil actions or as a means of discovery. Providing affidavits does not exempt witnesses from subsequent courtroom appearances during the course of a trial, nor does it exempt witnesses from appearing before a grand jury that is examining a case relating to which affidavits have been executed. Often the presentation of af-

---

AFFIDAVITS ARE USED WHEN

- Witnesses live far from the site of a trial
- Testimony is needed from a seriously ill person
- Appearing in court would create an undue hardship
- Appearing in court might jeopardize a witness's safety

fidavits eliminates the need for witnesses to appear in court, but there is no guarantee of that.

Affidavits cannot be used to try issues raised by the pleadings in a courtroom procedure. Witnesses from whom affidavits have been obtained can be subpoenaed if the court considers it necessary to secure additional testimony from them. Such witnesses may be called to give testimony in person during a trial.

Signing an affidavit in the prescribed and legal manner attests only to the truthfulness of the information it contains. If it can be shown that witnesses have willfully distorted or withheld pertinent facts, they may be prosecuted for perjury, one of the most serious charges that can be leveled against a witness.

The convenience of affidavits makes them valuable in the legal system, although they have obvious limitations, the most notable of which is that they preclude cross-examination. In some cases, depositions provide more effective means of obtaining information from witnesses who for one reason or another do not appear in court.

—*R. Baird Shuman*

See also Cross-examination; Depositions; Evidence, rules of; Notary publics; Perjury; Subpoena power; Testimony.

Age of majority

Particular age at which citizens are considered to be legally adults; the age was traditionally twenty-one years but has been regarded as eighteen since the 1970's

According to European legal tradition, children were considered adults at age twenty-one. When the United States was founded, this principle was generally assumed but was never stated in the U.S. Constitution. The only age requirements stipulated were those involved in holding federal office, which varied from twenty-five for representatives to thirty-five for the U.S. president.

When Americans reach the age of majority, as determined by their state of residence, they are entitled to own property and engage in financial transactions and can be held legally responsible for their signature on documents. Throughout U.S. history, however, only these basic rights have been guaranteed. The age of consent for other activities varies widely from state to state.

The age at which people may marry with parental consent varies from as low as twelve to as high as eighteen, although the marriage age without parental consent is eighteen in most states. The maximum age of compulsory education is usually sixteen, but it is as high as eighteen in some states. Motor vehicle license age requirements vary from fourteen to eighteen.

This situation was altered dramatically in the 1970's, at least partially as a result of controversy over the Vietnam War. Critics objected that eighteen-year-olds could be drafted to fight in the war but could not vote for or against the officials who made war policy. The result was the Twenty-sixth Amendment to the U.S. Constitution, ratified in 1971, which prohibited all states from denying the vote to citizens eighteen years of age or older. After the amendment became law, most states quickly lowered their legal age of majority to eighteen.

A number of controversies remained, however. Among them was the legal age for purchase of alcoholic beverages. When Prohibition was repealed by the Twenty-first Amendment in 1933, states were given full rights to regulate alcohol. The age of purchase varied among the states from eighteen to twenty-one years. In the wake of the Twenty-sixth Amendment many states lowered the drinking age to eighteen years old. In 1984, however, the U.S. Congress passed a law denying highway funds to states with drinking ages under twenty-one, and the Supreme Court upheld this law as constitutional. As a result, all states raised the drinking age to twenty-one. However, the power to regulate alcohol still remains with the states.

A more complex issue involves the age of majority and how it relates to the rights of minors. Complications have arisen when authorities have decided to try minors as if they were adults, making them subject to full adult criminal punishment. Complications may arise in respect to marriage among minors and the responsibilities of parents under eighteen years of age.

—*Marc Goldstein*

See also Competency; Criminal records; Family law practice; Juvenile criminal proceedings; Legal guardians; Probation, juvenile; Trial publicity.

AMERICAN BAR ASSOCIATION

Professional organization of attorneys that has sought to maintain high educational and ethical standards in the legal profession and has contributed significantly to shaping the American sense of justice

The development of the legal profession and the laws on which it is based occurred almost contemporaneously. Prior to the American Revolution, disputes were generally heard by laymen. "Attorneys" were often laymen who were tradespeople. Throughout most of the seventeenth century, lawyers were widely deemed to be individuals of poor reputation and moral character. They were viewed with suspicion by those in the more powerful strata of society. The law and lawyers were of little consequence to the majority of citizens, having little if any impact on their everyday existence.

With the dawn of the eighteenth century, the social milieu of the colonies began undergoing subtle change. Concepts of education as well as the founding of various educational institutions such as Yale, Columbia, and Princeton began changing the appearance of various professions. Newspaper publication was initiated in the colonies. Communication both within and among the colonies was vastly improved with the implementation of a government position, deputy postmaster general for the colonies, which significantly improved the exchange of information. Commerce flourished and property rights became central to the implementation of a merchant class and upper-class values. There was then a need for seasoned attorneys and judges. The reputation of those practicing law improved, as there were more disciplined, educated professionals expounding the rule of law.

Establishment and History of the ABA

Against this background, the first bar association of any kind was established in the colonies in New York in 1745. Others soon followed. Ironically, as the stature of the bar improved, the justice system itself came under increasing attack. Simeon E. Baldwin, a member of the Connecticut Bar Association, proposed that the Connecticut Bar Association form a committee under its auspices to investigate the formation of a national bar. This committee of senior lawyers concluded that such an association was desirable and circulated a letter which included a proposal that a body of delegates, representing the profession in all parts of the country, should meet annually for a comparison of views and friendly intercourse.

The first meeting was attended by one hundred lawyers from twenty-one states on August 21, 1878, in Saratoga Springs, New York. They determined to coordinate themselves as the American Bar Association and appointed committees to draft a constitution and by-laws. The constitution, which was adopted, states the primary objectives of the association in Article I. Its object was to "advance the science of jurisprudence, promote the administration of justice and uniformity of legislation throughout the union, uphold the honor of the profession of the law and encourage cordial intercourse among the members of the American Bar."

The organization's first president was James O. Broadhead of Missouri. The American Bar Association began with 289 members representing twenty-nine states. The association established a number of standing committees: on jurisprudence and law reform, judicial administration and remedial procedure, legal education and admission to the bar, international law, publications, and grievances. In early years, the association focused more on technical aspects of legal administration than on controversial social and economic public policy issues. Improvement of the law was a goal; revolutionary reformation and political polarization were not.

The early years of the American Bar Association found an organization struggling to establish itself among individual attorneys and local and regional bar associations as the representative of the profession. Focus was on organizing, building personnel, and determining policies. One of the major accomplishments in these early years was the establishment of the Association of American Law Schools for the sole purpose of improving legal education. Eventually the connection between the ABA and the AALS was broken, with the AALS maintaining an independent existence, overseeing the quality of legal education.

The Twentieth Century

In 1936, the ABA was completely reorganized. Focus shifted from an autonomous association of individuals to an association of limited autonomy operating within the framework of a house of delegates, representation of state and local bar associations, and respected juridical groups which maintained all powers relating to the administration and organization of the ABA.

In 2003 the ABA had more than 410,000 members, who represented all fifty states and the District of Columbia. It was said to be the largest voluntary organization in the United States. The association is far more complex than at its initiation, yet it still maintains many of the same goals. The goals continue to be met through an interplay of standing committees and special committees with operating units and sections. The mission of the ABA is to be the national representative of the legal profession, serving the public and the profession by promoting justice, professional excellence, and respect for the law. These goals are reflective of a more activist ABA, which plays a significant and vocal role in public and political discussions.

—*Murray Henner*

Suggested Readings

Overviews of various bar organizations include Glenn R. Winters, *Bar Association Organization and Activities: A Handbook for Bar Association Officers* (Ann Arbor, Mich.: American Judicature Society, 1954). For a history of the American Bar Association, see Charles Warren, *A History of the American Bar* (Buffalo, N.Y.: W. S. Hein, 1990), and Edson R. Sunderland, *History of the American Bar Association and Its Work* (1953). For an in-depth discussion on the role of the ABA in formulating policy and law, see *The ABA in Law and Policy: What Role?* (Washington, D.C.: Federalist Society for Law and Public Policy Studies, 1994). Also, see *ABA Compendium of Professional Responsibility Rules and Standards*. Chicago: Center for Professional Responsibility, American Bar Association, 2001.

See also Attorney confidentiality; Attorney types; Attorneys as fiduciaries; Bar associations; Bar examinations and licensing of lawyers; Grievance committees for attorney discipline; Judicial appointments and elections; Judicial conduct code; Law schools; Model Rules of Professional Conduct; Paralegals; Pro bono legal work; Unauthorized practice of law; Unethical conduct of attorneys.

Amicus curiae BRIEFS

Written briefs by persons or organizations that are not parties to the litigation in question

An *amicus curiae* ("friend of the court") brief gives an opportunity to people who may be affected by the decision of a particular case, but are not a party to the case, to influence the reasoning process that will lead judges to a decision. An *amicus curiae* brief explains rational arguments as to how and why a case should be decided a certain way. The judges or justices are not under any obligation to follow the line of reasoning set forth in the *amicus curiae* brief. *Amicus curiae* briefs are often filed in appeals that may affect a large category of people in the United States, such as cases dealing with broad public policy matters. These briefs may be filed only with the written consent of all parties or by permission of the recipient court.

See also Class action; Litigation; Public interest law; Supreme Court, U.S.

AMNESTY

General pardon made by government to persons who have been convicted of, or may be prosecuted for, a crime

Amnesty is a government action that grants immunity from prosecution to an identified group of people for a specified criminal offense. The term is derived from the Greek word meaning "oblivion," which is appropriate, because amnesty involves the "forgetting" of an offense. Although accused individuals do not have to exchange information or testimony to receive amnesty, they are expected to abide by all laws in the future. In some cases grants of amnesty are conditional, requiring a loyalty oath or community service. The difference between amnesties and pardons is not well defined, but amnesties are typically granted to persons before prosecution has taken place, while pardons are usually granted to persons after their trial and conviction.

In the United States the power to grant amnesty usually resides in the chief executive. Governors usually possess the power to grant amnesties for violations of state law. At the federal level, both the president and Congress can grant amnesties. The president's authority derives from Article II, section 2 of the U.S. Constitution, which gives the president the "Power to grant Reprieves and Pardons for Offences against the United States, except in cases of Impeachment." Congress may grant amnesties under the terms of the "necessary and proper" clause found in Article I, Section 8 of the Constitution. The U.S. Congress does not have the power to limit or place conditions on any presidential amnesties.

Presidents have generally granted amnesties in situations involving actions undertaken in protest against government policies. In 1795 President George Washington granted amnesty to participants in the Whiskey Rebellion, which was essentially a revolt against excise taxes. In 1865 President Andrew Johnson offered most ex-Confederates amnesty if they agreed to take a loy-

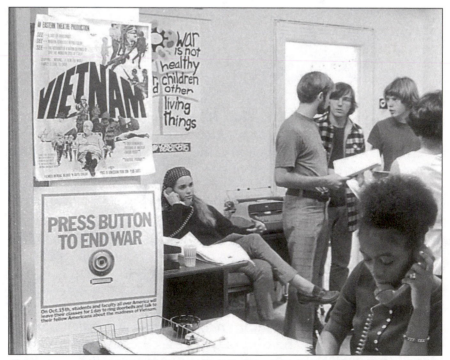

There was such widespread opposition to American involvement in the Vietnam War that President Gerald Ford was moved to offer amnesty to young men who had refused to serve in the military. (Library of Congress)

alty oath to the Union. These examples reveal the intent behind most amnesties: to end divisive conflicts within American society in order to achieve reconciliation and domestic tranquillity.

President Gerald R. Ford's 1974 decision to offer amnesty to individuals who had refused to serve in the Vietnam War illustrated both the confusion surrounding the meaning of the term "amnesty" and the political calculations involved in granting it. As late as March, 1974, Ford declared that draft evaders had to be tried in the nation's courts. However, upon succeeding President Richard M. Nixon as president the following August, Ford was advised by his cabinet officers that an amnesty program would speed the nation's recovery from the war. In addition, the American public would regard Ford as a conciliator, which would improve his political standing. Later that same month, Ford announced that draft evaders would have the opportunity to earn their reentry into American society. He called his proposal clemency rather than amnesty on the grounds that draft evaders would be required to perform some form of alternative nonmilitary service to the nation. Ford's action, commonly regarded as an example of conditional amnesty, was intended to appease Americans who opposed the unconditional pardon of persons who refused to perform military service during the Vietnam War.

—*Thomas Clarkin*

See also Appellate practice; Community service as punishment for crime; Immigration, legal and illegal; Immunity from prosecution; Legal immunity; Pardoning power.

ANNOTATED CODES

Orderly compilations of laws together with citations to court opinions interpreting these laws are crucial legal research tools

Legislative bodies at the national, state, and local levels regularly enact laws. Examples of lawmaking bodies include the U.S. Congress, state legislatures, and city councils. When legislative bodies pass laws, these enactments take their place among previously enacted laws. However, the collection of laws passed over a period of time can eventually become a bewildering assortment of legal prescriptions on a variety of topics, since legislative bodies pass new laws regularly and also amend and repeal old ones.

To bring order to this potentially confusing array of laws, federal, state, and local governments routinely incorporate legislative enactments into codes. These codes are orderly compilations of existing laws arranged by topic. For example, laws passed by the U.S. Congress are included in the United States Code.

In a code, legislative acts that amend previously existing laws appear with that law, and the various enactments still in force are generally arranged by subject matter. For example, laws on the protection of the environment appear in one place while laws on deportation appear in another. A code also reflects the repeal of laws by legislative bodies.

Once a legislative body passes a law, the work of interpreting it falls to the courts. Federal and state appellate courts routinely publish their decisions, including the decisions they render with respect to legislative enactments. These published decisions guide subsequent courts that may be called upon to interpret the same laws, since courts generally attempt to make their decisions harmonize with previously decided cases, which are called precedents. The respect for precedent is a standard feature of the U.S. legal system and is generally referred to as the doctrine of *stare decisis*, which literally means, "Let the decision stand." According to this legal doctrine, a court should, whenever possible, seek to make rulings consistent with the rulings by previous courts on the same subject. Thus, to understand a legislative enactment, one must generally have access not only to the text of the enactment but also to court opinions that have interpreted it.

Annotated codes assist lawyers and judges in conducting research on specific laws. These codes include not only the text of laws but also a brief description of cases and other legal authorities that have interpreted the law. These descriptions themselves are arranged topically, thus assisting researchers in finding cases that discuss the particular legal issues of interest to them. In addition, laws in annotated codes generally include cross-references to related laws in the same general field. For federal laws, the most widely consulted reference edition is the *United States Code Annotated* (St. Paul, Minn.: West Publishing). Furthermore, the laws of each state are published in annotated codes.

—*Timothy L. Hall*

See also *Black's Law Dictionary*; Judicial conduct code; Lesser included offense; Louisiana law; Model Penal Code; Statutes; Uniform laws; United States Code.

ANNULMENT

Judicial pronouncement that declares a marriage terminated and invalid

Annulment implies that a valid marriage never took place because of the inability of one or both partners to perform the responsibilities associated with marriage. Whereas an annulment denies that a marriage ever existed, a divorce acknowledges the existence of a marriage and then terminates it. Although most annulments occur during the first year of marriage, census records show that they have been granted as late as thirty years after marriage.

The statutes or legislation that determines the conditions for voiding a marriage are not uniform from state to state, and the grounds for annulment vary from one jurisdiction to another. In every case, however, these grounds must be clear, strong, and convincing before an annulment court will issue a decree to liquidate a marriage following legal proceedings. In many cases, corroborative evidence from other witnesses is required prior to any legal proceedings.

While the rule of law differs from one jurisdiction to another, the most common grounds for an annulment include the failure to conform to law, such as not obtaining a proper marriage license; previous marriage of one spouse that has not been terminated; failure of either spouse to have reached the age of consent, usually eighteen; either spouse's lack of the mental capacity to consent to marriage; marriage to a close blood relative, including a first cousin or anyone more closely related; either spouse's incurable incapacity to have sexual intercourse; either spouse's consent to marry as a result of force or duress caused by the other spouse; and the use of intentional deception to lure one of the parties into marriage, such as making false claims of wanting to have children.

If a spouse seeks to annul a marriage, it is typically necessary first to obtain legal counsel and file a signed and sworn complaint with a family court of jurisdiction detailing the grounds for voiding the marriage. Then the court serves the defendant with the complaint and the defendant responds in a specified amount of time with a written answer. If there is sufficient evidence based on the complaint and the response, legal proceedings occur and a timely decision is rendered.

If an annulment is granted by a court of jurisdiction, the marriage is considered never to have existed, but any children that may have come from the union are deemed legitimate. The court legally provides for an equitable distribution of marital property and debt, child custody, visitation rights, child support, alimony, and counsel fees.

In addition to a legal annulment of marriage, there are church annulments. Whereas a legal annulment requires a court order ruling that the marriage never existed, a church annulment is the declaration of a church authority that the marriage never existed. While the Roman Catholic Church acknowledges divorce only in exceptional cases, it does recognize annulments.

—*Alvin K. Benson*

See also Family law practice; Uniform laws.

APPEAL

Action taken by parties who seek review of their cases in higher courts after losing all or part of their claims in a trial

Courts in the U.S. judicial system generally fall into one of two categories: trial and appellate courts. Lawsuits begin in trial courts, in which parties call witnesses and present evidence and in which judges or juries pronounce verdicts. However, in many cases trials are not the end of the story for losing parties. Those who do not emerge victorious at a trial may frequently have a possibility of appeal.

The actual characteristics of the right of appeal vary widely depending on the type of proceeding involved—whether it is a criminal or civil case, for example—and the particular jurisdiction in question. A few generalities are possible, however. First, the right of appeal is not simply a right to air a case again in a higher court. Appellate courts do not listen to witnesses or allow the presentation of new evidence. They confine their review to legal as opposed to factual questions. Thus, to prevail on appeal one must normally convince an appellate court that the trial court made a legal and not simply a factual error. Second, appellate courts generally differ from trial courts in that appeals are heard by more than one judge. An appellate court normally consists of a number of judges, and appeals are considered either by the entire court or by smaller panels of appellate judges—commonly three. The U.S. Supreme Court, for example, consists of nine justices who collectively review decisions of lower courts.

In some cases, parties dissatisfied with the results of a trial have only a single chance to appeal to a higher court, such as a state supreme court. In many state judicial systems and in the federal system, however, there are two appellate courts: an intermediate appellate court, often called a court of appeal, and a supreme court. In these systems it is possible that one might lose at the trial and intermediate appellate levels and still be able to appeal to a supreme court.

Even in judicial systems that include more than one appellate court, these courts must not necessarily consider the appeals that come before them. In some state systems and in the federal system the highest appellate court has a great deal of discretion in determining which appeals it considers. For example, scarcely any cases are entitled to review by the U.S. Supreme Court. Instead, parties wishing such a review must file a petition for a writ of *certiorari* with the Court requesting review of a case. However, the Court turns down far more of these requests than it grants.

—*Timothy L. Hall*

See also Acquittal; Appellate practice; *Certiorari*, writ of; Convictions; Court types; Courts of appeals; Criminal procedure; Death row attorneys; Execution of judgment; Federal judicial system; *Habeas corpus*; Objection; Opinions; Supreme Court, U.S.; Trial transcripts.

Appellate practice

One of the hallmarks of modern Anglo-American law, a legal prac-
tice that provides checks on legal errors made during civil and
criminal trials

In the United States, in both the federal court system and in each
state court system, a party who loses at the initial trial level may
seek a review of that decision by taking an appeal to a higher
court. The party who files the appeal is generally referred to as the
"appellant," and the party opposing the appeal is generally referred to as the "appellee" or "respondent." In order to commence
an appeal, the appellant must file a notice of appeal within a specified number of days (usually thirty or sixty) after judgment is
entered. Frequently the appellant must briefly state the legal
grounds why he or she believes the decision of the trial court or
jury was wrong.

Procedure

Generally, the appellant has the responsibility to prepare the
"record on appeal," which includes copies of all relevant legal papers, transcripts, and evidence that the higher court will need to
decide the appeal. For example, if the appellant is challenging
a verdict in a criminal trial on the grounds that the trial judge
improperly admitted illegally obtained evidence, the appellant
must ensure that the appellate court has a transcript of the testimony of all witnesses relating to that particular issue.

Once the record on appeal has been prepared, both sides submit written briefs presenting legal arguments on each of the issues raised by the appeal. The appellant files the first brief, followed by the appellee (or respondent), and then generally the
appellant has the opportunity to file a reply brief.

The art of writing a good brief is to isolate one or more specific
legal errors in the trial court that directly resulted in a decision
that is contrary to law or is not supported by substantial evidence.
Generally, the law assumes that the decision in the trial court was
correct. Therefore, the burden is on the appellant to persuade the
higher court to reverse the lower court. Usually it is not the function of the appellate court to reconsider factual issues; those are
for the jury alone to decide. The appellate court is primarily con-

cerned with legal issues, such as whether evidence was properly admitted (or excluded), whether the judge gave the correct instructions to the jury, or whether the statute or regulation involved is constitutional. An appeal must be based on the appellate record; only in very rare instances may new evidence be presented on appeal.

Appellate judges are not interested in a rehash of all the evidence and arguments previously presented in the trial court. An appeal is not a "second chance"; it is an opportunity to identify mistakes that resulted in a miscarriage of justice. Some errors are not of sufficient weight to result in a reversal of the judgment; these are referred to as "harmless errors." Only errors that are prejudicial to the appellant and if corrected would make a difference in the result constitute "reversible errors."

The task of an appellate brief is to persuade. From the first sentence of the argument an appellant must catch the judges' attention. While the parties to an appeal are intimately familiar with their own case, the briefs are the first opportunity the appellate judges have to learn what the dispute is about. The appellant's briefs have to simultaneously tell a good story and convince the judges that they should reverse the judgment.

The brief filed by the appellee (or respondent) should have the opposite effect. It should reassure the appellate judges that the result in the lower court was correct, that any errors were slight (and therefore "harmless"), and that no grounds exist which require the appellate court to intervene.

Contrary to the portrayals in popular motion picture and novels, appeals are not decided by last-minute discoveries of new evidence or by a dramatic speech from a charismatic lawyer. A successful appeal is the product of hard work by tenacious lawyers and law clerks combing through mountains of evidence and transcripts and searching for legal precedents to support their arguments. In rare instances an appeal presents an issue of first impression—a novel legal question that has not been addressed before. Such appeals call for the most creative and innovative appellate lawyers who can extend existing court decisions and persuade the appellate court to establish new precedent.

Judicial Standard

The standard of review applied by the appellate court can often dictate the outcome of the appeal. Certain legal issues on appeal are subject to the "de novo" standard of review and others are subject to the "abuse of discretion" standard. Under the "de novo" standard the appellate court substitutes its own judgment for that of the trial court and reviews the evidence on a clean slate. Under the "abuse of discretion" standard the appellate court merely decides whether the trial court's rulings were reasonable and supported by substantial evidence. If so, the judgment will be affirmed, even if the appellate court would have reached a differ- ent result on its own.

Once the written briefs have been filed, the appellate court usu- ally sets the case for an oral argument. This is a live proceeding, at which attorneys for each side present arguments before the appel- lant court for and against the appeal. As with the written briefs, the appellant usually goes first, followed by the respondent. Most experienced attorneys representing appellants reserve some of their allotted time for rebuttal to respond to the points raised by the respondent's counsel.

Following oral argument, the appellate court usually takes the case under advisement. It is rare that the court will immediately announce its decision from the bench. However, often by the time of the oral argument the appellate judges will have met to discuss the case and sometimes will even have written a draft of their opinion. In those instances, the judges may use the oral argument to force the lawyers on either or both sides to concede a weak point or to clarify their positions. After conferring among them- selves, the appellate judges issue a decision, usually accompanied by a written opinion explaining the reasoning for either affirming or reversing the lower court decision. Any appellate court judge who disagrees with the majority of his or her fellow judges may issue a dissenting opinion explaining why he or she would have reached a different result.

Types of Appellate Courts

In the federal court system and most state court systems there are two levels of appellate courts. First, there is the intermediate level. This is usually known as the court of appeals and is made up of several judges, or justices as they are often called, of which generally a panel of three hears and decides each case. Next, there is the U.S. Supreme Court, which is composed of nine judges (or justices). While an appellant usually has an automatic right to an appeal to the intermediate appellate court, which is required to hear and determine the case, the Supreme Court has the discretion to decide whether or not to consider a further appeal if the appellant loses in the intermediate appellate court.

The appellate process exists because the law recognizes that the courts are not infallible and that on occasion the system should provide a mechanism to correct serious mistakes in order to assure the most fair and equitable judicial process possible.

—*Stephen F. Rohde*

Suggested Readings

For an engrossing story of a landmark appeal, see Anthony Lewis's *Make No Law: The Sullivan Case and the First Amendment* (New York: Random House, 1991). Henry Abraham offers a clear description of the differences among courts in *The Judicial Process: An Introductory Analysis of the Courts of the United States, England, and France* (7th ed. New York: Oxford University Press, 1998). There are numerous works on the U.S. Supreme Court. Two of the best treatments of the Court as a decision-making institution are David M. O'Brien's *Storm Center* (3d ed. New York: W. W. Norton, 1993) and Henry J. Abraham's *The Judicial Process* (6th ed. New York: Oxford University Press, 1993). A book that discusses how the Supreme Court decides what to place on its agenda is *Deciding to Decide: Agenda Setting in the United States Supreme Court* (Cambridge, Mass.: Harvard University Press, 1991) by H. W. Perry, Jr. Other useful studies include Donald R. Songer's *Continuity and Change on the United States Courts of Appeals* (Ann Arbor: University of Michigan Press, 2000), David G. Knibb's *Federal Court of Appeals Manual: A Manual on Practice in the United States Courts of Appeals* (St. Paul, Minn.: West Publishing, 2000), and Ann E. Woodley's *Litigating in Federal Court: A Guide to the Rules* (Durham, N.C.: Carolina Academic Press, 1999). Sara C. Benesh's *The U.S. Court of Appeals and the Law of Confessions: Perspectives on the Hierarchy of Justice* (New York: LFB Scholarly Publishing, 2002) the appellate process in the federal judicial system.

See also Amnesty; Appeal; Attorney types; *Certiorari*, writ of; Convictions; Court reporters; Court types; Courts of appeals; Criminal procedure; Federal judicial system; Judicial clerks; Judicial review; Opinions; Reasonable doubt; Reversible errors; Trial transcripts; Trials.

ARBITRATION

Submission of legal disputes to impartial persons or panels of persons known as arbitrators; the process may or may not lead to decisions that are binding or nonbinding on the parties

Arbitration commonly is a contractual agreement between parties to resolve disputes by requesting the assistance of impartial persons or panels of persons. A hallmark of commercial arbitration is its voluntariness. Parties agree by mutual consent to submit their disputes to arbitration instead of going to court. Arbitration may be binding or nonbinding. Binding arbitration occurs when parties to a dispute agree in advance to accept an arbitrator's decision as binding and final. Generally, there is no appeal from this decision unless it is demonstrated that the decision was procured through fraud or bias. Nonbinding arbitration is not final. After an arbitrator hears the dispute and issues a decision, the parties decide whether or not to accept the recommendations. If the parties do not accept the recommendations, the dispute continues and may be resolved in court.

In some jurisdictions, state law requires compulsory arbitration in particular kinds of disputes. For example, New York law may require that disputes between public employees and a government employer be resolved through arbitration. This form of arbitration is called compulsory arbitration, because it is required by law. Interest arbitration involves the resolution of disputes pertaining to the specific terms or meaning of contractual language. Grievance arbitration involves the resolution of disputes pertaining to the violation of terms of a collective bargaining agreement—that is, a labor agreement between an employer and a union. Arbitration is a more formal process than mediation. Under mediation neutral persons, or mediators, assist parties in reaching their own settlements. Unlike arbitrators, mediators do not have the authority to issue binding decisions. Thus, mediation is similar to settlement discussions with neutral persons present to assist the parties in reaching a satisfactory resolution. Both arbitration and mediation form part of an alternative dispute resolution process that encourages expeditious resolution of problems outside the courtroom.

Arbitration Procedure

The advantages of arbitration include confidentiality, specialized expertise, quick decision making, and less formality than court litigation. Additionally, arbitration is usually less expensive than lengthy court cases. The disadvantages include concerns about arbitration's informality, the enforceability of arbitration awards, and arbitrators' "split-the-difference" approach.

There are two ways to start the arbitration process. One is to agree to arbitrate prospectively. Upon entering into an agreement, before any disputes arise, the parties write into the contract an arbitration clause that basically states that the parties agree to submit disputes arising under the contract to arbitration. The second way to initiate arbitration is through an agreement by the parties to submit an existing dispute to arbitration. There are a number of profit and nonprofit organizations that provide arbitration services. The American Arbitration Association is an example of a private nonprofit organization that has been a central force in the area of alternate dispute resolution. Once an arbitration agreement has been reached, a party need only file a claim with the arbitration organization, pay the filing fee, and serve the defending party with notice of the arbitration claim.

Once the claim for arbitration is filed and fees are paid, a case administrator may be assigned to assist both parties on procedural matters. The first step for the parties is to select an arbitrator, who usually belongs to a panel provided by the arbitration association. The panel of arbitrators typically has extensive experience and training in the field involved. Usually the parties mutually agree on an arbitrator, but when they cannot, the arbitration association appoints somebody. Typically, most cases involve the appointment of one arbitrator, but large, complex cases may require the appointment of a panel. A panel usually consists of three arbitrators in order to prevent a tie vote. The arbitrator is required to disclose any relationships that may interfere with providing an impartial hearing.

The Hearing

The parties to a dispute select a convenient day and location for the arbitration hearing. Arbitrators usually charge an hourly fee, which is equally divided between the parties. While arbitration is less formal than courtroom litigation, it often requires careful preparation. Parties have the right to be represented by counsel or by other persons. While arbitration hearings are not governed by formal rules of evidence, the arbitrator must hear all material evidence to render a decision. The arbitrator decides what evidence is relevant. Thus, the arbitrator may accept evidence that would not be admitted by a judge in a trial. Both parties may make arrangements with a stenographer for a stenographic record of the proceedings. The arbitrator may require witnesses to testify under oath. The arbitrator's decision is based on facts and exhibits presented at the hearing.

Claimants (the parties submitting requests for arbitration) usually present their cases first, followed by the respondents. The parties to the dispute must attempt to convince the arbitrator of the soundness of their position. Then they provide opening presentations that briefly describe the controversy and the issues to be proved. Witnesses are called in systematic order and may be cross-examined. The parties provide closing statements at the conclusion of their presentations. After the arbitrator is satisfied that all questions have been addressed, the hearing is closed and the arbitrator has a period of time (usually thirty days) to issue an award. Some arbitration proceedings may call for expedited provisions that shorten the time for issuing a decision.

The Award

The award is the final decision of the arbitrator on the issues submitted by the parties. If an arbitration panel is involved in a case, its decision is based on a majority vote. The purpose of the award is to resolve the dispute. The award must be made within the time limits of the arbitration agreement and should decide each claim submitted. The decision is transmitted to the case administrator, who puts it into a standard form and resubmits it to the arbitrator for a signature. Once the decision is signed by the arbitrator, it is forwarded to the case administrator for transmission to the parties.

Arbitrators, unlike judges, are not required to write opinions explaining the reasons for their decisions. To do so could generate potential challenges by the losing party. Parties understand that by referring a dispute to arbitration they have expressed a preference for a final and nonreviewable award. They have also agreed to abide by the arbitrator's final award. Thus, the parties seek a decision from the arbitrator, not an explanation. Judicial review is, therefore, not compatible with the contractual agreement of the parties to submit disputes to binding arbitration. However, judicial review may be available on a limited basis in exceptional circumstances.

Grounds for judicial review of an arbitration award include arbitrator fraud or bias, the claim that the arbitrators exceeded the scope of their authority, and arbitrators' failure to provide the parties due process (fairness during the proceeding). A losing party may petition a court to vacate an award, while some jurisdictions provide specific statutory grounds for vacating awards. Judicial review is limited to addressing the defects in the arbitration procedure; it cannot be based on the sufficiency of the evidence or the merits of the case. If the rare circumstance arises that an award is vacated, the entire case is reopened, a new arbitrator is appointed, and the process starts anew.

Because the judicial resolution of disputes is often lengthy and expensive, individuals, businesses, and governments use a variety of alternative mechanisms to expedite dispute resolution. While the arbitration process is not without its critics, its advantages are noted by many. Private parties, lawyers, businesses, and governments view arbitration as a sensible way to expeditiously and inexpensively resolve disputes.

—*Robert N. Davis*

Suggested Readings

General discussions of arbitration include Steven C. Bennett's *Arbitration: Essential Concepts* (New York: ALM, 2002), Karl J. Mackie's *A Handbook of Dispute Resolution: ADR in Action* (New York: Routledge and Sweet & Maxwell, 1991), *Remedies in Arbitration* by Marvin Hill, Jr. (Washington, D.C.: The Bureau of National Affairs, 1981), Arnold M. Zack's *Arbitration in Practice* (New York: Industrial and Labor Relations Press, 1984), Arthur T. Ginnings's *Arbitration, A Practical Guide* (Aldershot, England: Gower Publishing Company Limited, 1984); Robert Coulson's *Business Arbitration—What You Need to Know* (New York: American Arbitration Association, 1980), Frances Kellor's *American Arbitration* (New York: Kennikat Press, 1972), and Frank Elkouri's *How Arbitration Works* (Washington, D.C.: The Bureau of National Affairs, 1985).

See also Attorney-client relationship; Breach of contract; Commercial litigation; Family law practice; Lawsuits; Mediation; Trials.

ARRAIGNMENT

Hearing at which an accused person is informed of charges being brought and is given the opportunity to plead; accused persons cannot be held without being charged

The Seventh Amendment to the U.S. Constitution provides that an accused person must be informed of the nature of the accusation being brought. The arraignment fulfills that right. At the arraignment, the accused is called by name, informed of the charges, and given the opportunity to enter a plea of guilty, not guilty, or *nolo contendere* (no contest).

If the charge is serious, an attorney may be present with the accused or may be appointed by the court if the accused requests. The defense may use the arraignment to determine the merits of the case and, if appropriate, attempt a plea bargain, pleading guilty to a lesser offense in return for a reduced sentence.

A plea of guilty or *nolo contendere* leads to immediate sentencing without trial. A plea of not guilty leads to a trial. *Nolo contendere*, which the court considers an implied confession of guilt, does not lessen liability in criminal matters. Such a plea may reduce liability in civil matters, however, because there is no confession of guilt.

See also Arrest; Criminal procedure; Defense attorneys; Lesser included offense; Liability, civil and criminal; Pleas; Plea bargaining.

ARREST

Process by which suspected offenders are formally taken into custody and transferred for processing into the criminal justice system; arrests are the point of entry into the criminal justice system and one of the main functions of police officers

An arrest takes place when a police officer has probable cause to believe that an individual has committed a crime. An essential part of the arrest procedure involves taking the suspect into secure custody. That is, persons suspected of committing crimes are

> ## Standard Police Operating Procedure
>
> The first police officer at the scene of a crime:
> 1. Arrests the offender, if present
> 2. "Freezes" the scene—that is, discovers and holds witnesses and others involved until they are identified and interviewed and prevents unauthorized persons from entering the crime area
> 3. Prevents persons present at the scene from destroying evidence
> 4. Secures all available information
> 5. Searches for and preserves evidence
> 6. Records all facts

taken to police stations against their will. When arrests take place, the suspected offenders are taken, often in handcuffs, to booking facilities at police stations, where their identities, fingerprints, and details of the crime are recorded.

Arrest is the point of entry into the criminal justice system for people who are caught violating the law. For some offenders, their journey through the criminal justice system continues to trial and sentencing. For others, whose cases are dismissed, the events following arrest are inconsequential. Regardless, every suspected offender apprehended by the police experiences the arrest procedure. The bulk of police officers' work involves arresting suspects.

Arrest Warrants

Police officers may arrest suspects only if they believe that there is probable cause to do so. Probable cause exists when a reasonable person would believe (given the evidence) that there is sufficient cause to bring a suspect into custody. The facts must reasonably point to the individual to be arrested. Probable cause is necessary whether an officer is arresting an individual with a warrant or without one.

Arrest warrants are given to police officers by judges, who must find probable cause before issuing them. An arrest warrant is a paper that authorizes an officer to arrest a suspect without actually seeing the suspect committing a crime. This paper must contain specific details about the nature of the offense committed, where the individual will be apprehended, and why a warrant is desired. An officer may arrest a suspect without an arrest warrant if he or she has seen the suspect violate the law. The majority of arrests are made without warrants.

Police officers make arrest decisions based on the information available about the offense and their past experience. Because of the large number of differences in arrestees and arrest situations, there is no way to anticipate all the situations police officers will encounter. Police officers are said to have "discretion" in the arrest decision, which means that they must use their own judgment in deciding whether to arrest a suspect. While they must always abide by the doctrine of probable cause, they must still rely on their own judgment. Some critics of police procedure have argued that the police have too much discretion in the arrest decision and that racism or sexism may play a part in some officers' decisions to arrest.

Arrest Procedures

Arrest involves taking a suspect into secure custody. A police officer making an arrest must have intent to arrest. Simply stopping a motorist to write a ticket or ask a question does not constitute intent to arrest. In some cases, an arrestee will voluntarily submit to the arrest procedure. When this occurs, there is no need for the officer to take the suspect into custody forcibly. In most cases, however, it is more difficult to take a suspect into custody, and some amount of force is required. Officers also must have authority to arrest a suspect. "Authority" refers to the power that police have to deprive a citizen of liberty through arrest. While ordinary citizens have limited powers to arrest someone suspected of committing a felony (in some states), they do not have the legal authority to take an offender into custody.

Finally, suspects must be informed that they are being arrested. That is, they are told that they are not merely being stopped for questioning but have been taken into custody because there is probable cause to believe that they committed a crime.

Rights of Arrestees

Special constitutional rights apply to people arrested by the police. They include the right to counsel and the right against self-incrimination. In other words, arrestees are entitled to attorney representation, and they are accorded the right not to incriminate themselves in a crime. This latter right was written into the Constitution of the United States to keep officers from coercing arrestees into confessing to a crime. Specifically, the Fifth Amendment to the Constitution states (in part) that an arrestee shall not "be compelled in any criminal case to be a witness against himself." Historically, arrestees were often physically assaulted or tortured in order to obtain confessions.

The U.S. Supreme Court case *Miranda v. Arizona* (1966) established that arrestees must be notified of their rights under the Constitution. They must be aware that they are entitled to an attorney and that if they cannot afford an attorney, one will be provided for them by the court. They are also notified that they have the right to remain silent, but if they choose to speak it can be used against them at their trial. This notification is called a Miranda warning, and it must be given to all arrestees immediately following their arrest.

—*Christina Polsenberg*

Suggested Readings

Police discretion is discussed extensively in Michael K. Brown, *Working the Street: Police Discretion and the Dilemmas of Reform* (New York: Russell Sage Foundation, 1988), and Jerome H. Skolnick, *Justice Without Trial: Law Enforcement in Democratic Society* (2d ed. New York: John Wiley & Sons, 1975). A detailed discussion of police arrest procedure and relevant Supreme Court cases can be found in Rolando V. Del Carmen, *Criminal Procedure for Law Enforcement Personnel* (Monterey, Calif.: Brooks/Cole, 1987). Carl J. Franklin's *Constitutional Law for the Criminal Justice Professional* (Boca Raton, Fla.: CRC Press, 1999), has several chapters on arrest procedures. A practical guide for the private citizen is *The Criminal Law Handbook: Know Your Rights, Survive the System*, by Paul Bergman, Sara J. Berman-Barrett (5th ed. Berkeley, Calif.: Nolo Press, 2003), which covers every stage of criminal cases in a question-and-answer format.

See also Arraignment; Bail system; Bench warrants; Citizen's arrest; Confessions; Criminal procedure; Criminal records; Diplomatic immunity; *Habeas corpus*; House arrest; Indictments; Juvenile criminal proceedings; Law enforcement; Miranda rights; Police; Presumption of innocence; Probable cause; Suspects.

Attachment

Court order to seize a person's property

In general, an attachment includes a writ, mandate, or other judicial order to take, apprehend, or seize a person, a person's goods, or a person's estate. As opposed to an arrest, an attachment can authorize taking a person's property, as well as the person. However, attachments issued against people are typically used only against those who are in contempt of court.

The attachment process is believed to have originated with the Romans and has existed in England for hundreds of years. In modern America attachments are used chiefly against debtors. In several older U.S. states attachments against property can be issued at the commencement of suits for debts in order to protect the person to whom the debt is owed. If the plaintiff wins the suit, the attached property can be sold to satisfy the claim. In other states, the plaintiff is required to post a bond or security for the payment of damages in case the court had no right to attach the property. Consequently, a person's property prior to the settlement of a case in court is typically attached only in special cases, particularly when the defendant is a nonresident of the state involved, is a fraudulent debtor, or is attempting to conceal property. After a court judgment, an attachment may be issued to seize a debtor's bank accounts, wages, or other intangible assets.

—Alvin K. Benson

See also Arrest; Attorney general of the United States; Bonds; Contempt of court; Execution of judgment; Garnishment; Justice Department, U.S.

ATTORNEY-CLIENT RELATIONSHIP

Rules governing the formation, maintenance, and dissolution of the working relationship between an attorney and a client

The most important but easily overlooked feature of the attorney-client relationship is that it is primarily a creature of contract law. That is, the terms of the relationship depend on the wishes of the parties. Although the relationship may be created by oral contract or may be implied from the course of conduct among the parties, it is generally recommended that the relationship be formalized through a written "retainer" agreement, which spells out with clarity the nature of the work for which the lawyer is being hired and the fee that will be paid by the client. A well-drafted retainer agreement should thus enable the parties to know, among other things, the nature, scope, and, if possible, duration of the work for which the lawyer is being hired, the manner and rate of compensation, the right of the parties to terminate or withdraw from the agreement, and the means for resolving disputes that arise in the relationship.

Scope of the Relationship

The varieties of attorney-client relationships that may be created by contract are numerous. Lawyers may be retained for single projects or as general counsel for an indefinite number of projects. They may be retained as litigators to try one or more cases or as counselors to render advice or draft documents relating to one or more transactions. Clients may be individual persons or legal or juristic persons, such as corporations, partnerships, labor unions, associations, or membership organizations. Finally, lawyers may be retained or appointed for clients by persons other than the clients. Thus, insurance companies frequently retain lawyers for policyholders and courts may appoint lawyers for indigent persons. Whoever pays the lawyer is not necessarily the client.

In some cases it may be difficult to tell precisely who the client of the lawyer is. For example, it is sometimes difficult to determine whether the general counsel of a corporation is the corporation's lawyer, the officers' lawyer, the employees' lawyer, or the board of directors' lawyer. Similarly, the attorney general of a state may be considered the lawyer for the state's executives or for the state's legislature. These issues may not matter for the most part because the interests of the various constituent groups represented by a lawyer may be identical. However, when they diverge, which happens not infrequently, it may raise difficult issues. Many of the difficulties can be avoided by a well-drafted contract that anticipates them and clearly resolves them ahead of time.

Extracontractual Regulation

In addition to contract law, the attorney-client relationship is regulated by a variety of rules that derive from the practice of law as a profession, not simply as a business enterprise. Some of these rules are ethical in the sense that they merely state principles of good behavior, while others are enforceable in the sense that their violation by the lawyer results in the imposition of penalties. Some of the rules are self-regulatory; that is, they are formulated and enforced by privately organized associations of lawyers, such as the American Bar Association (ABA) or the various city, county, or state voluntary bar associations. Other rules are mandatory because they are promulgated and enforced by official or quasiofficial bodies, such as state legislatures, state supreme courts, or mandatory bar associations. Most of these rules are disciplinary rather than remedial; that is, they are intended to regulate the conduct of lawyers and only incidentally to provide compensation to clients who are injured as a result of the violation of the rules.

In the event of injury to a client resulting from the conduct of a lawyer, the client may obtain relief either by arguing that specific conduct was a breach of the terms of the contract or that the conduct was tortious because it violated a common-law duty of care or loyalty that the attorney owed to the client. Such claims typically include malpractice, breach of fiduciary duty, violation of trust, or a claim for conversion (that is, for the return of misappropriated funds or property). Disciplinary rules constitute the most pervasive means of regulating the attorney-client relationship and are antecedent to the remedial measures that are available to the client and to the lawyer in the event of a dispute between them.

Ethical Rules and Their Enforcement

The ethical rules of the legal profession are highly developed, and they are central to the regulation of the relationship between the client and the lawyer. Although the rules in their particulars vary from one jurisdiction to another, their basic outlines are reasonably clear. The rules seek to balance three distinct interests: those of the client in obtaining zealous, competent, and effective representation or counseling; those of the lawyer in being adequately compensated for his or her services; and those of the judicial system (and society at large) in running and maintaining an effective and smoothly functioning machinery for dispensing justice. The resulting rules fall into three broad categories: zealous representation of the interests of the client, confidential treatment of client communications, and avoidance of conflict between the interests of the lawyer and those of the client. Assuring the full loyalty of the lawyer to the client's interests is a theme that runs through all three categories.

Generally speaking, ethical rules are intended to regulate the behavior of lawyers rather than to provide a substantive right to clients. They are thus typically enforced through administrative disciplinary proceedings before the promulgator of the rules, such as a bar association or the highest court of the state. Nonetheless, clients may obtain substantive vindication of rights that may flow to them indirectly under the ethical rules. Typically, most bar associations provide for a relatively nonadversarial method of resolving disputes between clients and their lawyers. Thus, arbitration, mediation, and other mechanisms of so-called alternative dispute resolution are usually available to a client who wishes to proceed against a lawyer outside the judicial system. In deciding the viability of a complaint filed by a client against a lawyer, panels employing forms of alternative dispute resolution typically consider the ethical rules in addition to whatever substantial legal rights the client may have.

Zealous Representation

Although every person is entitled to a lawyer when legal issues arise, there is no generalized obligation of any lawyer to represent any client. Once a lawyer undertakes to represent a client, however, the lawyer is required to do so both competently and zealously. That means that the lawyer must be diligent in gathering relevant information, analyzing that information, and in using that information for the purpose of representing the client's interests. Juxtaposed against such zealous representation is the extent to which the lawyer must take into account interests other than those of the client.

As a preliminary matter, there is the issue of how the client's interest is to be defined. Generally speaking, an overarching duty of a lawyer is to assist the client in understanding his or her real as opposed merely to nominal interests. Thus, a lawyer is always an adviser, never merely a person who records the facts or simply a hired gun. After an attorney has counseled a client, however, the legal system accepts as decisive the client's definition of his or her interest. A lawyer who disagrees with that definition or otherwise believes that his or her representation of the client's interest is antithetical either to the long-term interest of the client or to the lawyer's conception of what is right and just may withdraw from continuing to represent the client after due notice or, if there is pending litigation, with the approval of the court. Withdrawal from representation, however, ordinarily does not remove the lawyer's ethical obligation to maintain the confidentiality of client information, nor does it permit the lawyer to use that information in any manner that is adverse to the interests of the client.

There is one instance in which a lawyer may arguably act in a manner that appears inconsistent with the interest of the client: when the client intends to use the lawyer's services to perpetrate a crime or otherwise to injure other persons. Ethical rules vary about whether the lawyer is required simply to withdraw from representation of the client or whether he or she has an additional affirmative duty to disclose the client's putative wrongful act to the authorities. It seems clear that when a client intends to physically injure someone, the lawyer has an obligation to disclose this information either to the intended victim or to law-enforcement authorities. Much less certain are the lawyer's obligations when the putative injury would be financial or psychological.

Confidentiality of Client Information

Among lawyers it is widely accepted that possession of information is the most vital asset in the attorney-client relationship. The ethics rules are geared toward safeguarding this asset and assuring that it is used solely for the benefit of the client. Thus, a lawyer is required not only to keep confidential information disclosed to him by a client but is also required to keep confidential all information that comes into his possession or is developed by him while he represents the client. These so-called attorney-client and attorney work-product privileges may be waived by a client. Furthermore, they may be overridden under exceptional circumstances by social necessity, such as when the client is dead and the lawyer's disclosure of the confidential information is deemed necessary in order to safeguard the interest of the client. Confidentiality may also be overridden if the information has been disclosed to a third-party who is neither an agent of the client or the lawyer. Less clear-cut is the extent to which a lawyer may disclose information which, in the lawyer's professional judgment, would promote the interest of the client but which the client does not want disclosed. Another ambiguous circumstance arises when the client is incapable of deciding whether or not information should be disclosed. In a noteworthy decision in the late 1990's involving notes taken by a former friend and lawyer of President Bill Clinton, the U.S. Supreme Court held that the federal common-law rule against the disclosure of a client's confidential information continues to apply even after the death of the client.

Avoiding Conflicts of Interests

As a fiduciary, or a person with a special obligation to act on another's behalf, a lawyer owes a duty of loyalty to a client. The lawyer is required to treat the client's interest as would a prudent person managing his or her own property. This principle raises difficulties when a lawyer's interest is entangled with that of the client or when the interest of two clients are commingled. To deal with these situations, ethical rules create some presumptive rules, but these are not always sufficient or complete to deal with all situations.

As a preliminary matter, a lawyer is required to make every effort to avoid situations that would raise a conflict of interest. Thus, a lawyer ordinarily should not take on a new client whose interest is likely to conflict with that of a client already being represented by the lawyer, and a lawyer should not take on a client whose interest is potentially adverse to the lawyer's.

Similarly, after representation has begun, a lawyer should endeavor to avoid situations that would create conflict between the lawyer's interest and that of a client or among the interests of clients. A lawyer thus ordinarily should not commingle his or her assets with those of a client nor with the assets of different clients.

A lawyer should keep good records of transactions involving the assets of different clients and should avoid appropriating for his or her own benefit client opportunities, such as book, television, or movie contracts to a client's story. Above all, a lawyer is required to disclose to all potentially affected clients any likelihood of a conflict among the clients' interests or between those of the client and the lawyer. Finally, when a conflict is inevitable and a client cannot make a reasonably informed decision about whether to waive the conflict, the lawyer should discontinue representation.

Advocate or Court Officer

A perennial and seemingly intransigent problem in attorney-client relationships flows from the view of the litigator-lawyer as a dual representative of both the client and the judicial system. This view imposes on the lawyer both the duty to engage in zealous advocacy on behalf of the client and to zealously maintain the integrity of the judicial system. Many litigators, especially those involved in the criminal justice system, frequently encounter seemingly irreconcilable conflicts in upholding both demands. Increasingly, the issue has become not simply one of the ethical rectitude of the lawyer's practice or choices but of his or her own personal liberty and right to collect fees for representation.

Indeed, one of the consequences of the "War on Drugs" and the many rules that U.S. society has adopted to deal with drug trafficking has been the possible prosecution as coconspirators of lawyers who represent drug dealers and the potential forfeiture of their fees. Such action against lawyers calls into question the continuing vitality of such concepts as zealous representation, confidentiality, client privilege, and conflict of interest. Whatever may be the propriety of the developing doctrines in this area, they illustrate the simple truism that the rules of the attorney-client relationship, like much else in law, derive from and are reflective of societal structures and concerns. They are not fixed in time or place.

Breach of Contract and Malpractice Actions

As in other relationships, any one who is injured in an attorney-client relationship may seek redress for the injury in court. Typically such actions allege breach of contract, malpractice, or conversion. A lawyer or client may sue for breach of contract on the grounds that the other party has failed to perform an undertaking of the retainer agreement or other contract between the lawyer and the client. This claim is usually available to the lawyer for the purpose of collecting unpaid fees.

In addition to a breach of contract claim, a client may bring a malpractice claim for inadequate or poor representation of his or her interests by the lawyer. A malpractice action differs from a breach of contract claim in that it relates to what the lawyer did or did not do, not necessarily to what he or she promised to do. Finally, in conflict of interest situations a client arguably may be able to state a conversion claim—that is, that the lawyer misappropriated an opportunity or other asset that rightfully belonged to the client. All three claims are civil actions that are subject to standard rules of adjudication.

—*Maxwell O. Chibundu*

Suggested Readings

Exploring the role of lawyers in American society is a mainstay of current literature, both fiction and nonfiction. Such exploration invariably invites discussion of the relationship of the lawyer to the client. Illuminating general works on lawyer-client relations include Mary Ann Glendon's *A Nation Under Lawyers: How the Crisis in the Legal Profession Is Transforming American Society* (1994), Herbert M. Kritzer's *The Justice Broker: Lawyers and Ordinary Litigation* (1990), Saul M. Linowitz's *The Betrayed Profession: Lawyering at the End of the Twentieth Century* (1994), David Luban's *Lawyers and Justice: An Ethical Study* (1988). Several books have dealt with attorney-client relationships in specific settings. One dealing with bargaining and settlement is Herbert M. Kritzer's *Let's Make a Deal: Understanding the Negotiation Process in Ordinary Litigation* (1991). Kenneth Mann's *Defending White Collar Crime* (1985) deals with criminal defense work in the corporate setting. *Attorney-Client Relations in The United States* by Paul R. Rice (1993) discusses attorney-client privilege. Ethical issues of attorney-client relationships are considered in the American Bar Association's *ABA Compendium of Professional Responsibility Rules and Standards* (Chicago: Center for Professional Responsibility, American Bar Association, 2001) and *Ethical Standards in the Public Sector: A Guide for Government Lawyers, Clients, and Public Officials*, edited by Patricia E. Salkin (Chicago: Section of State and Local Government Law, American Bar Association, 1999).

See also Adversary system; Attorney confidentiality; Attorney fees; Attorney trust accounts; Attorney types; Attorneys; Attorneys as fiduciaries; Billable hours; Billing rates; Contingency fees; Defendants; Defense attorneys; Effective counsel; Legal services plans; Privileged communications; Solicitation of legal clients; Unethical conduct of attorneys.

ATTORNEY CONFIDENTIALITY

One of the central obligations owed by lawyers to their clients—the duty to preserve the confidentiality of their clients' secrets

The U.S. legal system values the relationship between attorney and client and seeks to protect its integrity. It believes in the first place that justice is best served when citizens are able to obtain legal advice. Not only does this advice protect important rights, but it also often provides the necessary information or counsel that prevents clients from violating the law. Moreover, in the U.S. system providing legal advice requires that lawyers know the facts of their clients' affairs. Because the answers to legal problems vary widely depending on the precise facts at issue, it is not possible for lawyers to provide competent advice without knowing the details of their clients' situations. Finally, the U.S. legal system reasons that clients do not divulge relevant facts to their lawyers unless the lawyers are inclined to and in a position to keep these facts secret.

Attorney-Client Privilege

To preserve client secrets and thus encourage clients to seek legal advice, U.S. law surrounds the attorney-client relationship with a two-fold protective screen. First, the law imposes an ethical requirement on lawyers not to divulge their clients' affairs without compelling necessity. Second, the law accords to clients an evidentiary privilege to prevent certain lawyer-client communications from being exposed in court proceedings. The ethical duty of confidentiality prevents lawyers from voluntarily disclosing client secrets; the evidentiary privilege prevents courts from forcing lawyers or clients to reveal the substance of their communications with each other.

The lawyer's duty of confidentiality is more expansive than the attorney-client privilege. This privilege generally protects only communications between lawyers and their clients that are delivered in confidential settings. Lawyers, however, have an ethical duty not to disclose any information about a client's affairs. This duty persists even if the information comes from a source other than the client and even if the information is not obtained under confidential circumstances.

Exceptions to the Duty of Confidentiality

The obligation of attorneys to preserve the confidences of their clients is not absolute. The laws of most jurisdictions deem a variety of interests as sufficiently weighty to justify exceptions to the general principle of confidentiality. The precise contours of these exceptions vary from jurisdiction to jurisdiction, but a majority of states have adopted a code of legal ethics proposed by the American Bar Association (ABA), referred to as the Model Rules of Professional Conduct, that specify the instances in which lawyers may depart from their normal obligations of confidentiality. The Model Rules elaborate a number of circumstances in which lawyers have the discretion to divulge the confidences of their clients and one circumstance in which lawyers must divulge confidential information.

In the first place lawyers may but are not required to divulge a client confidence when disclosure is necessary to prevent a client from committing a crime that could result in imminent death or serious bodily injury. In most jurisdictions a lawyer who knows that a client is about to harm another seriously would not be punished for declining to inform the police of the client's intent. In any event, this exception to the normal principle of confidentiality only applies to crimes which could result in death or serious bodily injury. It allows a lawyer to reveal a client's intent to commit murder but not a client's intent to perpetrate a financial fraud. Moreover, it permits lawyers to divulge information of dangerous future crimes but not crimes already committed. Thus, if a client confesses to a lawyer that the client has committed a murder, the lawyer could not reveal this fact, even anonymously, to the authorities.

EXCEPTIONS TO AN ATTORNEY'S DUTY OF CONFIDENTIALITY

- Disclosures necessary to prevent the client from committing a crime that will cause imminent death or serious bodily injury
- Disclosures necessary to establish a claim or defense of the lawyer in a lawsuit against the client
- Disclosures necessary to establish a defense of the lawyer when he or she is charged with participating in a client's wrongdoing or otherwise acting improperly in the representation of a client
- Disclosures necessary to rectify a client's perjury in a judicial proceeding

In the second place, the ABA's Model Rules permit lawyers to reveal client confidences when doing so is necessary to protect lawyers' own interests in certain circumstances. For example, a lawyer may disclose a confidence when necessary to prove a claim the lawyer has against a client. A client who requests that a lawyer perform some legal service and then refuses to pay for it may expect to be sued by the lawyer. In such an event, the lawyer may reveal in court that the client requested the service, even though this information would normally be protected by the duty of confidentiality. Similarly, a lawyer may reveal a client's secrets when necessary to defend against the claim that the lawyer wronged the client in the process of legal representation. The lawyer who is falsely accused of assisting a client in perpetrating a crime could probably reveal conversations in which the lawyer advised the client not to commit the crime.

These exceptions to the duty of confidentiality are within the discretion of individual attorneys, who may disclose such confidences but are not required to do so. In one instance, however, the American Bar Association's ethics rules actually command lawyers to reveal client confidences: in cases involving client perjury. When a client lies on the stand and a lawyer knows that the client has lied, the lawyer is generally required to take steps to protect the judicial proceeding from contamination. These steps might include persuading the client to tell the truth. However, if the client refuses to do so, a lawyer must, according to the ABA's ethics rules, disclose the client's perjury to the court. The lawyer's obligation to the court overrides normal obligations to the client. Moreover, the Supreme Court has held that a criminal defendant's constitutional rights are not violated when, in the face of persistent client perjury on the stand, a lawyer frightens a client by threatening to reveal the perjury to the court.

—Timothy L. Hall

Suggested Readings

Charles W. Wolfram's treatise on the ethical responsibilities of lawyers, *Modern Legal Ethics: Practitioner's Edition* (St. Paul, Minn.: West Publishing, 1986), contains a substantial discussion of the duty of confidentiality. For a detailed analysis of the American Bar Association's Model Rules of Professional Conduct including the rules on the duty of confidentiality, *The Law of Lawyering: A Handbook on the Model Rules of Professional Conduct* (2d ed. New York: Aspen Law & Business, 1996) by Geoffrey C. Hazard, Jr., and W. William Hodes is an important resource. Finally, Alan Dershowitz's *The Advocate's Devil* (New York: Warner Books, 1994), written by a well-known lawyer and Harvard legal scholar, is an engaging legal novel centered on the dilemma posed by the duty of confidentiality. William H. Simon's *The Practice of Justice: A Theory of Lawyers' Ethics* (Cambridge, Mass.: Harvard University Press, 1998), has chapters on confidentiality. See also *ABA Compendium of Professional Responsibility Rules and Standards* (Chicago: Center for Professional Responsibility, American Bar Association, 2001).

See also Arbitration; Attorney-client relationship; Attorneys; Attorneys as fiduciaries; Model Rules of Professional Conduct; Privileged communications; Unethical conduct of attorneys.

ATTORNEY FEES

Lawyers earn fees for legal services in a variety of ways—fees which the legal profession itself regulates to some extent

Lawyers, like other professionals such as physicians and accountants, derive their income largely from fees charged for the performance of legal services. Legal services and their costs vary widely, depending on clients' needs and the complexity and duration of their cases. As a corollary, legal fees assume a variety of forms, depending on the nature of the legal services provided and the wishes of lawyers and clients.

Forms of Attorney Fees

The three most common forms of fee arrangements between lawyers and clients are the hourly-rate fee, the flat fee, and the contingency fee. In most cases, lawyers charge clients for the time actually spent on their cases or affairs based on an hourly rate. This rate varies widely depending on the locale, the experience, and the prestige of the lawyer. Rates between one hundred and several hundred dollars per hour are not unusual. The hourly rate is especially appropriate for legal work the precise scope of which the lawyer and client cannot gauge in advance. When clients require relatively routine legal services and lawyers can easily predict the measure of work involved, they will sometimes charge a flat fee for their services. For example, a lawyer might charge two or three hundred dollars to prepare a simple will or seven hundred dollars to file a straightforward bankruptcy.

Finally, in some circumstances, lawyers and clients may agree that the lawyers' fees will consist of some percentage of a successful recovery. For example, persons who desire to sue others for injuries they have suffered in an automobile accident will generally find lawyers who agree to accept 30 to 40 percent of any recovery as a fee. If such suits are unsuccessful in yielding a monetary recovery, the clients would not owe the lawyers any fee. However, such clients would likely owe their lawyers for the expenses they incurred in filing and preparing the cases. The contingency fee arrangement is well suited to situations in which clients cannot afford to pay an hourly rate and the costs of the legal work (such as preparing a case for trial) are substantial.

Court Awarded Fees

Legal work can assume a variety of forms, many of which do not involve contested matters before a court. But in legal representations involving the prosecution or defense of lawsuits the traditional rule has been that the loser in a lawsuit is not required to pay the winner's attorney fees. This rule is often referred to as "the American rule," to distinguish it from the traditional British practice according to which the winner in a court matter is entitled to have the loser pay for the winner's attorney fees. It is widely believed that the American rule encourages people with novel or less weighty claims to bring lawsuits, since the most they risk is the cost of paying their own attorneys.

Although the traditional rule continues in force in most circumstances, the last half of the twentieth century saw federal and state governments adopt a variety of laws that alter this rule in particular contexts. Increasingly, laws permitting individuals to bring previously unrecognized claims against others often include a provision that these individuals, if successful, may recover their attorney fees from the losing parties. For example, laws that protect employees from job discrimination or consumers from unfair business practices routinely provide that successful employees or consumers are able to recover their attorney fees from the opposing side in a lawsuit. Similarly, the laws of many states provide that a person who sues another person on the basis of a written contract is entitled to recover attorney fees if the suit is successful. In these cases, the court awards attorney fees to the successful party along with whatever other relief the party is awarded. The court generally takes into account a variety of considerations in determining what fees are appropriate. Because these kinds of laws shift the normal responsibility for paying one's own attorney fees, they are frequently referred to as "fee shifting" laws.

Courts routinely award legal fees to criminal attorneys who represent indigent criminal defendants. The Sixth Amendment to the U.S. Constitution guarantees that criminal defendants in serious criminal cases are entitled to have an attorney provided to represent them if they are unable to hire one. In some locations local governments hire special attorneys called public defenders (or PAs), who work full-time to handle these types of cases. Public defenders earn a salary like other government employees. In circumstances in which a public defender is not available, a court simply appoints a lawyer from the local bar to represent an indigent defendant. In these cases, the appointed lawyer is normally entitled to be paid by the government for this appointed work, although the amount of payment is typically much lower than the attorney can normally earn in a criminal case.

Prepaid Legal Services Plans

The last several decades of the twentieth century saw an enormous increase in insurance-like plans to provide legal services to individuals. These plans allow persons access to at least some legal services, so that they do not face the prospect of unpredictable and perhaps daunting attorneys' bills. Such plans are generally financed by relatively small monthly contributions by persons or employers on behalf of employees. In return, persons receive the right to some specified legal services. Under such plans, members typically have the right to unlimited telephone advice from lawyers about legal problems and the right to some routine legal services, such as the preparation of wills or real estate sales contracts. Under more ambitious plans, members or employers make a greater monthly payment and are entitled to a specified amount of legal services covering a broader array of fields.

Prepaid legal services plans generally operate like insurance policies and are similar to prepaid medical or dental plans. Because not every member of a plan uses it or uses it to the full extent, the other members who use the plan are able to obtain legal services for less than if they had to purchase them individually. Moreover, lawyers who participate in such plans generally agree to accept lower hourly rates in return for the steady clientele the plans offer. Plan members are enthusiastic about such plans because they reduce legal fees. Lawyers endorse legal services plans because they ensure a steady stream of legal work and help to generate referrals.

Legal services plans generally involve a group of persons related by circumstances, such as trade union members who negotiate a legal service plan as an employee benefit. Commercially marketed plans have focused on more diffuse groups. For example, credit union members, credit card holders, and bank depositors increasingly find themselves offered the opportunity to join prepaid plans. The marketing of prepaid legal services plans has been widely successful, boosting these plans' membership to millions of members.

Legal and Ethical Restrictions on Attorney Fees

The law does not generally regulate the prices or fees involved in most contracts. Ordinarily, the parties to a contract are free to bargain for as much or as little as they wish. Legal fees, however, at least in principle, are not subject to the same kind of free-for-all approach. Lawyers in virtually every jurisdiction must conduct their practices subject to certain established ethical rules, and these rules regulate certain aspects of attorney fees. Moreover, in the area of contingency fee agreements, some states have placed limits on the amounts of fees lawyers can earn in particular contexts.

The key limit on attorney fees in most jurisdictions is that they must be reasonable. The reasonableness of a particular fee, however, turns on a number of factors, including the experience of the lawyer, the complexity of the matter, the results obtained because of the lawyer's services, the customary fee charged for a particular kind of service, and whether the fee is fixed or contingent. In practice, the standard of reasonableness is flexible enough so that a lawyer is not likely to be found in violation of it. Nevertheless, in exceptional cases, lawyers have been disciplined by courts and bar associations for charging excessive fees. In these circumstances, a lawyer may be denied recovery of all or part of the fee charged, forced to refund a portion of fees paid, or otherwise reprimanded for engaging in unethical conduct.

Unless a client and lawyer agree to a contingency fee, a lawyer need not prepare a written fee agreement, although the American Bar Association (ABA) recommends such an agreement in most cases. With respect to contingency fees, however, a lawyer must have a written agreement, which must spell out not only the percentage recovery to which the lawyer is entitled, but other details as well. For example, the agreement should specify whether the lawyer is entitled to the same percentage if a case settles soon after it has been filed as after a full trial or an appeal. In addition, the ethical rules that govern the conduct of lawyers in most states do not allow them to obtain a contingency fee in every kind of case. In particular, lawyers generally may not agree to a contingency fee in cases involving the defense of persons accused of crimes or in cases involving divorce or child-custody disputes. In such matters, lawyers must choose either an hourly or a flat fee.

—*Timothy L. Hall*

Suggested Readings

Books that offer practical advice to clients on lawyers and their fees include Tanya Starnes's *Mad at Your Lawyer?* (Berkeley, Calif.: Nolo Press, 1996), which discusses a variety of conflicts between lawyers and clients, including conflicts relating to fees and offers practical advice. *What Lawyers Do—And How to Make Them Work for You* by Daniel R. White (New York: E. P. Dutton, 1987) also includes some discussion on legal fees. In addition, for small business owners Dennis M. Powers's *Legal Expense Defense: How to Control Your Business' Legal Costs and Problems*, edited by Linda Pinkham (Grants Pass, Oreg.: Oasis Press, 1995), offers practical advice on the control of attorney fees. For a more scholarly perspective on legal fees and their impact on the legal profession, Maclin Fleming's *Lawyers, Money, and Success: The Consequences of Dollar Obsession* (Westport, Conn.: Quorum Books, 1997) and Michael H. Trotter's *Profit and the Practice of Law: What's Happened to the Legal Profession* (Athens, Ga.: University of Georgia Press, 1997) are important sources. Finally, *The Honest Hour: The Ethics of Time-Based Billing by Attorneys* by William G. Ross (Durham, N.C.: Carolina Academic Press, 1996) explores the ethical considerations behind hourly fees. Other studies of ethical issues include *Legal Ethics and Legal Practice: Contemporary Issues*, edited by Stephen Parker and Charles Sampford (New York: Clarendon Press, 1995), and *Ethical Standards in the Public Sector: A Guide for Government Lawyers, Clients, and Public Officials*, edited by Patricia E. Salkin (Chicago: Section of State and Local Government Law, American Bar Association, 1999).

See also Attorney-client relationship; Attorney salaries; Attorney trust accounts; Attorneys; Attorneys, court-appointed; Attorneys as fiduciaries; Bail bond agents; Bail system; Billable hours; Billing rates; Contingency fees; Court-awarded fees; Court costs; Law firms; Legal clinics; Legal services plans; Litigation expenses; Model Rules of Professional Conduct; Personal injury attorneys; Retainers; Solicitation of legal clients.

Attorney General of the United States

Cabinet-level officer who heads the federal Department of Justice and has responsibility for the impartial enforcement of federal law

The office of attorney general of the United States has existed since the administration of George Washington, the nation's first president. The office has, however, evolved into something quite different from what it was at the time of its creation.

Evolution of the Office

A major enactment of the first Congress under the U.S. Constitution was the Judiciary Act of 1789. It set forth the structure of the federal court system and created the office of attorney general. The law set forth no qualifications for the position other than that the person appointed be learned in the law. The president was to appoint the attorney general, subject to the consent of the Senate.

Washington wanted to appoint Edmund Randolph of Virginia to be the first attorney general. The Virginian was not eager to have the position, however, because Congress had appropriated funds for only a low salary without any allowance for expenses. Moreover, Congress had created no department for the attorney general to head, which meant that if Randolph were to need help with the work, or if he needed supplies, all such expenses would have to come out of his pocket. Congress apparently interpreted the position as that of legal adviser to the president and the heads of the executive departments and did not foresee the attorney general incurring expenses or being sufficiently busy to warrant a larger salary (even though the attorney general was to represent the United States before the Supreme Court). Edmund Randolph, who was Washington's personal attorney, accepted appointment as the nation's first attorney general because Washington was able to convince him that his private law practice would benefit from the prestige of the office.

Since the attorney general was not the head of an executive department, that official was not initially a member of the president's cabinet. During cabinet meetings, however, discussions often revolved around legal issues; therefore, Washington brought Randolph into his cabinet. This set the precedent for future attorneys general being considered regular members of the cabinet.

The office of attorney general underwent its greatest change when the Department of Justice was created. The bill creating it was signed into law by President Ulysses S. Grant on June 22, 1870. One of the things it did was create the position of solicitor general of the United States. The solicitor general became the official who represented the United States before the Supreme Court, with strong ties to the Court as well as to the Department of Justice. Attorneys general ceased to represent the United States regularly before the Court, which they had done in the early years, and became primarily administrators and presidential advisers. By the late twentieth century, the attorney general headed a large and complex organization. Among the major units of the Justice Department in the 1990's were the Criminal Division, Civil Division, Civil Rights Division, Antitrust Division, Tax Division, Immigration and Naturalization Service, Federal Bureau of Investigation, and Drug Enforcement Administration.

Politics and the Attorney General

Many twentieth century attorneys general were politically active persons who played major roles in the campaigns of the presidents who appointed them. Such was Attorney General Robert F. Kennedy. Although he did not have legal experience, his brother, President John F. Kennedy, appointed him attorney general because he relied on his advice and could be confident of his loyalty. President Richard M. Nixon appointed John Mitchell, his former law partner, who had managed his campaign.

Mitchell ultimately was discredited because he had been a major participant in the Watergate scandal. Presidents Gerald Ford and Jimmy Carter therefore sought attorneys general who would be less involved in the partisan politics of their administrations. Ford appointed Edward Levi, a law professor who was not even a registered member of a political party. Carter appointed Griffin Bell, who had been a federal appeals court judge of impeccable reputation. Carter and Bell had known one another since they were boys, but they had not maintained a close relationship over the years.

President Bill Clinton appointed Janet Reno, the first woman to hold the office of attorney general. Reno took an interest in chil-

Attorney General Janet Reno with President Bill Clinton. (Library of Congress)

dren's issues and in supporting the Immigration and Naturalization Service's efforts to prevent illegal immigrants from entering the United States. She sometimes displayed a degree of independence from the president who appointed her.

Judicial Selection

Attorneys general have played important roles in the process of selecting federal judges, who are appointed by the president with the consent of the Senate. President Dwight D. Eisenhower's attorney general, Herbert Brownell, worked hard at maintaining good relations with state and local Republicans as well as with the Senate Judiciary Committee. Attorney General Griffin Bell urged President Carter to create merit selection commissions to identify prospective nominees, including more minorities and women, which he did. The commissions were abandoned by succeeding presidents.

—Patricia A. Behlar

Suggested Readings

Overviews of the office of attorney general include H. Jefferson Powell, *The Constitution and the Attorneys General* (Durham, N.C.:

Carolina Academic Press, 1999), Nancy V. Baker, *Conflicting Loyalties: Law and Politics in the Attorney General's Office, 1789-1990* (Lawrence: University Press of Kansas, 1992); Cornell W. Clayton, *The Politics of Justice: The Attorney General and the Making of Legal Policy* (Armonk, N.Y.: M. E. Sharpe, 1992); U.S. Department of Justice, *200th Anniversary of the Office of the Attorney General, 1789-1989* (Washington, D.C.: U.S. Department of Justice, 1990). Works on or by specific attorneys general include Herbert Brownell, with John P. Burke, *Advising Ike: The Memoirs of Attorney General Herbert Brownell* (Lawrence: University Press of Kansas, 1993), and Victor Navasky, *Kennedy Justice* (New York: Atheneum, 1971).

See also Advisory opinions; Attorneys, United States; Attorneys general, state; Federal Bureau of Investigation; Judicial appointments and elections; Justice Department, U.S.; Law enforcement; Prosecutors.

ATTORNEY SALARIES

Attorney salaries climbed precipitously over the last half of the twentieth century, especially in large law firms

From the 1960's to 1990's the number of lawyers in the United States increased from just under 300,000 to just over 900,000. However, while the supply of lawyers increased, the demand for their services seemed to swell at an even faster pace. Consequently, many lawyers at the end of the twentieth century were working harder and making more money than their peers at mid-century.

Salaries for Lawyers in Private Firms

Most lawyers begin practice after gaining a doctor of jurisprudence (JD) degree from a nationally accredited law school, at which they spend three years as students, preceded, in most cases, by four years of undergraduate work. In the early 1960's these seven years of undergraduate and graduate education earned lawyers a salary of about $3,000 annually at private law firms. By the end of the 1990's, however, the same educational investment yielded starting salaries of more than $50,000 annually in many large firms and, for some of the most prestigious New York firms, more than $100,000. However, these figures represent upper limits of attorney salaries, since most starting lawyers work for smaller firms and earn substantially less than associates in larger law firms.

In law firms, beginning lawyers normally work as associates. Associates earn a salary, as opposed to sharing in the actual profits of the law firm. Most firms require that associates serve a term of years—typically between five and ten—in this salaried capacity. The firms then invite those associates who have worked hard and demonstrated exceptional legal skill to become partners. Unlike associates, partners generally do not receive an actual salary but a share in the firm's profits. During the probationary period served by associates before becoming partners, their salaries increase steadily but not meteorically. A study of attorney salaries conducted during the mid-1990's found that the average salary of fifth-year associates in private firms was $78,511, an increase of slightly less than $30,000 over average first-year salaries.

Partner compensation in private firms also grew steadily in the second half of the twentieth century. In 1960, for example, the average salary of partners in private law firms who had worked for twenty-five to twenty-nine years was $88,449. Over the ensuing years, this figure climbed rapidly to $127,400 in 1981, $156,64 in 1985, $181,843 in 1989, $204,157 in 1993, and $208,064 in 1996. However, even these figures are dwarfed by the salaries of partners in the nation's largest law firms. In the booming economy of the last years of the twentieth century, these firms generated for their partners average profits per partner of more than $300,000 annually. Average profits per partner in Baker & McKenzie, for example, a firm with more than two thousand lawyers—of which five hundred were partners—were $460,000 in 1997. The San Francisco firm of Brobeck, Phleger & Harrison L.L.P., with 552 lawyers, generated on average $560,000 for each of its 120 partners in 1997.

Salaries for Lawyers Outside Private Firms

The rosy picture for large-firm attorneys at the close of the twentieth century did not necessarily apply for other lawyers. In general, attorneys working outside private firms have seen steady income increases but not of the magnitude enjoyed by those working for big firms. For example, entry-level salaries for lawyers who begin work as prosecutors in criminal cases varied in the mid-1990's from around $25,000 to $45,000 per year. Prosecutors who had gained the highest posts available to them—district attorney in most jurisdictions—might expect to earn salaries ranging from the mid-$60,000's to approximately $125,000. Lawyers who worked in the mid-1990's for municipal governments generally earned salaries roughly comparable to those of their prosecutor colleagues. Lawyers with legal posts in state government offices earned slightly more as a rule. The highest ranking attorney for a state, the attorney general, earned in the late 1990's between $70,000 to $120,000 depending on the general prosperity and populousness of the state. Persons in entry-level legal positions in state governments tended to earn in the range of $30,000 annually.

If partners in large national law firms command the top rung of the legal salary ladder, public interest lawyers generally grasp the lowest. Perched beneath most other private or government-paid lawyers, public interest lawyers have seen salaries suffer from declining governmental budgets for public interest legal work of all kinds. By the late 1990's entry-level lawyers seeking to serve in legal aid offices could generally expect an annual salary of about $25,000, or barely half the average starting salary enjoyed by beginning attorneys in private firms. Career lawyers who choose to devote their legal lives to public interest work could seldom expect to see salaries exceeding $70,000 per year.

—*Timothy L. Hall*

Suggested Readings

Two solid sources for investigating historical and current trends in attorney salaries are Michael H. Trotter's *Profit and the Practice of Law: What's Happened to the Legal Profession* (Athens: University of Georgia Press, 1997) and Maclin Fleming's *Lawyers, Money, and Success: The Consequences of Dollar Obsession* (Westport, Conn.: Quorum Books, 1997). In addition, the leading national legal newspapers, *The National Law Journal* and *American Lawyer*, publish annual surveys of attorney salaries around the country. See, for example, "What Lawyers Earn," *National Law Journal* 20 (June 1, 1998). A helpful book on the increase in law firm size as a means of maximizing profits is *Tournament of Lawyers: The Trans-*

formation of the Big Law Firm by Marc Galanter and Thomas Palay (Chicago: University of Chicago Press, 1991). Clients seeking advice on dealing with attorneys, including matters relating to attorneys fees, should consult Tanya Starnes's *Mad at Your Lawyer?* (Berkeley, Calif.: Nolo Press, 1996). An American Bar Association guide to this subject is *Compensation Plans for Law Firms*, edited by James D. Cotterman (Chicago: ABA Law Practice Management Section, 2001).

See also Attorney fees; Attorneys, court-appointed; Billable hours; Billing rates; Law firm partners and associates; Law firms; Pro bono legal work; Public defenders; Public interest law; Retainers.

ATTORNEY TRUST ACCOUNTS

Funds held by lawyers on behalf of clients in special bank accounts or trust accounts that are separate from their other accounts under rules of legal ethics

Lawyers routinely hold client funds in their possession. Lawyers who oversee the administration of an estate may hold cash from the estate and from the liquidation of estate assets prior to distribution to beneficiaries of the estate. Lawyers engaged in real estate practice may briefly hold client funds necessary to close the real estate transaction. Trial lawyers may hold money intended to be paid in a settlement. Tax lawyers may hold client funds briefly before paying taxes on their clients' behalf.

Trust Account Rules

In these and other circumstances rules of legal ethics emphatically require that lawyers keep the funds of their clients separate from the lawyers' own funds. The Model Rules of Professional Conduct of the American Bar Association (ABA), the standards for attorney conduct in most states, require that lawyers maintain a separate bank account for client funds, commonly referred to as a "trust account." Thus, in most cases lawyers should have at least two bank accounts: one for the operating expenses of the legal

---

OBLIGATIONS OF A LAWYER HOLDING THE FUNDS OF A CLIENT

- To keep the funds in a bank account separate from the lawyer's own funds
- To notify a client when the lawyer receives funds belonging to the client
- To promptly transfer to a client funds to which the client is entitled once the lawyer receives these funds
- To provide an account of a client's funds upon the client's request

---

practice and one for the safeguarding of client funds. It is not sufficient for lawyers simply to keep close track of the amount of client funds on hand. The funds must actually be kept separate from lawyers' other funds.

Although lawyers may ultimately be entitled to some of the funds held in a trust account, they may not withdraw these funds until they are so entitled. For example, if a client gives a lawyer a retainer—an advance payment of legal fees—the lawyer must generally place the retainer in the trust account. Furthermore, the lawyer may not withdraw funds from the retainer until he or she has actually earned the funds. Similarly, even though a lawyer may be ultimately entitled to a percentage of funds held pending a real estate closing, he or she must wait until the closing and until the fee is actually due before withdrawing money from the trust account.

Lawyers have other responsibilities with respect to trust accounts. They must promptly notify clients or other parties once they have received funds that belong to them. Furthermore, lawyers must promptly deliver funds to clients or third parties who are entitled to the funds. And finally, lawyers are required to render a prompt accounting of funds upon the request of clients or third parties whose funds the lawyers have held.

Separate and Combined Accounts
Sometimes a lawyer separates particular clients' funds from those of other clients if they are substantial enough and to be held long enough to justify separate accounts. In these cases, a lawyer should establish interest-bearing accounts. More frequently, how-

ever, clients' funds are not substantial enough to justify this course. In these cases, the lawyer is permitted to deposit a client's funds into a general trust account containing other clients' funds.

Although general trust accounts may bear interest, lawyers are not entitled to the interest from clients' funds. In addition, banks have generally taken the position that it is impossible to allocate interest in an interest-bearing account to the various deposits in the account. Accordingly, at the close of the 1990's, forty-eight states had established programs either requiring or at least permitting lawyers to take the interest from their general trust accounts and turn this money over to state bar association for use in a variety of public causes, such as legal services for indigent persons. These programs are called Interest on Lawyers Trust Account programs (IOLTA). The programs were dealt a substantial blow at the close of the 1990's, however, in the U.S. Supreme Court's decision in *Phillips v. Washington Legal Foundation* (1998). This case held that the interest earned on all trust account funds belongs to the clients. Accordingly, state programs that took this interest for public purposes were possibly in violation of the takings clause of the Fifth Amendment to the U.S. Constitution, which prohibits government from taking private property for public purposes without just compensation.

Discipline of Lawyers for Trust Account Violations
In most states the state supreme court supervises attorney conduct, assisted normally by disciplinary committees of the state bar. These committees are generally quite vigorous in punishing lawyers who improperly handle funds in trust accounts. Punishments range from public or private reprimands to suspension from practice or even disbarment from the practice of law. Especially when lawyers take funds from their trust accounts to which they are not entitled, bar grievance committees and state supreme courts have often handed out stiff punishments. Even when a lawyer has returned money to the trust account after improperly removing it and even when clients have not been injured, state disciplinary authorities have often ordered that the lawyer be suspended or disbarred. A few states, to aid in the discovery of trust account abuses, have established systems that make spot checks of these accounts to determine whether they are being handled appropriately.

—Timothy L. Hall

Suggested Readings

Tanya Starnes's *Mad at Your Lawyer?* (Berkeley, Calif.: Nolo Press, 1996) discusses a variety of issues relating to attorney-client relationships and offers practical advice to clients in dealing with lawyers. For a discussion of the law concerning attorney trust accounts Charles W. Wolfram's *Modern Legal Ethics* (St. Paul, Minn.: West Publishing, 1986) is a useful treatise on legal ethics. *The ABA Guide to Lawyer Trust Accounts* by Jay G. Foonberg (Chicago: ABA Section of Law Practice Management, 1996) also offers a detailed discussion of the legal aspects of attorney trust accounts. Abuse of trust accounts may reflect broader currents within the legal profession. Maclin Fleming's *Lawyers, Money, and Success: The Consequences of Dollar Obsession* (Westport, Conn.: Quorum Books, 1997) and Michael H. Trotter's *Profit and the Practice of Law: What's Happened to the Legal Profession* (Athens: University of Georgia Press, 1997) contain discussions of modern lawyers' attitudes toward profit. The standards of the American Bar Association are laid out in *ABA Compendium of Professional Responsibility Rules and Standards* (Chicago: Center for Professional Responsibility, American Bar Association, 2001).

See also Attorney-client relationship; Attorney fees; Attorneys as fiduciaries; Litigation expenses; Model Rules of Professional Conduct; Paralegals; Retainers; Unethical conduct of attorneys.

ATTORNEY TYPES

Areas of legal specialization of the licensed professionals who provide advice and representation on legal matters for individuals businesses organizations and governments; examples include criminal corporate and taxation law

Licensed attorneys in the United States are permitted to handle virtually any legal matter that a client hires them to handle. The breadth of attorneys' authority in the United States contrasts with the organization of legal professions in some other countries. In Great Britain, for example, there is a traditional division within the legal profession between solicitors, who advise clients and prepare legal documents, and barristers, who present cases in court. Despite their authority to handle any area of law, U.S. lawyers usually specialize in specific tasks or legal subjects. Their specializations usually result from the needs of their employers or from the demands of their clients.

Training and Licensing of Attorneys

In the United States attorneys must generally have a four-year college degree and a degree from a law school accredited by the American Bar Association (ABA) or approved by a state supreme court. Graduation from law school requires three years of full-time study or four years of part-time study. During law school all students take a variety of required courses covering a broad range of legal subjects. In addition, depending on a particular law school's requirements, 30 to 60 percent of a student's courses may be electives. Many students use their elective choices to begin preparing for a career specializing in a particular field of law.

States require that law school graduates pass a bar examination and undergo a background check before becoming licensed attorneys. Each state has its own bar examination. Many states give a standard six-hour multiple-choice examination on general subjects, and each state requires of examinees that they answer essay questions focused on the laws of the state in question. Upon passing the bar examination, law school graduates become licensed attorneys who are permitted to handle the full range of legal matters, from writing a simple will to conducting a jury trial in defense of an accused murderer.

Because law students must pass the bar examination in order to become licensed attorneys and the examination covers a broad sweep of subjects, few students become specialists in particular areas of law while in law school. Instead, the jobs obtained by new attorneys largely determine what types of attorneys they will be.

It is not always easy for new attorneys to choose their own specializations. Beginning attorneys must compete for jobs, because U.S. law schools produce thousands of new law school graduates each year. Students whose grades place them at the top of their law school's graduating class or those who attend the most prestigious law schools are most likely to gain employment in the law firm, corporate, or government setting of their choice. Most other new attorneys have limited options and therefore find their specializations determined by the settings in which they happen to find employment. For example, if they are hired by a law firm that specializes in family law, they may become divorce lawyers.

Attorneys in Government

Attorneys employed by government agencies become specialists in the areas of law handled by their agencies. For example, attorneys who work for the Internal Revenue Service (IRS) or a state's treasury department handle tax matters on behalf of the government. Attorneys at the Environmental Protection Agency (EPA) or a state's natural resources department handle legal issues concerning land, water, and environmental pollution regulations. Other government attorneys specialize in matters affecting health care, education, transportation, housing, agriculture, and the other areas overseen by government agencies. These attorneys typically advise government agencies on how to follow stat-

---

TYPES OF ATTORNEYS

Bankruptcy attorney: represents people seeking to have their debts discharged by the court

Corporate attorney: employed by a law firm or corporation to draft contracts, arrange business deals, and handle other aspects of corporate law

Criminal defense attorney: represents people accused of crimes

Estate planning attorney: assists clients in addressing laws affecting inheritance by handling wills, trusts, and estates

Family law attorney: specializes in divorce, adoption, and child custody cases

Government attorney: employed by a government agency to represent the government and enforce governmental laws and regulations

Labor attorney: specializes in employment issues, including contract negotiations between labor unions and employers

Litigator: specializes in presenting cases in the courtroom during trials

Personal injury attorney: specializes in pursuing lawsuits against people allegedly responsible for a client's injuries

Prosecutor: investigates and pursues charges against people suspected of committing crimes

Tax attorney: advises clients on arranging business and personal affairs to minimize the imposition of taxes

utes enacted by legislatures and decisions issued by courts. They may also defend government agencies against lawsuits by individuals and businesses. Frequently they help to draft suggested new statutes when an agency seeks to have its authority expanded or otherwise altered by the legislature. Even the branches of military service have attorneys to handle all kinds of cases that arise affecting military personnel.

The enforcement of criminal laws is primarily handled by local prosecutors who typically work for county or city government. Attorneys who work for state attorneys general, the chief legal officials in each state, may have the authority to prosecute violations of certain state laws or to file civil lawsuits against corporations and individuals involved in illegal business practices. Such attorneys also defend the state against lawsuits, whether by large corporations or by imprisoned criminal offenders who claim that their rights have been violated. In the federal government, lawyers in the Justice Department prosecute federal crimes and handle lawsuits involving the U.S. government. In addition, the federal government and many counties have salaried attorneys, called public defenders, who represent criminal suspects who are too poor to hire their own attorneys. The Sixth Amendment to the U.S. Constitution provides a right to counsel, which means that even poor people must be provided with attorneys in criminal cases.

In the judicial branch of government, attorneys serve in various roles. Judges who preside over courtrooms and decide issues during trials are attorneys. The president of the United States chooses attorneys for the federal courts to serve as judges. In most states, voters play a role in either electing attorneys to become judges or in deciding whether judges have performed well enough to continue in office. Inexperienced attorneys called "law clerks" work for a year or two as assistants to federal judges, state appeals court judges, and some state trial judges. In addition, many appeals courts have staff attorneys who assist judges by reviewing cases and making recommendations about which cases deserve a full court hearing and which should receive a quick decision based solely on the initial papers filed with the court.

Interest Group Attorneys

Many organizations seek to use law as a means to advance their preferred public policies. They file lawsuits asking courts to issue orders declaring that the U.S. Constitution or a statute requires the government to operate in a particular manner. The most famous example of the use of law to change public policy involved civil rights attorneys in the 1950's who persuaded the U.S. Supreme Court to declare that racial segregation in public schools violates the Constitution's equal protection clause. Attorneys for interest groups focus on particular kinds of issues of concern to their organizations. These attorneys often feel deeply committed to the causes they represent. Unlike attorneys in private practice, who may represent any client that hires them, interest group attorneys often have passionate feelings about the cases they pursue. For example, attorneys for the American Civil Liberties Union (ACLU) handle cases in which individuals believe that the government has violated their rights to freedom of speech, freedom of religion, and other matters addressed by the Constitution's Bill of Rights. Interest group attorneys for other organizations specialize in such fields as environmental law, labor law, education law, and consumer protection law.

Attorneys in the Private Sector

Some attorneys work as employees of corporations. These corporate attorneys are responsible for the full range of legal matters involving the corporation. They draft contracts, ensure compliance with government regulations, and produce the necessary legal documents to set up corporations and partnerships. Other corporate attorneys work for law firms that are hired by businesses to handle such legal matters.

General practice law firms handle all types of legal cases, while other law firms specialize in specific areas of law. The areas of specialization within private legal practice touch upon nearly every area of human endeavor, especially activities regulated by the government or involving contractual relationships between private individuals or businesses.

Labor attorneys handle matters related to employment. Most notably, they represent unions or employers in labor contract negotiations. The lawyers help to determine the details of labor contracts and ensure that labor-related activities of unions and employers are consistent with relevant laws. In the employment field, attorneys also handle discrimination claims and workers' compensation claims by injured employees.

Family law attorneys address problems concerning family relationships. In particular, such attorneys advise individuals about divorce issues and represent clients in disputes over the division of financial assets and child custody. These attorneys may also draft legal documents for adoptions and for other matters affecting families.

Litigators specialize in preparing and presenting cases in courtrooms during trials. Often these specialists work for law firms and work closely with corporate attorneys in specific cases that arise when resolutions to contractual and other disputes cannot be easily negotiated. Personal injury attorneys often have significant expertise in litigation because they must make use of court procedures to seek compensation for their clients' injuries caused by other people or businesses. While many personal injury cases result in negotiated settlements, these attorney must be prepared to take their cases to trial, at which judges or juries may be required to decide on the issue of compensation.

Many attorneys specialize in providing advice to clients concerning financial matters. Attorneys who handle estate planning problems draft wills and create trusts in an effort to ensure that clients' assets are transferred properly after they die. Tax attorneys advise clients about how their business and personal financial dealings will be affected by tax laws. These attorneys also help clients legally avoid taxes that might otherwise be imposed.

—Christopher E. Smith

Suggested Readings

A description of the historical development of the legal profession is presented in Richard Abel's *American Lawyers* (New York: Oxford University Press, 1989). An analysis of the roles of lawyers in American society is presented in Jerold Auerbach's *Unequal Justice: Lawyers and Social Change in Modern America* (New York: Oxford University Press, 1976). Descriptions of the division between corporate lawyers and those who serve the needs of individual clients are presented by John P. Heinz and Edward O. Laumann in *Chicago Lawyers: The Social Structure of the Bar* (New York: Russell Sage, 1982) and by Marc Galanter and Thomas Palay in *Tournament of Lawyers: The Transformation of the Big Law Firm* (Chicago: University of Chicago Press, 1991). In contrast, descriptions of other types of lawyers are presented in Carroll Seron's *The Business of Practicing Law: The Working Lives of Solo and Small-Firm Attorneys* (Philadelphia: Temple University Press, 1996) and Donald Landon's *Country Lawyers* (New York: Praeger, 1990).

See also American Bar Association; Appellate practice; Attorneys; Attorneys, court-appointed; Attorneys, United States; Attorneys general, state; Bar associations; Court types; Death row attorneys; Defense attorneys; District attorneys; Family law practice; Law firm partners and associates; Legal services plans; Legislative counsel; Military attorneys; Personal injury attorneys; Prosecutors; Public defenders.

ATTORNEYS

Persons trained in the law and admitted by their states' highest courts to practice law in the states

An attorney is a person learned in the law who gives legal advice and is licensed to represent a person, or client, who hires the attorney. Originally, attorneys were minor court officials, tutored by judges or others with legal knowledge, who represented a client. The modern attorney is a graduate of an accredited four-year college and spends three years at an accredited law school to receive the degree of Juris Doctor. The graduate must pass an examination given under the auspices of a state's bar association. An attorney may perform legal duties related to both criminal and civil matters. In both venues, an attorney offers counsel concerning the law, drafts documents, and represents the client in court.

Much of the communication between attorney and client is subject to privilege (confidential) and may not be divulged to a third party unless the client agrees to it. For the attorney to do otherwise would be considered a serious breach of professional conduct. Attorney-client privilege is so important that an attorney must receive permission from the court to withdraw from representation of a client once proceedings are begun.

The professional conduct of attorneys is governed by the *Model Rules of Professional Conduct* (first published in 1984), established by the American Bar Association and accepted by individual state bar associations. A serious breach of professional conduct or ethics may subject an attorney to censure or suspension from practice and, in extreme cases, to disbarment.

An attorney may be in private practice, work for a private corporation, or work for the government. An attorney engaged in private practice, whether a sole practitioner, a member of a partnership, or a member of a large law firm, may handle diverse duties such as estate planning, business law, and civil or criminal litigation. Many law firms specialize in an area of law, so that the attorney becomes a specialist. An attorney may also have expertise that is unrelated to the firm's general practice but enhances the services offered to a client. The private-practice attorney is hired by, and works directly for, a client. The majority of lawyers are engaged in private practice.

Attorneys working for private corporations may represent the corporation in labor or contract negotiations and may handle routine litigation filed against the corporation. Major litigation, or any lawsuit that may take a long time to resolve, is often turned over to a private law firm hired for the purpose. Corporate attorneys may also provide low-cost or no-cost legal advice to employees of the corporation.

Attorneys engaged in government service may work directly for the U.S. Department of Justice or in any of the government's numerous agencies. The ultimate in government service may be election to the legislative or executive branch in either state or federal government. Because the business of government is law, attorneys are often considered particularly qualified to serve in elective offices.

See also Attorney-client relationship; Attorney confidentiality; Attorney fees; Attorney salaries; Attorney trust accounts; Attorney types; Attorneys, court-appointed; Attorneys as fiduciaries; Bar associations; Grievance committees for attorney discipline; Law firms; Legal services plans; Model Rules of Professional Conduct; Paralegals; Unauthorized practice of law; Unethical conduct of attorneys.

ATTORNEYS, COURT-APPOINTED

*Private-practice attorneys who are appointed by courts and paid
by the government to represent indigent criminal defendants*

The U.S. Supreme Court's decision in *Gideon v. Wainwright* (1963)
argued that the "right to counsel" in the U.S. Constitution's Sixth
Amendment requires the government to provide defense attorneys for indigent criminal defendants. Indigent defendants are
people accused of crimes who are too poor to hire their own attorneys. All levels of government—federal, state, and local—have
developed methods for providing attorneys for criminal defendants.

While the federal government and many large cities have full-
time salaried attorneys known as public defenders who handle
such work, most counties throughout the United States rely on
court-appointed attorneys to represent indigent defendants.
Court-appointed attorneys are private attorneys who are paid by
the government for accepting appointments from the court to represent indigent defendants. While most private practice attorneys
rarely or never accept criminal cases from indigent persons, some
attorneys who specialize in criminal law devote a substantial portion of their time working on court-appointment cases.

Appointment of Attorneys

Governments employ different mechanisms for appointing attorneys to handle specific cases. In some places, attorneys must
meet specific experience requirements in order to receive appointments to defend indigent persons against serious charges.
For example, recent law-school graduates may only be eligible to
receive appointments for misdemeanor cases, those in which the
potential punishment is probation or less than one year in a
county jail. Attorneys may need to handle a certain number of
cases or have criminal defense experience for a specific amount of
time before they are eligible for appointments to handle felony
cases, which are those cases with potential punishments exceeding one year in state prison. By contrast, in other counties any licensed attorney can have his or her name placed on a list for appointments in all kinds of criminal cases, even if they have no
prior experience in criminal cases. In these locations, attorneys

who are inexperienced or are unsuccessful in other areas of legal practice may see court-appointed criminal cases as an attractive means to gain income and experience.

The actual appointment of attorneys to specific cases generally occurs in one of two ways. In many courthouses the court clerk or court administrator assigns each new case to the next eligible attorney on the list of lawyers who have expressed a desire to take court appointments. This method produces an orderly and fair rotation of cases among local attorneys. By contrast, judges in other courthouses assume the power to select particular attorneys for each case. This method may help defendants if a careful judge uses the power to make sure that capable and experienced attorneys are matched with complex and controversial cases. On the other hand, there is also the risk that some judges will use this system to steer cases to attorneys who are friends, relatives, and political supporters, without regard for the quality of representation required by the defendant.

The Attorney's Responsibilities

The court-appointed attorney begins to represent the defendant shortly after the arrest is made. Sometimes the attorney is appointed in time to represent the defendant at the bail hearing. Even if the attorney is not appointed prior to the setting of bail, the attorney must be appointed before there is a preliminary hearing in which a judge examines whether there is enough evidence to proceed with the case against the defendant. Although many defendants waive their opportunity to have a preliminary hearing, especially if the evidence against them is overwhelming, the preliminary hearing may provide an opportunity for the defense attorney to learn about and challenge the evidence gathered by the police and prosecutor. The attorney seeks to persuade the judge to dismiss the case for lack of evidence or to convince the prosecutor to drop the charges.

The most important and frequent activity of court-appointed attorneys is negotiating with prosecutors about a possible plea bargain. The attorney discusses with the prosecutor the provable facts in the case and the defendant's prior record in the hope of getting an agreement on a reduction in charges or a specific sentencing recommendation in exchange for a voluntary plea of guilty. After the attorney has learned what deal the prosecutor is willing to offer, the attorney makes recommendations to the

---

RESPONSIBILITIES OF COURT-APPOINTED ATTORNEYS

- Represent the defendant during questioning
- Represent the defendant at the bail hearing
- Represent the defendant at the preliminary hearing
- Investigate the facts of the case
- Negotiate with the prosecutor for a plea agreement
- Advise the defendant about whether to accept the plea bargain
- Represent the defendant at trial if there is no guilty plea
- Make arguments to the judge about the appropriate sentence

---

defendant about whether or not to accept the plea agreement. Ninety percent of all criminal convictions are obtained through this plea bargaining process. Relatively few court-appointed cases ever go to trial. Trials occur when defendants face very serious charges, such as murder, so that the prosecutor is unwilling to offer any inducements to obtain a guilty plea. Thus, the job of court-appointed attorneys primarily involves talking to the prosecutor about plea agreements and then advising the defendant about what to do.

Problems with Court-Appointed Attorneys

There are many criticisms of the use of court-appointed attorneys. In many counties, attorneys are not appointed quickly enough to protect defendants' interests during bail hearings and other early stages of the criminal proceedings. Many counties pay such low fees to court-appointed attorneys that only inexperienced or unsuccessful attorneys are willing to handle cases for indigent criminal defendants. These attorneys may lack both knowledge about and interest in criminal law. The low fees may also discourage attorneys from taking cases all the way to trial.

Low fees can create an incentive for attorneys to assist prosecutors by persuading their clients to plead guilty as quickly as possible. In some courthouses, defendants may plead guilty after one short meeting with their attorneys. The speed of such plea bargains raises questions about attorneys' commitment to investigating their clients' cases and negotiating carefully with the prosecutor. Many court-appointed attorneys feel that they have few options other than to seek a quick plea bargain, because the low fees do not provide them with enough money to hire the investigators and expert witnesses used by attorneys for affluent clients. Some commentators argue that indigent defendants are better served by full-time, salaried public defenders who have chosen criminal defense work as a career. However, many counties find that it is less expensive to rely on court-appointed attorneys.

—*Christopher E. Smith*

Suggested Readings
   The need of indigent criminal defendants to have representation by attorneys is demonstrated in *Gideon's Trumpet* (New York: Random House, 1964) by Anthony Lewis, the story of the U.S. Supreme Court's decision on the right to counsel. The pitfalls of relying on inexperienced court-appointed attorneys for complex murder cases is presented in John C. Tucker's *May God Have Mercy: A True Story of Crime and Punishment* (New York: W. W. Norton, 1997). The best-known study of private practice criminal defense lawyers is Paul B. Wice's *Criminal Lawyers: An Endangered Species* (Beverly Hills, Calif.: Sage, 1978). An overview of systems for representing indigent defendants is presented in Robert Spangenberg's "Indigent Defense Systems in the United States" in *Law and Contemporary Problems* 58 (1995). More recent studies include H. Richard Uviller's *The Tilted Playing Field: Is Criminal Justice Unfair?* (New Haven, Conn.: Yale University Press, 1999) and David Cole's *No Equal Justice: Race and Class in the American Criminal Justice System* (New York: New Press, 1999).

See also Attorney types; Bail system; Death row attorneys; Defense attorneys; Effective counsel; Indigent criminal defendants; Legal clinics; Miranda rights; Plea bargaining; Pleas; Preliminary hearings; Privileged communications; Pro bono legal work; Public defenders; Trials.

ATTORNEYS, UNITED STATES

*Chief legal representatives of the U.S. Department of Justice in its
ninety-four regional offices, responsible for supervising the local
operations*

The ninety-four United States attorneys stationed in the United
States, Guam, Puerto Rico, and the Virgin Islands are appointed
by the Department of Justice and report to the director of the Executive Office for United States Attorneys, who in turn reports to
the deputy attorney general of the United States. United States attorneys work cooperatively with the United States marshals assigned to their offices and supervise the work of assistant United
States attorneys and special assistant United States attorneys in
their jurisdictions.

United States attorneys coordinate the work of their offices,
which deal with legal situations that include such responsibilities
as doing regional investigations of matters about which other
branches of the Department of Justice need information. Their offices, for example, might be asked to gather data about federal
prisoners being considered for pardons and transmit such information to the Office of the Pardon Attorney.

See also Attorney general of the United States; Attorney types;
District attorneys; Federal Bureau of Investigation; Federal judicial system; Legislative counsel.

ATTORNEYS AS FIDUCIARIES

*Special responsibilities of attorneys when receiving or holding the
money or other property of their clients*

The attorney-client relationship requires a high level of confidence, good faith, and trust. Lawyers also have a fiduciary relationship with the court and the society at large. The lawyer's fiduciary duties are prescribed in the Rules of Professional Conduct of
the American Bar Association (ABA). A lawyer shall not reveal

confidential information relating to the representation of a client unless the client consents after consultation with the lawyer. Lawyers are authorized to make disclosures about clients appropriate to carrying out their duties of representation. Keeping confidences is essential to the attorney-client relationship.

Lawyers have a fiduciary relationship when receiving or holding moneys or other property of the client. The Rules of Professional Conduct require that all property of clients be kept separate from lawyers' personal properties. Lawyers must promptly notify a client of the receipt of funds, securities, or other properties. Lawyers must maintain complete records of all funds, securities, and other properties coming into their possession. Client funds must be kept in separate interest-bearing accounts and not be commingled with attorneys' own funds. The Code of Professional Responsibility provides that an attorney shall "not consciously influence a client to name him or her as an executor or trustee." Attorneys must avoid even the appearance of impropriety in assisting clients with trust or estate administration.

Attorneys may be bound by a fiduciary relationship in holding property in trust or serving as trustees. They may have a fiduciary relationship if serving as executors or administrators of estates. Attorneys are required to act in the utmost good faith and not take advantage of clients in their business dealings with clients. Business dealings with clients presents a situation of potential conflict of interest between the lawyer's role of business partner and fiduciary. Attorneys have a fiduciary duty to avoid business dealings that conflict with the interests of clients.

The Model Rules of Professional Conduct prohibit business transactions with clients unless they are fair and reasonable to the clients, fully disclosed, and clients are given an opportunity to seek independent counsel. Clients must consent to business transactions in writing after full disclosure of potential adverse interests. An attorney conducting business aspects of the practice of law must adhere to the highest business standards of the community. While the fiduciary duty applied in dealings with clients is not expected of a lawyer in business dealings with third parties, the lawyer must act in utmost good faith when representing a client.

Lawyers frequently serve in a business capacity in the course of representation. For example, lawyers may be asked to serve as directors or officers of corporations. The law requires utmost good faith if any of these business dealings involve clients. The substantive field of trusts and estates requires that lawyers handle client moneys as fiduciaries. Attorneys violating the fiduciary relationship are subject to sanctions by the grievance committees of the relevant state bar association. Attorneys violating the fiduciary duty owed clients may also be subject to professional malpractice lawsuits. Breach of fiduciary duty owed clients is a cause of many legal malpractice lawsuits.

—*Michael L. Rustad*

See also American Bar Association; Attorney-client relationship; Attorney fees; Attorney trust accounts; Attorneys; Commercial litigation; Model Rules of Professional Conduct; Unethical conduct of attorneys.

ATTORNEYS GENERAL, STATE

Chief legal officers of individual states who serve as counselors for state government agencies, legislatures, and the citizenry, providing legal advice and legal representation for state agencies and the public on diverse matters such as drug abuse, the environment, business regulation, and criminal appeals

The development of state attorneys general in the United States can be traced to England. The king of England had specially designated lawyers to represent his legal interests. The attorney general of England served as legal adviser to the king and all government departments and was responsible for all litigation. During the American colonial era, the attorney general provided legal advice to the king and governance over the colonies. After the revolution, American officials adapted the English version of the office of attorney general to govern their own legal interests. Constitutional provisions were enacted to create the office of the attorney general to have jurisdiction of legal affairs of the federal government. As the new nation grew, the states also adopted the office of attorney general, and many had constitutional provisions for the office.

Attorneys general are popularly elected in forty-three states, appointed by the governors in five states and six jurisdictions, appointed by the state supreme court in Tennessee, and selected by the state legislature in Maine. New legislation and conceptions of the office have significantly expanded the powers and duties of the state attorneys general. There is much diversity in the role of the attorney general from state to state.

In response to needs identified by governors and legislatures, attorneys general have become active in areas of consumer protection, antitrust law, toxic waste, child-support enforcement, organized crime, and many other areas. The most common duties of the attorney general involve controlling litigation concerning the state, serving as chief legal officer, writing opinions which clarify law, acting as public advocate, enforcing criminal law, and investigating issues of public interest.

Public advocacy is a growing field for attorneys general in nearly all states. In addition to providing legal service in such areas as consumer protection and child-support enforcement, relatively new areas of concern for states' chief legal officers include utility regulation and advocacy regarding the provision of services to crime victims. These new areas of interest put attorneys general in the position of being the initiator of legal action, or plaintiff, which is a role reversal that provides a new opportunity to implement and interpret public policy. One of the most important functions of the state attorney general is writing opinions. Opinions clarify law for the executive and legislative branches. Attorneys general use their opinions to identify legislative oversight that is in need of correction and to resolve issues that are not likely to be solved through litigation.

See also Administrative law; Attorney general of the United States; Attorney types; Criminal justice system; Prosecutors; State courts; State police.

BAIL BOND AGENTS

Type of insurance agents who provide financial instruments to courts to ensure that released defendants will make all subsequent court appearances as required

Bail bond agents are insurance providers who work with high-risk companies and clients. One of the services they provide is to offer criminal defendants the opportunity to be released from jail pending the conclusion of their criminal court actions by the posting of their bail bonds. This type of bond is generally known as a surety bond. The bail bond agent writes the clerk of the court a promissory note. The agent ensures that the defendant will appear for all scheduled court appearances. If the defendant fails to appear, the bail bond is forfeited and the clerk may cash the promissory note.

For their services bail bond agents collect fees, typically 10 percent of the price of the bail bonds. Agents may refuse to write bail bonds in particular cases or may require collateral interest in an amount above the typical 10 percent fee. If defendants fail to appear, the clerk of the court may grant the agents a grace period to locate the defendants and return them to the court.

Bail bond agents found themselves in a shrinking market as the 1990's came to a close. Abuses by agents and their reliance on poor defendants as clients have encouraged courts to develop other types of bonds or to do away with surety bail bonds altogether.

—*Michael L. Barrett*

See also Arrest; Attorney fees; Bail system; Bonds; Defendants; Due process of law; Personal recognizance.

BAIL SYSTEM

System that allows persons accused of criminal offenses to be released prior to their court appearances by securing funds to assure their appearance in court

The United States bail system operates on the premise that some individuals can be released prior to their appointed court date by leaving an amount of money with the court. Individuals are expected to return for their subsequent court appearance to have the amount of bail returned to them. Many argue that this practice discriminates against poor arrestees who cannot afford a monetary bail and thus must remain incarcerated while awaiting trial.

Tradition in English Law

The bail system in the United States is rooted in the traditional court systems of England. In feudal England (prior to the Battle of Hastings in 1066), law was dispensed by judges who would travel from county to county. Sheriffs would typically keep accused offenders in local jails with the promise to turn the offender in when the judge returned. As the number of offenders increased and jail space became limited, offenders were occasionally entrusted to the custody of a friend or relative who would ensure their appearance. In some cases, these individuals were required to sign a bond promising a specific sum of money to the king if the accused failed to appear when the judge next visited the area.

Over time (and eventually in the American colonies), the practice of having an individual step forward for an accused was replaced by the use of financial security, or monetary bail. In exchange for freedom prior to trial, the accused would deposit a certain amount of money with the court, which would be returned following appearance. Even before the colonization of America it was recognized that the practice discriminates against individuals who cannot afford to leave a monetary bail. Arrestees who could not afford to leave bail were frequently incarcerated until their appearance at trial, a time period which could encompass years. Thus, the first formal regulations governing the use of bail were written in England in the year 1275. These statutes set forth specific conditions under which bail could be imposed, defining which crimes were "bailable" and which were not. That is, they specified for which crimes bail must be denied and the accused must be incarcerated prior to trial. Laws forbidding excessive bail eventually appeared in England, but not until they were included in the English Bill of Rights in 1688.

History of the American Bail System

Like the English system, early Americans also protected against excessive bail. The Eighth Amendment to the U.S. Constitution begins with the phrase, "Excessive bail shall not be required." The meaning of this phrase, however, has not been successfully decided by the U.S. Supreme Court. For example, does excessive bail refer to the defendant's ability to pay, or does it relate to the seriousness of the crime committed? In addition, is there a constitutional right to bail?

The Judiciary Act of 1789 gave offenders a right to bail unless arrested for a capital offense. For a capital offense, maximum penalties can consist of life imprisonment or death. Assuming that these offenders may be likely to flee, considering the severity of punishment, bail is typically denied. Thus, every defendant in a noncapital case was guaranteed to receive bail. The appropriate amount of bail was not discussed in the Judiciary Act of 1789.

A recommended or appropriate amount of bail was not dealt with in the United States until 1951, when the Supreme Court, in *Stack v. Boyle*, decided that bail must be of sufficient amount to ensure the defendant's appearance at trial. In other words, the amount of bail must be enough to assure the defendant's appearance, but it cannot be more than that amount, or else it would be considered excessive. The vagueness of this decision has left many experts speculating about the appropriate amount of bail.

Bail Reform

During the 1960's, it became apparent that the United States bail system was not operating as it was designed. Judges were accused of having an excessive amount of discretion in setting amounts for bail. In addition, judges were responsible for setting bail based on which defendants were at high risk for flight and which were not. These decisions were supposed to be based on criminal characteristics, such as the seriousness of the crime committed and prior appearance history. It became clear, however, that among the factors taken into account in the assessment of flight risk were race and sex. Thus, judges' decisions were discriminatory against certain racial groups and against male offenders.

Another form of discrimination emerged in the practice of pretrial detention. Although the primary purpose of bail is to assure a defendant's appearance at trial, there is another purpose. Preventive detention is the practice of holding an arrestee prior to trial so that he or she does not commit any crimes during the time between arrest and court appearance. If a defendant is deemed to be a danger to the community during the pretrial period, a high amount of bail might be set in order to keep the arrestee locked up. Judges are responsible for making the determination regarding the "dangerousness" of an offender. Again, it was found that these decisions were influenced by noncriminal characteristics such as sex and race. Thus, the type of discrimination that appeared when assessing risk of flight also occurred when judges attempted to assess how likely an offender was to commit a crime while awaiting trial.

In the face of these problems, the first bail reform movement developed. Beginning in the early 1960's, bail came to the forefront as a serious problem within the criminal justice system. The Bail Reform Act of 1966 was an attempt to limit judicial discretion and remove discrimination from the bail process. There were two important developments that came from the Bail Reform Act of 1966. First, judges were expected to release all defendants on their own recognizance unless the judge had some good reason to set bail. In other words, the judge had to have solid grounds for setting bail. Second, "pretrial service agencies" were created to collect information about defendants, thus allowing the judge to have more—and more correct—information about each defendant.

Although preventive detention was a reality in the bail system, there were no laws in the United States stating that it was legal. The second bail reform movement occurred in the early 1970's, and it focused on the issue of legalizing preventive detention. In 1970, the District of Columbia enacted a law which authorized the detention of arrestees without bail if they were deemed a danger to the community. This was the first statute to set standards for the detention of arrestees for preventive reasons.

The issue of preventive detention was not a legal one until the year 1984. In this year, the United States bail system was a central focus of the Comprehensive Crime Control Act of 1984. The Bail

Reform Act of 1984 legitimated two federal judicial practices that were informally used before 1984. First, this act gave judges the power to assess defendants on their level of "dangerousness" to the community if released. It gave federal judges the legal right to use preventive detention. While the District of Columbia had its own provisions for preventive detention in 1970, it was not until 1984 that federal judges were given that right. Second, judges were given the right to deny bail in certain circumstances. Traditionally, bail was denied to offenders arrested for capital crimes; the Bail Reform Act of 1984 permitted judges to deny bail to those offenders who were judged to be at extremely high risk for nonappearance. Most notable in this group of offenders were drug traffickers, who were usually able to make extremely high bail and then flee the country.

The Bail Reform Act of 1984 was challenged in 1987, when *United States v. Salerno* was heard before the Supreme Court. This case challenged the idea of preventive detention, arguing that incarcerating alleged offenders violates their right to due process of law. Opponents of preventive detention argue that incarcerating offenders because of *potential* threat violates the presumption of innocence to which every arrestee is entitled. The Supreme Court did not agree with Salerno and upheld the judicial right to preventive detention. As long as judges have convincing evidence that the offender is likely to commit a crime while awaiting trial, they may set bail at a level higher than the typical amount.

Types of Bail

Judges must make a decision for every offender regarding the likelihood that the offender will appear for trial. They take several factors into account in making this decision, usually including prior arrest record, whether the defendant has appeared at previous hearings, stable family ties, and steady employment. After judges weigh these factors, they make a determination about how likely the defendant is to appear at trial. If offenders are classified as good risks—that is, if they are likely to appear for trial—they are typically released on their own recognizance. Release on recognizance (ROR) allows offenders to remain free before trial with the expectation that they will appear at the appropriate time.

Not all offenders are judged as good risks for appearance. For those expected to be bad risks, or those who are unlikely to appear at trial, some type of bail is usually required. While bail itself involves leaving some type of financial security with the court, the type of security can vary. The most obvious type of bail is typically called a cash bond, and this occurs when the defendant turns over money in the exact amount of bail to the court. Money is not the only type of bail that a defendant can leave with the court. In some cases, a defendant can post a property bond instead, which entails leaving property (personal possessions) with the court to ensure appearance. If the defendant does not appear for the next court appearance, all money and property is forfeited to the court.

Courts are aware that not everyone has the financial ability to post the exact amount of bail or to put up a substantial amount of property. For these individuals, a deposit bond is available. In a deposit bond, the accused offender deposits only a portion of the full bail amount to the court. If the defendant fails to appear, the deposit is kept by the court. If the defendant appears for trial, the majority of the bond is returned, with a small percentage kept by the court to cover court costs.

Finally, the most common type of bail is a surety bond. In this arrangement, a third party (not the court nor defendant) promises the court that if the defendant does not appear, they will turn over the amount of bail to the court. In exchange for this service, the defendant pays a fee to the third party. Usually, this third party is a bailbondsman.

Bailbondsmen

When defendants are required to pay bail prior to release, they may enlist the aid of a bailbondsman in securing funds. Bondsmen are independent businessmen who loan bail money to defendants with only a small amount of cash used as a fee. Bondsmen typically require 10 percent of the amount of bail for the fee. They use part of this fee to purchase a surety bond from an insurance company, which actually pays the bail if the defendant does not appear. In addition, bondsmen usually require some collateral as assurance that the defendant will not default on the loan. Many bond businesses also serve as pawn shops in their spare time, selling the collateral left by those who jump bail. Not all defendants will qualify for a bondsman's services. If defendants have a prior history of jumping bail, they will most likely be denied the bondsman's service.

Even those defendants judged as good risks for the bonds-man's service sometimes jump bail. When a defendant fails to appear for trial after securing a bondsman, the bailbondsman has legal authority to retrieve the defendant. The bondsman hires in-dividuals referred to as "bounty hunters" or "skip tracers," peo-ple who search for those who jump bail. These skip tracers have virtually unlimited discretion in apprehending the defendant. Unlike state and local police officers, skip tracers are allowed to cross state lines to retrieve individuals who jump bail and are al-lowed to enter a residence without an arrest warrant.

A major criticism of the bailbondsman trade is the ease with which corruption can flourish. Officers of the court, for example, are sometimes paid by bondsmen to refer defendants to their of-fices. These officers are typically given kickbacks for each defen-dant referred to the bondsmen. Judges are not immune from inap-propriate behavior—some judges may set unreasonably high bail so that defendants are forced to utilize the bondsman's services. In return for these "referrals," judges are paid by the bondsman. Finally, the bondsman trade also discriminates against indigent offenders, as most poor people cannot afford the fees.

Trends and Statistics

Approximately half of all defendants are held prior to trial, ac-cording to 1991 statistics. This figure includes individuals who do not make bail (44 percent of all defendants) and those who are held without bail (9 percent of all defendants). Only about 18 per-cent are released on their own recognizance. The amount of bail also varies across individuals and is usually dependent on the se-riousness of the crime committed and prior criminal record. Prop-erty offenders are likely to receive lower bail (under $2,500), while violent offenders are more likely to receive high bail (some-times over $20,000).

Of those who are released prior to trial, about one-fourth fail to appear for trial. Drug offenders are most likely to jump bail, and public order offenders are most likely to appear for trial. There also appears to be a relationship between the type of bond and rates of appearance. For example, offenders who are released on their own recognizance and offenders who leave a deposit bond have the highest rates of failure to appear. Offenders who use a bondsman are most likely to appear at their appointed court date.

—*Christina Polsenberg*

Suggested Readings

The Criminal Law Handbook: Know Your Rights, Survive the System, by Paul Bergman, Sara J. Berman-Barrett (5th ed. Berkeley, Calif.: Nolo Press, 2003), covers all aspects of criminal cases, including bail, in a question-and-answer format. A survey of the history of the American and English bail systems can be found in Ronald Goldfarb, *Ransom: A Critique of the American Bail System* (New York: Harper & Row, 1965). The felony bail process is summarized in Roy B. Flemming, *Punishment Before Trial: An Organizational Perspective of Felony Bail Processes* (New York: Longman, 1982), and an overview of bail reform in the United States can be found in Wayne H. Thomas, Jr., *Bail Reform in America* (Berkeley: University of California Press, 1976). Bail reform is also discussed in Samuel Walker, *Taming the System: The Control of Discretion in Criminal Justice, 1950-1990* (New York: Oxford University Press, 1993). Information on released and detained defendants is contained in the Bureau of Justice Statistics' annual *Sourcebook of Criminal Justice Statistics* (Washington, D.C.: U.S. Government Printing Office). For studies of financial inequities in the bail system, see H. Richard Uviller's *The Tilted Playing Field: Is Criminal Justice Unfair?* (New Haven, Conn.: Yale University Press, 1999) and Carl J. Franklin's *Constitutional Law for the Criminal Justice Professional* (Boca Raton, Fla.: CRC Press, 1999).

See also Arrest; Attorney fees; Attorneys, court-appointed; Bail bond agents; Bonds; Criminal procedure; Cruel and unusual punishment; Defendants; Eighth Amendment; Parole; Personal recognizance; Prosecutors.

BAILIFFS

Court officials responsible for maintaining order in courtrooms

In the judicial sense, a bailiff is an officer of the court who is specifically charged with the duty of preserving and protecting order in a courtroom, thereby allowing proceedings to continue unimpeded. During trial, the bailiff serves as the liaison between judge and jury. The bailiff ensures that the jury is present in the courtroom when required and is responsible for maintaining the integrity of the jury. Bailiffs are generally appointed to their positions by the judge in whose courtroom the bailiff serves. A bailiff may be a private individual or a sheriff's deputy.

Bailiffs also serve in other capacities. A bailiff may be appointed by the court to act as guardian of a mental incompetent, in which case the bailiff must report regularly to the court. A bailiff may also stand in the place of an owner of lands or goods, as a manager, and owes an accounting of that management to the owner.

See also Clerks of the court; Competency; Jury sequestration; Officers of the court; Trials.

BANKRUPTCY

Legal process through which debts that cannot be paid in full are discharged through a federal court; the inability to pay debts as they become due is also called insolvency

The concept of bankruptcy, or debt cutting, goes back at least as far as the Old Testament. Both Deuteronomy (15:1-6) and Leviticus (25:1-55) set forth rules for the legal cancellation of debts. The ancient Greek statesman Solon canceled debts in Athens in 594 B.C.E. These independent responses to debt indicate the complex natures of economies ranging from agricultural to capitalist.

Article I, section 8 of the U.S. Constitution provides that Congress shall have the power "to establish . . . uniform Laws on the subject of Bankruptcies throughout the United States." The intent was to give creditors long-arm jurisdiction to reach debtors fleeing from one state in the republic to another. Debtors' prisons existed in America until the early nineteenth century.

The longest continuous legislation was the Bankruptcy Act of 1898, which prevailed until the passage of the Bankruptcy Reform Act in 1978, effective October 1, 1979, which has been variously amended in 1980, 1984, 1986, 1990, and 1994. These amendments have generally limited and narrowed the access of debtors to broad bankruptcy relief. The goal of bankruptcy is to provide a

Laws relating to bankruptcy are adjudicated through federal courts. (Digital Stock)

fresh start for the honest debtor. The cause of bankruptcy may be poor business decisions, loss of employment or reduced income, divorce, substance or gambling abuse, illness and lack of health insurance, improvidence, and the uncertain shifts in a capitalist economy.

Current statute provides for types of bankruptcies known as Chapters 7, 9, 11, 12, and 13. Chapter 7 is a general liquidation, sometimes called straight bankruptcy; Chapter 9 is for municipalities (such as California's Orange County in 1994); Chapter 11 generally is for businesses that may liquidate or reorganize; Chapter 12 is for family farmers (introduced in 1986); and Chapter 13 is commonly called the wage earner's plan. Chapters 7 and 13, the most frequently used by individual or married debtors, are usually referred to as consumer bankruptcies. Bankruptcies may range from a few thousand dollars in a consumer Chapter 7 to several billion dollars in a Chapter 11.

Exemptions
In bankruptcy certain of the debtor's property is protected from creditors. In the nineteenth century, state statutes specifically exempted items such as cattle, sheep, a horse and wagon, bedding, and a family Bible from execution. The list includes

household goods, tools of the trade, and automobiles. States may adopt the generous federal exemptions or use state exemptions. About thirty-three states chose not to use the federal exemptions, thus creating wide diversity in exemptions. The federal homestead exemption is $15,000 per individual debtor and $30,000 for a married couple. In Florida, Iowa, Kansas, Minnesota, Texas, and Washington, 100 percent of the debtor's homestead is exempt from creditor claims. In seventeen other states the homestead exemption is $7,500 or less. Workers' compensation and employment benefits are also generally exempt. There is some concern about the good-faith motives of debtors planning bankruptcy who move from stingy to generous jurisdictions.

The U.S. Bankruptcy Court is part of the Department of Justice. There is a United States Trustee network at the national, regional, and state levels. At the local level, a Chapter 7, 12, or 13 trustee manages the disposition of the case. Before 1978 a referee served the function of the trustee. From filing to discharging Chapter 7 takes three to five months. Most Chapter 7 cases do not contain assets for the trustee to distribute to creditors. A Chapter 13 bankruptcy runs from three to five years. Chapter 13 has a superdischarge, because it discharges problems such as fraud that cannot be discharged in a Chapter 7.

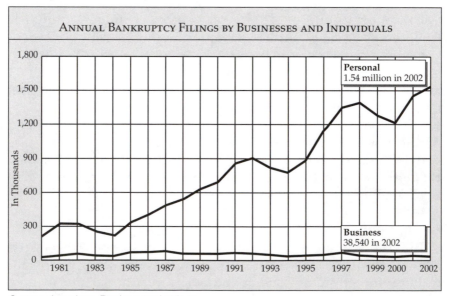

Source: American Bankruptcy Institute

Litigation in bankruptcy court is heard by a bankruptcy judge who is appointed by the president of the United States for a renewable fourteen-year term. There are two types of proceedings: motions and adversary proceedings.

Types of Debts and Dischargeability

There are three types of debt: Secured (lien on collateral); priority (taxes, wages, and certain other specified claims); and unsecured (everything else, including medical bills, credit cards, and back rent). In addition, there are administrative claims and executory contracts (leases and the like). Congress has determined that some debts cannot be discharged. These include child support, alimony, personal injury claims based on automobile accidents involving alcohol, willful and malicious action, student loans under certain circumstances, criminal restitution, and some taxes.

Section 362 of the bankruptcy code, which is called the automatic stay, provides injunctive relief against creditors. It stops creditor harassment, lawsuits, foreclosure, eviction, and garnishment. There are exceptions to the automatic stay, however. For example, it does not stop the prosecution of a criminal charge or the collection of child support. Bankruptcy is only a civil court matter. Filing fees are $160 for debtors, $200 for Chapter 12, and $800 for Chapter 11, making bankruptcy court one of the most expensive court costs within the American judicial system. Preferences involve the improper payment of selected debts on the eve of filing bankruptcy. After they receive a discharge, the code provides that certain lenders and employers are proscribed from discriminating against the discharged debtor "solely" on the basis of filing bankruptcy.

The number of bankruptcies filed increased considerably after the passage of the 1978 code. There is some correlation between bankruptcy and the state of the economy. In 1980, 331,098 cases were filed. By 2002 this number had risen to 1,577,651. More than 97 percent of these filings were consumer cases, the rest were business.

The 1994 Bankruptcy Reform Act created a National Bankruptcy Review Commission to report to Congress on the effectiveness of the 1978 code and subsequent amendments in the late twentieth century American economy.

—*Oliver B. Pollak*

Suggested Readings

A humane overview is provided in Teresa A. Sullivan, Elizabeth Warren, and Jay Lawrence Westbrook, *As We Forgive Our Debtors: Bankruptcy and Consumer Credit in America* (New York: Oxford University Press, 1989). *Collier on Bankruptcy* (15th ed. New York: Matthew Bender, updated regularly) is a technical treatise. Douglas G. Baird, *The Elements of Bankruptcy* (Westbury, N.Y.: Foundation Press, 1992), is also helpful. For a thorough historical survey of bankruptcy, see F. Regis Noel, *A History of the Bankruptcy Law* (New York: William S. Hein, 2002). Detailed texts on bankruptcy law include William D. Warren and Daniel J. Bussel, *Bankruptcy* (New York: Foundation Press, 2002); Charles J. Tabb and Ralph Brubaker, *Bankruptcy Law: Principles, Policies, and Practice* (Cincinnati: Anderson, 2003); and *Bankruptcy Anthology*, edited by Charles J. Tabb (Cincinnati: Anderson, 2002).

See also Commercial litigation; Court types; Foreclosure; Judgment proof; Justice Department, U.S.; Long-arm statutes; Release.

BAR ASSOCIATIONS

Professional organizations of attorneys established to support the practice of law, legal issues, and their members

Membership in some bar associations is mandatory for those who want to practice law within particular states. Mandatory bar associations have the power to control who may practice, discipline members, and control members' activities. They also engage in informal activities. The membership in other bar associations is voluntary; such associations have no official powers to control the practice of law but serve to advance legal institutions, act as advocates for legal issues, and lobby for the legal interests of their members. Bar associations that have official regulatory powers and engage in informal activities are referred to as unified bar associations.

The most common examples of mandatory bar associations are state bar associations. These associations set standards for admission to practice law within their states, have disciplinary powers to sanction members, collect required fees from members, and generally control the profession. These powers are given to the state bar association by the highest court in the state, the state legislature, or both. These associations are extremely powerful within their states, and some have expanded their activities to include the review and endorsement of judicial appointments and lobbying on impending legislation. As mandatory bar associations have moved into these other areas, they have been increasingly criticized.

The most prominent example of a national voluntary bar association is the American Bar Association (ABA). Although membership in the ABA is not a prerequisite for the practice of law, the ABA engages in many activities to promote law and lawyers. The public is a principal beneficiary of the ABA's work. There are other voluntary bar associations that promote special areas of practice through offering their members continuing education, providing expertise for legislators and administrative agencies, and encouraging scholarship. Such associations as the American Intellectual Property Law Association, the Federal Bar Association, and the Maritime Law Association are examples of such professional bar associations that serve both their members and the public. Most of these voluntary bar associations have nonattorney members and members of the academic community who work with practicing lawyers.

There are hundreds of local bar associations that do not have regulatory powers yet are active in local legal activities, providing benefits to the public. Attorneys in most counties and many larger cities have organized these bar associations. Initially such associations served a social function. However, such activities have been eclipsed by public benefit and awareness programs. County and city bar associations serve as referral agencies for local attorneys, encourage their members to engage in legal support for underrepresented groups such as children and elders, and publish guides and legal aids for the public. Some of the larger bar associations maintain law libraries that are often open to the public. Most state bar associations have Web sites, and some county and city bar associations also have Web sites.

—*J. Denny Haythorn*

See also American Bar Association; Attorney-client relationship; Attorney types; Attorneys; Bar examinations and licensing of lawyers; Grievance committees for attorney discipline; Judicial conduct code; Legal clinics; Model Rules of Professional Conduct; Pro bono legal work; Unauthorized practice of law; Unethical conduct of attorneys.

BAR EXAMINATIONS AND LICENSING OF LAWYERS

Examinations administered by the National Conference of Bar Examiners and many state boards of law examiners to graduates of accredited law schools (or, in rare cases, to individuals who may qualify to take the examination based on study and internship under the direction of a licensed attorney) in order to certify their qualifications for admission to the practicing bar of the state

A primary objective of the American Bar Association (ABA) at its inception, as written in its constitution, was "to advance the administration of justice and uniformity of legislation throughout the union, uphold the honor of the profession of the law, [and] encourage cordial intercourse among the members of the American Bar." To this end, one of the original standing committees established was that on legal education and admission to the bar. At that time, each of the states had its own standards for admission to the state bar. The ABA's section on legal education was the first organizational section created in 1893 to supplement the standing committee on legal education. In 1898, this section invited members of state boards of law examiners to meet in conjunction with the annual meeting of the American Bar Association. The purpose was to discuss the similarities and discrepancies in how the state boards administered their responsibilities.

Discussion topics included the organization of examining boards, the nature and scope of the exams, grading, eligibility requirements, ratio of failing grades, fees, exams for moral character, and retesting. A committee was appointed to study the feasibility of forming a National Association of Bar Examiners. In

1900, this committee suggested that representatives of the state boards meet contemporaneously with the annual ABA meeting to discuss the various aspects of legal education.

At the 1904 annual meeting of the ABA it was resolved "that it is desirable that the members of the Boards of Law Examiners in the different states form an association for the purpose of adopting uniform methods in their work establishing and maintaining standards of excellence." No significant changes occurred until the standing committee's presentation of nine recommendations in 1918. These included the recommendation that state bar membership be contingent on more than successful completion of a course of legal study at an accredited law school. Further requirements should take the form of passing a state examination under the direction of the highest appellate court of that state. In 1921, the ABA adopted the resolution that "graduation from a law school should not confer the right of admission to the Bar, and . . . every candidate should be subjected to an examination by public authority to determine his fitness."

The National Conference of Bar Examiners is a permanent agency that assists the state boards in carrying out their mandates. Every state administers its own examination for licensure in that state, commonly known as the bar exam. Generally, these exams may be separated into three parts: an exam testing one's knowledge of the canon of ethics of the profession; an objective, or multiple-choice exam covering generalities of law in all disciplines (focusing on aspects of constitutional law, criminal law, contracts, evidence, torts, and real property, known as "multistate" subjects); and an essay portion focusing on aspects of state law.

The bar exam is considered a comprehensive testing of an applicant's knowledge of the law. Each state weighs the various aspects of the examination differently. Some states do not administer a "multi-state" examination at all. The bar examination's overt purpose is to indicate to the public, as well as to the legal profession itself, that a candidate for licensing is well equipped to assist in the general appreciation of justice.

Suggested Readings

An overview of the organization of various bar organizations and examinations administered is Glenn Winters, *Bar Association Organization and Activities: A Handbook for Bar Association Officers*

(Ann Arbor, Mich.: American Judicature Society, 1954). For a discussion of the role of the bar association in licensing, see *The ABA in Law and Policy: What Role?* (Washington, D.C.: Federalist Society for Law and Public Policy Studies, 1994). The final chapter of Robert H. Miller's *Law School Confidential: The Complete Law School Survival Guide: by Students, for Students* (New York: St. Martin's Griffin, 2000) is on strategies for the bar examination.

See also American Bar Association; Attorney types; Bar associations; *Black's Law Dictionary*; Law schools; Unauthorized practice of law.

BENCH WARRANTS

Orders issued by courts in session for immediate arrests of persons for the purpose of allowing matters at bar to continue without lengthy delay in obtaining warrants

A bench warrant, issued by the court, is an order that follows the failure of earlier attempts to resolve a problem. It permits police to seize a person, but not usually property, immediately. The bench warrant may be issued in a case of contempt, a refusal to abide by an order of the court. The court may have issued a written order requiring the performance of certain duties, such as payment of support, or during a trial the court may have issued an order that is not obeyed, such as an order to a witness to disclose certain information. A bench warrant also follows if the court issues a subpoena or another order commanding a witness to appear and testify at trial, but the witness ignores the order. The bench warrant differs from a warrant issued by the court which permits search and seizure of persons and property for evidence.

See also Arrest; Contempt of court; Probable cause; Search warrant requirement; Subpoena power.

BILL OF RIGHTS, U.S.

First ten amendments to the U.S. Constitution that contain the Constitution's most concentrated statement of civil liberties

The Bill of Rights consists of the first ten amendments to the U.S. Constitution, although some scholars believe that the differences between the first eight and the final two mean that only the first eight should really be counted. The first eight provide specific prohibitions against government action, while the last two appear to be more explanatory. British common law had evolved many rights that British citizens had in relation to their government, but these rights were not necessarily granted to American colonists; this was one of the grievances that led to the American Revolution. There was a direct relationship, in fact, between certain British actions and certain amendments in the Bill of Rights.

Not only grievances against the British but also fear of the potential power of the national government under the newly proposed Constitution led to the Bill of Rights. Some opponents of the proposed document seized on the lack of a list of citizens' rights as an argument against adopting the Constitution. The inclusion of a Bill of Rights was accepted by the Constitution's proponents as a means to sway undecided voters to vote for ratification. Still, not all proponents liked the idea. In one of the Federalist Papers, Alexander Hamilton argued that the entire Constitution was so limited as to be itself a "Bill of Rights," that no further list was needed, and that there might even be the danger that a narrow list of rights would be regarded as the only rights people had. To meet Hamilton's objection, the Ninth Amendment stated explicitly that the mere enumeration of these rights was not meant to preclude other rights belonging to Americans. The Ninth Amendment and the Tenth Amendment (which reserves power to the states and people, respectively) therefore are explanatory and do not have the same character as the first eight. The decision to promise inclusion of a Bill of Rights was a great strategic success for the Constitution's proponents and was a key feature in several wavering states' support for the new union.

Early in the First Congress under the new Constitution, James Madison led in suggesting the amendments that, after committee

James Madison, who later became the fourth president, is credited with principal authorship of the Bill of Rights. (White House Historical Society)

deliberation, became the text of the Bill of Rights. There were twelve amendments, but only ten were ratified initially. In contrast with the twentieth century celebration of the Bill of Rights, at their centennial in 1891 there was almost no mention of them. At that time they were understood to apply only to the federal government, which was not significantly involved in regulating individual behavior. Even after the passage of the Fourteenth Amendment, which the Supreme Court later used to extend the Bill of Rights to the states, the actual incorporation of these rights for use of citizens against either level of government did not come until much later. In the twentieth century, the "selective incorporation" process applied most essential provisions to the states under the "due process" clause of the Fourteenth Amendment.

Modern Significance of the First Four Amendments

The First Amendment's promise that "Congress shall make no law" establishing religion or blocking the free exercise of religious belief, speech, press, peaceful assembly, or petition is of core importance to the whole realm of free expression. Of all the sections of the Bill of Rights, the provisions of the First Amendment were the first to be incorporated under the due process clause of the Fourteenth Amendment and applied to the states. All of its sections have been the subject of considerable litigation.

Most scholars believe that the Second Amendment's language— "a well regulated militia, being necessary to the security of a free state, the right of the people to keep and bear arms, shall not be infringed"—is misunderstood by those who attempt to find in it a broad individual right to own unregulated firearms. Adopted because of the British attempt to disarm the colonial militias before the Revolution and the fear that the new U.S. national government might do the same, this amendment has never been interpreted by the Supreme Court to establish an absolute individual right to own guns or to bar regulation of them. It has not been applied to state regulation of firearms. The amendment was intended to prevent national disarmament of state militias, which is no longer a substantial concern. Clearly, Congress cannot regulate guns in such a way as to disarm state militias, but not much more is banned by this amendment. For example, *United States v. Miller* (1939) held that a ban on sales of sawed-off shotguns did not violate the amendment, since these guns would not be used by a militia.

The Third Amendment was written in response to British stationing of troops in the homes of civilian colonists without compensation for the service—purportedly to cut the cost of the army needed to defend against American Indians, but probably also as a device for controlling rebellious colonists. The Third Amendment bans such a practice: "No soldier shall, in time of peace be quartered in any house, without the consent of the owner, nor in time of war, but in a manner to be prescribed by law." The Supreme Court has not heard any cases contesting the Third Amendment because the language is so clear, the quartering of soldiers in civilian houses is impractical in modern times, and the amendment has not been applied to the states under the incorporation theory.

The Fourth Amendment's promise—"the right of the people to be secure in their persons, houses, papers, and effects, against unreasonable searches and seizures, shall not be violated, and no warrant shall issue but upon probable cause, supported by oath or affirmation, and particularly describing the place to be searched, and the persons or things to be seized"—arose out of British colonial practices. Although British citizens had gained some protection against unreasonable searches and seizures in England itself, the British government did not extend this protection to the colonists. To protect citizens from such abuses by the new national government, the requirement for a search warrant provided an important judicial control on search and seizure actions by the police.

Although the police may both search and seize, they must obtain court approval, which is to be granted only with probable cause. Any material seized through an unreasonable search and seizure may be found inadmissible as evidence in federal courts,

THE BILL OF RIGHTS

Amendment I. Congress shall make no law respecting an establishment of religion, or prohibiting the free exercise thereof; or abridging the freedom of speech, or of the press; or the right of the people peaceably to assemble, and to petition the Government for a redress of grievances.

Amendment II. A well regulated Militia, being necessary to the security of a free State, the right of the people to keep and bear Arms, shall not be infringed.

Amendment III. No Soldier shall, in time of peace be quartered in any house, without the consent of the Owner, nor in time of war, but in a manner to be prescribed by law.

Amendment IV. The right of the people to be secure in their persons, houses, papers, and effects, against unreasonable searches and seizures, shall not be violated, and no Warrants shall issue, but upon probable cause, supported by Oath or affirmation, and particularly describing the place to be searched, and the persons or things to be seized.

Amendment V. No person shall be held to answer for a capital, or otherwise infamous crime, unless on a presentment or indictment of a Grand Jury, except in cases arising in the land or naval forces, or in the Militia, when in actual service in time of War or public danger; nor shall any person be subject for the same offence to be twice put in jeopardy of life or limb; nor shall be compelled in any criminal case to be a witness against himself, nor be deprived of life, liberty, or property, without due process of law; nor shall private property be taken for public use without just compensation.

Amendment VI. In all criminal prosecutions, the accused shall enjoy the right to a speedy and public trial, by an impartial jury of the State and district wherein the crime shall have been committed, which district shall have been previously ascertained by law, and to be informed of the nature and cause of the accusation; to be confronted with the witnesses against him; to have compulsory process for obtaining Witnesses in his favor, and to have the assistance of counsel for his defence.

Amendment VII. In Suits at common law, where the value in controversy shall exceed twenty dollars, the right of trial by jury shall be preserved, and no fact tried by a jury, shall be otherwise reexamined in any Court of the United States, than according to the rules of the common law.

Amendment VIII. Excessive bail shall not be required, nor excessive fines imposed, nor cruel and unusual punishments inflicted.

> **Amendment IX.** The enumeration in the Constitution, of certain rights, shall not be construed to deny or disparage others retained by the people.
>
> **Amendment X.** The powers not delegated to the United States by the Constitution, nor prohibited by it to the States, are reserved to the States respectively, or to the people.

under a legal doctrine known as the "exclusionary rule," which was applied to the states as a result of incorporation in *Mapp v. Ohio* (1961). In the early history of the United States, searches and seizures were largely physical acts, but later, as of *Katz v. United States* (1967), the Court held that electronic eavesdropping and wiretapping also require a warrant from a judge based on probable cause.

The Fifth Amendment

The Fifth Amendment is so comprehensive that each section must be examined separately. The first section provides that "no person shall be held to answer for a capital, or otherwise infamous crime, unless on a presentment or indictment of a grand jury, except in cases arising in the land or naval forces, or in the militia, when in actual service in time of war or public danger." While the grand jury (not the petit jury which sits at a trial) is one of the oldest institutions in Anglo-American law, its use has declined, and this right has not been incorporated and applied to the states. Many states do not use a grand jury and proceed to a trial with an indictment or presentment by the prosecutor.

The second section prohibits "double jeopardy": "Nor shall any person be subject for the same offense to twice be put in jeopardy of life or limb." The double jeopardy provision covers only criminal cases and was not applied to the states until the case *Benton v. Maryland* (1969). The double jeopardy provision is important as a safeguard against a government that seeks to retry a person until it finally gains a conviction, as the British did in colonial times. It is an important individual protection against the government, but the provision does not always prohibit a retrial if a mistrial has occurred or if the defendant appeals a conviction.

The third widely known provision of the Fifth Amendment protects against self-incrimination "Nor shall [any person] be

compelled in any criminal case to be a witness against himself."
Churches' and monarchs' ancient practice of torturing people to
force them to confess to crimes was gradually overcome in England in the sixteenth and seventeenth centuries, and it was natural for Americans to include protection against it. The Supreme
Court did not consider this right so fundamental that it needed to
be applied to the states until the case of *Malloy v. Hogan* (1964).
Those who testify before some congressional committees are not
protected by this section, although most congressional committees voluntarily allow witnesses "to take the Fifth." With this exception, the U.S. legal system does provide a broad, significant
protection against self-incrimination.

The fourth section states, "Nor [shall any person] be deprived
of life, liberty, or property, without due process of law." Identical
words are used in the Fourteenth Amendment, and subsequent
judicial interpretation has applied the due process clause of the
Fourteenth Amendment to all the other protections included in
the Fifth Amendment and many other protections as well. For
most of U.S. history, the Supreme Court has treated the due process clause of the Fifth Amendment as if it were redundant
(merely reincorporating the procedural due process guarantees
listed elsewhere). On some occasions, the due process clause has
been interpreted as meaning that substantive due process issues
(such as reasonableness or fairness) can also be examined under
the Fifth Amendment. The Fifth Amendment was used in this
way to strike down national economic legislation under a substantive due process concept early in the twentieth century, but
the Court has increasingly departed from this practice without
completely abandoning the substantive due process notion. Specifically, the Supreme Court has allowed this section of the Fifth
Amendment to be used to resolve substantive due process questions in the civil rights area. This represents a substantial shift in
the meaning of substantive due process. In *Bolling v. Sharpe* (1954),
the Court included the legal equal protection concept of the Fourteenth Amendment under the due process portion of the Fifth
Amendment. In this way, the notion of equal protection of the law
was applied on the federal level, whereas previously it had applied only on the state level through the Fourteenth Amendment.

The last provision, "nor shall private property be taken for
public use without just compensation," represented an attempt
by the Framers to limit the power of eminent domain, or the gov-

ernment's power to reclaim private land for society's benefit. Clearly, in war property owners might need to yield their property for the good of all, or lose it to the enemy. Such situations make any limit on government difficult, so the U.S. drafters should be credited for trying. This restraint has been seriously weakened in the twentieth century. As the courts have stopped second-guessing legislatures on what constitutes a "public purpose," the phrase has become vague and meaningless. The Supreme Court has even allowed the government to take land from one private party and sell it to another for a commercial use, so that all any owner can do is haggle over the sales price. Even this is difficult, because "just compensation" should match the "fair market value," which implies a willing seller. This was the first portion of the Bill of Rights to be incorporated under the due process clause of the Fourteenth Amendment—in *Chicago, Milwaukee and St. Paul Railway Co. v. Minnesota* (1890), and even more clearly so in a second case, *Chicago, Burlington and Quincy Railroad Co. v. Chicago* (1897).

The Sixth Amendment

The Sixth Amendment enumerates basic rights for those accused of committing crimes. First, "in all criminal prosecutions, the accused shall enjoy the right to a speedy and public trial, by an impartial jury of the state and district wherein the crime shall have been committed, which district shall have been previously ascertained by law." These are virtually the same words used in Article III of the Constitution; clearly, the Framers were convinced that these rights were absolutely vital. These rights, which had evolved over time in Anglo-Saxon law, had not been extended to the American colonists by the British, and the Framers wanted to avoid the possibility of similar difficulties recurring. These provisions did not apply to the states until *Duncan v. Louisiana* (1968).

A second speedy, public trial section was applied to the states in *Klopfer v. North Carolina* (1967). Klopfer had been indicted by North Carolina for criminal trespass for taking part in a sit-in demonstration in a restaurant. At the trial, the jury failed to reach an agreement; the resulting mistrial allowed the state to retry Klopfer. The state elected to delay the trial indefinitely, but the U.S. Supreme Court ruled unanimously against North Carolina, stating that the resulting uncertainty and delay deprived Klopfer of his liberty without due process of law. "Public" trials have turned out to be an even more difficult issue for the courts because they readily bring the rights of the accused into conflict with the rights of the press under the First Amendment.

The Sixth Amendment's requirement of an impartial jury has been used on occasion to prevent racial discrimination in the selection of local juries as well as discrimination based on sex, nationality, and religion. Prior to the American Revolution, the British had hauled American colonists across the Atlantic to stand trial in England. Not only was the expense prohibitive for the accused colonist, but also the chances of bringing witnesses in the accused's defense or of a fair trial were nonexistent. Thus the right to a "local" jury was included to prevent the federal government from doing the same to residents of various states. Other rights basic to the common-law tradition of the Anglo-Saxon judicial tradition, including the right to be informed of the nature and cause of an indictment, to be confronted by witnesses, to have compulsory process (subpoenas) for obtaining reluctant witnesses in one's behalf, and to have the assistance of counsel for defense, are also in the Sixth Amendment.

Notable among the Sixth Amendment guarantees applied to the states is the right to the assistance of counsel in the defense of criminal cases, as established in the case *Gideon v. Wainwright* (1963). Prior to this time, the right to counsel in capital cases had been granted to criminal defendants, but until 1963 it was not clear that all defendants in criminal proceedings should have counsel provided. Later, the more controversial *Escobedo v. Illinois* (1964) and *Miranda v. Arizona* (1966) cases provided for the assistance of counsel not only at the trial but also at the time an accused is arrested by the police.

Provisions of the Seventh and Eighth Amendments

The Seventh Amendment states, "In suits at common law, where the value in controversy shall exceed twenty dollars, the right of trial by jury shall be preserved, and no fact tried by a jury, shall be otherwise reexamined in any court of the United States, than according to the rules of common law," providing guarantees in federal civil cases. Because civil cases are held to be less directly related to an individual's basic rights and civil liberties, and because the original limit of twenty dollars is unrealistically low, the Supreme Court has not applied the Seventh Amendment to the states.

The Eighth Amendment provides that "excessive bail shall not be required, nor excessive fines imposed, nor cruel and unusual punishments inflicted." The ban on excessive bail (not yet applied to states) means that bail should not be set higher than would be reasonable to ensure the presence of the defendant at the trial. It also allows the denial of bail when no bail could guarantee the presence of the accused at trial, as in capital cases or those where the accused might commit other crimes pending trial. The prohibition of excessive fines has been extended to states; it means that an indigent person does not have to pay a fine, since failure to pay a fine cannot result in imprisonment unless imprisonment is otherwise a penalty for the same crime.

Controversy has emerged over the Eighth Amendment's prohibition of cruel and unusual punishment, since opponents of capital punishment argue that it is "cruel and unusual." Throughout U.S. history, however, capital punishment has existed in most states, and the prevailing view is that capital punishment is not cruel and unusual. Former U.S. Supreme Court Justices Harry A. Blackmun, William J. Brennan, and William O. Douglas have maintained that public sensibilities have gradually changed and that capital punishment is now, by nature, "cruel and unusual." These justices did not persuade a court majority to this view, but in *Furman v. Georgia* (1972) a majority did rule that capital punishment as administered in the various states was cruel, unusual, and discriminatory in its impact because vastly more blacks were executed than whites. Subsequently, many states revised their capital punishment laws, and the revisions were upheld.

The Ninth and Tenth Amendments

The Ninth Amendment was added to try to overcome the objections of those who opposed adding a Bill of Rights for fear that such a list would lead people to conclude that only those rights would be protected. The Ninth Amendment states, "The enumeration in the Constitution, of certain rights, shall not be construed to deny or disparage others retained by the people." The Ninth Amendment has been used principally to include a broad range of rights under the general notion of privacy, which can be found in the Fourth, Fifth, and Sixth Amendments.

Technically, the Tenth Amendment adds nothing to the Constitution, because it simply makes explicit what everyone regarded as understood: that the power of the federal government consisted in certain delegated or enumerated powers which could not expand. The Framers considered it important, however, to make clear that certain rights were retained by the states or the people, so they added the words "The powers not delegated to the United States by the Constitution, nor prohibited by it to the states, are reserved to the states respectively, or to the people."

—*Richard L. Wilson*

Suggested Readings

An accessible introduction to this complex subject is *The Bill of Rights*, edited by Thomas T. Lewis (2 vols., Pasadena, Calif.: Salem Press, 2002). A helpful volume of general scholarship is Henry J. Abraham and Barbara A. Perry's *Freedom and the Court* (6th ed. New York: Oxford University Press, 1994). For a contrary view on incorporation, see Raoul Berger, *The Fourteenth Amendment and the Bill of Rights* (Oklahoma City: University of Oklahoma Press, 1989). A comprehensive examination of each element of the entire Bill of Rights can be found in Eugene W. Hickok, Jr., ed., *The Bill of Rights: Original Meaning and Current Understanding* (Charlottesville: University of Virginia Press, 1991). A comprehensive symposium on the entire Bill of Rights can be found in Geoffrey R. Stone, Richard A. Epstein, and Cass R. Sunstein, eds., *The Bill of Rights in the Modern State* (Chicago: University of Chicago Press, 1992). Akhil Reed Amar's *The Bill of Rights: Creation and Reconstruction* (New Haven, Conn.: Yale University Press, 1998) looks at the Bill of Rights from a historical perspective.

See also Arraignment; Change of venue; Civil rights and liberties; Common law; Constitution, U.S.; Counsel, right to; Criminal procedure; Cruel and unusual punishment; Double jeopardy; Due process of law; Eighth Amendment; Exclusionary rule; Fifth Amendment; Immunity from prosecution; Legal immunity; Presumption of innocence; Probable cause; Search warrant requirement; Self-incrimination, privilege against; Speedy trial requirement; Subpoena power.

BILLABLE HOURS

Common method by which lawyers charge their clients set rates for the hours they devote to their cases

Lawyers often charge clients by the hour for legal time spent on client matters. These hourly rates vary widely depending on factors such as the locality, the experience of the lawyer, and the lawyer's expertise or prestige. Typical rates vary from one hundred to several hundred dollars per hour.

Lawyers routinely divide their time between billable and nonbillable hours. Billable hours are those spent directly for particular clients and for which lawyers seek payment from their clients. Nonbillable hours are those that lawyers spend on activities for which they cannot bill clients. Hours spent on continuing professional education, office management, recruiting new lawyers to join a firm, and pro bono (free) legal work are examples of nonbillable hours. Many lawyers accept as a rule of thumb that they must work approximately ten hours a day to bill eight hours.

Most lawyers do not bill for the precise number of minutes spent working for a client. Instead, they use minimum billing increments, normally either one-tenth or one-quarter hour increments. For example, if lawyers make a three-minute telephone call on behalf of clients, they will probably bill them either for the equivalent of six minutes (a tenth of an hour) or fifteen minutes (a quarter of an hour). Lawyers typically justify this practice by arguing that a three-minute telephone call actually consumes more than three minutes of their time, because they also must perform such activities as thinking about what they want to say and finding telephone numbers.

Law practice has become more competitive, and law firms have become more conscious of the billable hours their attorneys work. These hours, after all, represent a law firm's chief and perhaps even exclusive source of income. Many law firms have specific expectations as to the number of billable hours their lawyers must generate each year. Especially for lawyers who work on a salaried basis for the firm, who are called "associates," annual billable hours are often a key factor in the determination of associate compensation and advancement to the rank of "partner"— that is, a lawyer who shares in the profits of the firm and in the firm's management. Expectations of billable hours for associates have ranged from 1,500 to 2,400 annually, depending on the location and size of the firm. Moreover, billable hours are often an important component in the determination of what share of the firm's profits a partner receives.

—*Timothy L. Hall*

See also Attorney-client relationship; Attorney fees; Attorney salaries; Attorneys; Billing rates; Court-awarded fees; Law firm partners and associates; Litigation expenses; Pro bono legal work.

BILLING RATES

Hourly rates charged by lawyers for legal work; rates vary widely and depend on lawyers' seniority, location, and expertise

Lawyers routinely bill clients for each hour of legal service they provide. However, lawyers' hourly rates depend on a number of factors. Lawyers' experience and expertise are perhaps the most important variables in establishing billing rates. Recent law school graduates seldom charge as much as more experienced attorneys. Similarly, lawyers with only general knowledge of a field of law are seldom able to command the same fee as experts. Geographical location affects billing rates as well. Thus, lawyers practicing in major cities generally charge more per hour than lawyers in smaller communities.

Bearing these variations in mind, lawyers' hourly billing rates may be as low as $75 and as high as $400 or even $500. The higher rates tend to be charged by corporate attorneys with special legal expertise. Although lawyers are generally free to obtain whatever fee a client is willing to pay, in theory at least it is possible for a fee to be excessive. Rules of legal ethics prohibit lawyers from charging unreasonable fees, although these rules are seldom used to challenge hourly billing rates.

—*Timothy L. Hall*

See also Attorney-client relationship; Attorney fees; Attorney salaries; Attorneys; Billable hours; Contingency fees; Court-awarded fees; Legal services plans; Litigation expenses; Model Rules of Professional Conduct.

BILLS OF ATTAINDER

Legislative acts that punish specific individuals or groups without a trial in a court of law—a form of legislation forbidden by the U.S. Constitution

In English common law, bills of attainder were legislative pronouncements of death sentences. Lesser punishments such as forfeiture of property or loss of a job were known as bills of pains and penalties. Under U.S. law, all legislative punishments are known as bills of attainder and are forbidden. For legislation to be a bill of attainder it must contain three elements: a clear and definite punishment, the absence of a judicial trial, and a clear specification of individuals or groups to which it applies. The legal standard for each of these elements is high, or else the ban on bills of attainder would seem to apply to almost any legislation that burdens some groups or individuals but not all. Many bills of attainder have been *ex post facto* laws (laws applied retroactively "after the fact"), but they need not necessarily be so.

See also Constitution, U.S.; Cruel and unusual punishment; Eighth Amendment; *Ex post facto* laws; Forfeiture, civil and criminal.

Black's Law Dictionary

First published in the late nineteenth century, the premier legal reference book in the English language

The first edition of *Black's Law Dictionary: Definitions of the Terms and Phrases of American and English Jurisprudence, Ancient and Modern* by Henry Campbell Black (1850-1927) was published in 1891. The seventh edition (1999) of this standard legal resource had as its editor in chief noted legal lexicography Bryan A. Garner. For more than a century the book has served as a useful reference to both general and legal professionals.

The volume's strengths rest on its readability, the comprehensiveness of its entries, and its thorough documentation of specific cases and cross-listings. In addition to more than 1,600 pages of definitions of legal terms, the seventh edition includes a collection of legal maxims, the text of the U.S. Constitution, a historical table of the U.S. Supreme Court, and a table of British regnal years.

The most recent edition expanded explanations of changes that occurred after the important sixth edition appeared in 1990. In addition to using thousands of citations to update or revise earlier entries, the sixth edition had added 4,500 new definitions. *Black's Law Dictionary* also includes substantive and clear explanations of the application of laws to such standards and models as the Uniform Commercial Code (UCC), Restatements of the Law, the Model Penal Code, and the Federal Rules.

—*William T. Walker*

See also Annotated codes; Bar examinations and licensing of lawyers; Law schools; Model Penal Code; Uniform laws.

BONDS

Legal or credit instruments that promise to pay money at designated times under certain conditions

A bond protects the government, individuals, or companies against loss through the dishonesty of others or the failure of others to fulfill certain contracts or obligations. The promise to pay money as part of a bond agreement may be conditional or unconditional. If conditional, the promise to pay depends upon the occurrence or nonoccurrence of a specified event. For example, a bail bond is forfeited if the defendant does not appear at the designated time as ordered by a court. In cases in which the defendant does not have the amount of money or property to cover the bail set by the judge, the defendant may use the services of a bail bond agent to procure a bail bond. The bail bond agent is paid a percentage of the bail amount (usually 10 to 20 percent), and the bond agent then posts an insurance bond with the court, ensuring that the dollar amount of the set bail will be paid should the defendant fail to appear.

Many businesses and service organizations use another type of conditional bond known as a fidelity bond. In this case, the employees are bonded against any loss from fraud or other dishonesty in the performance of their jobs. Workers at banks, brokerage firms, and other financial institutions are examples of bonded employees, and many government officials are also bonded for the performance of their duties.

Performance and completion bonds are commonly used in the construction industry. These bonds provide for the payment of a penalty if a building contractor does not complete work on a structure by the stated date. Since construction projects typically involve large sums of money, it is customary for the obligated party to procure a bond issued by a surety company.

Conditional bonds are also often required when litigation occurs. Most jurisdictions have statutes that require a losing party in civil actions to furnish a surety bond as security to guarantee the payment of costs that may be awarded on an appeal. In cases in which a suit begins by attaching a defendant's property, the suing party generally must furnish a bond for any loss or damage the defendant may sustain.

Unconditional bonds are commonly used in financing corporate and governmental borrowings and are usually sold to investors through banks or brokers. These investment bonds resemble promissory notes in that they are evidence that the maker is indebted to the holder and that the bonds will pay interest and principal at given times. Bonds issued by a sovereign nation rely for their security entirely on the buyer's confidence in the taxing power and stability of the issuing government.

When a mortgage on real estate is issued as security for a loan, such as in the purchase of a home, an unconditional bond often accompanies the transaction. The bond evidences the debt, while the mortgage represents the security for the debt. Instead of a bond, a mortgage note is sometimes used.

—*Alvin K. Benson*

See also Arrest; Attachment; Bail bond agents; Bail system; Contracts; Parole; Personal recognizance.

Breach of contract

Failure to fulfill an important obligation that one has agreed to perform

A party that fails to keep a promise in an oral or written agreement is guilty of a breach of contract, unless a legal defense is available. For example, if someone borrows money and does not pay it back when due, he or she has committed a breach of contract. If someone agrees to pay a house painter $5,000 to paint a house, $2,500 at the beginning and $2,500 at the conclusion of the work, and the homeowner pays the first installment but not the second when the job is completed, that person is guilty of a breach of contract.

Elements of Breach of Contract

To constitute a breach of contract, the obligation that has not been performed must be material. It must go to the heart of the agreement and not be merely incidental or insignificant. Thus, if the homeowner actually paid the second installment but it was three days late, it would not be a breach of contract. The object of the agreement must be legal. The law does not recognize as a breach of contract the failure to pay an illegal gambling debt, a commission to an unlicensed broker, or a usurious interest rate.

Any formalities required by an agreement must first be met before there is a breach of contract. Thus, if the agreement to lend money contains a provision that no default in payment shall constitute a breach of contract unless the lender gives written notice and the borrower fails to pay within ten days after receipt of the notice, those requirements must be satisfied before the borrower is deemed to be in breach of contract.

Many agreements contain promises that are dependent on each other. The failure of one party to perform his or her obligations may excuse the other from performing contractual obligations. Thus, the first party is in breach but not the second. For example, if the house painter has agreed to apply a base coat and then two top coats of paint but skips the base coat and applies only one top coat, the homeowner is excused from the obligation to pay the second installment. In fact, due to the breach of contract, the house painter could be ordered to refund the first installment and could also be held liable for the cost of removing the paint so that another painter could start from scratch.

A party may also be excused from a breach of contract due to an "act of God," also known as a *"force majeure."* Certain events beyond a party's control, such as fires, floods, wars, civil insurrections, or strikes, which prevent a party from performing its obligations, excuse the party from being held liable for breach of contract. For example, if the house is hit by lightening after the painter is only partially finished with the job, there has been an act of "force majeure." The painter is excused from painting the rest of the house and the homeowner is excused from paying the second installment; neither party is guilty of a breach of contract. Likewise, if the painter has agreed to paint the house by a set deadline but a strike by the employees of all paint manufacturers intervenes, thereby delaying the job for two months past the deadline, the painter is not in breach of contract unless it is found that the painter agreed to purchase all the paint needed at the outset of the job and failed to do so.

The law requires that people act reasonably in carrying out their contractual obligations. Requirements or matters of taste known to one party but not disclosed and agreed to by the other cannot form the basis of a breach of contract. For example, if the painter and homeowner agreed that the house would be painted dark blue but after the job was finished the homeowner refused to pay because the color clashed with his curtains, the homeowner, not the painter, would be in breach of contract.

If a party clearly and unequivocally repudiates an agreement prior to the time when performance is due, it constitutes an anticipatory breach of contract. For example, if a borrower declares without qualification that he or she has no intention of repaying the debt on the date due, the lender has the option of treating the repudiation as an anticipatory breach, in which case the lender may sue immediately or wait until the due date and then sue.

In addition to being in breach of contract for failing to perform obligations, a person can be in breach of contract for preventing or seriously hindering the other party's performance. For example, if the homeowner has a locked gate to the property and keeps it locked or leaves town without opening it so that the painter is unable to paint the house, the homeowner is liable for breach of contract.

Remedies

There are several remedies available when there has been a breach of contract. Suing for damages is the most common remedy. For example, the lender may sue the borrower for repayment of the loan with interest, and the house painter who finishes the job on time may sue for the balance of the contract price. A party could also sue for rescission and restitution. For example, if the painter abandons the job shortly after beginning it, the homeowner may sue to rescind the agreement and get back the initial installment of $2,500.

A party may elect to sue for specific performance, which is a court order requiring that the other party complete the performance of their obligations. For example, the homeowner could sue the painter for specific performance, requiring him to complete the painting job. However, in some states personal services are not subject to specific performance. A party may also seek an injunction to prevent a breach of contract. For example, the painter may seek an injunction requiring the homeowner to unlock the gates so that he can gain access to the property to finish the work.

A party may sue another party for ejectment. For example, if the painter takes a liking to the house and refuses to leave or goes so far as to claim that the house is his or hers, the homeowner may sue to obtain a court order instructing the sheriff or marshal to physically eject the painter and declare that he or she has no right, title, or interest in the property (except possibly a lien in case the homeowner has not paid the last installment on the painting job).

Finally, in rare cases in which a breach of contract is the result of gross negligence or other wrongful conduct, a party may sue for tort damages, including punitive damages under certain circumstances. For example, if the homeowner is injured by a falling paint can that the painter left precariously on the roof or from toxic chemicals the painter should not have been using, the homeowner may sue for general damages, medical expenses, pain and suffering, and possibly punitive damages.

—Stephen F. Rohde

Suggested Readings

General treatises on U.S. contract law include Hugh Collins's *Regulating Contracts* (New York: Oxford University Press, 1999), Claude D. Rohwer and Gordon D. Schaber's *Contracts in a Nut-*

shell (St. Paul, Minn.: West Publishing, 2000), John D. Calamari and Joseph M. Perrillo's *Contracts* (3d ed. St. Paul, Minn.: West Publishing, 1987), Richard A. Lord's *Williston on Contracts* (4th ed. Rochester, N.Y.: Lawyer's Cooperative, 1990), E. Allan Farnsworth's *Contracts* (2d ed. Boston: Little, Brown, 1990), and *Corbin on Contracts*, edited by Joseph M. Perillo (rev. ed. St. Paul, Minn.: West Publishing, 1993). An extensive and thorough review of contract law can be found in *Restatement of the Law, Second, Contracts* (Philadelphia: American Law Institute, 1981). *Oxford Essays in Jurispudence. Fourth Series*, edited by Jeremy Horder (New York: Oxford University Press, 2000), includes a chapter on breach of contract.

See also Arbitration; Civil actions; Commercial litigation; Contracts; Damages; Declaratory judgments; Lawsuits; Negligence; Statutes of limitations; Uniform laws.

BURDEN OF PROOF

Duty to prove a disputed charge or allegation in a court of law—a responsibility closely associated with the the constitutional right to due process of law

Few ideas are more central to litigation—and therefore more disputed—than that of the "burden of proof." Stated in simple terms, the issue concerns who (the plaintiff or the defendant) must bring forward evidence on a particular issue at a trial, as well as the quantity or quality of the evidence that must be brought forward. The answers to these questions are affected by whether the trial is a civil or a criminal one and by the definition of the "elements" of the claim or case.

The general rule is that in a criminal case, the government (the prosecution) must prove all elements of the offense "beyond a reasonable doubt." This rule has been upheld by the Supreme Court, most notably in *In re Winship* (1970). The rule in civil cases is less straightforward. The plaintiff has the burden of proving all material elements of his or her claim. In the majority of cases the required standard of proof is that of "preponderance of the evidence"—in other words, that it is "more likely than not" that the truth of the matter is as told by the plaintiff. In some cases, however, a higher burden is imposed on the plaintiff, usually phrased in some combination of the words "clear," "convincing," and "unequivocal," as in "clear and convincing evidence."

Even if the plaintiff satisfies the burden of proof, a defendant may, in a civil case, avoid liability by satisfying what is called an "affirmative defense." For example, the law may say that a person who goes onto another person's land without invitation is a trespasser who may be liable in damages to the owner of the land, but it may add that if the trespasser openly occupies the land for twenty-one years, then ownership of the land shall pass to the trespasser. In this situation, even though a plaintiff successfully shows ownership of land and its uninvited occupation by the defendant, the defendant may still win if he or she can prove under one of the standards above that he or she has openly occupied the land for the prescribed period of time. One of the most difficult questions in law is determining what constitutes an "affirmative defense" (in which the burden of proof is on the defendant), and what is simply a regular defense (under which the burden remains with the plaintiff).

Whether the standard for the burden of proof is expressed in terms of the "preponderance of the evidence" or a higher burden, and whether a given element of a case must be proved by the plaintiff or the defendant, is related to society's conception of fairness—its interest in distributing the rights at issue. One question, for example, would be which party society believes to have the easier access to the necessary information or evidence with which to meet the burden.

See also Civil law; Criminal justice system; Directed verdicts; Discovery; Due process of law; Evidence, rules of; Litigation; Prosecutors; Standards of proof; Testimony.

CAPITAL PUNISHMENT

State execution of convicts for purposes of punishment or to deter future crime

During the colonial period and the founding of the United States, the execution of convicts was not only routine but also a public spectacle. The hangman's noose, a humane alternative to beheading, was employed with a liberality that would disturb modern sensibility. In eighteenth century England, for example, it is estimated that approximately 240 crimes were punishable by death, with the sentence commonly carried out in the town squares. In contrast to millennia of practice, the nineteenth and twentieth centuries have seen a gradual civilization of punishment. Incarceration replaced execution for most crimes. Hangings were removed from public view and placed instead behind prison walls. The abolition of physical torture as a legitimate part of punishment followed, eventually culminating in efforts to also circumscribe the infliction of psychological pain. Thus, the noose was replaced by electrocution, followed by the gas chamber, and then by lethal injection, all in a search of a humane method of depriving the convict of life, as the ultimate punishment. In the eyes of many ethicists, legal scholars, and moral leaders, the fulfillment of this historical trend would be the abolition of capital punishment altogether. In the United States, one of the last democratic nations retaining the death penalty, this debate has often acquired a constitutional dimension.

The Death Penalty and the Constitution

It is clear from the text of the Constitution that the Framers envisioned executions as a part of their legal regime. The Fifth Amendment provides that "no person shall be held to answer for a capital, or otherwise infamous crime" absent an indictment by a grand jury. It further provides that no person shall "be subject for the same offense to be twice put in jeopardy of life or limb" nor be "deprived of life, liberty, or property, without due process of law." The Fourteenth Amendment, adopted after the Civil War, similarly commands that no state shall deny any person "life, liberty, or property, without due process of law." Proponents of a contractual constitution, interpreted according to the historical intent of its Framers, are on apparently solid ground when they contend that the Constitution, in principle, sanctions capital punishment.

Opponents of the death penalty point to the same pair of due process clauses, promises of legal fairness, to condemn the application of the death penalty as arbitrary, capricious, even, in the words of Justice Potter Stewart, "freakishly imposed." They also point to the Fourteenth Amendment's requirement that states accord all persons the "equal protection of the laws" and raise questions concerning possible racial bias in the meting out of death sentences. Finally, and most tellingly, the Eighth Amendment's proscription of "cruel and unusual punishments" might provide a flat ban on capital punishment. The latter seems to have been adopted to end corporal punishments or the infliction of torture. However, in *Weems v. United States* (1910), the Supreme Court held that a constitutional principle "to be vital must be capable of wider application than the mischief which gave it birth." Abolitionists contend that these clauses create evolutionary constitutional rules, progressively driven by contemporary moral theory, that proscribe the death penalty, regardless of accepted practice at the time of their adoption.

Judicial appeals to contemporary morality are always risky, especially regarding an emotionally contentious subject such as capital punishment. However, it is difficult to reconcile the death penalty, as practiced in the United States, with any of the common theoretical justifications for punishment. The death penalty is obviously not intended to accomplish the rehabilitation of the offender. There is little evidence in support of any general deterrence produced by the death penalty beyond that already achieved by incarceration and considerable evidence against the claim. Incapacitation of dangerous or repeat offenders can also be accomplished by means short of execution.

Retribution, the theory that crime is a moral offense that must be redressed by the infliction of proportional pain to expiate the original offense, might justify capital punishment for heinous crimes, especially first-degree murder. The biblical injunction of "an eye for an eye and a tooth for a tooth" is a concise summary of retributive punishment. The problem is that retribution, if consistently followed, is a nondiscretionary punishment—a sentence proportional to the crime *must* be carried out, with no room for mercy or selection. Proponents of capital punishment who appeal to retribution would have to countenance the execution of all defendants convicted of crimes for which capital punishment is authorized. The result would be a rate of executions unprecedented in U.S. history. Public opinion overwhelmingly supports capital punishment. However, polls and jury behavior also show that Americans want the death sentence to be employed sparingly.

The modern Court's initial foray into death penalty law was not encouraging to abolitionists. In *Louisiana ex rel. Francis v. Resweber* (1947), the Court rejected the contention that a second attempt at executing a prisoner, the electric chair having malfunctioned the first time, was either double jeopardy or cruel and unusual punishment. Despite the Court's permissive attitude, the number of executions in the United States was already in decline. National statistics on executions date only from 1930, with 1935 the largest single year, with 199 executions. By the 1960's this number had declined to a trickle. Since the early 1980's, however, the number of annual executions in the United States has again been rising, especially in southern states. Between 1997 and 2002, an average of seventy-seven executions were carried out each year.

The Death Penalty Moratorium

Encouraged by the Court's activism in civil rights and defendants' rights cases, death penalty opponents in the 1960's began a campaign to enlist the Court in the cause of abolition. The Legal Defense Fund (LDF) of the National Association for the Advancement of Colored People, later joined by the American Civil Liberties Union, orchestrated a threefold attack on capital punishment. First, the routine exclusion of "scrupled" jurors, those opposed to the death penalty on principle, was said to result in nonrepresentative juries skewed toward conviction and execution. Second, the determination of guilt and passing of sentence in a single trial procedure put defendants in an untenable position of having to offer evidence in mitigation of a crime they also contended they did not commit. Finally, the nearly complete discretion accorded juries in deciding when to impose death (the only sentencing question juries are called on to decide) resulted in an unpredictable, arbitrary, and discriminatory application of the death penalty.

In *Witherspoon v. Illinois* (1968), the Court banned the blanket exclusion of all scrupled jurors merely by virtue of their voicing objections to capital punishment. The state could still exclude those who would automatically or invariably vote against a death sentence, but not those expressing only "general objections" to capital punishment. The practical result of *Witherspoon* was to require commutation or resentencing of nearly all death sentences for prisoners then on death row. Until further litigation sorted out all potential *Witherspoon* claims, a de facto moratorium on capital punishment had been achieved. From 1967 until 1977, no executions were carried out in the United States.

Further LDF challenges to capital punishment were in the works. In *Furman v. Georgia* (1972), a fragmented Court adopted the third LDF critique of the death penalty as then practiced in all the states authorizing capital punishment, that unguided jury discretion produced arbitrary results. Only Justices William J. Brennan, Jr., and Thurgood Marshall held capital punishment to be cruel and unusual punishment per se in contravention of the Eighth Amendment. Dissenters William H. Rehnquist, Warren E. Burger, Lewis F. Powell, Jr., and Harry A. Blackmun found no constitutional prohibition to unbridled jury discretion to mete out death and would have deferred on the issue to state legislative politics (although the latter eloquently expressed personal misgivings concerning capital punishment). This left Justices William O. Douglas, Potter Stewart, and Byron R. White to cast limited but decisive votes against Georgia's capital punishment statute.

Douglas expressed concerns that the death penalty was applied disproportionately to poor and socially disadvantaged defendants, in effect reading into the Eighth Amendment an equality requirement. Stewart held that the rare imposition of death made capital punishment cruel and unusual in the minority of cases in which it was imposed. White agreed, arguing that its infrequency deprived the death penalty of any deterrent effect or ability to meet the test of retribution. For the first time, the Court had struck down a death sentence as cruel and unusual punishment. However, the long-term impact of *Furman* depended on the continued support of either Justice White or Justice Stewart, both centrists whose opposition to capital punishment seemed weak.

Public reception of *Furman* was immediate and hostile. Within a few years, thirty-five states had reenacted death penalty statutes purporting to meet the Court's objections. Three possibilities seemed available in the wake of *Furman*. States could enact mandatory death penalty statutes, imposing death in all cases where the death penalty was available, without discretion. This seemed to meet the objections of the Douglas, Stewart, and White bloc but would also have resulted in a large number of executions. A second option was to forgo death as a punishment altogether, but this seemed politically unlikely given the climate of public opinion. The third option was to enact guided discretion statutes, supplying juries with a host of aggravating and mitigating circumstances that would be considered in a separate sentencing phase of the trial, following a previous determination of guilt. This procedure met the LDF's second challenge to capital punishment, that the combined procedures for determining guilt and sentence imposed untenable choices on the defense. It also seemed to meet the issue of jury discretion head on, with neither the unpopular abolition of capital punishment nor the volume of executions that might follow adoption of mandatory capital punishment laws.

These laws came under the Court's scrutiny in *Gregg v. Georgia* (1976). Actually a compendium of five cases testing mandatory death penalty statutes in North Carolina and Louisiana and guided discretion statutes in Georgia, Texas, and Florida, *Gregg* also resulted in a badly fragmented Court. Justices Brennan and Marshall continued their per se opposition to the death penalty. Chief Justice Burger, along with Rehnquist, Blackmun, and White, voted to uphold all five death penalty regimes.

As with *Furman*, the Court's decision rested on the centrists, now Justices Stewart, Powell, and John Paul Stevens. They approved of Georgia's death penalty regime, requiring a bifurcated procedure that separated the determination of guilt from the passing of sentence. In addition, before death could be imposed, a jury had to find beyond a reasonable doubt that at least one of ten aggravating circumstances had been met. Mitigating circumstances were also to be considered, and all death sentences were subject to mandatory appeal. Thus, a death penalty regime based on guided jury discretion now passed constitutional muster. The decision for a companion case, *Woodson v. North Carolina* (1976), specifically banned mandatory death sentences.

It is not at all clear that the death penalty regime approved in *Gregg* is able to meet the objections of jury discretion and arbitrary application of capital punishment that underlie *Furman*. Although subsequent litigation struck down jury guidelines that were deemed too vague, juries were still called on to consider unique circumstances pertaining to each case. Further inconsistency was introduced into the application of the death penalty through such practices as prosecutorial charging discretion, plea bargaining, and executive clemency. It thus appeared that *Gregg* marked a changed political sentiment on the part of the Court, perhaps even, as a practical matter, overruling *Furman*. With the decision in *Gregg*, the Court signaled a green light to executions. The death penalty moratorium came to an end in January of 1977, when the state of Utah executed Gary Gilmore by firing squad.

Race and the Death Penalty

The interest of the LDF in capital punishment should have surprised no one. It was long known that the death penalty was applied most frequently to society's outcast groups, especially the poor and members of minority groups. Over half of the convicts executed for all capital crimes between 1930 and 1995 were African Americans, far exceeding their proportion of the nation's population. Even more striking, of the 450 executions for rape between 1930 and 1965, more than 90 percent involved African American convicts. Criminologist Marvin Wolfgang, in a 1966 study, found that of 119 convicted rapists executed in twelve southern states between 1945 and 1965, 110 were black. The question remained as to whether these discrepancies could be explained by nonracial factors, such as a propensity to commit more heinous crimes.

A research team lead by David Baldus studied more than 2,400 criminal homicide cases in Georgia, from 1973 to 1980, tried under the death penalty regime approved in *Gregg*. Taking account of more than 230 separate characteristics of each case, they employed sophisticated statistical analysis to weigh the effect of each in producing death sentences. Their results found that, when adjusted for legitimate nonracial factors, the race of the *defendant* did not result in a strikingly disproportionate application of the death penalty. However, a strong correlation was uncovered between the race of the *victim* and the passing of a capital sentence.

In raw numbers, white or black killers of white victims were eleven times more likely to receive the death penalty than were killers of African American victims. Even when nonracial variables were factored in, killers of white victims were executed 4.3 times as often as were killers of black victims. The discrepancy was inexplicable, except by the inference that race prejudice continued to affect the death penalty regime, even after *Gregg*. In fact, the race of the victim proved to be a stronger predictor of a capital sentence than such factors as the defendant's prior history of violence, that the victim was a police officer, or that the killing occurred during an armed robbery. The supposition drawn from these results was that prosecutors, when faced with the killer of an African American victim, were less likely to seek the death penalty or more likely to accept a plea bargain eliminating death. Alternatively, juries, even guided statutorily by nonracial aggravating and mitigating circumstances, were less likely to impose death for the killing of a black victim, perhaps valuing the life of a black person less highly than that of a white victim.

These data formed the basis for the LDF's next challenge to capital punishment, in *McCleskey v. Kemp* (1987), as violating both the Eighth Amendment and the equal protection clause of the Fourteenth Amendment. Such a disparate racial impact would seem to call into question the effectiveness of *Gregg* in eliminating the arbitrary or discriminatory factors in applying the death penalty that had informed *Furman*. However, writing for the Court, Justice Powell held that to make an equal protection claim, McCleskey had to demonstrate that either the Georgia legislature or the jury in his particular case was motivated by racial animus or a discriminatory purpose. The social background data revealed in the Baldus study were insufficient to make even a *prima facie* case that McCleskey had personally suffered from racial discrimination and, in any event, were more appropriately considered in a legislative forum. Similarly the discrepancy revealed in the Baldus study was insufficient to demonstrate a violation of the Eighth Amendment because it did not offend society's evolving standards of decency. Justices Brennan, Marshall, Stevens, and Blackmun dissented.

In *Furman* and *Gregg,* the Court had sought to remove arbitrary and capricious factors, presumably including racial prejudice, from the application of the death penalty in the United States. However, with *McCleskey,* the Court appeared to be turning its back on that promise by foreclosing the last avenue for arguing for the per se unconstitutionality of capital punishment. It did find in the Eighth Amendment limits to the kinds of crimes that could be deemed capital offenses. In *Coker v. Georgia* (1977), the Court found a capital sentence disproportionate to the crime of rape and therefore barred by the Eighth Amendment. Similarly, *Enmund v. Florida* (1982) barred the death penalty for a felony murder in which the defendant did not commit, nor intend or contemplate, the killing. However, this ruling was modified in *Tison v. Arizona* (1987) to permit sentencing to death of a codefendant in a felony murder in which there was major participation in the felony combined with reckless indifference to human life. These rulings indicate that the Court views the Eighth Amendment as imposing substantive limits on the death penalty, at least concerning the issue of proportionality.

At the end of the twentieth century, thirty-eight states authorized the death penalty for first-degree murder. The federal government also authorized death for certain homicides, as well as for espionage, treason, or running a large-scale drug enterprise, but has not carried out a single capital sentence since 1963. On January 1, 2003, the number of prisoners on death row throughout the United States was 3,692. By that date, more than eight hundred convicted prisoners had been executed since 1977. Death row inmates are overwhelmingly poor and uneducated and disproportionately African American and southern. Many have suffered from inadequate assistance of counsel at trial. The most significant modern innovation by the Court has been the increasing of restrictions on the availability of federal *habeas corpus* review of state death penalty convictions and sentences. The apparent goal of the Court is to permit the states to apply post-*Gregg* death penalty law, largely absent federal judicial supervision.

—*John C. Hughes*

Suggested Readings

Bohm, Robert M. *Deathquest: An Introduction to the Theory and Practice of Capital Punishment in the United States*. Cincinnati: Anderson, 1999.

Coyne, Randall, and Lyn Entzeroth. *Capital Punishment and the Judicial Process*. Durham, N.C.: Carolina Academic Press, 2001.

Crump, David, and George Jacobs. *A Capital Case in America: How Today's Justice System Handles Death Penalty Cases from Crime Scene to Ultimate Execution of Sentence*. Durham, N.C.: Carolina Academic Press, 2000.

Haines, Herbert H. *Against Capital Punishment: The Anti-Death Penalty Movement in America, 1972-1994*. New York: Oxford University Press, 1999.

Henderson, Harry. *Capital Punishment*. New York: Facts on File, 2000.

Martinez, J. Michael, William D. Richardson, D. and Brandon Hornsby, eds. *The Leviathan's Choice: Capital Punishment in the Twenty-first Century.* Lanham, Md.: Rowman & Littlefield, 2002.

Palmer, Louis J., Jr. *Encyclopedia of Capital Punishment in the United States.* Jefferson, N.C.: McFarland, 2001.

Sarat, Austin. *When the State Kills: Capital Punishment and the American Condition.* Princeton N.J.: Princeton University Press, 2001.

Simon, Rita J., and Dagny A. Blaskovich. *A Comparative Analysis of Capital Punishment: Statutes, Policies, Frequencies, and Public Attitudes the World Over.* Lanham, Md.: Lexington Books, 2002.

Zimring, Franklin E. *The Contradictions of American Capital Punishment.* New York: Oxford University Press, 2003.

See also Bill of Rights, U.S.; Criminal justice system; Cruel and unusual punishment; Death row attorneys; Eighth Amendment; Execution of judgment; *Habeas corpus*; Military justice; Military tribunals; Sentencing; Verdicts.

CASE LAW

Entire body of reported cases forming all or part of the law in a particular jurisdiction; a defining characteristic of common law legal systems, which use cases to declare rules and principles of law

The common law, as developed in England and transplanted to colonial America, was unwritten and based on custom. It had no authoritative statement in a code or statute such as may be found in civil law systems. Legal rules and principles were "found" or "declared" by judges as they decided cases. A judicial decision can be viewed in two parts: first, the decision on who won and the relief granted, and second, the reasoned explanation of the judge in reaching the decision. It is the reasoned explanation which gives rise to a case law system, even if the reasons must be skillfully extracted or inferred from the written decision.

Cases, including their explanations, are used to decide future cases. If the facts of a future case are similar to the facts of an old

In 1870, when Christopher Columbus Langdell was dean of Harvard Law School, he introduced the "case method" of teaching, in which the process and evolution of law is stressed through the study of individual cases. The system was soon adopted by most other law schools. (Courtesy of Art & Visual Materials, Special Collections, Harvard Law School Library)

case, the rule or principle of the old case will be used to decide the new case. The old case is called a precedent, and the general procedure whereby courts use old cases to decide new ones is called *stare decisis*. Over time *stare decisis* causes a refinement of old rules and principles, adapting them to changes in law and society. In addition, judges will change an old rule or principle if they believe it is wrong, outdated, or otherwise unacceptable. For example, the law of products liability changed in the early twentieth century as judges rejected established legal rules which did not allow consumers to recover damages when injured by defective products except under the most extreme circumstances. The common-law rules allow recovery in most circumstances.

Case law is also used to interpret positive law, such as constitutions, statutes, and administrative regulations. This is particularly true if the language of the positive law is open-ended, vague, ambiguous, susceptible to different interpretations, or simply ill-defined. A court which applies the positive law in a particular case will announce a decision accompanied by a reasoned explanation. This explanation will be read by lawyers to discover a legal rule or principle, which will then be applied to future cases arising under the same or a similar positive law. For example, cases arising under the free speech clause of the First Amendment to the United States Constitution have created a rich case law defining the boundaries of protected speech. The Constitution does not define what is meant by freedom of speech, so it is up to the courts to give meaning to this concept as they decide individual cases.

See also Civil law; Common law; Contracts; Court calendars; Liability, civil and criminal; Opinions; Precedent; Supreme Court, U.S.

CAUSE OF ACTION

Fact or facts specifying the reasons for filing a lawsuit

A plaintiff begins a lawsuit by filing a complaint. In the complaint the plaintiff identifies the cause of action, or reasons for asking for judicial relief. The cause of action specifies the situation or facts that would entitle the plaintiff to a judicial proceeding. A cause of action might be articulated in a sentence or it might be very detailed. Plaintiffs do not need to establish the exact legal theory they will use in the trial, and they may plead hypothetical or contradictory claims. Modern courts have a liberal attitude toward the contents of causes of action, because the emphasis is on providing defendants fair notice of the grounds of the cases against them. Defendants can then learn more about the plaintiff's claim through discovery or other pretrial procedures.

It is possible for a court to find a failure to state a cause of action, however. If the plaintiff fails to provide sufficient facts to support a case, the defendant will move to dismiss for failure to state a cause of action. Such a motion was once referred to as a "demurrer" but has since come to be denoted under federal rules as a failure to state a claim upon which relief can be granted.

The term "cause of action" has been variously defined over the years. From the mid-nineteenth century until 1938 the procedure for pleading a legal case in the United States was called code pleading. Code pleading emphasized the facts in the cause of action and did not seek to narrow down a single issue in the pleading or rely on discarded English common law. The problem with code pleading was that the cause of action was difficult to pinpoint. Pleaders were supposed to plead the "ultimate facts," but legal conclusions and evidentiary facts were hard to discern from "ultimate facts." Thus, if a plaintiff in a trial could not prove the exact law or the exact facts articulated in the cause of action, the case would likely be dismissed.

Ultimately, code pleadings became as confusing as the pleadings in English courts of equity or common law. In 1938 the Federal Rules of Civil Procedure (FRCP) were adopted at the federal level and in many jurisdictions. The FRCP adopted a procedure for pleading a legal case called "notice pleading," in which the terms "facts" and "cause of action" were replaced by a rule specifying that pleadings must contain a short and plain statement of the claim. The intent of the rule was to place less emphasis on the pleadings and more emphasis on the case itself. While the term "cause of action" was eliminated from the wording of the federal rule, it is still used to designate the reason for advancing a lawsuit.

—Ann Burnett

See also Civil actions; Civil law; Class action; Commercial litigation; Dismissal; Lawsuits; Negligence; Probable cause; Release; Shareholder suits.

Certiorari, WRIT OF

Written order issued by the Supreme Court exercising discretionary power to direct a state supreme court or federal court of appeals to deliver records in a case for review

The U.S. Constitution and Congress determine the Supreme Court's jurisdiction to review cases. Article III of the Constitution and various congressional statutes grant the Court two main areas of jurisdiction: original and appellate. To relieve the Court of its rapidly growing caseload burden, Congress established the federal circuit court of appeals with the Judiciary Act of 1891. The act also authorized the Court to review final decisions in certain categories of cases through the issuance of writs of *certiorari*.

Although the Constitution does not expressly grant the Court *certiorari* jurisdiction in the state courts, the Court may grant *certiorari* for those state court decisions that implicate federal law.

Statutes limit *certiorari* jurisdiction to federal questions that have been decided in final judgments of the states' highest courts. The Court may review final judgments or decrees of the states' highest court if the validity of a treaty or statute of the United States is questioned. It may also review a state court decision if a state statute is viewed as violating the Constitution, treaties, or laws of the United States. The Court may not review a case involving federal law if the state court's decision can be upheld purely on state law.

The Court reviews the majority of its cases through appellate jurisdiction. Within its appellate jurisdiction, the power to grant or deny *certiorari* gives the Court discretion in determining which cases it will review. The passage of the Judiciary Act of 1925 greatly expanded the Court's *certiorari* jurisdiction in an effort to reduce its overwhelming docket of cases. The act also enhanced the Court's status and power by largely allowing it to set its own agenda. Since the act's passage, the number of *certiorari* petitions greatly expanded, and by the 1970's, writs of *certiorari* were responsible for 90 percent of the Court's caseload.

The Court reviews petitions for writs of *certiorari* solely at its discretion. If the Court grants *certiorari*, it agrees to review the judgments in question in that case. It will generally simply issue its decision to either grant or deny *certiorari* without giving any explanations for the decision. *Certiorari* is essential to the Court's functioning because of the high number of cases brought to it each year. In the late twentieth century, the Court granted full review to about 160, or 3 percent, of the nearly 5,000 cases submitted through petitions for writs of *certiorari* each year. If the Court decides not to hear a particular case by denying the petition for a writ of *certiorari*, there are almost no other avenues that the petitioner can pursue to have the lower court's judgment reviewed.

The Court grants writs of *certiorari* only for compelling reasons. It pays special attention to resolving conflicts among the federal courts of appeals, the federal district courts, and the state courts on important legal principles or issues of law.

Petitions

A party to any civil or criminal case in which a judgment was entered by a state court of last resort or a U.S. court of appeals may petition for a writ of *certiorari* requesting the Supreme Court to review the lower court's judgment. A party may also petition the Court for a writ of *certiorari* in a case in which a judgment was en-

tered by a lower state court if the state court of last resort has issued an order denying its discretionary review. Parties involved
in the same judgment may file a petition jointly or separately. The
person petitioning the Court for a writ of *certiorari* is known as the
"petitioner" and the opposing party as the "respondent."

The petition must be accurate, brief, and clear in its presentation of the information necessary for the Court to review the case.
The petition contains the questions the petitioner wishes the
Court to review, when and how these questions were raised, and
the names of the parties involved in the proceeding of the court
that rendered the judgment in question. It also includes citations
of the courts' and administrative agencies' opinions and orders issued in the case, the basis for the Court's jurisdiction, and the constitutional provisions, treaties, statutes, ordinances, and regulations involved in the case. All this information is necessary for the
justices to review the petition and make a sound judgment on
whether the Court should review the case.

Review of Petitions

The Court may review cases on appeal, by certification, by an
extraordinary writ, or by *certiorari*. The Court must review cases
on appeal, meaning that Congress has mandated review of that
type of case, whereas the Court may grant or deny *certiorari* at its
discretion. Because Congress eliminated most categories of appeals in 1988 and original jurisdiction represents only one or two
cases a year, the majority of the cases the Court hears are those
granted *certiorari*.

Each justice handles the petitions for *certiorari* sent to the Court
differently; however, justices generally either depend on memos
written by their own law clerks or those prepared by clerks in the
certiorari pool. Some justices have one of their law clerks read the
petition and prepare a memo for them recommending what action the Court should take. Other justices use the *certiorari* pool
that began in 1972 at the behest of several justices. In the pool, the
petitions are divided randomly among the clerks, and the clerks
read each petition assigned to them and prepare a single memo
for all the justices. The justices' individual clerks then receive the
memos and may mark them for their particular justice. These
memos contain a brief summary of the case, the relevant facts, the
lower court's decision, the parties' contentions, an evaluation of

the petition, a recommendation for action, and any additional information necessary to an understanding of the case.

Cases the justice feels are worthy of review are added to the Court's list of petitions to be voted on by all the justices. The justices then discuss these cases at their twice-weekly conferences. The Court also schedules several daylong conferences in September to discuss those petitions that have accumulated over the Court's summer recess. About 70 percent of the petitions for *certiorari* do not make the discussion list and are automatically denied *certiorari*. The chief justice announces those cases that the justices will discuss, and the justices then vote in order of seniority on whether to grant or deny *certiorari*. The justices may speak on an individual case if they feel it merits discussion rather than simply a vote. The Court will grant *certiorari* if four of the nine justices are in favor of the petition. The justices developed this informal rule of four after the 1891 Judiciary Act broadened the Court's discretionary jurisdiction. The rule became public knowledge in 1924. Clerks, secretaries, and visitors may not be present at these conferences, and the Court does not release its votes on *certiorari* petitions to the public. Justices who dissent from the decision to either grant or deny *certiorari* rarely publish their dissent or their reasons for dissenting.

If the Court grants the petition for a writ of *certiorari*, the Court clerk will prepare, sign, and enter the order and notify the council of record and the court whose judgment is in question. The clerk will also schedule the case for briefing and oral argument before the Court. A formal writ of *certiorari* will not be issued unless specially directed. If the Court denies *certiorari*, the clerk will prepare, sign, and enter the order and notify the counsel of record and the court whose judgment was in question. A denial of *certiorari* simply means that the Court will not review the case. It does not mean that the Court agrees with the lower court's ruling although that ruling will stand. The denial of *certiorari* does not constitute a ruling on any legal issues raised by the case although some scholars would argue that it is an informal indication of the Court's position.

—*David Trevino*

Suggested Readings

Robert G. McCloskey's *The American Supreme Court* (Chicago: University of Chicago Press, 1994) offers a good general introduction to the Supreme Court and its jurisdiction. Doris Marie Provine's *Case Selection in the Supreme Court* (Chicago: University of Chicago Press, 1980) and Lee Epstein and Jack Knight's *The Choices Justices Make* (Washington, D.C.: Congressional Quarterly, 1998) both offer an overview of the Court's vital process of deciding which cases it will review. Other useful works on this subject include David C. Frederick's *Supreme Court and Appellate Advocacy: Mastering Oral Argument* (St. Paul, Minn.: West Publishing, 2003); *Judicial Review and Judicial Power in the Supreme Court*, edited by Kermit L. Hall (New York: Garland, 2000); Cass R. Sunstein's *One Case at a Time: Judicial Minimalism on the Supreme Court* (Cambridge, Mass.: Harvard University Press, 1999); and *The Supreme Court Compendium: Data, Decisions, and Developments*, by Lee Epstein and others (Washington, D.C.: CQ Press, 2003).

See also Appeal; Appellate practice; Clerks of the court; Federal judicial system; Indigent criminal defendants; Judicial clerks; Supreme Court, U.S.

CHAIN OF CUSTODY

Procedural matter regarding the custody of real evidence

Chain of custody, also called "chain of possession" or "chain of evidence," is an account of the storage and preservation of real evidence, which is evidence provided by material objects such as a weapon used in committing a crime or bloodstained clothing found at a crime scene. The term also applies to the storage of blood or hair samples taken for chemical or deoxyribonucleic acid (DNA) analysis. The party offering the evidence must prove that it is the same object retrieved from the crime scene and that the object has not been tampered with while in the possession of law-enforcement authorities. For this reason, many police departments have a locked property room in which to store evidence.

Maintaining chain of custody is often complicated, because grand juries, prosecutors, and defense attorneys are permitted to examine evidence prior to the trial. To solve this problem, logs recording the whereabouts of an item of evidence and the identities of individuals coming into contact with it are usually kept. Chain of custody is usually proven through the testimony of a law-enforcement official, who can identify the evidence and affirm that it was stored in a protected area. In cases in which the chain of custody cannot be proven or is in doubt, the court can declare the evidence inadmissable or rule that the value of the evidence in determining guilt is diminished.

—*Thomas Clarkin*

See also Discovery; Evidence, rules of; Police; Standards of proof.

Change of venue

Removal of a legal proceding from the locality in which a case is filed to another location, where the interests of justice might be better served

"Venue" concerns the place at which a case is to be tried. The appropriate venue for civil cases is typically the county in which the defendant resides, events underlying a controversy occurred, or where subject matter such as land is located. For criminal actions, Article III, section 2 of the Constitution specifies that a trial shall occur in the state where the underlying offense was committed. The Sixth Amendment provides for a jury from the state and district where the crime was committed.

A case filed originally in one location may be moved to another place under certain circumstances. A criminal defendant, for example, may seek a change of venue on the grounds that a fair trial cannot be obtained in the original venue. In civil cases, a case may be transferred from one venue to another for the convenience of the parties or witnesses or in the interests of justice generally.

See also Commercial litigation; Hearings; Juries; Jurisdiction; Jury sequestration; Speedy trial requirement; State courts; Trial publicity; Trials.

CITIZEN'S ARREST

Arrest without a warrant made by a private citizen rather than by an officer of the law—a procedure that allows private citizens to detain perpetrators of felony offenses or breaches of the peace and allows law enforcement officials to call for citizen assistance when making arrests

The concept of citizen's arrest has its roots in English common law, formalized in the Statutes of Winchester in 1285. During the first century of United States history, citizen's arrest was abused for individual self-interest, such as bounty hunting, causing most states to restrict citizen's arrest laws in the nineteenth century. Some of these restrictions limited citizen's arrests by making citizens responsible for wrongful arrests and by placing boundaries on ways of getting information that led to arrests. In *Aguilar v. Texas* (1964), for example, restrictions were placed on the use of citizen informers: The informant must be reliable and credible, and the informant's information has to be corroborated. In addition, the resulting arrest must comply with the standards of "probable cause" contained in the Fourth Amendment.

Although citizens in all states may make arrests for both felonies and misdemeanors, usually the arrests involve a breach of peace committed in the presence of the arresting citizen. Other crimes, especially in the case of felonies, need not be committed in the arrester's presence if the arrester has reasonable cause for believing that the person arrested has committed the crime. When a citizen makes an arrest without the assistance of a police officer, the arrester is responsible for turning the arrested person over to an officer of the law as soon as possible. In other instances, a police officer may request the help of a citizen in making an arrest. In these instances, because the private citizen is legally bound to assist the officer, the officer is responsible for the actions of the private citizen assisting in the arrest.

Most arrests made under citizen's arrest laws are not, however, made by private citizens. Most are made by other individuals or groups covered by these laws, including postal inspectors, private security personnel, bank guards, store employees detaining shoplifters, customs inspectors, private investigators, and state and federal agents. Because not all these groups are registered or licensed, accurate statistics regarding their numbers and their arrests are impossible to obtain.

The degree of physical force that can be used is a critical issue in making a citizen's arrest. State laws vary on the degree of physical force allowable. Deadly force in making a citizen's arrest is generally reserved for situations of protecting other people, and private citizens making such arrests act at their own legal peril in using deadly force. In contrast, when a citizen assists a police officer in making an arrest or in preventing an escape, deadly force may usually be used for self-defense, for the defense of a third party, or at the authorization of a police officer. Because the assisting citizen cannot take time to verify an officer's authority, good-faith assistance is justified, even if the officer misdirects the assisting citizen.

Private policing by individual citizens and private groups increased during the 1990's. Even though psychologists and sociologists contend that most citizens avoid intervening in situations of criminal activity, citizens are forming groups such as neighborhood watch groups to lower crimes of theft and personal injury. These groups are especially strong in neighborhoods with high rates of crime and understaffed police forces.

See also Arrest; Common law; Informants; Law enforcement; Police.

CIVIL ACTIONS

Procedures for handling noncriminal cases, ranging from initial decisions to file lawsuits to the final judgments

In civil actions laws have not been broken and statutes have not been violated. Thus, the state does not prosecute a defendant, as in a criminal action, but persons or entities who feel that they have been wronged decide to file lawsuits against other persons or entities. Civil actions involve multiple steps and are usually a lengthy process, although they can end at any point before the final judgment.

Beginning the Action

The first step in the process is deciding to sue. Potential litigants must decide if their grievances can be addressed by the law. Often, individuals have problems that cannot be resolved by a court of law, making it fruitless to attempt to sue. Potential litigants also must determine the probability of winning their lawsuits, ascertaining if the potential defendant, witnesses, and documents can be found and if the case is strong. Finally, potential litigants must decide if it is worth the money and time to pursue a lawsuit.

After deciding to sue, plaintiffs must select the appropriate court. The court must have jurisdiction over the subject matter of the case. In other words, the court must have the power to decide the type of case at hand. For example, the jurisdiction of probate courts is to adjudicate wills. The court must also have jurisdiction over the persons involved. Usually this means that defendants must reside in or be found in the jurisdiction in which they are being sued.

When the court has been selected, plaintiffs must let the defendants know that they are being sued. Notice is accomplished through the service of process, in which defendants are given a summons directing them to appear in court. If they do not appear and answer the summons in court, a default judgment is entered in favor of the plaintiffs.

In the summons, defendants receive the complaint, the first element in what is termed the pleadings. The complaint specifies

---

QUESTIONS TO CONSIDER BEFORE PURSUING A LAWSUIT

- Are there alternative methods of dispute resolution?
- Will monetary payment be a satisfactory means of relief?
- Will the defendant be able to pay monetary damages?
- How much will the lawsuit cost the litigant?
- If the court orders the defendant to comply with an order or restriction, how easy will it be to enforce?
- Will the remedy be sufficient?
- Will the litigant earn a bad reputation by suing?
- Will the lawsuit open the litigant's life to unwelcome public scrutiny?
- Will the litigant's lawsuit antagonize people who are important or influential?

the cause of action against the defendant and provides the facts and reasons for instituting the lawsuit. The second part of the pleadings consists of the defendants' answer to the complaints against them. Defendants must either move to dismiss the complaint for failure to state a cause of action or answer it. Sometimes plaintiffs reply to defendants' answer, constituting the third element of the pleadings. No response on plaintiffs' part usually signifies that they deny the answer.

Pretrial

Before a trial can take place, the parties exchange information about the opposition's case through the discovery process. The primary method of discovery is the deposition, in which attorneys have the opportunity to question opposing witnesses. The deposition is conducted in an examination format and is transcribed. Discovery can also include written interrogatories that ask for specific information, orders for production of documents and evidence, and orders for physical examinations in which the injured party is examined by a doctor of the defendant's choosing.

If defendants feel after discovery that, regardless of the facts, they should win based on the law, they supplement the pleadings with additional documents and move for a summary judgment. If the judge grants the summary judgment at this point, a judgment in favor of the defendant is entered. If the parties do not settle the case at this point, a trial date is set. Sometimes trials occur years after being placed on a judge's court calendar. If either party wants a jury, jury selection is the first step in the trial process. Attorneys and the judge ask questions of prospective jurors, whereby challenges for cause remove jurors with clear biases and prejudices toward the case and peremptory challenges remove jurors without explanation. If neither party requests a jury, the judge determines the outcome of the case.

Trial and Appeal

After the jury is selected, the trial begins and the plaintiff makes an opening statement, followed by the defendant. Opening statements allow the parties to acquaint the jurors with the key facts of the case. Then the plaintiff's attorney examines witnesses who support the case and the defense attorney has the opportunity to cross-examine them. After the presentation of the plaintiff's witnesses, the defense attorney might move for a directed verdict, claiming that the plaintiff has not presented a *prima facie* case, or a case that is true or valid on first view. If a case is *prima facie*, the plaintiff has met the burden of proof and there is enough evidence to proceed with the defense's case. If the motion for directed verdict is granted, the trial is over; if it is not granted, the defense presents its witnesses.

After all the evidence has been submitted, the lawyers deliver their closing arguments. The plaintiff begins, followed by the defendant, and then concluding with a rebuttal from the plaintiff. Closing arguments are persuasive speeches designed to sway the jury toward a particular side. Then the judge provides jury instructions that have been discussed and agreed upon by both attorneys. The jury deliberates, reaches a verdict, and a judgment is entered.

Finally, the losing party has a chance to appeal the verdict to the next higher court based on any number of factors, including juror misconduct, excessive damage awards, and an error in admitting evidence. An appeal is made in the form of a written brief and through oral argument before the appellate court. The appellate court rules on matters of law, not evidence; it does not rehear the trial. After hearing the appeal, the court can affirm, reverse, or modify the lower court's decision. After the appeal, the judgment is final and cannot be challenged in another proceeding.

—Ann Burnett

Suggested Readings

For an examination of the federal court system, consult *Guide to the Federal Courts* (Washington, D.C.: WANT Publishing, 1984). Some basic texts outlining civil action include *The Twenty-First Century Family Legal Guide*, by Joseph W. Mierzwa (Highlands Ranch, Colo.: ProSe Associates, 1994), and *Introduction to Law and the Legal System*, by Harold J. Grilliot and Frank A. Schubert (4th ed. Boston: Houghton Mifflin, 1989). For a legal scholar's perspective, see *An Introduction to the Legal System of the United States*, by E. Allan Farnsworth (3d ed. Dobbs Ferry, N.Y.: Oceana, 1996). An excellent, readable legal text is *Civil Procedure: Examples and Explanations* by Joseph W. Glannon (2d ed. Boston: Little, Brown, 1992). Other useful works on this subject include Thomas Glyn Watkin's *An Historical Introduction to Modern Civil Law* (Brookfield, Vt.: Dartmouth, 1999); Jay Tidmarsh and Roger H. Trangsrud's *Complex Litigation: Problems in Advanced Civil Procedure* (New York: Foundation Press, 2002); Jay Tidmarsh's *Complex Liti-*

gation and the Adversary System (New York: Foundation Press, 1998); and Lawrence M. Friedman's *American Law in the Twentieth Century* (New Haven, Conn.: Yale University Press, 2002).

See also Appeal; Breach of contract; Cause of action; Directed verdicts; Discovery; Dismissal; Lawsuits; *Nolo contendere* pleas; Summary judgments; Trials; Witnesses.

CIVIL LAW

Division of law, sometimes called "private law," that applies to the rights governing conduct among individuals who resort to the courts for redress; goals of civil law include compensation in the form of money damages or equitable relief and the returning of the injured party to the status quo

Two major subdivisions of the law are criminal law and civil law. Because a crime is considered an offense against society, the government initiates criminal actions through the office of the public prosecutor or district attorney. Criminal law seeks to punish the wrongdoer for violating societal rules, generally through imposition of a penalty in the form of a fine payable to the state or imprisonment. Criminal law also aims to serve as a deterrent to other citizens in society. A basic premise of the criminal law concerns the presumption of innocence of the accused until proven guilty beyond a reasonable doubt. If that burden is not met, then the accused is released.

Civil cases, on the other hand, are primarily brought by private individuals or organizations against persons or entities who have allegedly injured or wronged them. Civil law seeks to compensate the plaintiff (the person initiating the lawsuit) for a wrong through an award of monetary damages or a remedy in equity. In most civil cases, the plaintiff must prove his or her case by the preponderance or weight of the evidence—which essentially means merely tipping the scales slightly in the plaintiff's direction. Other civil cases sometimes require proof by clear and convincing evidence, a standard more demanding than preponderance of the evidence but below the burden of proof required in criminal

---

SPECIFIC AREAS OF CIVIL LAW

- Agency
- Antitrust and unfair competition
- Bankruptcy
- Business organizations
- Commercial paper
- Constitutional civil rights
- Contracts
- Domestic relations
- Entertainment and sports
- Estates and trusts

- Immigration
- Insurance
- Intellectual property
- International relations
- Labor and employment
- Property
- Sales
- Secured transactions
- Taxation
- Torts

---

cases. Certain cases (such as battery) are actionable in independent criminal and civil proceedings.

Damages

The civil law awards money damages to right any wrong done to a plaintiff, assuming that the plaintiff has prevailed at trial. Damages awardable in a civil case are of four types: compensatory, punitive, nominal, and liquidated. Compensatory damages attempt to compensate the plaintiff for pecuniary (monetary) losses—past, present, and future—which resulted from the defendant's wrongful conduct. In awarding compensatory damages, the court attempts to put the plaintiff in the same financial position as existed before commission of the wrong or prior to the breach of contract. The law will not put the party in a better position. Recovery for future losses is not permitted for remote, speculative, or indirect consequences.

Punitive or exemplary damages punish the wrongdoer for unconscionable, willful, or wanton conduct. They also are awarded to deter others from similar conduct. Punitive damages are awarded to the plaintiff over and above the compensatory amount. They are additional damages for a civil wrong and are not a substitute for criminal punishment. In order to receive punitive damages, therefore, the plaintiff must prevail at trial.

Nominal damages, generally a token sum (such as one dollar), are awarded to vindicate a plaintiff's claim or establish a legal right in cases where no evidence of specific harm exists. Liquidated damages are stipulated in a contract by the parties as the amount to be paid as compensation for loss in the event of a breach.

Equity

Civil law may be subdivided into law and equity. Law, referring to the original common-law courts that developed in medieval England, granted money damages according to rigid and strict rules and procedures. Grievances where money was not the remedy sought were brought before a British religious and political leader called a chancellor, sometimes referred to as the "king's conscience." Attempting to mitigate the harshness of strict rules and statutes, equity courts applied flexible principles of fairness and discretion in individual cases. Instead of relying on rules of law to reach decisions, courts of equity use as guidelines in the decision-making process equitable maxims, or short statements containing the gist of equity law.

The dual system of law and equity became part of the American legal system. In fact, until the courts were merged and integrated in 1938, law and equity courts were completely divided, each having a separate administrative system. Distinctions between the two still exist in principle; the threshold requirement for entering equity is the existence of an incomplete or inadequate remedy at law. Because jury trials are unavailable in equity, the judge acting as chancellor has the discretion to fashion an appropriate remedy in the case.

Among equitable remedies are injunctions, or judicial orders directing another to act or refrain from acting in a certain manner; reformation, used to rectify or reform an agreement to reflect the true intention of the parties; rescission, or cancellation of an agreement because of mistake, duress, fraud, or undue influence; and specific performance, requiring the defendant to fulfill contractual obligations. Hybrid actions seeking both common law and equitable remedies may be brought in one lawsuit, with the legal issues decided by a jury and the equitable issues by a judge/chancellor.

Certain landmark constitutional cases have been decided following equitable principles. Those include *Brown v. Board of Education* (school desegregation, 1954) and *Regents of the University of California v. Bakke* (racial quotas and preferential admissions programs, 1978).

—*Marcia J. Weiss*

Suggested Readings

Excellent starting points on this subject are Thomas Glyn Watkin's *An Historical Introduction to Modern Civil Law* (Brookfield,

Vt.: Dartmouth, 1999) and *Civil Justice in Crisis: Comparative Per-spectives of Civil Procedure*, edited by Adrian A. S. Zuckerman (New York: Oxford University Press, 1999). Civil law is also covered in such introductory law texts as Harold J. Grilliot and Frank A. Schubert, *Introduction to Law and the Legal System* (5th ed. Boston: Houghton Mifflin, 1992), and Beth Walston-Dunham, *Introduction to Law* (2d ed. St. Paul, Minn.: West Publishing, 1994). Books on equity include Peter Charles Hoffer, *The Law's Conscience: Equitable Constitutionalism in America* (Chapel Hill: University of North Carolina Press, 1990), and Gary L. McDowell, *Equity and the Constitution: The Supreme Court, Equitable Relief, and Public Policy* (Chicago: University of Chicago Press, 1982). A readable comparison of common law and civil law traditions, including historical development and the emergence of equity courts, is John Henry Merryman, *The Civil Law Tradition: An Introduction to the Legal Systems of Western Europe and Latin America* (2d ed. Stanford, Calif.: Stanford University Press, 1985). More specialized works include Guozhang Huang's *Introducing Discovery into Civil Law* (Durham, N.C.: Carolina Academic Press, 2003) and David A. Dittfurth's *The Concepts and Methods of Federal Civil Procedure* (Durham, N.C.: Carolina Academic Press, 1999).

See also Case law; Cause of action; Class action; Common law; Contracts; Damages; Equitable remedies; Lawsuits; Liability, civil and criminal; Louisiana law; Standards of proof; Statutes; Torts.

CIVIL RIGHTS AND LIBERTIES

Civil rights are generally understood to be rights that a government affirmatively promises to protect; in contrast, civil liberties are generally understood to be rights or liberties that a government promises not to violate

Late twentieth century America was increasingly preoccupied with arguments over civil rights and civil liberties. However, rarely has any distinction been made between civil rights and liberties. While many recognize that litigation is increasing in America, few inquire as to why this is occurring. The explosion in civil

FIRST AMENDMENT CONTROVERSIES

Issue	Reasons to Limit	Reasons Not to Limit
Does the First Amendment protect the right of members of the Native American Church to smoke peyote as part of their religious rituals?	Peyote is a controlled substance. To permit its use might endanger the lives of the user and others.	The free exercise of religion by the Native American Church requires the use of peyote. Freedom of religion should not be infringed.
Does the First Amendment protect the right of art galleries to display artworks that may be considered obscene or offensive?	The First Amendment does not protect pornography or obscenity. A work considered offensive by the community, should not be displayed.	Freedom of speech and freedom of the press imply free expression. Art is in the eye of the beholder.
Does the First Amendment protect those who burn the American flag in violation of state laws?	The flag is the country's most important symbol. State governments ought to be allowed to protect it.	Burning the flag is as legitimate an act of protest as speaking out against a government policy. Preventing flag-burning would be banning a form of political expression.
Should schools and public libraries ban books that contain racially offensive terms?	Use of some racial terms is offensive and may lower the self-esteem of minority students.	Censorship restricts the flow of ideas. Students would be prevented from reading literature written when such terms were more acceptable.
Should the press be allowed to print all government documents?	The press's freedom should be restricted to ensure national security.	All government decisions should be exposed to the will of the people.
Should newspapers and the media be allowed access to participants in a trial before a verdict has been delivered?	Unlimited discussion of trial-related matters in a public forum may infringe upon rights to due process.	Matters of public concern should be open for discussion.

rights litigation is enormous. Between 1960 and 1980, the total number of civil rights lawsuits jumped from 200 to more than 25,000. This total was far in excess of the growth in the population and outstrips almost every other form of litigation in terms of its rate of increase. Some scholars and jurists believe that the expansion of civil rights legislation has increasingly put civil rights in conflict with civil liberties. To fully understand this requires examining the history of both phrases and the distinction between the two.

Many authors regard civil liberties as negative promises by or negative commands to the government not to do certain things. The U.S. Constitution's Article I, sections 9 and 10 (the prohibitions against specified federal and state government actions) and the entire Bill of Rights (the first ten amendments) are clearly lists of negative commands. The First Amendment's wording that "Congress shall make no law respecting an establishment of religion" is only one of a long list of such commands. Other negative commands in the Bill of Rights include, "No Soldier shall, in time of peace be quartered in any house," "No person shall be held to answer for a capital, or otherwise infamous crime, unless on a presentment or indictment of a Grand Jury," and "Excessive bail shall not be required."

Negative commands would not help very much if a government did not also act affirmatively to protect its citizens from improper acts by others. Purely negative commands need to be balanced with certain affirmative obligations, and these are properly known as civil rights. These are particularly important to individuals or groups discriminated against in the past, such as African Americans, Hispanics, and women. There is also an overlap between civil liberties and civil rights. A negative promise that the government will not interfere with free speech implies an affirmative promise that the government will protect individuals who express their opinions, even in the face of majorities that wish to silence them. Civil liberties have a longer, clearer relationship to American government that do civil rights. The negative commands in the U.S. Constitution preceded affirmative promises.

The Fourteenth Amendment

From the founding of the United States until after the Civil War, the U.S. Supreme Court held that the Constitution protected state governments (and only indirectly their citizens) from the federal government's power. After the Civil War, the U.S. Congress sought to redress this problem by inserting language in the Constitution that would reverse this situation.

While the Fourteenth Amendment's first section has four parts, the most important is the first, which reads: "All persons born or naturalized in the United States and subject to the jurisdiction thereof, are citizens of the United States and of the State wherein they reside." This statement sought to undo the pre-Civil War notion of citizenship, under which each person was primarily a citizen of the state in which he or she resided and, only secondarily, a citizen of the United States. This constitutional language appeared to mean that all persons, African American or white, were to be citizens both of the United States and of the states in which they lived and that African Americans could not be denied citizenship as they had been in the Southern states. This allowed the U.S. Constitution to reach through the boundaries of the states to affect each individual citizen.

The Fourteenth Amendment also states: "No State shall make or enforce any law which shall abridge the privileges or immunities of citizens of the United States; nor shall any State deprive any person of life, liberty, or property, without due process of law; nor deny to any person within its jurisdiction the equal protection of the laws." From a reading of the plain meaning of the text, these words would seem to reverse the Court's previous view. Having amended the Constitution in this fashion, it would appear that the American people overturned the older view by ratifying the Fourteenth Amendment through their various state legislatures.

The Supreme Court did not initially adopt this posture. However, from the 1920's through the 1960's they finally did so under the doctrine of selective incorporation, which holds that parts of the U.S. Bill of Rights are so basic to the notion of due process that the states cannot deny them to any persons residing within their borders. Thus, the words "Congress shall make no law . . ." have come to mean that no government within the United States shall make any law that abridges the freedom of speech or press.

The Supreme Court did not make much progress in advancing toward incorporation until the 1950's and 1960's, when changes in the composition of the Court made it possible to move beyond the First Amendment to incorporate eventually nearly all of the important sections of the Bill of Rights. Thus, civil liberties against the actions of both the federal government and state governments are a comparatively recent addition to the understanding of civil liberties in the United States.

Striking Down Segregation

The Supreme Court did not initially protect civil rights. As a result of a series of decisions, the late nineteenth century Supreme Court treated the Fourteenth Amendment as if it did not exist for ordinary citizens. A white butcher in New Orleans was not considered to be covered by the Fourteenth Amendment, because the Court said the original intent of those who had proposed the amendment was merely to bring African Americans to the level of whites. African American citizens could not claim protection under the amendment if a state provided any kind of remotely comparable separated facilities, even if they were quite unequal in fact. From the modern perspective, the Fourteenth Amendment seemed not to provide much protection for its citizens.

For nearly sixty years the Court did not go very far toward reversing itself on civil rights until changes in the composition of the Court made it possible to move toward protecting civil rights by applying the equal protection clause of the Fourteenth Amend-

Signs such as that on the rest room door began disappearing from public accommodations after the passage of the federal Civil Rights Act of 1964. (Library of Congress)

ment, making civil rights available to all citizens. The first decision in this direction was *Brown v. Board of Education* (1954), which overturned *Plessy v. Ferguson* (1896) by deciding that separate but equal was an impossibility because segregated schools were inherently unequal.

By overturning *Plessy*, the Court announced a new jurisprudence with revolutionary implications. Perceiving this, some legal scholars wrote searching challenges to *Brown*, but the Court won, not simply because it was the highest court in the land but also because its interpretation of the Fourteenth Amendment more closely corresponded to the original language than did the earlier view. In fact, segregated schools had not been equal to integrated schools, and the separate but equal doctrine had been used fundamentally to discriminate against African Americans by maintaining grossly unequal facilities.

State action was the principal focus toward which *Brown* was directed, because southern states had been taxing all of their citizens—African Americans and whites—but had been using tax revenues to unequally benefit whites over African Americans. Since African American citizens had no effective way to vote in most southern states, they had no political remedy to fight against this discrimination. It was this abusive use of the coercive power of the state that gave the Supreme Court its greatest moral claim to set aside segregation in the schools and other facilities.

The Court, the least powerful of the national institutions, must lead largely by persuading the populace that its decisions are correct. U.S. courts have sufficient legitimate strength to force national and state executive branches to respond to court orders. Persons who defy the courts find themselves in great difficulties. However, in *Brown* the Court sought to persuade not individuals but large masses of people, who were strengthened because they could counterpose the force of the states' political subunits to the courts. Many southern states responded to *Brown* by erecting state legal and constitutional barriers to the Supreme Court decision, continuing to use their coercive power to deny African Americans equal protection. At the same time, they did not protect African American citizens from private groups, such as the Ku Klux Klan.

Lacking the support of the U.S. government's executive and legislative branches, the Court's power was not sufficient to achieve the end of segregation. From the 1954 *Brown* decision to the passage of the 1964 Civil Rights Act, a decade passed in which the courts struck down discriminatory laws in the southern states, a process so slow and tedious that only 1 percent of southern students attended integrated schools by 1964. Only after the passage of the 1964 and 1965 Civil Rights Acts did all three branches of the national government begin to strengthen the uniformity of the U.S. federal system by providing equal protections. Only when these acts were enforced by a sympathetic administration in the 1960's did real progress toward eliminating this improper use of southern state governmental power begin to have effect.

Private Acts of Discrimination

The problem was complicated because it was not a question of merely striking down a handful of laws that gave preference to whites over African American citizens but a whole fabric of law that protected privileges acquired over years of discrimination. The constitutional system often protects minorities by slowing change. Within the nation as a whole, white southerners were a protected minority that used the legal system to maintain their previous benefits. While legislation should not be retroactive, the legal system should also be equal, or legitimacy will erode.

The attempt to redress all segregation was still more difficult because many discriminatory acts were in the domain of activities long regarded as private and beyond the legitimate scope of governmental activity. Given the past benefits many people derived from segregation, citizens could rely on the constitutional/legal structure to resist integration. The U.S. Supreme Court could strike down statutes and state constitutional provisions one after the other. However, when they had rendered the legal system presumably neutral, they still found schools largely segregated because of private decisions made by citizens without any overt governmental support.

Nowhere was this clearer than in the segregation of northern schools, which turned out to be based on residential housing patterns. When the Court found that decisions by local authorities deliberately brought about the segregation of schools, they could strike them down. However, they could do far less when discrimination was not the result of deliberate governmental action. However, this is what the notion of civil rights entails: affirmative guarantees that the government will act fairly toward all individuals.

Civil Rights and Civil Liberties in the 1990's

Groups other than African Americans, particularly women, claim to have suffered discrimination in the past. Such groups were similarly not granted equal protection of the laws in the late 1800's despite their pressing claims at that time. By the 1990's political issues in the civil rights area focused on the Fourteenth Amendment's last section, which calls on Congress to pass appropriate remedial legislation. Civil rights issues are heavily dependent on affirmative legislation passed by the U.S. Congress, the quality of which is in doubt. Some believe there has been a decline in the quality of the legislation passed by Congress. Much critical legislation is excessively vague, so that attempts to improve civil rights for U.S. citizens create conflicts with constitutional protections of civil liberties.

Worse, Congress not only passes vague legislation on its own but also delegates its law-making powers to various administrative agencies that are authorized to establish such rules and regulations having the force of law as may be necessary to remedy whatever problem is at stake. This has created a situation in which everyone's rights and liberties are limited, especially regarding free speech.

Insofar as the U.S. Supreme Court interprets cases, it interprets laws passed by Congress. The Court, instead of striking this legislation as overbroad, has damaged the situation by handing down vague rulings of its own. Inevitably, contradictions arise in which Congress, the courts, and citizens must decide whether they wish to sacrifice civil liberties or civil rights in important cases.

Examining the case of women's rights, it is important to know that modern attempts to promote gender equality and protect women's rights rest on the 1964 Civil Rights Act. Sex, meaning gender, was added to the legislation in an effort to have it killed by southern senators who were convinced that the logic of civil rights law would mean that not only racial minorities but also women would have to be protected. Supporters of the 1964 Civil Rights Act simply denied that the addition of sex or gender to the act would have any impact on women, and the act passed with the words included.

Sexual Discrimination

Initially, women did not have much protection and sought to be protected by a new constitutional amendment, the Equal Rights Amendment (ERA). The ERA failed to win a sufficient number of states to be added to the Constitution, but other federal legislation resting on the Fourteenth Amendment strengthened the status of women in their efforts to end job discrimination in employment. In the end southern senators were right that the status of women changed as the result of the inclusion of gender protection in the 1964 Civil Rights Act.

In the 1990's the United States coped with this vague legislation, and the Supreme Court continued to interpret the vague offerings of Congress on the status of women and civil rights. This vague legislation has helped the status of some women, but other women have been harmed by the legislation. In the employment area, many women in the late twentieth century were employed in jobs and professions to which they previously lacked access. The gap in pay between men and women has grown smaller. There remains a gap overall, but it may be due to the relatively younger age of women in some professions as much as to residual discrimination. Complaints about the entry of women into the highest echelons of business and government continue.

Progress in this area is apparently sufficient so that the focus of gender equality has shifted to the area of sexual harassment, of which there are two forms: *quid pro quo* sexual harassment and hostile environment harassment. The ban on the former presumably seeks to prosecute cases in which favors are granted or withdrawn based on whether sexual favors are given or withheld by the aggrieved party. The ban on the latter presumably deals with harassment designed to discourage women from entering certain jobs or professions. Actions qualifying as forms of harassment are very broadly and vaguely defined.

Consent as a defense against charges that sexual harassment has occurred was called into doubt in the late twentieth century. The U.S. Supreme Court has determined that the question of whether there must be a demonstrated job or monetary loss for sexual harassment to have occurred is unnecessary. The question of liability is strict in the case of businesses but virtually nonexistent in the case of educational institutions.

While sexual harassment was once thought to be perpetrated only by men against women, it came to be viewed in the late twentieth century as an act that either men or women could perform. It could occur between men and men or women and women. In 1998 the Supreme Court determined that sexual harassment could occur between heterosexual men. In other words, sexual interest was no longer seen as a necessary element in sexual harassment. Sexual harassment may involve actions or behaviors that do not have any sexual content because of the nearly infinite range of words and behavior that may be double entendres. Any person in an educational or employment setting who touches—however tangentially—anyone else or who speaks to anyone else may be accused and convicted of sexual harassment without regard to the gender or sexual orientation of any of the parties. Concrete, tangible, and objective evidence is not necessary for a finding of fault. Some find this to be excessively vague.

Another controverial area has been homosexuals' demands for job protection, the right to marry members of the same sex, and the legal availability of health care benefits to same-sex partners. These questions have generated exceptional controversy. Despite improvements in the status of homosexuals, opposition remains strong.

Persons with physical or mental disabilities and handicaps are protected by the Americans with Disabilities Act (1990), a congressional enactment in line with the Fourteenth Amendment. Here the critical vagueness appears to concern the definition of disability. A court case expanded the definition of disabilities to include reproductive disability. Should this definition be upheld, the number of persons considered to have disabilities will grow dramatically. Coupled with the vagueness inherent in what constitutes discrimination, the prospects for further litigation are considerable.

On the subject of racial discrimination—once the core issue of the civil rights struggle—further progress has been complicated not only by the progress made in the past but by a backlash by whites and conservative members of various minority groups to some of the more ambitious conceptions of affirmative action.

—*Richard L. Wilson*

Suggested Readings

The best way to approach this complex subject is to turn to works such as *A Reader on Race, Civil Rights, and American Law: A Multiracial Approach*, edited by Timothy Davis, Kevin R. Johnson, and George A. Martínez (Durham, N.C.: Carolina Academic Press, 2001); William Cohen and David J. Danelski, *Constitutional Law: Civil Liberty and Individual Rights* (New York: Foundation Press, 2002); and *The Lanahan Readings in Civil Rights and Civil Liberties*, edited by David M. O'Brien (Baltimore: Lanahan Publishers, 1999). An excellent work of general scholarship is Henry J. Abraham and Barbara A. Perry's *Freedom and the Court* (6th ed. New York: Oxford University Press, 1994). For a cogent statement of the case against the Court's current understanding of civil rights, readers may refer to Raoul Berger's *The Fourteenth Amendment and the Bill of Rights* (Norman: University of Oklahoma Press, 1989). A comprehensive examination of the elements of the Bill of Rights can be found in *The Bill of Rights: Original Meaning and Current Understanding*, edited by Eugene W. Hickok, Jr. (Charlottesville: University of Virginia Press, 1991) and *The Bill of Rights in the Modern State*, edited by Geoffrey R. Stone, Richard A. Epstein, and Cass R. Sunstein (Chicago: University of Chicago Press, 1992). Ronald J. Fiscus's *The Constitutional Logic of Affirmative Action*. (Durham, N.C.: Duke University Press, 1992) presents a tightly logical argument written in support of the concept of affirmative action as a part of the package of rights known as civil rights. An opposing view can be found in Kent Greenwalt's *Discrimination and Reverse Discrimination*. (New York: Knopf, 1983). For excellent analyses of the dangers of vague delegations of power see David Schoenbrod's *Power Without Responsibility: How Congress Abuses the People Through Delegation* (New Haven, Conn.: Yale University Press, 1993). Also useful is Shmuel Lock's *Crime, Public Opinion, and Civil Liberties: The Tolerant Public* (Westport, Conn.: Praeger, 1999). Stephen J. Schulhofer's *The Enemy Within: Intelligence Gathering, Law Enforcement, and Civil Liberties in the Wake of September 11* (New York: Century Foundation Press, 2002) examines the erosion of civil liberties after the terrorist attacks on the United States of September 11, 2001.

See also Bill of Rights, U.S.; Constitution, U.S.; Due process of law; Effective counsel; Federal Bureau of Investigation; Justice Department, U.S.; Presumption of innocence; Pro bono legal work; Reversals of Supreme Court decisions by Congress; State courts.

CLASS ACTION

Lawsuit brought by or against many individuals or organizations who share a common legal interest; such suits give individuals with similar small claims greater chances for justice

The modern class action originated in the English court of chancery in a procedure known as the bill of peace, which allowed persons with a common complaint to gain justice against a larger group or a more powerful wrongdoer. In the United States, prior to the nineteenth century, these ideas were embodied in the Federal Equity Rules, regulations outside the state and federal codes. In the nineteenth century, state codes made class actions legal actions at the state level. In 1938, federal courts followed.

Groups that want to initiate a class action must convince a judge that the complaints of individual members bringing the suit are sufficiently similar that justice is better served by processing the group action rather than individual actions. In addition, the judge must be convinced that absent class members will be fairly represented. Once the class action is under way, those bringing the action must try to find others who will be bound by the findings of the court, so that they may participate in or voice their objections to the representation.

Class actions are most commonly used in cases involving the environment, securities, antitrust regulation, racial or sexual discrimination, unfair employment practices, and governmental benefits. Class actions have also been used by prisoners who believe the conditions of their confinement are unlawful and by consumers who can show a systematic pattern of misrepresentation of a product.

Since the early 1970's, the number of class action suits has greatly increased. Much of the increase probably reflects changes in the legal profession, specifically in fields of substantive law, and in the rising fees from class action suits. The class action also provides a way to bring important social issues to light, and such issues received increasing attention. Despite the increase in class actions in general, the trend has been to eliminate class actions from federal courts and get them into state courts.

Class actions have their drawbacks. Leaders of a class action can be bought off by an opponent to the detriment of others in the group. Members of the group may lose heart during the time-consuming legal process. The results represent an anomaly to the general rule that everyone has the right to a day in court because those results are ultimately binding on all class members, regardless of whether they participated in the case.

See also *Amicus curiae* briefs; Breach of contract; Cause of action; Civil law; Commercial litigation; Lawsuits; Shareholder suits.

CLERKS OF THE COURT

Court officers responsible for keeping track of proceedings and exhibits

Clerks of the court are the administrative arm of the judicial system in the United States and a part of the different levels of the court system ranging from the justice of the peace, or magistrate court, to the U.S. Supreme Court. Historically, they were responsible for maintaining the records and dockets of the king's courts in England. The office was imported to the United States during the colonial era.

The responsibilities of clerks of the court vary depending on the court system. In some states clerks' duties are confined to the internal operations of the court, including assembling trial lists, receiving fines and fees, maintaining court records, receiving criminal warrants and forwarding them to pros-

Among the responsibilities of clerks of the U.S. Supreme Court is scheduling oral arguments for cases that the Court has decided to hear. (Library of Congress)

ecutors, and summoning prospective jurors. In other states, clerks may also serve as county treasurers, auditors, and secretaries to county commissioners and probate judges. At the federal level clerks of the court are responsible for the internal operations of the courts.

Despite these responsibilities, only a few states require that clerks of the court possess certain minimum qualifications. Normally, they are elected at the county level for four-year terms. The only requirement for holding office is that they be qualified electors in the jurisdictions in which they serve. At the federal level clerks of the court are appointed by judges.

—*William V. Moore*

See also Bailiffs; *Certiorari*, writ of; Court calendars; Court costs; Judicial clerks; Officers of the court; Subpoena power; Trials.

COMMERCIAL LITIGATION

Court actions involving business and corporate clients in state and federal courts, governmental agencies, and alternative dispute resolution tribunals

Commercial litigation encompasses the fields of banking, bankruptcy, business torts, corporate law, computer law, construction law, defamation, employment law, environmental law, insurance, bad faith, intellectual property litigation, products liability, professional negligence, unfair competition, and the Uniform Commercial Code (UCC).

Role of Commercial Litigators

Many commercial litigators belong to the Litigation and Business Law Sections of the American Bar Association (ABA), which have specialized committees devoted to antitrust, business torts, insurance, product liability, securities, and criminal defense litigation. Commercial litigators represent their clients at all levels of the state and federal courts. Large law firms frequently form specialized legal departments to litigate commercial matters, such as contract, insurance, banking, and intellectual property disputes.

Commercial litigators must be skilled at gathering facts, drafting complaints, determining jurisdiction and venue, conducting depositions, examining and cross-examining expert and fact witnesses, understanding evidence issues, and employing trial techniques of persuasion. Commercial litigators frequently represent their clients before federal and state appellate courts.

They must be skilled at selecting arbitrators and representing their clients in less formal arbitrations and minitrials. Binding arbitration is frequently called for by contracts between commercial parties. Commercial disputes are increasingly resolved by private alternative dispute resolution, including arbitration, mediation, and other forms of binding and nonbinding dispute resolution. Commercial litigators are frequently consulted when firms draft arbitration clauses. The American Arbitration Association has specialized panels dealing with commercial litigation.

Types of Commercial Litigation

Business torts are common-law causes of action that regulate the relations among businesses. Business torts litigation may involve the breach of fiduciary duties (breach of trust), misrepresentation or fraud, and tortious interference with contract. Corporate fiduciaries, partners, or trustees are held to a high duty of care, loyalty, confidentiality, and good faith. Fiduciary liability is imposed against those who misappropriate or mishandle retirement funds by the Employee Retirement Income Security Act of 1974 (ERISA). Commercial litigation based on the concept of the fiduciary may be found in actions against stockbrokers, trustees, real estate agents and brokers, and majority shareholders.

Interference with contract is traditionally divided into two torts: interference with contract and interference with economic relations. Interference with contractual relations includes inducing breach of an existing contract, whereas interference with economic advantage protects the interests of future contractual relations. The essence of these torts is the intent of a defendant to entice a third party to breach its contractual relations with a plaintiff, creating damage to the business.

Commercial litigators frequently litigate causes of action under the federal Securities Act of 1934, which creates a cause of action for the fraudulent sale of securities. Unauthorized trading, fraud, and churning (which occurs when a broker initiates exces-

SPECIALIZED COMMERCIAL COURTS

Delaware: Delaware's Court of Chancery is a specialized court dealing with corporate matters.

New York: New York has instituted specialized commercial courts. The commercial division was a pilot project of the New York State Supreme Court. The Commercial and Federal Litigation Section of the New York State Bar Association and the *National Law Journal* conducted a survey of 198 in-house litigation counsel in New York County. Most in-house counsel viewed the concept of the commercial court favorably. Litigants in New York County have litigated commercial disputes in specialized merchant courts since 1993. The commercial court concept was extended to Rochester, New York, in 1995.

New Jersey: In 1996 New Jersey launched a special program for the handling of complex commercial litigation at the trial level. The New Jersey system tracks litigation depending on the complexity of the case. One track is specially devoted to complex litigation.

Wisconsin: Wisconsin has experimented with specialized courts to hear business cases.

Other states: A number of other states have considered proposed legislation to create commerce or commercial litigation courts.

sive numbers of transactions for personal gain) may also be the basis for federal securities litigation. The Racketeer Influenced and Corrupt Organizations (RICO) statute of 1970 is frequently asserted as a cause of action in commercial litigation. A federal jury awarded $134 million in punitive damages to a former commodities brokerage firm for fraud and racketeering committed by former employees in 1992. RICO provides statutory remedies of treble damages and attorney fees to the victims of fraud.

Commercial litigators increasingly represent their clients in bankruptcy cases. Secured creditors such as banks and other institutional creditors frequently have representation in bankruptcy proceedings. Lawyers representing their clients in a corporate bankruptcy case must be familiar with Article Nine of the UCC, the Bankruptcy Code, commercial debt restructuring, workouts, finance and economics, and business law.

Commercial litigators represent corporations, authors, writers, computer scientists, and other owners of intellectual property rights. Litigators with a specialty in intellectual property handle a wide range of intellectual property disputes involving patents, trademarks and trade dress infringement, software infringement, copyrights, trade secrets, and unfair competition. Claims of misappropriation of trade secrets and confidential information may arise out of lawsuits by departing employees.

Product Liability

The Dalkon Shield contraceptive device, the synthetic hormone DES that was administered to millions of pregnant women to reduce the risk of miscarriage, the morning sickness drug Bendectin, and breast implants are examples of products that have led to mass torts arising out of the design and distribution of unreasonably and dangerously defective products. Litigating complex multidistrict product liability cases involves difficult jurisdictional issues. The courts have been reluctant to order class actions in adjudicating mass toxic substances litigation. Commercial litigators frequently review product promotional literature and conduct product safety audits to prevent product liability.

Many toxic torts cases result in disputes over insurance companies' duty to defend, pay defense costs, and settle claims. Insurance coverage for environmental liability may involve disputes over contractual liability exclusion and coverage.

Measurement of Damages

Commercial litigators frequently employ experts such as economists to measure damages in complex litigation. Experts are sometimes required to assess corporate control transactions and the effects of insider trading. Commercial litigation is frequently high stakes litigation. For example, an Alaska jury awarded plaintiffs $5 billion in punitive damages arising out of Exxon's oil spill in Prince William Sound, Alaska, in 1989. In 1987 Pennzoil received $3 billion in punitive damages and $7.53 billion in compensatory damages arising out of a business torts case based upon interference with contract.

—*Michael L. Rustad*

Suggested Readings

Thomas J. Shroyer's *Accountant Liability* (New York: John Wiley, 1991) examines liability and damages faced by accountants. Peter Chinloy's *The Cost of Doing Business: Legal and Regulatory Issues in the United States and Abroad* (New York: Praeger,

1989) examines the impact of commercial litigation, compliance, and costs on modern business enterprises. William Cerillo's *Proving Business Damages* (New York: John Wiley Law Publications, 1991) is the best guide to remedies for antitrust, unfair competition, fraud, and other business torts. Paul A. Batista's *Civil Rico Practice* (New York: John Wiley & Sons, 1997) provides an overview of RICO and every aspect of civil racketeering law. The American Bar Association's Section of Litigation has published a book on many of the most important commercial litigation theories, rules, remedies, and defenses: George F. McGunnigle, Jr., *Business Torts Litigation* (Chicago: American Bar Association, 1992). David Owen's article on "The Intellectual Development of Modern Products Liability Law: A Comment on Priest's View of the Cathedral's Foundation" was published in volume 14 of the *Journal of Legal Studies* in 1985. Edward F. Mannino's *Business and Commercial Litigation: A Trial Lawyer's Handbook* (Charlottesville, Va.: Michie, 1997) deals broadly with the issue of commercial litigation and business law, as does Jay M. Feinman's *Law 101: Everything You Need to Know About the American Legal System* (New York: Oxford University Press, 2000), which has chapters on ligitation and business law. A central issue in commercial litigation is contracts, which are well covered in Marvin A. Chirelstein's *Concepts and Case Analysis in the Law of Contracts* (New York: Foundation Press, 2001), Dalia Marin and Monika Schnitzer's *Contracts in Trade and Transition: The Resurgence of Barter* (Cambridge, Mass.: MIT Press, 2002), Edward Avery Harriman's *Elements of the Law of Contracts* (Holmes Beach, Fla: Gaunt, 2003), and Hugh Collins's *Regulating Contracts* (New York: Oxford University Press, 1999).

See also Arbitration; Bankruptcy; Breach of contract; Contracts; Damages; Law firms; Liability, civil and criminal; Litigation; Torts; Uniform laws.

COMMON LAW

System of jurisprudence used in the United Kingdom, the United States, and some Commonwealth countries that fits current legal problems into case-based systems of law that stress precedent and continuity over time

Except for Louisiana, which uses a civil law system derived from the French Napoleonic Code (enacted in 1804), the states of the United States and the District of Columbia use their own modified version of case-based common-law jurisprudence. In case-based common-law jurisprudence judges compare the facts and issues in current cases to those in previous cases and reach decisions based on analogy between the current and past cases.

Americans decided to retain the common law after becoming politically independent from England in 1776, despite serious attempts in the early period of nationhood to sever legal and political ties to the mother country. The civil law of continental Europe based on Roman law as modified by statute and compilations such as the Napoleonic Code would have been a possible alternative.

Historical Origins

The common-law system developed in what are now England and Wales after the Norman Conquest of the British Isles in 1066. From the twelfth to the fourteenth centuries the common-law courts became an effective tool of the royal government in its attempts to centralize public administration, and lawyers became trained functionaries in a specialized body of knowledge. While the common-law system faced competition from prerogative courts in the sixteenth and seventeenth centuries, the English regarded the common-law system as a valued and effective bulwark of their rights against the Crown. After England colonized North America, the common-law system formed the basis of American law. In addition, British colonization carried the common-law system to Canada, with the exception of Quebec. Australia and New Zealand still use variants of common-law jurisprudence, and the common law also influences many other former British colonies.

Common-law systems are characterized by evolutionary growth

and change. In the United States the common-law system works within the constraints of the Constitution adopted in 1789 and its later modifications. For this reason U.S. and British common-law rules now differ significantly. Ironically, modern U.S. law is closer to the eighteenth century system described by Sir William Blackstone's *Commentaries on the Laws of England* (1765-1769) than is modern British law. Strongly influenced by Blackstone and other contemporary English writers on the common law, the Founders expected that the common law would be embodied in the laws of the several states. Thus the Seventh Amendment to the U.S. Constitution states:

> In Suits at common law, where the value in controversy shall exceed twenty dollars, the right of trial by jury shall be preserved, and no fact tried by a jury, shall be otherwise reexamined in any Court of the United States, than according to the rules of the common law.

In addition to the Seventh Amendment's explicit reference to the common-law tradition, the Constitution recognized this tradition in four other key respects. First, the Constitution included a written prohibition against any impairment of contracts (Article I, section 10). Second, the Fourth Amendment's prohibition against arbitrary search and seizure echoed a 1765 decision by England's Lord Chief Justice Charles Pratt Camden. Third, the Second Amendment's guarantee of the right to bear arms reflected the codification of the common law in the English Bill of Rights of 1689. Fourth, the Fifth Amendment's prohibition against forced self-incrimination can be related to the abolition of the English Star Chamber in 1642 by a parliament determined to maintain the supremacy of the common law and abolish non-common-law courts.

Federal Common Law

There is no federal common-law system in the United States, since forty-nine state court systems have over time adopted British common law in different ways. (The single exception is Louisiana, which has French roots) While there were century-long attempts to develop a federal common law on the basis of the case of *Swift v. Tyson* (1842), American jurisprudence has never overturned *Erie Railroad Co. v. Tompkins* (1938), in which Supreme

Court justice Louis Brandeis remanded a tort suit to the federal district court in Pennsylvania for trial under Pennsylvania substantive law and federal procedural law. In *Erie Railroad Co. v. Tompkins* Brandeis overturned Supreme Court justice Joseph Story's decision in *Swift v. Tyson*. Story had desired to create a uniform body of commercial law supervised by the federal courts, which amounted to a federal common law. In contrast to Story, Brandeis believed that the Constitution made no provision for a federal common law of any kind, either civil or criminal.

Despite *Erie Railroad Co. v. Tompkins*, modern legal thought recognizes some judge-created principles frequently called federal common law. These principles can be overturned by statute and are generally procedural or jurisdictional rather than constitutional in nature. When it applies, federal common law must be adopted by state courts.

Comparison

The common-law system of jurisprudence is normally contrasted to the civil-law system of jurisprudence used in France, Germany, Spain, and other continental European countries. Civil-law systems have their roots in Roman law as modernized by the Napoleonic Code and are characterized by less reliance on precedent than common-law systems and more reliance on judicial decision making and statutory promulgations. Judges and legislatures are the driving forces in the development of civil law, and civil law thus contrasts with the case-based tradition of building on precedent that is found in the common law. There are other differences between common-law and civil-law systems. For example, the jury system is characteristic of common-law but not of civil-law systems. In common-law systems criminal law is accusatorial rather than inquisitional. Common-law systems generally require that courts exclude significant evidence that could be included in civil-law cases.

The common-law system is a case-based system of jurisprudence that relies on precedent and the concept of *stare decisis* (the doctrine of following rules handed down in previous judicial decisions). Common-law judges examine a body of case law showing how courts have treated similar problems in the past and attempt to fit current problems into previously established patterns. Common-law systems use the collective memory of their societies to place some restraint on legal thinking that reflects the fads of the moment. Some critics of common law complain that under common-law systems the dead hand of the past rules the present to the public detriment. Other critics of common law see precedent breaking down under the stress of contemporary so-cial-reform efforts to make society more egalitarian and more strictly subject to majority rule.

Future Projections

Despite the changes U.S. law has undergone under the influ-ence of twentieth century commerce, the common law is still cen-tral to contemporary American justice. When aspiring lawyers prepare for the Multistate Bar Examination, they study very tradi-tional versions of the common law of contracts, criminal law, property law, and torts. While the common law of contracts was supplanted in the twentieth century by the Uniform Commercial Code (UCC) in dealings between merchants, the common-law legacy defining contracts as bargained-for exchanges between in-dividuals with reciprocal consideration still exists.

Although the types of common-law crimes have been supple-mented by other offenses and redefined by statute in every state, the most serious crimes defined by U.S. criminal law are those that were tried by medieval English courts. Common-law prop-erty rules have proven even more resistant to change than con-tract and criminal law. It would probably be correct to say that a post-Reformation sixteenth century English lawyer would under-stand most modern legal practice in the United States. Common-law tort rules have been strengthened by new constructs, such as product liability law (a contract/tort hybrid), and workers' com-pensation law. However, early tort rules still help citizens to win their day in court when they suffer civil wrongs.

In the United States courts apply common-law rules when no statute exists to govern the question at hand. State courts also ap-ply common law when a statute has been repealed and no replace-ment adopted. Given continuing American support for the legacy of Anglo-American common-law systems, extremist groups have been appropriating the term "common law" in reference to extra-judicial common-law courts of their own creation. Such courts are supported by individuals who believe that they can interpret the law as they see fit without reference to established governmental forms. Groups such as the American Patriot Network disseminate their own views of what they call common-law systems through the Internet. Isolated from mainstream thought, these groups may believe that they are restoring the long-lost virtues of Anglo-American common law.

—*Susan A. Stussy*

Suggested Readings

An excellent summary of the roots of the U.S. common-law system is historian Norman F. Cantor's *Imagining the Common Law: Common Law and the Foundations of the American Legal System* (New York: HarperCollins, 1997.) Although he is clearly more interested in the medieval origins of the common law, Cantor also provides an excellent account of seventeenth and eighteenth century attempts to organize and rationalize the common-law tradition. The passage of the common law from England to America receives scholarly treatment in the easy-to-read *Common Law and Liberal Theory: Coke, Hobbes, and the Origins of American Constitutionalism*, by James R. Stoner, Jr. (Lawrence: University Press of Kansas, 1992.) For those seeking to examine the origins of the common-law systems of contract law, criminal law, torts, and property law, Supreme Court justice Oliver Wendell Holmes, Jr.'s *The Common Law*, edited by Mark De Wolfe (Cambridge, Mass.: Harvard University Press, 1963), is worth reading. For late twentieth century examinations of Holmes's classic study, see *Holmes and the Common Law: A Century Later*, with contributions by Benjamin Kaplan, Patrick Atiyah, and Jan Vetter (Cambridge, Mass.: Harvard Law School, 1983.) These scholars analyze Holmes's work from the standpoint of modern Anglo-American law. Gordon Tullock's *The Case Against the Common Law* argues that the common-law system of the United States is essentially obsolete (Durham, N.C.: Carolina Academic Press, 1997). *Comparative Legal Traditions: A Nutshell*, jointly authored by three law professors, Mary Ann Glendon, Michael W. Gordon, and Michael Osakwe, provides a lucidly written comparison of civil law, common law, and socialist legal systems (St. Paul, Minn.: West Publishing, 1982). See also John Hamilton Baker's *The Common Law Tradition: Lawyers, Books, and the Law* (Rio Grande, Ohio: Hambledon Press, 2000), Francis Alan Roscoe Bennion's *Understanding Common Law Legislation: Drafting and Interpretation* (New York: Oxford University Press, 2001), and the American Bar Association's *Common Law, Common Values, Common Rights: Essays on Our Common Heritage* (San Francisco: American Bar Association, 2000).

See also Bill of Rights, U.S.; Case law; Civil law; Constitution, U.S.; Contracts; Ignorance of the law; Lawsuits; Louisiana law; Model Penal Code; Precedent; Statutes.

COMMUNITY SERVICE AS PUNISHMENT FOR CRIME

Punishment that involves unpaid work in the community rather than incarceration—a system that is commonly used as an alternative to incarceration; it helps alleviate jail overcrowding and avoids the costs of incarceration

When an individual commits a crime, a judge has many options as to punishment. Community service is one option that allows the offender to be punished without the state having to pay the high costs of imprisonment. An offender is typically sentenced to a certain number of hours (anywhere from forty to two hundred) of community service instead of being incarcerated. Some jurisdictions use community service in combination with other punishments, such as monetary fines.

Community service is viewed as restitution, or a punishment that makes an offender "pay back" society for the crime committed. The types of community service available to a judge are too great to mention, but typically include some kind of work to better the community, such as cleaning litter off the streets or lecturing about the dangers of certain criminal behaviors. For example, individuals convicted of driving under the influence of alcohol sometimes lecture to high school students about the possible effects of committing this particular crime.

See also Amnesty; Parole; Pro bono legal work; Restitution; Sentencing.

COMPENSATORY DAMAGES

Monetary awards to a plaintiff that compensate for injuries or losses sustained; the two general types of compensatory damages—general and special—are distinct from punitive damages

Compensatory damages, sometimes called actual damages, are intended to compensate a plaintiff in a civil case for an injury or loss caused by the wrongful action or misconduct of another person (the defendant). The purpose is to return the plaintiff to the position he or she was in before the loss occurred. For example, car A does not stop at a stop sign and hits car B in the intersection. The driver of car B is injured, and she is taken to the hospital. Compensatory damages, paid by the driver of car A (or his insurance company) will pay her medical and hospital expenses. Compensatory damages are distinct from punitive damages, which are awards beyond compensatory damages that are intended to punish and make an example of the wrongdoer.

Two subdivisions of compensatory damages are general damages and special (or consequential) damages. General damages require a causal relationship between the wrongful act and the loss. The loss is something that can normally be foreseen to occur as a consequence of the defendant's act. An injured driver, for example, would be expected to have medical bills.

Special damages are those which stand separately from expected damages. They may be payable for an indirect loss, yet the wrongdoing of the defendant must be the proximate cause of the loss. In the example given, the injured driver may also collect amounts for "pain and suffering" and for lost income during the period she is unable to work.

See also Civil law; Damages; Indemnity; Punitive damages; Torts.

COMPETENCY

Ability to make decisions and commitments required of citizens with a rational understanding of their probable consequences

Rational understanding is a legal prerequisite to making decisions such as those involved in signing a contract, agreeing to medical treatment, making out a will, testifying in court, making a major purchase, and even defending oneself against criminal charges in court. People who make out wills, for example, are expected to know the nature and amount of their assets, the identity of potential heirs, and have logical reasons for the disposition of their property. People who consent to medical treatment are expected to be able to comprehend the potential benefits and risks accompanying such treatment. Defendants in criminal cases are expected to be able to understand the charges against them, the trial procedure itself, and the risks and benefits of such alternative defense strategies as accepting a plea bargain. Even making everyday purchases requires a knowledge of elementary arithmetic and a rational capacity to allot money to essentials.

Since legal competency is generally assumed, legal issues arise in cases in which this assumption is challenged. Such cases most clearly define the meaning of the term. One limitation on the assumption of competency is age. Children and adolescents younger than eighteen years of age, the age of majority, are not generally considered capable of making significant contractual commitments.

A major category of cases in which competence has been questioned involves adults who suffer from mental illness or mental defect. At one time institutionalization in a mental hospital was widely accepted as a self-evident criterion of incompetence. Increasingly, however, lack of competence is determined through examinations of patients by mental health professionals. Such examinations focus on patients' understanding or lack of understanding of the particular procedures and choices in relevant areas. At subsequent judicial hearings patients' inability to understand the choices involved in specific areas, such as making a will or health care, must be corroborated by the testimony of these expert witnesses.

The consequences of a finding of incompetence by a court is different for criminal and civil matters. If criminal defendants are found incompetent to stand trial, they undergo treatment under institutional auspices and are reevaluated at a later time. At that time they may be found to be competent to stand trial or, if unimproved, they may be committed to an institution. If persons are found incompetent to administer their civil affairs, a guardian is appointed to administer these affairs for them. Guardianships may be established in financial matters (guardianships of estate), such personal matters as residence (guardianships of the person), or in specific matters such as medical treatment.

In order to invalidate a previously made contract or will, someone thereby disadvantaged may later try to show that the contracting individual was incompetent. To show this, it must be established that this individual suffered from a disturbed mental condition at the time and that the agreement resulted from this disturbed condition. Since the determination of any previous mental condition is somewhat speculative, proof of this is often difficult.

—Thomas E. DeWolfe

See also Age of majority; Bailiffs; Defendant self-representation; Effective counsel; Legal guardians.

CONFESSIONS

Voluntary admissions of guilt of crime that may or may not be admissible as evidence against the criminal defendants making the confessions

In criminal law a confession is a voluntary statement by persons who have been charged with a crime acknowledging their guilt for the offense. Typically a confession discloses some or all of the physical details of the crime as well as the defendant's share in its commission. Confessions may be "judicial" or "extra-judicial." The former are given in court before a judge or magistrate. A plea of guilty to a criminal charge is a simple judicial confession. Extrajudicial confessions can be made to any person, including police officers.

The Fifth Amendment to the U.S. Constitution provides that "No person . . . shall be compelled in any criminal case to be a witness against himself." This provision has important impact on both judicial and extrajudicial confessions. In American courts criminal defendants have an absolute right not to testify at trial, and the prosecution may not suggest to the jury that their refusal to testify is an indication of guilt. In other words defendants are under no obligation to give an accounting of themselves, and it is incumbent on the government to prove beyond a reasonable doubt that they have committed the crime of which they are accused. By contrast, legal systems in most other countries follow the European continental model and do not provide this guarantee. Should defendants refuse to say anything about the crime for which they are standing trial, the tribunal may take their refusal into account as one of the circumstances of the case.

At issue in extrajudicial confessions is whether or not they are voluntary. An involuntary confession is not admissible in evidence. Until 1966, except under special circumstances, the burden of proving that a confession was coerced and therefore not voluntary was placed primarily on the defendant. Although all forms of physical coercion were unconstitutional the courts had to develop a long and detailed set of rules to determine when or whether unfair psychological coercion had taken place. The rules had become very complex.

The Miranda Case

In 1966 the U.S. Supreme Court clarified confession law in its ruling in *Miranda v. Arizona*. Ernesto Miranda had been arrested for rape in Arizona. After two hours of interrogation by Phoenix police officers he confessed. Neither physical nor psychological coercion was applied by the investigating officers. At trial, Miranda moved to suppress his confession on the grounds that custodial interrogation—that is, when an arrested person is questioned by the police—is inherently coercive. The trial court disagreed, and Miranda was convicted on the basis of his victim's testimony as well as his confession, which the court admitted into evidence.

Miranda's appeal eventually reached the Supreme Court, which agreed with him about interrogation: "Compulsion [is] inherent in custodial surroundings." The Court held that the coercive effect of being questioned in private by law-enforcement officers can only be offset by requiring that arrested persons be given a warning or statement of their rights. After Miranda's initial conviction was overturned, Arizona retried him. The victim's testimony alone was sufficient for the court to find Miranda guilty again. He was sentenced to nine years imprisonment.

Under *Miranda*, an arrested defendant must be warned by the police of his right to remain silent, his right to counsel (including assigned counsel if he is indigent), and that anything he says can be used against him in court. Only if the defendant "voluntarily, knowingly, and intelligently" waives his right to silence may questioning take place.

When the *Miranda* case was first handed down, many law-enforcement officials and students of the criminal justice system believed that it would be enormously harmful. Then as now, most criminal prosecutions depend on incriminating statements given by the defendant. But the fact is that few defendants fully understand or are able to operationalize their rights under *Miranda*. Studies have shown that the great majority of defendants do in fact give either inculpatory or false exculpatory statements. The causes of confession which are most commonly identified by psychologists are isolation, despair, the need for companionship and social approval, and feelings of guilt. These operate whether the defendant has been warned or not and account for the continuing prevalence of confessions in American criminal cases, despite the "Miranda warning" issued by police officers.

Since 1966 only one major modification in the *Miranda* doctrine has been made. This occurred in *Quarles v. New York* (1984). In *Quarles*, the defendant, who had just been arrested in a supermarket and was therefore in custody, was believed to have hidden a loaded pistol nearby. Before the arresting officers warned Quarles of his rights they asked him where he had hidden the gun. He revealed the pistol's location to them and was later prosecuted for carrying a concealed weapon without a license. He objected that the discovery of the gun was the result of an unlawfully coerced confession. The Supreme Court held that because the motive of the arresting officers was to safeguard the public rather than accumulate evidence, Quarles's answer to the question was admissible. This case established a "public safety" exception to the *Miranda* rule. In 2000 the Supreme Court reaffirmed its committment to the Miranda doctrine in *Dickerson v. United States*, a decision in which the justices declined to overrule the long-established precedent.

The Modern Role of Confessions

By the end of the twentieth century, the American system of criminal justice came to rely almost exclusively on confessions, both judicial and extrajudicial. Of every hundred arrests, excluding simple traffic offenses, roughly 48.5 defendants plead guilty to something, usually a lesser-included offense of the crime for which they had been arrested. Charges are never brought against fifty of the defendants (many of these are juveniles who undergo some kind of diversionary process that does not involve formal conviction). It can be seen that only 1.5 percent of arrested persons actually come to trial and contest the charges brought against them. Plea bargaining has become the dominant American criminal justice institution. The rules regulating confessions substantially define the procedural content of justice in the United States.

—*Robert Jacobs*

Suggested Readings

Two works that focus on the subject of confessions are *Criminal Interrogation and Confessions*, by Fred E. Inbau et al. (Gaithersburg, Md.: Aspen Publishers, 2001), and Sara C. Benesh's *The U.S. Court of Appeals and the Law of Confessions: Perspectives on the Hierarchy of Justice* (New York: LFB Scholarly Publishing, 2002). A good general treatment of American law that discusses confessions and the *Miranda* rules is Lawrence M. Friedman's *American Law: An Introduction* (New York: W. W. Norton, 1988). Insight into the techniques of police interrogation as well as a discussion of legal rules is found in *Criminal Interrogation and Confessions*, 3rd edition, by Fred E. Inbau, John E. Reid, and Joseph P. Buckley (Baltimore: Williams & Wilkins, 1986). The psychological pressures placed on arrestees to confess are covered in O. John Rogge, *Why Men Confess* (New York: Da Capo Press, 1971). Liva Baker's *Miranda: Crime, Law, and Politics* (New York: Atheneum, 1983) provides a broad perspective on the role of confessions in the American system and the politically charged issues that they engender. A good collection of articles relating confession law to public policy is *Police Interrogation and Confessions: Essays in Law and Policy* (Ann Arbor: University of Michigan Press, 1980), edited by Yale Kamisar.

David Thoreson Lykken's *A Tremor in the Blood: Uses and Abuses of the Lie Detector* (New York: Plenum Trade, 1998) considers the use of lie detectors in evoking confessions.

See also Arraignment; Arrest; Defendants; Due process of law; Evidence, rules of; Exclusionary rule; Fifth Amendment; Lesser included offense; Miranda rights; Perjury; Plea bargaining; Self-incrimination, privilege against; Testimony; Trials.

CONSENT DECREE

Court-supervised or sanctioned settlement agreement in cases involving an institutional change of organizations such as prisons, mental hospitals, or schools

Consent decrees are equitable remedies in which the parties agree to a given remedial plan to correct organizational conditions. Broad equitable powers are given the judge supervising a consent decree. Judges may, for example, have the power to appoint special persons to complete audits of an organization. Consent decrees are frequently employed in litigation that involves organizational changes, such as increasing the numbers of minorities or improving conditions. There has been a large number of consent decrees to eliminate poor conditions in state prisons, mental hospitals, and criminal justice agencies.

Government agencies such as the Equal Employment Opportunity Commission (EEOC) enter into consent decrees with private employers to reduce institutional discrimination. The federal government has entered into a number of consent decrees with major universities to implement federally mandated goals. It is common to enter consent decrees to monitor compliance with affirmative action goals. The consent decree sets forth an employment and business plan of affirmative action. The duties and responsibilities for compliance are set forth in the consent decree. Courts have the power to modify consent decrees as events unfold and frequently appoint persons to monitor compliance. Monitors make recommendations to the defendants in areas in which defendants have obligations under the consent decree. If the defendants fail to meet their obligations, the monitors may report infractions to the court. Courts afford defendants the opportunity to be heard before taking necessary action based on monitors' reports. One frequently litigated issue is when a court terminates a consent decree because institutional reform is completed.

—*Michael L. Rustad*

See also Class action; Declaratory judgments; Equitable remedies; Injunctions; Release; Restraining orders, temporary.

CONSTITUTION, U.S.

Foundation document that defines the structure and powers of the U.S. national government and lays the basis for the U.S. legal systems

The U.S. Constitution was created in an effort to design a workable, strong national government for the American states that had freed themselves from the British Empire through the Revolutionary War. The Constitution replaced the Articles of Confederation, which were regarded as an ineffective basis for a strong national government because they did not grant the federal government sufficient powers with respect to economic and military matters. The Constitution represented a new attempt to design an effective national government for a diverse set of states that expected to retain many powers for themselves.

Article I of the Constitution describes the structure and powers of Congress, the national legislative body. Article II describes the president's role and powers. Article III describes the judicial branch of the national government. Section 1 of Article III established the Supreme Court and describes the protected tenure and compensation provided for Court justices to ensure that they have sufficient insulation from political pressures to be able to make proper decisions. Justices serve "during good Behavior," which can effectively mean for life. Moreover, Congress cannot reduce the justices' salaries; therefore, other branches of government cannot threaten the justices with loss of income to pressure

AMENDING THE U.S. CONSTITUTION

Amendments allow the Constitution to change as the United States changes. They can be proposed in either of two ways: by a two-thirds vote of both houses of the U.S. Congress or by a special convention called by Congress upon the request of two-thirds of the state legislatures. To date, however, only the first method has been used.

After an amendment is proposed, it must be ratified by three-fourths of the states, either by their legislatures or at specially called ratifying conventions. Only then is it added to the Constitution.

These requirements for amendments ensure deliberate, often slow, consideration of changes but also allow needed and popular changes to be accomplished. Amendments to the earlier Articles of Confederation, which the Constitution replaced in 1789, required unanimous consent of the states. That unrealistically strict requirement prevented needed changes. For example, two amendments proposed for the Articles would have addressed the pressing need for improving government finances. Both failed to achieve the required unanimous consent of the states. Indeed, it might be said that the inadequacy of the amendment process under the Articles of Confederation played an important role in the move to create a new constitution for the United States.

their decisions. In addition, only the Supreme Court is established by Article III. All other federal courts are created by Congress and therefore can be altered or even abolished by Congress.

The Constitution also specifies that Supreme Court justices shall be appointed by the president and confirmed by the Senate. Because justices may serve on the Court for decades, the selection of a Court member is often one of a president's most important decisions. Most presidents are able to appoint at least one justice to the Court, but some presidents, including President Jimmy Carter, are never able to appoint a justice because no one on the Court dies, retires, or resigns during their term in office.

Article IV of the Constitution discusses the obligations of states to each other, such as respecting each other's court judgments. Article V describes the process for amending the Constitution. Article VI declares that the Constitution and laws made under the authority of the Constitution shall be the supreme law of the land and that states shall respect the Constitution and federal laws. This is an important provision because it helped to establish the broad scope of the Court's power. When the Court interprets the Constitution, it is establishing legal rules for the entire nation to follow. Article VII notes that nine states needed to ratify the Constitution in order to give it effect.

The original Constitution was amended twenty-seven times. The first ten amendments, called the Bill of Rights, describe the protections that individuals possess against interference by government. These protections include many familiar rights, such as freedom of speech, freedom of religion, and the right to trial by jury. Although these rights originally protected citizens only against actions by the federal government, the Court subsequently interpreted the Constitution as providing most of these protections against violations by state and local governments. Other amendments have changed the way in which U.S. senators are selected, limited the president to two terms in office, abolished slavery, granted voting rights to women, and announced the plan for who would take charge in the event that the president and vice president should die or become disabled while in office. The Court is frequently asked to interpret the amendments to the Constitution, especially those amendments that grant rights to individuals. The Court's interpretations of these amendments define the extent to which individuals' constitutional rights protect them against actions by government.

Constitutional Interpretation

Because the Constitution was drafted by an assembly of representatives from various states, its wording is the product of negotiation and compromise. Therefore, many of the document's words and phrases are ambiguous. Even those phrases whose meaning appears to be relatively clear may require interpretation when they are applied to unanticipated situations. It falls to the Court to take primary responsibility for interpreting and applying the Constitution. The Court is given opportunities to interpret the Constitution when legal cases are brought forward involving disputes about the Constitution's meaning. Typically these cases involve either a challenge to the exercise of power by a government agency or a claim that a government employee, such as a police officer or prosecutor, has violated the rights of an individual. These questions about the Constitution's meaning are given initial decisions by lower federal courts or by state courts before they reach the Supreme Court. The Court has authority to pick and choose which constitutional issues to decide. If the Court does not wish to decide an issue, it simply leaves intact the prior decision by a lower federal or state court.

Justices often disagree with one another about how the Constitution should be interpreted. Many justices have their own theories about the proper approach to constitutional interpretation. Justice Hugo L. Black often argued that the justices should pay careful attention to the literal meaning of the Constitution's words and not add their own preferred meanings to interpretations of the document's words and phrases. When other justices decided in *Griswold v. Connecticut* (1965) that the Constitution contains a right to privacy that protects married couples' choices about birth control, Black argued that there could be no right to privacy because the word "privacy" did not appear anywhere in the Constitution. Similarly, Justice Clarence Thomas argued that the Constitution must be interpreted according to the meanings originally intended by the people who wrote the document. Therefore, when other justices applied the Eighth Amendment's prohibition against cruel and unusual punishment to protect prisoners from abuse and mistreatment within correctional institutions in *Helling v. McKinney* (1993), Thomas asserted that the people who wrote the Eighth Amendment at the end of the eighteenth century never intended for the provision to protect incarcerated people. Thomas claimed that the Eighth Amendment does not apply to the treatment of convicted offenders in prison.

In contrast, Chief Justice Earl Warren believed that the meaning of the Constitution can change as society changes. Warren and several of his colleagues believed that the Constitution embodies ideals of human dignity that are flexible enough to adapt to new situations that arise in society. Therefore, in *Trop v. Dulles* (1958), Warren declared that the cruel and unusual punishment clause of the Eighth Amendment must be defined according to the evolving standards of decency that develop as society progresses. Critics of Warren's approach to constitutional interpretation complain that such flexible interpretation merely permits justices to say that the Constitution means whatever they want it to mean. Critics of Thomas's approach, in contrast, complain that interpretation by original intent locks society into the rules of the eighteenth century without recognizing that society has changed drastically, with the emergence of new problems and different values. In general, the majority of justices take a flexible approach to constitutional interpretation, but many of them are self-conscious about the risks of interpreting the Constitution inappropriately according to their own personal values and are generally cautious about announcing new meanings for the document's provisions.

The Court and the Constitution

The nature of the constitutional questions brought to the Court changed along with American society, according to the particular controversies that affected government and society at different moments in history. During the first eighty years of the Constitution's history, the Court faced significant questions about the constitutional provisions defining the powers of government. The constitutional governing system of the United States was, in effect, an experiment. It was uncertain whether the scheme of government established by the Constitution would succeed and endure. The Court helped solidify the success of the Constitution through decisions addressing disputes about governmental powers. In *McCulloch v. Maryland* (1819), the Court interpreted the Constitution as barring states from imposing taxes on the federal government and its agencies. Without the Court's decision, the federal government would have been weaker and more vulnerable to assertions of authority by the states. In *Gibbons v. Ogden* (1824), the Court asserted the authority of the federal government to regulate interstate commerce when states had begun to assume such powers for themselves. The Court's decision helped to strengthen the federal government and diminish the risk that states would use economic policies to compete with one another and thereby harm the national economy.

The Court's decision in *Marbury v. Madison* (1803) established judicial review, which is the power of judges to review and invalidate actions by other branches of government. Judicial review is a very significant power that is not expressly stated in the Constitution. The Court asserted the existence of the power and then employed it to strike down a congressional enactment. By establishing and using the power, the Court made the judicial branch a powerful, equal partner with the other branches of government and helped establish a workable balance of power between the three branches of government.

The Court cannot solve all disputes about governmental power through its interpretations of the Constitution. Some disputes are worked out through political conflicts between the legislative and executive branches of government. During the Civil War (1861-1865), these disputes were resolved by warfare. The war served to settle debates about the relationship of the federal government with the states when the states that asserted their independence and autonomy under the Confederate flag lost the war. For the Court, the end of the war simply brought forward new issues about the meaning of the Constitution in a country undergoing the processes of industrialization and urbanization. The Court also faced questions about the legal protections possessed by newly freed slaves.

At the close of the Civil War, the Thirteenth, Fourteenth, and Fifteenth Amendments (the Civil War Amendments) were added to the Constitution. These amendments sought to prohibit slavery, protect people's legal rights from violation by state and local governments, and prevent racial discrimination in voting rights. Between the end of the Civil War and the dawn of the twentieth century, Court decisions affecting racial discrimination did little to improve the lot of African Americans. In the *Slaughterhouse Cases* (1873), the Court declined to identify specific rights protected by the Civil War Amendments. When southern states began enacting extensive, systematic laws to segregate African Americans in schools and other public places and services, the Court endorsed these discriminatory laws in *Plessy v. Ferguson* (1896). These cases in the late nineteenth century demonstrated that the Court's justices have no special capacity to recognize truth and justice. As human beings who happen to have been selected to serve, they are always susceptible to following and reflecting the prevailing attitudes and prejudices of their era. Few whites believed that African Americans were equal to them as human beings during the nineteenth century, and the Court's interpretations of the Constitution reflected this view.

In the late nineteenth century and early twentieth century, the Court faced many issues concerning economic regulation and social welfare. Many new social problems developed as the country experienced significant industrialization, urbanization, and immigration. Federal and state governments responded to these problems by enacting legislation to protect workers. However, the Court used its power of judicial review to systematically invalidate laws mandating minimum wages, laws establishing permissible working hours, and laws intended to limit the exploitation of child laborers. For example, in *Hammer v. Dagenhart* (1918), the Court declared that the federal government lacked the authority under the Constitution to regulate the transport and sale of goods made by child laborers. The Court's decisions impeded governmental regulation of the economy until the 1930's, when the composition of the Court changed significantly and the Court began to defer to legislative and executive decisions about economic regulation.

After the 1930's, the Court took a more active interest in interpreting the constitutional amendments that established rights for individuals. In a series of cases over the course of several decades, the Court applied most of the provisions of the Bill of Rights against the states by declaring that they had been incorporated into the due process clause of the Fourteenth Amendment. Before this time, the Bill of Rights protected citizens against actions by only the federal government. Because the Fourteenth Amendment was intended to give individuals rights against actions by state and local government, it became the vehicle through which the Court's interpretations of the Constitution applied other rights against the states. In the course of broadening the definitions of constitutional rights, the Court moved aggressively against racial discrimination. Using the equal protection clause of the Fourteenth Amendment, the Court prohibited racial discrimination in public schools in *Brown v. Board of Education* (1954). The Court also interpreted constitutional provisions about congressional power to permit the enactment of statutes against discrimination by private businesses and individuals in *Katzenbach v. McClung* (1964). By the end of the 1970's, the Court had identified new rights affecting racial equality, gender equality, protection of defendants in the criminal justice process, freedom of speech and religion, and many other aspects of American life.

In the final decades of the twentieth century, the Court's composition changed in a conservative direction. The new justices reconsidered many of the prior decisions expanding rights for criminal defendants and others. In new decisions interpreting the Bill of Rights, the Court reshaped constitutional law by narrowing the scope of many rights and permitting states to have greater authority over their own affairs. The Court also limited the authority of the federal government to enact legislation under the claim of economic regulation. In *United States v. Lopez* (1995), the Court declared that Congress lacked the authority to create a statute making it a crime to carry a gun in a schoolyard. In a move back toward the nineteenth century decisions that imposed clear limits on federal authority, the Court decided that states should regulate such matters because they were not directly related to interstate commerce and the economic matters that the Constitution clearly placed under federal authority.

The Constitution provided the design for the U.S. system of government. On its own, however, the Constitution could not ensure that the government would be durable and workable. The Court made major contributions to the stability and workability enjoyed by the Constitution through its decisions interpreting the document in order to define the powers of government and clarify the extent to which individuals possess protected constitutional rights.

—*Christopher E. Smith*

Suggested Readings

A detailed history of constitutional law is presented in Melvin Urofsky's *A March of Liberty: A Constitutional History of the United States* (New York: Alfred A. Knopf, 1988). Detailed examinations of Court decisions interpreting the Constitution are found in Daniel Farber, William Eskridge, and Philip Frickey's *Constitutional Law: Themes for the Constitution's Third Century* (St. Paul, Minn.: West Publishing, 1993) and Gerald Gunther's *Constitutional Law* (11th ed., Mineola, N.Y.: Foundation Press, 1985). The theories and approaches employed by the Court justices in interpreting the Constitution are discussed in John H. Garvey and T. Alexander Aleinikoff's *Modern Constitutional Theory* (3d ed., St. Paul, Minn.: West Publishing, 1994) and Michael McCann and Gerald Houseman's *Judging the Constitution* (Glenview, Ill.: Scott, Foresman, 1989). The personal stories of individual citizens who took their constitutional claims all the way to the Supreme Court are presented in Peter Irons's *The Courage of Their Convictions* (New York: Free Press, 1988) and Ellen Alderman and Caroline Kennedy's *In Our Defense: The Bill of Rights in Action* (New York: William Morrow, 1991). The procedures and processes used by the Court in interpreting the Constitution are discussed in David O'Brien's *Storm Center: The Supreme Court in American Politics* (2d ed., New York: W. W. Norton, 1990). A practical handbook for lay people is Jay M. Feinman's *Law 101: Everything You Need to Know About the American Legal System* (New York: Oxford University Press, 2000).

See also Bill of Rights, U.S.; Bills of attainder; Civil rights and liberties; Common law; Eighth Amendment; Equal protection under the law; *Ex post facto* laws; Federal judicial system; Fifth Amendment; Judicial review; Legal immunity; Reversals of Supreme Court decisions by amendment; Supreme Court, U.S.

CONTEMPT OF COURT

Conduct that obstructs a court's administration of justice or undermines its dignity; a court's power to punish contempt helps to safeguard the efficient administration of justice by assuring that its orders are complied with and its basic dignity preserved

Contempt of court has its origins in the period when all English courts were part of the Curia Regia, or court of the sovereign. Dis-

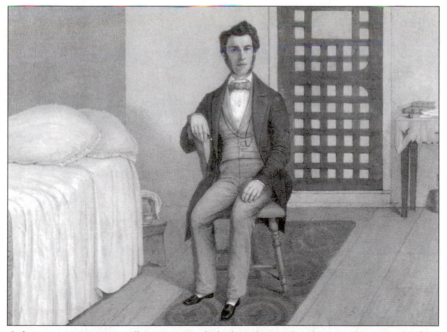

A famous contempt ruling occurred during the early nineteenth century when the abolitionist Passmore Williamson was jailed for giving "evasive evidence" in a trial. Since that time, the U.S. Supreme Court has limited the contempt power of courts to prevent abuses. (Library of Congress)

paragement of either the sovereign or his courts was punishable as contempt. Contempt of court includes disregard for, or disobedience of, a court's order as well as misbehavior in the presence of the court which tends to bring the authority and administration of the law into disrespect. Contempts are usually classified as being either civil or criminal in nature. A civil contempt is one involving disobedience of an order of the court rendered on behalf of one party. Criminal contempt involves disrespect of the court itself or conduct which undermines the court's dignity. Civil contempts are remedied by a fine intended to recompense the party for whose benefit an order was made. Criminal contempts are subject to punishment in the form of a fine or imprisonment.

See also Attachment; Bench warrants; Immunity from prosecution; Jury duty; Perjury; Subpoena power.

CONTINGENCY FEES

Common legal fee arrangements, especially in personal injury cases, that require clients to pay their lawyers only if the lawyers obtain successful legal result in their behalf

Lawyers often charge their clients a specified hourly rate for legal work. This hourly rate, however, may easily be out of the reach of persons who have limited financial means. In consideration of this reality, lawyers sometimes agree to accept a fee only upon the successful completion of a case. This kind of agreement is most common in the personal injury context. A person who has been injured by another and seeks to sue for damages usually finds legal representation on a contingency fee basis, whereby the person agrees to pay a lawyer a specified percentage—often between 30 and 40 percent—of any recovery the lawyer obtains from the opposing side. Thus, if the lawyer negotiates a settlement with the opposing side or wins a verdict at trial for $100,000, the lawyer under a one-third contingency fee contract would be entitled to approximately $33,000. However if the lawyer obtains no recovery, no fee whatsoever is due.

A contingency agreement often permits lawyers to obtain very attractive fees for the amount of work devoted to a case when they are successful. In fact, some jurisdictions, determining that contingency fee agreements may actually allow lawyers to recover excessive fees, have put caps on such fees. Statutory fee ceilings reduce the size of contingency fees in particular kinds of cases—for example, in medical malpractice cases against doctors.

In addition to the fee ceilings that some states have placed on contingency fee arrangements, the ethical rules that govern the practice of law impose additional restrictions on such fees. The rules of most states regulating legal ethics require that contingency fee agreements, unlike other legal fee agreements, be in writing. Furthermore, most states do not permit lawyers to work on a contingency fee basis in two kinds of cases: when they represent defendants in criminal cases and clients in divorce, alimony, and child support matters. For example, lawyers may not agree to arrangements in which they are to be paid by criminal defendants only in the event of not guilty verdicts. Nor may they agree to represent persons in divorce proceedings for a percentage of marital property or alimony settlements. Contingency fees in criminal cases and in the family law context have generally been viewed as encouraging lawyers to fight for results that are not necessarily in the public interest. Criminal lawyers working on a contingency fee basis in criminal cases might be reluctant to engage in plea bargaining if their fees depend on obtaining a finding of not guilty. Similarly, divorce lawyers might be reluctant to suggest reconciliation as in their clients' best interests if their fees depend on expensive settlements.

—Timothy L. Hall

See also Attorney-client relationship; Attorney fees; Billing rates; Court-awarded fees; Family law practice; Legal clinics; Litigation expenses; Personal injury attorneys; Public interest law; Solicitation of legal clients.

Contracts

Voluntary agreements among two or more parties that are enforceable under the law; contracts are a foundation of business and commerce in a free economy

In their simplest forms, contracts represent legally enforceable agreements that have been voluntarily entered into between two or more parties. Contract law in the United States is based on common-law principles derived from the English system of case law and case precedent. In the United States much of the contract law relating to commercial transactions has been codified in uniform statutes. These statutes are embodied in Article 2 of the Uniform Commercial Code (UCC). The statutes have been adopted by most states, thereby providing a cohesive and consistent body of rules. Article 2 has some limitations in that it does not apply to all types of contracts. For example, real estate and personal service contracts are not governed by Article 2. Any contract not governed by the UCC is governed by common-law contract principles. Contract law in other countries is based on a civil law system. However, all contract law, wherever found, is based on the basic principle of agreement between contracting parties.

Types of Contracts

Contracts are of two basic types: bilateral and unilateral. A bilateral contract is an exchange of promises in which an offer is accepted by a promise of performance. A unilateral contract involves an offer that is accepted by an act of performance. A typical unilateral contract is an offer of reward. The promise to pay a reward is accepted by an individual performing the act specified in the reward offer. The party who makes an offer is called the offeror and the party to whom the offer is made is called the offeree. Once a valid offer exists, the act of acceptance forms the contract. Therefore, the party who has the power to make a contract is the offeree.

Contracts can be expressed or implied. An expressed contract is an agreement that is stated orally or in writing. An implied contract is of two types: implied in fact or implied in law. In an implied-in-fact contract the agreement is implied from the conduct of the individuals, even though nothing has been expressed.

In an implied-in-law contract nothing has been expressed nor can any type of agreement be implied from the conduct of the parties. Nonetheless, the law treats the circumstances as if a contract existed in order to prevent a party from being unjustly enriched to the detriment of the other party. An implied-in-law contract is often referred to as a quasicontract, because it is a legal fiction created by the law to ensure fairness.

Not all agreements are enforceable under contract law. For an agreement to be enforceable certain elements must be present in the agreement. These elements are a valid offer, a valid acceptance, consideration, capacity, and lawful subject matter. If any of these elements are missing, the agreement is not legally enforceable.

Although most contracts need not be in writing to be enforceable, it is a good practice to memorialize agreements with some type of writing. The writing need not be formal; a handwritten agreement is usually sufficient. In most cases the agreement need not be witnessed. Although the agreement should be signed by both parties, the only signature that is required is the signature of the party against whom the contract is being enforced. The writing should be dated and contain the parties' names and any important and material terms to the bargain. It should be clear and unambiguous. Any changes to written agreements should be initialed.

Contracts need not be written by attorneys. However, attorneys can play an important role in contract negotiations and in drafting contracts. A well-drafted contract serves to structure the parties' expectations and bring certainty and predictability to the contractual relationship, especially in the event that a contractual dispute should arise. Additionally, the contract provisions can have a major impact on the rights of the parties. Attorneys are trained to identify potential problem areas and draft contract provisions favorable to their clients. The attorney's role is especially important when a contract involves complex matters or substantial obligations between parties.

Offer
For an offer to be effective the offeror must intend to make an offer, the offer must be sufficiently definite in its terms, and it must be effectively communicated to the offeree. Offers made in jest, anger, or in undue excitement are not considered valid, be-

cause the offeror lacks serious intent. Moreover, preliminary negotiations, expressions of opinions, and advertisements do not
constitute offers.

An offer must be sufficiently definite in its terms. Because the essence of a legally enforceable contract is an agreement, an offer cannot be accepted unless the offeree and the offeror know to what
they are agreeing. This is often called a "meeting of the minds."
The standard of definitiveness required for an offer to be valid is
"reasonable definiteness." Reasonableness is a flexible standard
and varies depending on the circumstances.

For an offer to be accepted it must be effectively communicated
to the offeree. Communication is generally effective when the
offeree receives and understands the offer. Any time before it is
accepted, an offer can be revoked by the offeror. This is true even
if the offeror promised to keep the offer open for a specified time.
The only way to make an offer irrevocable for a specified time is
for the offeree to pay compensation to the offeror for keeping the
offer open. This is called an option contract. The offer can also be
terminated by the offeree. The offeree can terminate the offer by
rejecting it or by making a counteroffer, whereupon the original
offer is terminated. However, the offeror can revive the original
offer by making it again. The offer can also be terminated by operation of the law. The law automatically terminates the offer after a
reasonable lapse of time if the subject matter of the offer is destroyed, if the offeror dies or becomes incompetent, or if a change
occurs in the law that makes the subject matter of the offer illegal.
However, these occurrences must take place before the offer is accepted.

Acceptance

An acceptance indicates a manifestation of the offeree to agree
to the terms of the offer. The offeree has the power of acceptance,
and after the offer is accepted a contract is formed. Only the party
to whom the offer is made has the power of acceptance. A unilateral contract is accepted by performance, while a bilateral contract is accepted by a promise of performance. For an acceptance
to be valid it must be unequivocal and must be communicated to
the offeror.

The common-law "mirror-image rule" states that the acceptance must be the mirror image of the offer. Therefore, the acceptance must contain an assent to the terms of the original offer.

Generally, if additional, different, or new terms are stated in the acceptance, this acceptance constitutes a counteroffer and terminates the original offer. Generally, the offeror cannot interpret silence on the part of the offeree as valid acceptance. Only if the offeree specifically states that silence constitutes an acceptance will a contract be formed.

> ## ELEMENTS OF A CONTRACT
>
> In order for a contract to be valid, the following criteria must be met:
> - A valid offer must exist
> - The contract must be validly accepted
> - There must be consideration
> - There must be capacity to understand the contract
> - The contract must have lawful subject matter

Acceptance is effective when it is communicated to the offeror. Effective communication takes place when an offeror receives the acceptance. However, under the common-law "mailbox rule," or "acceptance-upon-dispatch rule," an acceptance can also occur when it is deposited in the mail. This creates an unusual situation, because the contract can be formed before the offeror knows of its acceptance. The acceptance will be valid even if it is lost in the mail and is never received by the offeror. In order for these rules to apply, the acceptance must be properly dispatched or mailed by a method authorized by the offer.

Consideration

For an enforceable contract to be formed, an offer and acceptance must be supported by consideration. Consideration is something of legal value given in exchange for promises. It is the "bargained-for-exchange." Consideration must not necessarily be in the form of money. Consideration can consist of any legal detriment or legal benefit incurred in exchange for promises. Therefore, if offerees give up a something to which they have a legal right, this is sufficient to satisfy the element of consideration.

Not all agreements are enforceable. Promises to make a gift or other gratuitous promises are not considered enforceable, because they lack consideration. A promise that is based on some past consideration is not enforceable, because the past act was not the exchange bargained for in the agreement. A preexisting duty imposed by a prior contract is also not consideration, because no additional legal detriment was incurred. Lastly, refraining from performing an act that is illegal is not consideration, because it is a prior duty imposed by the law.

Capacity

In order for an enforceable contract to be formed, the parties must have the capacity to understand the nature, substance, and obligations under the agreement. If either party lacks the capacity to enter into a contract, the contract will be voidable. In other words, an enforceable contract may be formed that the party who suffers from incapacity may choose to cancel or disaffirm. Under this doctrine only the party who suffers the incapacity has this power.

Generally, minors who have not reached the age of majority are considered to lack the capacity to enter into an enforceable contract. Although the age of majority can vary slightly from state to state, eighteen years of age is the most common age at which parties are considered to have the capacity to enter into contracts. Therefore, if a person under the age of majority enters into a contract and chooses to disaffirm it, the other party may not enforce it. Incapacity can also occur as a result of intoxication or mental incompetence. If parties were so intoxicated by alcohol or drugs that they were unable to understand the nature of the agreements they reached, they may choose to cancel them. Likewise, individuals who lacked the mental capacity to understand the nature of transactions to which they were party may choose to void such contracts.

Legality

Agreements involving a subject matter that is against the law or public policy are not enforceable by either party. Such contracts are considered void, and the courts will not provide relief to either party. Contracts contrary to statute could include gambling agreements, agreements to commit a crime, or contracts in which a party does not possess a regulatory license, such as a state license to practice medicine or sell real estate.

Agreements against public policy include immoral contracts, contracts containing clauses relieving a party from liability for their negligence or willful misconduct, or contracts that are extremely unfair or oppressive. Some contracts with an anticompetitive impact, such as those that restrain trade, may also be void as against public policy. For example, a contract that prevents a party from opening a competing business within a certain geographic area would be void. However, such provisions are permitted when they are ancillary or part of another contract and are reasonable. For example, employment contracts and contracts for the sale of businesses that contain noncompetition clauses are considered permissible.

Defenses to Contract Enforcement

The law provides certain defenses to contract enforcement. If one of the defenses applies, performance will be discharged and the contract will not be enforced. Generally, the courts allow contracts to be rescinded. Rescission undoes contracts, returning the parties to their original positions.

If both parties are mistaken about a material fact in the agreement, the contract is not enforceable. A mutual mistake of fact must relate to a material element of the contract. Generally, a material element is one that was important to the parties' decision to enter into the agreement in the first place. Mutual mistakes of facts must relate to factual matter, such as the existence, identity, or subject of the agreement. Mutual mistakes of value are not sufficient to be a defense to contract performance. A mutual mistake of value could occur when the parties to a contract knew the object of the agreement but were mistaken as to its true value. Unilateral mistakes, those in which only one person is mistaken, are not considered to be a valid defense to a contract.

Fraud or innocent misrepresentations are also defenses to contract performance. Fraud involves a party's intention to deceive another party about a material fact, thereby causing the innocent party damage. Innocent misrepresentation takes place when a party did not know that what they were stating was false and when no intent to deceive was thus present.

Other standard defenses include duress and undue influence. Duress occurs when a party is forced to enter into a contract by threats of wrongful acts by the other party. Undue influence generally occurs where a person is in a position of power and influence and uses that position to unfairly persuade another person to enter into a contract.

Under the statute of frauds, certain types of contracts must be in writing. The lack of a writing is a defense to performance. Contracts involving an interest in land must be in writing. These include the sale of real property, mortgages, leases, and easements.

However, in many states statutes specify that leases for less than one year must not be in writing. Contracts that cannot reasonably be performed within one year must be in writing. Promises to pay the debt of another, such as guaranty contracts, must also be in writing. The statute generally requires that promises made in consideration of marriage and prenuptial agreements must be in writing if they are to be enforceable.

Rights, Duties, and Performance

Generally, parties to a contract have certain rights and duties imposed by their agreement. The rights under a contact may be transferred to another party. For example, the right to receive payment under a contract may be transferred to a third party. The transfer of a contractual right is called an assignment. Generally, most rights are assignable. However, contracts sometimes contain antiassignment clauses. The duties under a contact can also be transferred to other parties. The transfer of a duty is called a delegation. Not all duties may be transferred. For example, a duty under a personal service contract that involves special expertise or skill or a duty that would materially alter the risk involved in the contract may not be delegated.

A contract can be discharged in many ways. Performance can be discharged by the parties completing their obligations under the contract. Once performance is complete, the contract is discharged. The contract performance can also be discharged by agreement between the parties. For example, the parties could mutually agree to cancel the contract or substitute a new contract. The contract performance can also be discharged by operation of the law. For example, states have a statute of limitations for contracts. The statute of limitations specifies a certain amount of time in which a party must institute legal action after a breach of contract. If the specified time expires, the party may no longer enforce the contract. The expiration of the statute of limitations discharges performance by operation of the law. Performance can also be discharged because of impossibility—such as may be caused by one party's death.

Remedies

A remedy is the mechanism by which the law enforces a contract or provides a form of compensation for damages incurred because of a breach. The underlying purpose of contract remedies is to compensate nonbreaching parties as if the contract was fully performed. Punishing the breaching party is not a purpose of contract remedies. Therefore, punitive damages are not generally recoverable in a contract action. Additionally, the courts generally require that nonbreaching parties mitigate their damages. Mitigation of damages means that parties must take reasonable action to reduce or minimize the damages they would suffer because of a breach.

Historically, two categories of remedies are available to a nonbreaching party: legal and equitable remedies. Legal remedies involve the compensation of a nonbreaching party by requiring that the breaching party pay the nonbreaching party the amount necessary to compensate for the "loss of the bargain." Equitable remedies are provided if the legal remedy does not adequately compensate the nonbreaching party. For example, if the subject matter of a contract is unique, such as real estate the court may order the breaching party—for example, the seller—to perform or transfer the real property to the buyer. This equitable remedy is called specific performance.

—*Bruce E. May*

Suggested Readings

General treatises containing thorough discussions of the U.S. law of contracts include Marvin A. Chirelstein's *Concepts and Case Analysis in the Law of Contracts* (New York: Foundation Press, 2001), *Contracts in a Nutshell*, by Claude D. Rohwer and Gordon D. Schaber (St. Paul, Minn.: West Publishing, 2000), John D. Calamari and Joseph M. Perrillo's *Contracts* (3d ed. St. Paul, Minn.: West Publishing, 1987), Richard A. Lord's *Williston on Contracts* (4th ed. Rochester, N.Y.: Lawyer's Cooperative, 1990), E. Allan Farnsworth's *Contracts* (2d ed. Boston: Little, Brown, 1990), and *Corbin on Contracts*, edited by Joseph M. Perillo (rev. ed. St. Paul, Minn.: West Publishing, 1993). For a general introduction to the law of contracts see *Introduction to Basic Legal Principles* (5th ed. Dubuque, Iowa: Kendall/Hunt, 1991), by Benjamin N. Henszey et. al. For a comparison among contract law in the United States and others countries see K. Zweigert and H. Kotz's *An Introduction to Comparative Law* (2d ed. New York: Clarendon Press, 1992). An extensive and thorough review of contract law can be found in *Restatement of the Law, Second, Contracts* (Philadelphia: American Law Institute, 1981).

See also Bonds; Breach of contract; Case law; Civil law; Commercial litigation; Common law; Equitable remedies; Lawsuits; Litigation.

CONVICTIONS

Guilty verdicts in criminal trials

The term "conviction" is generally used to denote that a jury has determined that a defendant is guilty as charged. It may also refer to the stage in a legal proceeding at which the accused admits guilt. The conviction is typically followed by a judgment in which the court announces the consequences, or the sentence, that follows from the conviction. A jury may find the defendant guilty of the crime charged or of a lesser included offense. If a jury is inconsistent in its verdicts—for example, if it finds one defendant guilty and a codefendant not guilty or guilty of a lesser offense—this inconsistency does not invalidate the conviction. If persons are tried in nonjury bench trials, their guilt or innocence is determined by magistrates or judges. Guilty findings in such trials are called summary convictions.

A conviction is also the written record of the proceedings against a defendant found guilty. In this sense a conviction must contain information about the charges, the plea, the evidence, the verdict, and the penalty. If defendants are convicted, they may appeal their convictions and ask higher courts to review the record for errors of law. If appellate courts find errors in earlier proceedings, they may dismiss the case or set aside the conviction. The latter decision allows the prosecution to ask for a new trial in the hope of gaining a valid conviction. Convicted defendants may also bring collateral attacks on their convictions. That is, they may seek relief on the grounds that their convictions were invalid by applying for a writ of *habeas corpus* (an application to a court to consider whether a person in custody is being held lawfully). This procedure is most commonly used in the federal courts.

—*Mary Welek Atwell*

COUNSEL, RIGHT TO

Opportunity for defendants in criminal proceedings to be represented by lawyers, as guaranteed by the Sixth Amendment to the U.S. Constitution and a Supreme Court interpretation of the Fourteenth Amendment

Although the Sixth Amendment of the U.S. Constitution appeared to contain the right to legal counsel, the exact meaning of that provision was unclear until interpreted by Congress and the Supreme Court. In 1790, while the Sixth Amendment was still being ratified, Congress passed the Federal Crimes Act, which required that defendants in federal capital cases be provided with legal representation. The Court extended this same protection to all federal criminal cases, regardless of whether they involved the death penalty, in *Johnson v. Zerbst* (1938).

Special Circumstances Doctrine

Although some states required the appointment of lawyers even before the Sixth Amendment was ratified, there was no national code of due process that obligated the states to provide legal help for people accused of crimes. It was not until 1932 that the Court imposed even a limited requirement on state courts to provide legal counsel, and as late as 1963, some states still refused to pay for lawyers for poor defendants.

In *Powell v. Alabama* (1932), the first Scottsboro case, the Court, by a 7-2 majority, overturned Alabama's convictions of nine African American youths for raping two white women. The young men had been given a *pro forma* trial and sentenced to death. Although they had received court-appointed lawyers, the attorneys provided a weak defense. The trial judge behaved in an overtly biased fashion toward the defendants, and evidence that might have cast doubt on Alabama's case was never presented by the young men's lawyers. In his majority opinion, Justice George Sutherland did not extend the right to counsel to all state criminal cases, but he did establish the "special circumstances" doctrine. The Court ruled that in state capital cases where there were special circumstances, such as the illiteracy of the defendant, state trial judges were obligated to appoint competent lawyers to represent the accused. For more than thirty years, the special circumstances doctrine would be the law of the land, requiring state courts to appoint legal counsel in only the most obvious and serious situations of defendant need.

A Reconsideration

Although the Court had the opportunity to apply the right to counsel to all state criminal cases in *Betts v. Brady* (1942), it declined to do so, sticking to the case-by-case scheme it had prescribed in the *Powell* case. It was not until the 1963 case of *Gideon v. Wainwright* that the Court finally retired the special circumstances doctrine. Clarence Gideon was a drifter with a history of committing petty crimes. He was accused of breaking into a pool hall and stealing some money and liquor. Although Gideon asked the trial judge to appoint him a lawyer, the judge, relying on *Betts*, refused to do so. After a failed attempt at defending himself, Gideon was sentenced to a long term in prison. Gideon appealed his conviction on Sixth and Fourteenth Amendment grounds to the Supreme Court.

The Court had been looking for just the right case to overrule what most of them considered a flawed decision in *Betts v. Brady*. To reverse *Betts*, the Court needed a case in which an intelligent person, denied a lawyer, had been unable to successfully defend himself. Because Gideon was an intelligent man, there could be no question that the trial judge might have improperly denied him special circumstances status. Likewise, because Gideon was white, there could be no question of possible racial discrimination to muddy the waters. The charges against Gideon were not complicated. Gideon was an intelligent man, with a sympathetic, even helpful trial judge, who failed miserably to defend himself against noncomplex charges. This made *Gideon* the perfect case to overrule the special circumstances doctrine, and on March 18, 1963, a unanimous Supreme Court, speaking through Justice Hugo L. Black, applied the right to counsel to all state criminal proceedings.

In *Argersinger v. Hamlin* (1972) and *Scott v. Illinois* (1979), the Court extended the right to counsel to misdemeanor trials that resulted in jail sentences but not to those that resulted in fines or lesser punishment.

The Pretrial Period

Gideon left many important questions unanswered, including at what point in the criminal investigation a suspect who requested a lawyer had to be provided with one. In *Escobedo v. Illinois* (1964), the Court ruled that a suspect asking for counsel during a police interrogation had to be granted representation.

In *Miranda v. Arizona* (1966), the Court went a step further, requiring the police to advise suspects of their right to a lawyer even if they did not ask to speak with an attorney. According to the Court, a person suspected of committing a crime should be provided with a lawyer at the moment that individual ceases being one of several possible suspects and becomes the principal focus of the criminal investigation. The decisions in these two cases showed that, in the Court's collective mind, the Sixth Amendment right to counsel was firmly connected to the Fifth Amendment's protection from compulsory self-incrimination.

—*Marshall R. King*

Suggested Readings

Feinman, Jay M. *Law 101: Everything You Need to Know About the American Legal System.* New York: Oxford University Press, 2000.

Garcia, Alfredo. *The Sixth Amendment in Modern American Jurisprudence.* Westport, Conn.: Greenwood, 1992.

Horne, Gerald. *"Powell v. Alabama": The Scottsboro Boys and American Justice.* New York: Franklin Watts, 1997.

Lewis, Anthony. *Gideon's Trumpet.* New York: Vintage, 1989.

Tomkovicz, James J. *The Right to the Assistance of Counsel: A Reference Guide to the United States Constitution.* Westport, Conn.: Greenwood Press, 2002.

Wice, Paul B. *"Miranda v. Arizona": "You Have the Right to Remain Silent . . ."* New York: Franklin Watts, 1996.

See also Bill of Rights, U.S.; Criminal justice system; Presumption of innocence; Suspects.

COURT-AWARDED FEES

Attorney fees that courts require the losing sides in lawsuits to pay for the prevailing parties

Traditionally, American law has provided that the opposing sides of a lawsuit pay their own attorney's fees, regardless of who wins or loses. Increasingly, however, modern state and federal statutes have provided that prevailing parties in certain kinds of cases may have their attorney fees paid by their litigation opponents. These kinds of laws are sometimes referred to as "fee-shifting statutes." In the case of such statutes, the court that presides over a case will determine the amount of fees to be paid to the prevailing party's attorneys. For this reason, these kinds of attorney fees are frequently called "court-awarded" fees. Normally, courts awarding such fees consider the number of hours prevailing attorneys have devoted to a case and other general evidence of how much the service of these attorneys is worth.

Court-awarded fees are most common in connection with federal or state statutes designed to protect certain parties from unfair or unlawful treatment. For example, state laws protecting consumers from unfair business practices frequently provide that consumers who sue businesses under the laws for unfair treatment and prevail may have their attorney fees paid by the businesses. Similarly, federal laws prohibiting particular kinds of employment discrimination routinely include fee-shifting provisions. Victims of discrimination who successfully prove their claims in court are frequently awarded their attorney fees. That is, the opposing side is ordered to pay these fees.

The purpose of court-awarded fees in these contexts is to encourage persons who could not normally afford legal representation to pursue their claims. For example, a consumer who has been injured by a shady business practice might not have suffered serious enough harm to justify paying a lawyer to redress that harm in court. Consequently, the consumer might be forced to endure the harm. But a fee-shifting law allows consumers to obtain redress in such cases. If a seller deliberately misrepresents the qualities of a car and, as a result, a consumer purchases it for $2,000 more than it is worth, the consumer might not be in a position to hire a lawyer to pursue this $2,000 claim, since attorney fees to file and prosecute a lawsuit might easily exceed $2,000. A fee-shifting provision in a consumer protection statute, however, might provide that the consumer, if successful in prosecuting the $2,000 claim, will also receive payment for the attorney fees. This enables the consumer to pursue the claim.

—*Timothy L. Hall*

See also Attorney fees; Billable hours; Billing rates; Contingency fees; Court costs; Lawsuits; Litigation expenses; Trials.

COURT CALENDARS

Written lists of legal proceedings that are awaiting trial or other set-tlements in particular courts; scheduling of cases that are awaiting settlement may have important consequences for the parties involved

Court calendars, which are known as trial lists or dockets, are kept by officials known as clerks of the court. Information contained in a court calendar includes the date and time that a case will be heard, the name of the presiding judge, and the names of the two sides involved in the case, as in "*Smith vs. Jones*" or "*State vs. Brown*." A more detailed court calendar known as a special calendar also includes such information as the names of the attorneys representing the parties involved in the case and an estimate of the time required to hear the case. The special calendar may be maintained by the clerk or a judge.

The dates and times that cases will be heard are set during a court session known as a calendar call. The scheduling of a case during a calendar call may be significant to the parties involved. Both sides will want to schedule the case far enough in the future to ensure that they have time to prepare their arguments. If a case is not scheduled to be heard within a reasonable time, however, one side or the other may suffer the consequences of a delay in justice.

—*Rose Secrest*

See also Case law; Civil actions; Clerks of the court; Court types; Officers of the court; Speedy trial requirement; Trials.

COURT COSTS

Filing fees that courts require litigants to pay when they file legal actions; such costs are based on schedules that are usally determined by state legislatures

Court costs are the fees required by courts to file an action or proceeding. In many states court costs are assessed for noncriminal traffic infractions. For example, a defendant charged with a traffic offense of reckless driving may be assessed a fine of $100 plus $57 in court costs for a total of $157. Each state's schedule of court costs varies. Some states impose the same court costs irrespective of the offense. A growing number of states calibrate court costs to the seriousness of the offense.

There is a growing trend in the law for court costs to be distributed for statutorily mandated law-enforcement purposes. In Indiana, for example, an additional $2 in court costs is imposed for law-enforcement education. Texas allocates the proceeds from uniform court costs to abused children's counseling, crime-stoppers assistance, and other law-enforcement purposes. A 1997 Texas statute provides that $3 from court costs be allocated to municipal court building security. This court cost applies to all misdemeanor convictions. A time payment fee of $25 is imposed on every person convicted of a felony or misdemeanor. Court costs are also applied to persons ordered to pay fines or restitution. Many other states have expanded court costs in a similar manner. The Federal Rules of Civil Procedure allow prevailing parties to obtain court costs unless the court directs otherwise.

—*Michael L. Rustad*

See also Attorney fees; Clerks of the court; Court types; Litigation expenses; Trials.

COURT REPORTERS

Professional employees of courts who create stenographic records of legal proceedings

Court reporters produce verbatim records of words spoken in trials, depositions, or other legal proceedings. On the basis of their stenographic training, and with the aid of special stenographic equipment, court reporters can record human speech at rates in excess of 225 words per minute. Some reporters serve in an official capacity for courts or other legal bodies and record and produce transcripts of proceedings as needed. Most court reporters, however, provide freelance services to lawyers who conduct pretrial depositions. In these proceedings, lawyers question witnesses under oath but without the presence of a judge. Court reporters record these depositions and produce transcripts of them for the lawyers involved. Modern court reporters are making increased use of computers to produce transcripts from their stenographic recordings and even to produce virtually instantaneous displays of testimony during trials.

Court reporters must receive training in stenographic recording and transcription, as well as in the basic vocabulary and concepts of law. A variety of colleges and universities provide this training in connection with undergraduate degree programs. In addition, aspiring court reporters can generally obtain training from independent court reporting institutes. Training generally requires two or more years of study. In many states, court reporters must also pass official examinations and be licensed before they can do court reporting work.

—Timothy L. Hall

See also Cross-examination; Depositions; Litigation expenses; Trial transcripts; Trials.

COURT TYPES

Every state has courts of specialized limited and general jurisdiction; a separate hierarchy of federal courts parallels the fifty state judiciaries; in many states efforts have been made to reduce the number of court types

In contrast to Japan and many European countries, the United States has a highly complex network of courts. In nations with unitary political systems, such as France, there is a single judicial hierarchy. Because of federalism, however, there are two sets of trial and appellate courts in the United States, one state and the other federal. At the state level many courts of original jurisdiction can hear only a single type of case, such as that dealing with wills (probate courts) or claims for small amounts of money. Courts differ also in whether jury trials are possible, in what types of procedures are used and in what types of remedy judges can provide complaining parties. Selecting the correct court in which to file a complaint is so complicated that most law schools offer students a course called "Conflict of Laws" to help them make the right choice.

Types of Jurisdiction

There are a number of fundamental characteristics that distinguish one court from another. Jurisdiction is the power, or authority, of a particular court to hear a case. Courts of original jurisdiction, or trial courts, hear cases for the first time. Courts of appeal review the decisions of trial judges to determine if they made any reversible errors. Courts of common law can provide monetary compensation to injured plaintiffs in civil suits. Equity courts, or chancery courts, issue injunctions, which are orders to act or to refrain from acting in a particular way, such as polluting a river. The right to trial by jury can be exercised in common law and criminal courts but not in equity courts. Courts of specialized jurisdiction can hear only one type of case. Courts of limited jurisdiction hear several kinds of cases but not all.

The most important state trial courts are the civil and criminal courts of general jurisdiction, which can hear and determine any case. State courts hear cases involving state law, while federal courts determine legal disputes arising under the U.S. Constitution or federal laws. There are circumstances, however, in which a state court can hear a case that requires the interpretation of federal law and in which a federal court can determine controversies arising under state legislation. In the former type of case, the losing party may appeal to the U.S. Supreme Court after the state supreme court has rendered its decision. Criminal courts try cases in which the government seeks punishment of a defendant for violating the law. Civil courts resolve disputes between private parties in which a complainant alleges harm as a result of a defendant's failure to fulfill a legal duty. A court of record is a trial court whose determinations of fact are final.

Criminal Courts

States have established a variety of judicial tribunals to handle criminal cases. Municipal courts are trial courts of limited jurisdiction with the authority to determine misdemeanor cases. Other names for criminal courts of limited jurisdiction are justice or general sessions courts. Night court, or police court, is available in many large urban areas to process cases in which defendants are charged with petty offenses, such as public drunkenness. Police forces in populous cities issue citations ordering drivers caught breaking the law to appear in traffic court. In rural areas, justices of the peace often hear cases involving minor criminal charges. Municipal courts preside over preliminary hearings to determine if evidence is sufficient to hold over felony defendants for trial in superior court. Felonies are prosecuted in criminal courts of general jurisdiction, often called superior or county courts. It is in these courts that most jury trials occur. Other names for such bodies are circuit, district, or criminal courts.

CRITERIA FOR CHOOSING THE APPROPRIATE COURT

- Is the complaint a civil or criminal one?
- Is the applicable law state or federal?
- Is the case just beginning or has a judge already made a decision?
- If a crime is involved, is it a misdemeanor or a felony?
- If the case is a civil one, is the plaintiff asking for monetary compensation or an injunction?
- How much money is the plaintiff demanding?
- Is the suit between residents of different states?

Civil Courts

Trial courts of limited and general criminal jurisdiction in most states have the power to determine civil controversies. Municipal courts may hear legal disputes in which the amount of compensation requested is relatively low, usually under $30,000. County and superior courts hear civil cases in which the monetary amount in dispute exceeds that. Most states have established a court of specialized jurisdiction, or small-claims court, to make the civil courts more accessible to ordinary citizens. In these courts parties typically are not represented by lawyers, the filing fees are low, and the waiting period before trial is relatively short. The jurisdiction of small-claims courts is typically confined to cases not exceeding $5,000.

Probate courts exercise jurisdiction over wills, estates, and guardianship questions. Probate judges determine how the assets of deceased persons are to be allocated and who is legally responsible for frail elderly or mentally incompetent persons. Family law courts, or domestic relations courts, process divorce cases and resolve often contentious issues of child custody, visitation, child support, alimony, and the division of property.

Family law court judges have broad equitable powers. Youths charged with delinquency or youths in need of protection appear in family law or juvenile courts. Juvenile courts are civil courts; they do not mete out punishment, but rather provide treatment. In mediation court, or conciliation court, judges help parties negotiate mutually acceptable compromises rather than impose solutions to conflicts. In states with unified judicial systems, such as California, the trial court of general jurisdiction, the superior court, may sit as a probate court, juvenile court, family law court, and conciliation court.

Appellate Courts

While trial courts consist of a single judge, appellate courts are collegial bodies with three or more judges. They review trial courts' decisions on the request of losing parties. A reversible error is one that is so egregious that a trial judge's decision must be overturned. In general, appellate courts can only reverse a trial judge's interpretation of the law and not the trial court's determinations of fact. This rule exists to prevent appellate judges from undermining the jury system. In the United States, each loser in a trial has the right to one appeal. A consequence of this tradition is that some appellate courts have no control over their dockets. They must hear and decide every appeal that is filed.

The final court of appeal is the state supreme court (known in New York as the Court of Appeals). If a case involves matters of state law only, the decision of a state supreme court cannot be further appealed. In many states, the state supreme court is the only appellate court. In twenty-five states, however, there are intermediate courts of appeal. In these states the state supreme court enjoys discretion over the cases it wishes to review. Some states have separate intermediate courts of appeal for criminal and civil cases.

Several states, including New Jersey, Virginia, and California, have taken steps to simplify their judicial hierarchy. Their goal is to establish an integrated judicial pyramid embracing only a few kinds of trial courts and a single type of intermediate appellate court.

Federal Courts

Article III of the U.S. Constitution authorizes Congress to establish trial and appellate courts to determine cases arising under federal law, cases involving foreign ambassadors, and suits between citizens of different states. The federal courts of general trial jurisdiction are the ninety-four U.S. district courts. Federal jury trials occur in the district courts. They have both civil and criminal jurisdiction. Federal law requires that judges give preference to criminal over civil cases when scheduling trials.

There are a number of federal trial courts of specialized jurisdiction. Each district court has a bankruptcy unit. Bankruptcy courts determine whether petitioners can be relieved of the obligation to repay debts. Magistrate judges handle misdemeanor trials and many of the procedural disputes that must be resolved before a trial in the district court can begin.

Appeals of district court decisions are made to one of the thirteen U.S. courts of appeals. The judges sit in panels of three. They also hear appeals from the decisions of federal administrative agencies, such as the National Labor Relations Board (NLRB) and the Federal Communications Commission (FCC). The courts of appeal must accept for review all appeals. A specialized federal court is the U.S. Court of International Trade. It reviews the rulings by federal customs inspectors governing tariffs on imported goods.

When a federal question is at issue, appeals of decisions of the U.S. courts of appeals and the state supreme courts may be filed with the U.S. Supreme Court. The U.S. Supreme Court has complete discretion and only grants review to approximately 1 percent of the cases that are filed before it. All nine justices of the U.S. Supreme Court participate in the decision of every case accepted for review.

From time to time the U.S. Congress has established tribunals to assist administrative agencies in the performance of their adjudicative functions. U.S. Tax Court, for example, was set up to hear taxpayers' appeals of decisions of the Internal Revenue Service (IRS). Such so-called Article I courts differ from their Article III counterparts in the judges' tenure. Article I judges serve for a limited number of years while Article III judges are appointed for life. There are four other federal legislative courts: the U.S. Court of Federal Claims, the U.S. Court of Military Appeals, the U.S. Court of Veterans Appeals, and territorial courts. The Court of Federal Claims adjudicates plaintiffs' claims for compensation from the federal government. The Court of Military Appeals is a body of civilian judges who hear appeals from military courts-martial. The Court of Veterans Appeals reviews decisions of the Board of Veterans Appeals denying benefits to former military personnel. Appeals from the Court of Federal Claims, the Court of International Trade, and the Court of Veterans Appeals must be filed with the U.S. Court of Appeals for the Federal Circuit. The federal territories Guam, the Virgin Islands, and the Northern Mariana Islands have territorial courts, which can hear matters involving both local and federal law. Because Puerto Rico has its own set of local courts, the territorial court in Puerto Rico has the same jurisdiction as a U.S. district court.

—*Kenneth M. Holland*

Suggested Readings

For a comprehensive guide to the court system, consult Christopher E. Smith's *Courts and Trials: A Reference Handbook* (Santa Barbara, Calif.: ABC-CLIO, 2003). S. L. Alexander's *Covering the Courts: A Handbook for Journalists* (Lanham, Md.: University Press of America, 1999) is also useful for comprehensive information. Henry Abraham offers a clear description of differences among courts in *The Judicial Process: An Introductory Analysis of the Courts of the United States, England, and France* (7th ed. New York: Oxford

University Press, 1998). There are more than two thousand federal and state courts. Listings of the various types of courts are available in *BNA's Directory of State and Federal Courts, Judges, and Clerks* (Washington, D.C.: BNA Books, 1997) and *Want's Federal-State Court Directory 1998: All Fifty States and Canada* (New York: Want Publishing, 1997). The *BNA Directory* includes state court structure charts, which show the routes of appeal for all courts of record. The 1997 edition includes listings of Internet sites for federal and state courts. Lenore Banks examines from a citizen's viewpoint the daunting task of selecting the correct court in *The Judicial Maze: The Court System in New York State* (Albany, N.Y.: League of Women Voters, 1988). Court unification is a theme in *Improving the Quality of American Justice, 1987-1997* (Alexandria, Va.: State Justice Institute, 1997). *"Doing Justice" in the People's Court: Sentencing by Municipal Court Judges*, by Jon'a Meyer and Paul Jesilow (Albany: State University of New York Press, 1997), examines all aspects of the workings of municipal courts and their judges.

See also Attorney types; Bankruptcy; Courts of appeals; Criminal justice system; Federal judicial system; Jurisdiction; Night courts; Small-claims courts; Supreme Court, U.S.; Trials.

COURTS-MARTIAL

Military trials, which are equivalent to civilian criminal trials, that judge major infractions of military law by members of the armed forces

To preserve discipline and ensure order, military commanders have three ways to punish violations of the rules, regulations, and laws governing the Army, Navy, Air Force, Marine Corps, Coast Guard, and National Guard: administrative action, nonjudicial punishment, and court-martial. In administrative action the commander punishes by withdrawing common privileges with the offender's acquiescence. In nonjudicial punishment a small-unit commander tries minor infractions and assesses limited penalties. Courts-martial can consider any accusation of misconduct as defined in the Uniform Code of Military Justice (UCMJ) of 1950, published and elaborated in the *Manual for Courts-Martial* (1995). The sentences of some courts-martial include long-term imprisonment and the death penalty. Punishments under administrative action or nonjudicial punishment are internal military affairs; conviction by court-martial becomes part of a person's permanent criminal record.

All officers, enlisted personnel, and reservists on active duty are subject to the UCMJ, and each branch of the armed forces has jurisdiction over members of all the other branches. The Supreme Court has ruled that military courts cannot try civilians (*Ex parte Milligan*, 1866) or civilian employees of the services, even under martial law (*Duncan v. Kahanamoku*, 1946), except when civilian courts are not functioning. Courts-martial have exclusive jurisdiction over all purely military offenses, such as disobedience of orders or desertion. An action violating both military and civilian law can be tried either by court-martial or by a civilian court, although local civilian authorities usually have precedence over military courts.

Generally similar to civilian criminal courts, courts-martial nevertheless differ in their pretrial procedures, their questioning of witnesses, their method of reaching verdicts, and the variety of punishments they may impose. Three types of courts-martial exist: general, special, and summary. They differ in the crimes they judge and in the severity of punishment they may impose. All three are ad hoc courts convened by a commanding officer to judge a specific case or a small number of related cases. In general and special courts-martial, the "accused" (not "defendant," as in civilian courts) has the right to counsel; in summary courts-martial, counsel may be excluded if military circumstances require it.

Pretrial Procedure

The responsible officer, such as a company commander in an infantry regiment, acts as the accuser of subordinates suspected of having violated a provision of the UCMJ, who must be warned that any statements they make can be used against them during judicial action. The responsible officer can prefer charges and recommend the type of court-martial to the next higher-level commander, such as a battalion commander. This higher-level commander may convene either a summary court-martial or a special court-martial to hear the charges. This procedure, known as an "Article 32 investigation," performs the same function as a grand jury in civilian law. However, the accused has several rights not granted to civilian defendants, including the power to cross-examine witnesses and to submit and examine evidence.

The investigating officer reports the findings to an officer who has the authority to convene a general court-martial. That commander may convene the court, refer the charges back to a lower court, or drop the charges. If a general or special court-martial is initiated, the convening authority also appoints the trial counsel, a commissioned officer certified as a competent military lawyer by the service's judge advocate general, and the defense counsel, who must likewise be a certified military lawyer. In some cases the accused may also hire a civilian lawyer.

During the discovery phase of a court-martial proceeding attorneys take depositions from witnesses, gather documentary evidence, and arrange for the appearance of witnesses. The equivalent of the prosecuting attorney in a civilian court, the trial counsel must provide the defense with copies of documents and papers relating to the charge, reports of physical or psychological examinations performed on the accused, and a list of witnesses to be called. The defense must also disclose the names of its witnesses to the trial counsel. The accused may agree at this time to a plea bargain, as in civilian courts. A military judge may grant the accused or witnesses transactional immunity, which protects them from trial for one or more offenses under the UCMJ, or testimonial immunity, which excludes later trial action based on statements made in depositions or in court.

Conduct of Courts-Martial

The president of the United States, service secretaries, or high-ranking commanders, usually generals or admirals, convene general courts-martial. Those who convene courts-martial select members of their command to act as members of the court. The court consists of five to seven officers; one must be a qualified military judge, who is the presiding officer, and the rest fulfill much the same function as a civilian jury. Enlisted accused may request that one-third of the court be enlisted personnel. Except in capital cases, the accused can choose to be tried before a military judge alone.

The presiding officer instructs the members of the court on points of law, controls the proceedings, rules on questions of law and procedure, issues judgments on questions of fact, rules against trial participants who are in contempt of court, and may summon witnesses in addition to those called by the court and defense counsel. The court takes testimony, assesses the evidence, and may directly question witnesses, unlike the jury of a civilian court. The panel then retires to discuss the verdict, which must be based strictly on the evidence presented in court. Finally, after instruction from the presiding officer on the consequences of different verdicts, the panel votes. A two-thirds majority is required for conviction, which means that there is never a deadlocked jury, as in civilian courts. Court is reconvened and the verdict announced. If the accused is acquitted, the proceedings end and the accused is released.

If the accused is convicted, the sentencing phase begins. The court again hears arguments from the trial counsel and defense counsel in favor of a specific punishment and reviews pertinent evidence, such as records of previous convictions. The panel deliberates once more and votes by secret written ballot on the sentence. General courts-martial may impose any punishment authorized under the UCMJ. While a simple majority vote is sufficient for most sentences, such as dismissal from the service and dishonorable discharge, three-fourths of the panel must approve a sentence of imprisonment for ten years or more and a unanimous vote is required to impose the death penalty.

Special courts-martial convene under the authority of commanders of small units, such as regiments, or small installations, and consist of three members, unless the accused chooses to be tried by a military judge alone. Enlisted accused may also demand that one member of the panel be enlisted. A special court-martial verdict may include a bad conduct discharge if the court includes a military judge. Otherwise, the court may convict the accused to as many as six months of confinement, forfeiture of two-thirds pay for six months, hard labor for three months, or reduction in rank.

Unlike general and special courts-martial, which can try officers, a summary court-martial has power only over enlisted personnel. A commander of the rank at least of captain (lieutenant in the Navy or Coast Guard) is the convening authority and appoints the single member of the court. When no other commissioned officer is available, convening authorities in courts-martial may appoint themselves. The purpose of the court is to hear charges of minor offenses promptly. For accused noncommissioned officers, the presiding officer may impose sentences not to exceed forfeiture of two-thirds of one month's pay, restriction for two months, or reduction of one rank. Accused who are in the forth enlisted pay grade or below may receive one month's confinement or hard labor for forty-five days as well.

After adjourning a court-martial, the trial counsel must notify the accused's commander or the convening authority of the verdict and sentence, and this officer executes the court's decision by ordering confinement, the withholding of pay, or imposing other punishments. The military judge or convening authority may call for post-trial sessions to correct errors or rectify improper procedures by reopening the proceedings. A complete record of a court-martial's proceedings is assembled and forwarded to an appropriate reviewing authority.

Reviews and Appeals

The provisions for review and appeal of decisions by courts-martial are as varied as those for civilian courts, but they invest considerable review authority in individuals as well as appellate panels. Lawyers in the office of the staff advocate general, a unit under the authority of the local commanding general or admiral, review the conduct and decisions of courts-martial to ensure that proper procedures were followed. The convening authority also reviews the verdict of a court-martial and may vacate or reduce a sentence.

The accused has two years in which to appeal a conviction to the service's judge advocate general. After examining court-martial records, the judge advocate general may modify or set aside the findings or refer the case to the court of criminal appeals for the appropriate branch of the service. This court may modify a sentence but may not vacate it or alter the changes made by the convening authority. The judge advocate general may then refer the case to the Court of Appeals for the Armed Forces, whose three judges are appointed for fifteen-year terms by the president of the United States and confirmed by the U.S. Senate. The accused may also petition this appeals court. Furthermore, the Court of Appeals for the Armed Forces must review all verdicts that affect general or flag officers and death sentences, which, if approved, may be carried out only upon orders from the president.

Federal courts may review courts-martial when their jurisdiction is questioned or when the accused petitions for writs of *habeas corpus* (applications to a court to consider whether a person in custody is being held lawfully). The U.S. Supreme Court may review decisions of the Court of Appeals for the Armed Forces and return cases to the lower court for further hearings or direct the president or service secretary to act upon its directives.

—Roger Smith

Suggested Readings

Comprehensive guides to court-martial procedures include Francis A. Gilligan and Fredric I. Lederer's three-volume *Court-Martial Procedure* (Charlottesville, Va.: Lexis Law Publishing, 1999) and Michael J. Davidson's *A Guide to Military Criminal Law* (Annapolis, Md: Naval Institute Press, 1999). *Manual of Courts-Martial* (Washington, D.C.: Government Printing Office, 1995), produced by the Joint Service Committee on Military Justice, explains how courts-martial are conducted, details their jurisdiction and sentences, and publishes the punitive articles of the UCMJ. *Military Justice Trial Procedure* (Washington, D.C.: Headquarters, Department of the Army, 1973) is a how-to manual for lawyers. *They Call It Justice* (New York: Viking Press, 1977), by Luther West, a military lawyer, and *Military Justice Is to Justice as Military Music Is to Music* (New York: Harper and Row, 1969), by Robert Sherrill, are both somewhat bitter indictments of the influence of local commanders on court-martial proceedings and were inspired by cases from the Vietnam War. In *Justice Under Fire* (New York: Charterhouse, 1974) Joseph W. Bishow, Jr., argues that military law affords as many guarantees of due process, and sometimes more, than civil law. Outlines of court procedures and celebrated cases illustrating them are in *United States Law and the Armed Forces* (New York: Praeger, 1972). Lawrence A. Frost's *The Court Martial of General George Armstrong Custer* (Norman: University of Oklahoma Press, 1968) provides an entertaining account of a celebrated trial.

See also Martial law; Military attorneys; Military justice; Military police; Military tribunals; Trials.

COURTS OF APPEALS

Intermediate federal appellate courts, situated immediately below the Supreme Court in the judicial hierarchy, that hear the majority of appeals from federal trial courts and federal regulatory commissions

In the late 1700's the Supreme Court was overburdened with cases, so Congress took steps to ease its burden. With the Judiciary Act of 1789, Congress created two lower courts, the circuit courts of appeals and the federal district courts. Initially, Supreme Court justices presided over the courts of appeals, riding from city to city to hear cases and sitting on circuit court panels with one district court judge. Because of the strain this placed on the Supreme Court justices as well as a general dissatisfaction with the way these courts were functioning, Congress passed the Judiciary Act of 1801, which eliminated the circuit riding practice. However, a year later, the practice was restored; it lasted until the 1840's, when it fell into disuse. The 1891 Judiciary Act assigned all appellate functions to the circuit courts of appeals, separating these courts from the old circuit courts, which retained jurisdiction over capital cases, tax cases, and some diversity cases until they were abolished at the end of 1911. In 1948 the circuit courts of appeals were renamed as the courts of appeal.

Court Functions

The twelve circuit courts of appeals serve specific geographical areas. The District of Columbia has its own circuit, which is somewhat different in nature from the others because of the district's wealth of appeals from the decisions of administrative agencies and its lack of cases arising from the states.

The courts of appeals have mandatory jurisdiction, which means that, unlike the Supreme Court, they cannot choose the cases they hear but must hear every appeal that comes to them. This makes for a very large docket, and many legal experts worry about the judges' increasing workload. Although the Supreme Court's decisions are reviewable only by constitutional amendment in constitutional cases and congressional enactment in others, the courts of appeals are subject to overruling by the Supreme Court.

Because the Court tends to reverse the cases it takes, some experts think there is some incentive for the judges on these courts to decide in accordance with the clearest Supreme Court pronouncement on the subject in order to avoid reversal. However, others argue that because the Court very seldom reviews the decisions of these courts, any compliance on the part of the courts of appeals with the Court occurs for other reasons. Lower court judges may simply deem it their duty to comply with the Court because it holds moral authority over them. Lower court judges may comply with the Court because they perceive their role to be one of subordination and obedience or because it is easier to simply cite the Court precedent than to develop their own sound legal reasoning. They may also be looking to maintain a good reputation so that they might one day be elevated to the Court or to another high post within the government, such as attorney general. Whatever the reason, increasingly, it appears that the decision making in these lower courts is in some ways dependent on the decision making in the Court. Therefore, to understand decision making in the courts of appeals, it is necessary to comprehend the relationship between the courts of appeals and the Supreme Court.

The courts of appeals hear many types of cases and disputes that the Supreme Court deems too inconsequential to consider, and therefore their rulings on those cases are relatively more final. The Court trusts that these lower courts will decide cases as it would if it were able to hear all disputes arising in the United States. However, this is not necessarily the case. Therefore, these lower courts exert some level of influence on the Court because they enact some policies basically on their own.

Internal Reviews

The courts of appeals are also monitored internally. Generally, the circuits split the workload among three-judge panels, the membership of which is under the control of the chief judge of the circuit. Sometimes, because of a shortage of judges, district court judges, senior or retired circuit and district court judges, or retired Supreme Court justices sit on these panels as well. However, in rare instances, the entire circuit is asked to sit on an appeal, reviewing the decision of one of the three-judge panels. This means that, in some circuits, there will be twenty-eight judges hearing oral arguments in a given case. These reviews are called *en banc* (full-court) hearings. The judges hear arguments, write opinions, and perform an error-correction function. However, on the lower courts, in both regular hearings and *en banc* hearings, separate opinions (concurrences and dissents) are far less frequent than they are on the Supreme Court. In addition, at least on some circuits, the assignment of the majority opinion is random, while on the Supreme Court, it usually is deliberate. This makes for some substantive differences between the two federal appellate courts that manifest themselves in differences in decision making.

—Sara C. Benesh

Suggested Readings

Benesh, Sara C. *The U.S. Court of Appeals and the Law of Confessions: Perspectives on the Hierarchy of Justice*. New York: LFB Scholarly Publishing, 2002.

Carp, Robert A., and Ronald Stidham. *The Federal Courts*. 3d ed. Washington, D.C.: Congressional Quarterly, 1998.

Epstein, Lee, ed. *Contemplating Courts*. Washington, D.C.: Congressional Quarterly, 1995.

Howard, J. Woodford, Jr. *Courts of Appeals in the Federal Judicial System*. Princeton, N.J.: Princeton University Press, 1981.

Knibb, David G. *Federal Court of Appeals Manual: A Manual on Practice in the United States Courts of Appeals*. St. Paul, Minn.: West Publishing, 2000.

Songer, Donald R. *Continuity and Change on the United States Courts of Appeals*. Ann Arbor: University of Michigan Press, 2000.

Woodley, Ann E. *Litigating in Federal Court: A Guide to the Rules*. Durham, N.C.: Carolina Academic Press, 1999.

See also Appeal; Appellate practice; Court types; Defense attorneys; Federal judicial system; Opinions; Supreme Court, U.S.

CRIMINAL JUSTICE SYSTEM

Total complex of local, state, and federal laws, policing forces, prosecuting offices, court systems, and correctional facilities and programs in the United States

The American criminal justice system encompasses all the laws, procedures, and institutions that communities employ to apprehend, prosecute, and punish those who violate the property or persons of others.

State and Local Systems

Within the United States, criminal justice is primarily a state and local concern. More than nine-tenths of all crimes are dealt with at the state and local levels. Similar proportions apply to the personnel who work in criminal justice and to the expenditures that go to combat crime. The crimes that most concern average citizens—property crimes such as burglary and violent crimes such as robbery and assault—are typically violations of state, not federal, laws. The criminal justice systems of other countries contrast sharply with the American system in this regard. Outside the United States, most criminal offenses are defined by national laws; in most other countries, national, not local, institutions respond to violations of criminal codes.

The American system commonly designates the most serious crimes as felonies; in most jurisdictions, these are crimes that can be punished by prison sentences of at least a year. Lesser offenses are designated as misdemeanors—crimes for which punishments cannot exceed a year in jail. Felonies include most violent crimes, such as murder, rape, and robbery; some of the most serious property crimes, such as burglary; and drug trafficking. Misdemeanors typically include less serious crimes, such as simple thefts, vandalism, and disorderly conduct. In some cases repeated commission of a misdemeanor can elevate the crime to a felony.

Police

County sheriffs and city and town police bear the chief responsibility for responding to most property and violent crimes. As of June, 2000, such agencies employed more than 600,000 sworn officers and another 250,000 civilians throughout the United States.

Nationally, more than two-fifths of all criminal justice expenditures go toward police protection. In the vast majority of cases the police learn about crimes through calls from victims or witnesses; the police are rarely the first to learn about them. According to the National Crime Victimization Survey, which began in 1973, as many as three-fifths of crimes that are committed are never reported to the police, ranging from three-quarters of all thefts to about two-fifths of all aggravated assaults. Overall, only about half of violent crimes are reported to police. In 2000, more than eleven million crimes of seven major types were reported to police; these included murder and non-negligent manslaughter, rape, robbery, aggravated assault, burglary, theft, and motor vehicle theft.

The sheer number of criminal acts limits most police activity to simply responding to crimes after they are committed. Police work thus consists mostly of tasks such as going to the scenes of crimes, interviewing witnesses, gathering physical evidence, searching for suspects, and preparing investigative reports. In the past—especially in the nineteenth century, when municipal police forces were first established—most police activity involved maintaining order within communities rather than responding to crimes. This activity included preventing unruly—but not necessarily illegal—behaviors, prohibiting loitering or vagrancy, and checking on shops and businesses after closing hours.

Many Americans have called for the police to involve themselves more actively in the communities they serve by engaging in what is usually called "community policing": walking beats instead of cruising randomly in squad cars, establishing storefront offices to increase police visibility, meeting with community groups to identify problems, and other such proactive measures. Pilot projects of community policing in American cities provide evidence that such programs increase citizens' feelings of personal security and confidence in the police. Whether such programs actually reduce crime, however, is less certain.

A major impediment to adopting community policing more widely is the enormous demand that merely responding to present crime levels places on police resources. In 1992 local police were able to make arrests in only a fifth of the major crimes brought to their attention, including 65 percent of the murders, 52 percent of the rapes, 24 percent of the robberies, 13 percent of the burglaries, and 20 percent of the thefts. For all crime types, arrests totaled just over fourteen million. The largest categories of arrests were for driving under the influence of alcohol (1.6 million), assaults (1.6 million), theft (1.5 million), and drug law violations (1 million).

Prosecutors and Courts

Once an arrest is made, the case is turned over to a prosecutor, a public official who is charged with representing the people in the action against the defendant. Typically, most serious property and violent crimes are handled by the office of the county prosecutor, usually called the district, or state's, attorney. In most jurisdictions district attorneys are elected officials; they are often assisted by dozens or even hundreds of assistant district attorneys. Lesser offenses may be prosecuted by municipal attorneys, and specialized offenses—such as consumer fraud and commercial

---

KEY QUESTIONS IN THE CRIMINAL JUSTICE PROCESS

- What acts should be prohibited or punished?
- What punishments or rehabilitative methods are called for or allowed?
- Has the law been broken?
- Should crimes or suspicious acts be reported to the police?
- Should suspects be investigated or interrogated?
- Should suspects be arrested?
- Should an arrested suspect stay in jail or be released on bail or personal recognizance?
- Should suspected offenders be indicted or prosecuted and, if so, on what charges?
- Should a case be dropped, diverted, or prosecuted?
- Should a case be brought to trial?
- Should a jury trial or a bench trial be sought?
- Should defendants plead guilty or plea bargain?
- Should defendants be found guilty on all counts?
- Should convicted offenders be incarcerated or be placed under community supervision?
- Should incarcerated offenders be released into the community?
- Should probation or parole be revoked if parolees violate the law or the conditions of their status?

law violations—may be handled by prosecutors in the offices of state attorneys general.

Prosecutors perform several distinct functions: screening cases before charges are filed in court, interviewing victims and witnesses in preparing for trials, presenting evidence before grand juries, trying cases in court, and handling appeals. Although defendants cannot be convicted without proof "beyond a reasonable doubt," a lesser standard—"probable cause"—determines whether defendants should stand trial. Either before a grand jury or in a preliminary hearing, the prosecutor must show that a crime probably occurred and that the defendant under arrest probably did it. Although most states allow either a preliminary hearing or grand jury in felony cases, some states require a grand jury proceeding before an accused felon can go to trial.

Unlike trial juries, which usually comprise twelve members, grand juries typically have up to twice that number. They meet secretly and do not follow most of the standard rules of evidence that apply in courtroom trials. Also in contrast to trials, defendants typically have no right to counsel in grand jury proceedings. Although in British and American legal history grand juries were originally instituted to protect citizens from overzealous prosecutors, modern critics contend that they have developed into agents serving the state.

Courtroom Procedures

Trials are adversarial proceedings between prosecutors, who have the burden of proving guilt, and defendants, who are represented either by private attorneys or by public defenders (or other attorneys appointed by the courts) if they cannot afford private counsel. All trials are presided over by judges, who may be appointed or elected. Under American law all persons charged with serious crimes have the right to trial by jury. Juries serve as the triers of fact; they determine whether defendants committed the acts with which they are charged in violation of the criminal law. The judges are responsible for all legal rulings, particularly in applying the rules of evidence to the actual proceedings. When defendants choose not to exercise their right to trial by jury, the judges become the triers of fact. In some jurisdictions prosecutors can request jury trials even when defendants do not.

Pleas

Although every defendant has the right to go to trial for the determination of guilt or innocence, most defendants in most jurisdictions plead guilty rather than contest their cases at trial. Nationally, about 90 percent of felony convictions result from guilty pleas; 6 percent result from jury trials and 4 percent from bench trials (in which judges determine guilt or innocence). Critics have charged that the high rate of guilty pleas indicates two dangerous flaws in the system. On the one hand, it may imperil public safety when prosecutors reduce charges and potential punishments in exchange for guaranteed convictions; on the other hand, it may be unfair to innocent defendants who may be tempted to plead guilty in return for substantially reduced punishments rather than take chances on being convicted in a trial.

Sentencing

In 2000, nearly 984,000 persons were convicted of felonies in state courts in the United States, up from 830,000 in 1990 and 583,000 in 1986 (there are no national data on misdemeanor convictions, but these are almost certainly several times more common than felony convictions). Just under a fifth of the 1990 felony convictions were for violent crimes; a third were for property crimes; another third were for drug offenses; and the balance were for other crimes. Among the felony convictions were 11,000 for murder or non-negligent manslaughter, 18,000 for rape, 47,000 for robbery, 54,000 for aggravated assault, 110,000 for burglary, and 168,000 for drug trafficking. Of all the persons convicted of felonies in 1990, 29 percent were sentenced to probation (a period of supervision in the community as an alternative to incarceration), 25 percent were sentenced to local jails for less than a year, and 46 percent were sentenced to state prisons. These proportions remained roughly constant through the year 2000.

Sentencing systems throughout the United States are of two main types: determinate and indeterminate. In determinate sentencing systems a judge who sentences a convicted felon to prison designates a specific number of years, and the offender must serve this time, minus credits for behaving well in prison ("good time") or for involvement in educational or job training programs. Such sentence reduction credits can reach as high as half the formal sentence, depending on individual state laws. In indeterminate sentencing systems, the judge designates a range of years, such as ten to twenty years in prison, and the actual time served is determined by a parole board once the inmate becomes eligible for release. The result of these sentencing systems is that inmates of state prisons in the United States serve an average of only 35 percent of their maximum sentences.

Judges have traditionally had three basic options available when sentencing convicted felons: probation, several weeks or months in local jails, or a year or more in state prison. As expansion of the nation's prison population accelerated in the 1980's, a growing number of jurisdictions began experimenting with "intermediate sanctions." Punishments that are more severe than normal probation but less severe than incarceration, these include more intensive probation supervision, house arrest (sometimes monitored electronically with ankle bracelets), community service, and restitution to victims. Some proponents of such sanctions defend them as appropriate and less expensive alternatives to incarceration. Others support their use as alternatives to probation but regard them as insufficiently severe to use in place of incarceration.

Death Penalty

By the mid-1990's, the federal government and about three-fourths of the states had authorized the death penalty for certain specified offenses, principally murder. In 1990 there were 23,440 reported murders in the United States, about 11,000 murder convictions, 265 murderers sentenced to death, and 23 executions. Another 108 persons convicted of murder were removed from death rows through successful appeals of their convictions or sentences during that same year. Between 1976—when the U.S. Supreme Court reinstated the death penalty—and 1992, state courts sentenced a total of 3,979 persons to death and executed 188. Inmates who were actually executed spent an average of seven and a half years on death row. By the end of 1992, 2,575 prisoners were on death rows throughout the nation. This number rose steadily until 2000, when it reached 3,600, then began to drop.

One of the most controversial justice issues relating to the administering of capital punishment is the question of whether the race of convicted murderers or their victims affects courtroom decisions to impose the death penalty. While blacks are disproportionately represented on death row, compared to their share of the American population, whites arrested for murder are more likely to be sentenced to death than blacks arrested for murder. Of the inmates on death row at the end of 1992, for example, just over half were white non-Hispanics, two-fifths were black, and 8 percent were Hispanics.

Correctional System Populations

By the end of 1993, 859,000 persons were inmates in state prisons; another 90,000 were in federal prisons, and 450,000 more were in local jails. About half of the latter were serving sentences; the rest were awaiting trial. These figures for state and federal prisoners are almost three times greater than those for 1980. Despite the amount that prison populations increased, nearly three-fourths of the 4.9 million offenders under correctional supervision in 1993 were not incarcerated, but were under supervision in the community. Of those under supervision, 2.8 million were on probation and 909,000 were on parole (a period of supervision after release from prison).

According to surveys of state prison inmate populations, about 11 percent are serving time for murder and non-negligent manslaughter, 9 percent for rape or other sexual assault, 15 percent for robbery, 8 percent for assault, 4 percent for other violent crimes, 12 percent for burglary, 13 percent for drug trafficking, and 28 percent for other crimes. Many state prison inmates have extensive prior records: Four-fifths have at least one prior conviction, three-fifths have at least two, more than half have at least three, and almost a fifth have at least six prior convictions. Sixty percent of those sent to state prisons are return prisoners; 25 percent are beginning at least their fourth terms. Altogether, 93 percent of state prison inmates are either convicted violent offenders or convicted recidivists (repeat offenders).

Federal Criminal Justice System

Although the federal criminal justice system accounts for less than 5 percent of all felony convictions in the country and less than 10 percent of all prison inmates, the federal government enforces hundreds of criminal laws covering such offenses as counterfeiting, interstate drug trafficking, immigration violations, assaults on federal officials, terrorism, espionage, and violations of federal regulations concerning such matters as environmental pollution and commercial transactions. There are more than fifty separate federal law enforcement agencies. The principal bodies include the Federal Bureau of Investigation, which investigates a wide variety of federal offenses; the Drug Enforcement Administration (DEA), which concentrates on drug law violations; the Bureau of Alcohol, Tobacco, and Firearms (ATF), which is especially important in monitoring weapons violations; the Secret Service, which investigates counterfeiting and threats to the safety of the president; and the Immigration and Naturalization Service (INS), which investigates immigration law violations.

Responsibility for prosecution of federal offenses falls on the Department of Justice; it is headed by the attorney general, who is appointed by the president and confirmed by the U.S. Senate. Federal trials are conducted in federal district courts. Appeals of their decisions are made to federal appeals, or circuit, courts. The small fraction of such appeals that reach the Supreme Court usually raise basic constitutional questions or involve contradictory rulings from federal appeals courts in different parts of the country.

The compositions of prison populations reveal the differences in focus between state and federal criminal justice systems. For example, nearly half of all state prison inmates serve time for committing violent crimes, compared with under a fifth of federal prisoners. Conversely, while about a fifth of state prisoners serve sentences for drug offenses, almost three-fifths of federal prisoners serve time for such crimes; three-quarters of them are incarcerated for drug trafficking.

Resources Devoted to Criminal Justice

In 1990, federal, state, and local governments in the United States spent $74 billion for civil and criminal justice. This figure, which includes police protection, prosecution and courts, and corrections (prisons, jails, probation, and parole), accounted for 3.3 percent of all government spending in the nation that year. State and local governments devoted between 6 and 7 percent of their budgets to criminal justice, the federal government less than 1 percent. Nationally, criminal justice agencies employ about 1.6 million persons full-time. Nearly half work for police or investigative agencies; about a third work in corrections.

—*Joseph M. Bessette*

Suggested Readings

Excellent surveys of criminal justice for lay readers include Jay M. Feinman's *Law 101: Everything You Need to Know About the American Legal System* (New York: Oxford University Press, 2000) and *The Criminal Law Handbook: Know Your Rights, Survive the System*, by Paul Bergman and Sara J. Berman-Barrett (5th ed. Berkeley, Calif.: Nolo Press, 2003). The latter book covers all stages of criminal cases in an accessible question-and-answer format. The federal government's Bureau of Justice Statistics publishes the annual *Sourcebook of Criminal Justice Statistics* (Washington, D.C.: Bureau of Justice Statistics). As its title implies, Samuel Walker's *Popular Justice: A History of American Criminal Justice* (New York: Oxford University Press, 1980) surveys the history of the subject. Other overviews include Geoffrey P. Alpert, *The American System of Criminal Justice* (Beverly Hills, Calif.: Sage, 1984); H. Frank Way, *Criminal Justice and the American Constitution* (North Scituate, Mass.: Duxbury Press, 1980); George F. Cole, *The American System of Criminal Justice* (Belmont, Calif.: Wadsworth, 1992); and Howard Abadinsky, *Law and Justice: An Introduction to the American Legal System* (2d ed. Chicago: Nelson-Hall, 1991). An excellent survey of key issues is James Q. Wilson's *Thinking About Crime* (Rev. ed. New York: Basic Books, 1983). Richard C. Monk has edited a useful collection of nineteen essays on criminal justice controversies: *Taking Sides: Clashing Views on Controversial Issues in Crime and Criminology* (2d ed. Guilford, Conn.: Dushkin, 1991). For a sociological perspective on criminal justice, see *Multicultural Perspectives in Criminal Justice and Criminology*, edited by James E. Hendricks and Bryan Byers (Springfield, Ill.: Charles C Thomas, 2000) and *The System in Black and White: Exploring the Connections Between Race, Crime, and Justice*, edited by Michael W. Markowitz and Delores D. Jones-Brown (Westport, Conn.: Praeger, 2000). A critical examination of the system is William T. Pizzi's *Trials Without Truth: Why Our System of Criminal Trials Has Become an Expensive Failure and What We Need to Do to Rebuild It* (New York: New York University Press, 1999).

See also Attorneys general, state; Counsel, right to; Court types; Criminal records; *Ex post facto* laws; Felonies; Judges; Justice Department, U.S.; Juvenile criminal proceedings; Law enforcement; Misdemeanors; Multiple jurisdiction offenses; Presumption of innocence; Principals (criminal); Prosecutors; Public defenders.

CRIMINAL PROCEDURE

Stages and points at which particular decisions are made in the criminal justice process that are mandated by statutes and constitutional judicial decisions; the procedural steps are designed to ensure that correct decisions are made about guilt and innocence and that authorities respect the rights of criminal defendants

Every country has the authority to decide how it will determine which individuals will be punished for committing crimes. In some systems, the police or the army may have complete authority to identify and punish wrongdoers. The individual suspect may have no ability to question the law enforcement officers' decisions or swift imposition of punishment. In the United States, however, criminal procedure has been established to try to ensure that only guilty defendants receive punishment and to protect the public from abusive practices that police and prosecutors might employ in investigating, convicting, and punishing suspected criminals.

Historical Background

American criminal procedure, like other aspects of law, traces its roots to legal practices in England. The practice of using trials as a procedural mechanism to determine guilt and innocence began in England. Originally, England used physical trials to identify guilty offenders. Suspects were forced to place their hands in boiling oil, for example, or fight in a public duel with the assumption that God would protect the innocent but injure the guilty during such events. Eventually, the church discontinued its sponsorship of such events and England gradually shifted to the use of trials involving the presentation of testimony and the use of witnesses and jurors. Juries assumed an important role by protecting the public against abusive decisions by prosecutors. If there was insufficient evidence of guilt presented by the prosecutor, then the jury could acquit the defendant and the defendant would go free. The American jury trial, a key component of criminal procedure, developed from these English origins.

The U.S. Constitution

The first ten amendments to the Constitution, commonly known as the Bill of Rights, contain several provisions that mandate procedures to be followed in the investigation, prosecution, and punishment of criminal offenders. The Fourth Amendment protects people against "unreasonable searches and seizures." It also requires that search warrants and arrest warrants be supported by probable cause and that they specifically describe places to be searched and persons or things to be seized. The Fifth Amendment requires indictment by a grand jury before serious charges are prosecuted. The amendment also provides protection against compelled self-incrimination and the possibility of being tried twice for the same offense. The Sixth Amendment provides rights to speedy and public trials by impartial juries, as well as the right to be informed of charges, to obtain relevant documents and witnesses, to be confronted by adverse witnesses, and to have the assistance of a defense attorney. The Eighth Amendment prohibits excessive bail and fines and bans cruel and unusual punishments. The Fourteenth Amendment, which was added to the Constitution in 1868, provides additional rights to due process and equal protection of the laws. All of these provisions help to shape the procedures used in criminal cases by defining suspects' rights, limiting the authority of police, prosecutors, and judges, and mandating elements that must be incorporated into the legal process.

The provisions of the Bill of Rights originally applied only in federal court cases concerning defendants accused of violating criminal laws enacted by Congress. From the 1920's through the 1960's, the U.S. Supreme Court made many decisions that incorporated individual provisions of the Bill of Rights into the due process clause of the Fourteenth Amendment and made them applicable in state criminal cases. The only federal constitutional right concerning criminal procedure that has not been incorporated is the Fifth Amendment right to be indicted by a grand jury. State courts are not required by the Supreme Court to use grand juries, but many use such proceedings on their own. States are required to abide by all of the other provisions of the Bill of Rights concerning criminal procedure.

State and Federal Criminal Justice System
The legislatures for each state have the authority to design procedures that will be used within their state courts to process the cases of criminal defendants. Congress possesses this authority with respect to the federal courts. In addition, all court systems

must obey the U.S. Supreme Court's decisions that apply to them and mandate the use of certain procedures or respect for specific rights. State court systems must also obey the decisions of their own state supreme courts. The highest court in each state has the authority to interpret its state constitution and apply those decisions to the procedures used in processing criminal cases within that state. If legislatures want to change the kinds of procedures used within their own state's courts, they can enact reforms as long as those reforms respect the relevant provisions of the state and federal constitutions as interpreted by the state supreme court and the U.S. Supreme Court.

Because each state legislature and Congress possess the power to design procedures for the courts under their authority, there are differences in the criminal procedures used in different court systems. Although certain requirements of the U.S. Constitution which apply to all court systems, such as the use of defense attorneys and the availability of jury trials, provide common elements to all systems, other aspects of states' criminal procedure are quite different, especially with respect to preliminary proceedings.

Pretrial Proceedings

Immediately after an arrest is made by police officers, the individual arrested by the police is processed through the various steps of the state or federal court's criminal procedure. Two issues are decided shortly after arrest: first, whether the defendant will be released from custody on bail while the case is being processed; second, whether there is enough evidence to justify pursuing charges against the person arrested.

The process for setting bail varies from state to state and from county to county within states. If the suspect is arrested for a minor charge, the police may have the authority to release the suspect after fingerprinting, photographing, and obtaining relevant personal information. The person may be released on his or her "own recognizance," which means that the suspect does not have to post any amount of money with the police or court in order to gain release. The person merely signs a promise to appear at scheduled court dates. The person may also be required to post a set amount of money which will be forfeited if he or she fails to appear in court. It is more common for bail to be set by judges in an initial court hearing, and judges will always handle bail decisions when a person is charged with a very serious crime.

In some state constitutions, there is a right granted for each defendant to have bail set. Judges, however, will set a very high bail, perhaps even in the millions of dollars, if they do not want the person released while the case is being processed. In the federal courts and some states, the judge can deny bail by finding that the person would endanger the community if released or by deciding that no amount of money would guarantee that the person would return to court. In other states, suspects arrested for the most serious crimes, such as first-degree murder, may not be eligible for bail at all.

If a suspect was arrested through a decision by a police officer rather than through an arrest warrant issued by a judge upon the presentation of evidence, then the suspect is entitled to an initial hearing to make sure that evidence exists to support the arrest. The U.S. Supreme Court has interpreted the Fourth Amendment's prohibition on unreasonable seizures to require that initial hearings be held within forty-eight hours after a warrantless arrest (*County of Riverside v. McLaughlin*, 1991).

People who are arrested have a right to have an attorney represent them in court. The police must inform them of this right before any questioning takes place (*Miranda v. Arizona*, 1966), and defendants who are too poor to hire an attorney have a right to have an attorney provided for them by the government (*Gideon v. Wainwright*, 1963; *Argersinger v. Hamlin*, 1972). Attorneys need not be provided immediately after arrest if the police do not intend to question the suspect or if the suspect agrees to answer questions without an attorney present. Attorneys must be made available, however, to represent defendants at arraignments in which an initial plea is entered and at preliminary hearings in which a judge determines whether there is enough evidence to proceed with the case. Attorneys can also seek to have bail set or the amount of bail reduced by presenting arguments at a bail hearing.

At the arraignment, the court officially informs the suspect of the charges against him or her and gives the suspect the opportunity to plead "guilty" or "not guilty." Very few suspects plead guilty at felony arraignments, because their attorneys have just begun to work for them, and even if they will plead guilty eventually, as most defendants do, their attorneys need time to develop plea bargain proposals. It is more common for guilty pleas to be entered immediately in traffic courts or in misdemeanor cases, because defendants usually face only fines or probation and are anxious to get the cases resolved quickly. At preliminary hearings, prosecutors must present enough evidence to persuade a judge that sufficient grounds exist to proceed in a case against the defendant. In some states, arraignments and preliminary hearings take place in lower level courts, often called municipal courts or district courts. After these initial proceedings, felony cases will be transferred to upper-level courts, often called superior courts, circuit courts, or courts of common pleas. Defendants frequently waive formal proceedings for arraignments and preliminary hearings because they are aware of the charges and they already know that enough evidence exists to move the cases forward.

Some states and the federal government use grand jury proceedings to make the final determination about whether sufficient evidence exists to prosecute a defendant on serious charges. Grand juries are composed of citizens drawn from the community who meet in secret proceedings to hear witness testimony and examine the prosecutor's other evidence to determine whether charges should be pursued. The suspect has no right to be present in the grand jury proceedings. Defense attorneys are barred from the courtroom when grand juries meet. If the grand jury believes that charges are justified, it issues an indictment against the defendant.

Defense Attorneys and Criminal Procedure

Beginning with the preliminary hearing, defense attorneys file motions in an effort to have evidence excluded or to learn more about the evidence possessed by the prosecutor. Motions provide the basis to protect the defendant's rights against unreasonable searches and seizures. The defense attorney often argues during the preliminary hearing and subsequent pretrial motion hearings that specific evidence should be excluded from trial because it was obtained in violation of the defendant's rights.

The defense attorney also often initiates plea negotiations with the prosecutor. More than 90 percent of defendants whose cases are carried forward past grand jury indictments or preliminary hearings eventually enter guilty pleas in exchange for agreements about what punishment will be imposed. Although felony defendants have a right to have their cases decided at trial under constitutional rules for criminal procedure, most defendants prefer to make a plea agreement. Such agreements frequently produce lighter punishments than those that might have been imposed after a trial. Defendants' guilty pleas may be entered at any point in the process, from the arraignment through the middle of a jury trial.

The Trial Process

Defendants who face felony charges are entitled to a jury trial. Many defendants choose to have a bench trial before a judge alone rather than a jury if their case is controversial or if they believe that a judge will be fairer or more understanding. Misdemeanor defendants are entitled to jury trials under some states' laws, but they may have only bench trials under the laws of other states. The U.S. Supreme Court has said that the Sixth Amendment's right to trial by jury applies only to serious charges (*Blanton v. North Las Vegas*, 1989).

Under the Supreme Court's interpretations of the Sixth Amendment right to an impartial jury and the Fourteenth Amendment right to equal protection, jurors must be drawn from a fair cross-section of the community, and jurors cannot be excluded because of their race or gender. Through a process called *voir dire*, the prosecutor and defense attorney question potential witnesses and ask the judge to exclude those who might be biased because of their attitudes or personal experiences.

Although the federal government and most states use twelve-member juries in criminal cases, many states use six- to eight-member juries for misdemeanor cases. Six states use six- or eight-member juries for felony cases. The Supreme Court has declared that six-member juries must reach unanimous verdicts (*Burch v. Louisiana*, 1979), but non-unanimous verdicts are permissible for convicting defendants before twelve-member juries if permitted under a state's laws (*Apodaca v. Oregon*, 1972).

At the trial stage of criminal procedure, the prosecutor and defense attorney present evidence, question witnesses, and raise objections to each other's evidence and arguments. Each attorney attempts to persuade the jury or judge (in a bench trial) about the defendant's guilt or innocence. A conviction requires a finding of guilt beyond a reasonable doubt. In considering whether the evidence presented by the prosecutor achieves that standard, jurors must follow the judge's instructions about how to interpret the relevant law and evidence. Throughout the trial, the judge must follow the relevant laws of procedure and evidence that govern the state or federal court in which the trial is being conducted. The relevant laws are created by the state legislature for state courts and by Congress for the federal courts, and then they are refined and clarified by decisions of appellate courts, such as the state supreme court and U.S. Supreme Court. Decisions by the U.S. Supreme Court guide trial judges with respect to constitutional rights, such as those concerning double jeopardy, compelled self-incrimination, and confrontation of adverse witnesses, that can arise in the context of a trial.

Post-trial Procedures

After the jury or judge reaches a verdict, a defendant who is found guilty will be sentenced by the trial judge. In some states, juries determine the sentence in death penalty cases. Death penalty cases have special hearings in which the judge or jury must consider aggravating and mitigating circumstances, which are any circumstances making the crime or criminal especially deserving or not deserving of execution. Every sentence imposed for a crime must follow the punishments established by the legislature for that crime. The sentence must not violate the Eighth Amendment's prohibitions against excessive fines and cruel and unusual punishments.

Convicted defendants have a right to appeal their convictions by filing legal actions in appellate courts. These legal actions allege that the trial judge made specific errors which violated relevant laws or the defendant's constitutional rights. In most states, such appeals go first to an intermediate appellate court, usually called the state court of appeals, and then may be pursued in the state supreme court. In twelve states, however, there is no intermediate appellate court, so appeals go directly to the state supreme court. A few states have special appellate courts that hear only criminal appeals. There is a right to counsel only for the first appeal (*Douglas v. California*, 1963). Any subsequent appeals may have to be prepared and presented by the convicted offender unless he or she can hire an attorney or unless the relevant state law provides assigned counsel for convicts beyond the first appeal. Unsuccessful appeals to state supreme courts can subsequently be filed in the U.S. Supreme Court, but the nation's highest court accepts very few cases for hearing.

Convicted offenders can also file writs of *habeas corpus*, a traditional legal action from English history that permits a person to seek release or a new trial through a claim of wrongful detention. In the American system, prisoners must be able to show that their federal constitutional rights were violated in the course of the case and conviction. Very few prisoners prevail in such actions, but several thousand *habeas corpus* petitions are filed in the federal courts each year.

—*Christopher E. Smith*

Suggested Readings

A comprehensive and readable review of criminal procedure, including constitutional rights, is contained in Rolando V. del Carmen, *Criminal Procedure: Law and Practice* (3d ed. Belmont, Calif.: Wadsworth, 1995). This volume covers each stage of criminal procedure, with special attention given to relevant U.S. Supreme Court cases. More in-depth coverage of legal cases is provided by Yale Kamisar, Wayne R. LaFave, and Jerold H. Israel, *Modern Criminal Procedure: Cases, Comments, and Questions* (6th ed. St. Paul, Minn.: West Publishing, 1986). Reviews of the Supreme Court's criminal procedure decisions in the 1970's and 1980's are presented in John Decker, *Revolution to the Right: Criminal Procedure Jurisprudence During the Burger-Rehnquist Court Era* (New York: Garland, 1992), and Alfredo Garcia, *The Sixth Amendment in Modern American Jurisprudence* (New York: Greenwood Press, 1992). The history of criminal procedure is reviewed in David Bodenhamer, *Fair Trial* (New York: Oxford University Press, 1992), and Henry Abraham, *Freedom and the Court* (5th ed. New York: Oxford University Press, 1988). Bodenhamer's book in particular provides a brief, readable perspective on the development of criminal procedure. For international perspectives on the subject, see Christoph Johannes Maria Safferling *Towards an International Criminal Procedure* (New York: Oxford University Press, 2001). Useful books for lay readers include Jay M. Feinman's *Law 101: Everything You Need to Know About the American Legal System* (New York: Oxford University Press, 2000) and *The Criminal Law Handbook: Know Your Rights, Survive the System*, by Paul Bergman, Sara J. Berman-Barrett (5th ed. Berkeley, Calif.: Nolo Press, 2003). The latter presents its information in an easy-to-use question-and-answer format.

See also Appeal; Arraignment; Arrest; Bail system; Convictions; Criminal justice system; Defense attorneys; Due process of law;

Execution of judgment; Forfeiture, civil and criminal; Preliminary hearings; Presumption of innocence; Prosecutors; Public defenders; Suspects; Trials; Verdicts.

CRIMINAL RECORDS

Official documents listing persons' past convictions for misdemeanors and felonies; such records may also list arrests that do not result in conviction

A criminal record allows police agencies and courts to know the history of an individual's arrests and convictions for statute violations. It is often used as a sentencing tool in evaluating a convicted person's eligibility for probation and parole. Alien residents who are convicted of felonies are automatically deported if found, and aliens with serious criminal records cannot be admitted to the United States legally.

Local, state, and federal law-enforcement agencies and courts all compile criminal records. Effective national coordination of criminal records is a clear goal of the Federal Bureau of Investigation (FBI) and other law-enforcement agencies, but there are still holes in the system of record keeping that make it difficult to track mobile offenders, particularly low-level misdemeanants.

Data Collection

The FBI has national responsibility for the compilation of criminal records. These records are stored at the FBI's Criminal Justice Information Services (CJIS) division, which is headquartered in Clarksburg, West Virginia. The CJIS is the world's largest fingerprint repository; it cooperates with both national and international law information agencies. As of May, 1997, CJIS had over 219 million fingerprint cards. Of these over 132 million were criminal record cards and over 187 million were civil record cards.

Although submission of records to the CJIS is voluntary for state and local law-enforcement agencies, data submission increased in the late twentieth century. The CJIS also receives the fingerprints of aliens who seek permanent residence, naturalization, and asylum in the United States, as well as the fingerprints of Americans seeking to adopt children abroad.

In some states, state law requires those arrested for felonies and class A and B misdemeanors to be fingerprinted, and two sets of fingerprint records are made so that both local authorities and the state bureau of investigation can maintain appropriate records. Juveniles charged with offenses that would be felonies or class A and B misdemeanors for adults also must submit fingerprints. Minor misdemeanors slip through the cracks of states' recording systems.

Private and Public Use of Criminal Records

In addition to law-enforcement, court, and corrections use of criminal records, private citizens increasingly seek access to criminal records. Employers must know whether they are hiring individuals with criminal histories that raise serious concern about their fitness to deal with vulnerable populations in day-care centers, schools, summer camps, and nursing homes.

If an employer fails to do a background check and hires an employee whose record would have indicated that they posed a potential threat, the employer can be sued for negligent hire. Judgments average more than $1 million per case. Specialized search firms have proliferated to meet employer needs to learn of potential employees' criminal histories and other potentially damaging background information. Potential employees must often sign a consent form agreeing to a criminal record check or forfeit further consideration for employment even in low-level jobs.

Law-enforcement agencies use criminal records to track offenders over time. While juvenile records were once sealed when juvenile offenders became adults, many states make them available to courts sentencing former juvenile felons for adult crimes.

Prosecutors and courts use criminal records in determining how serious punishment should be for particular crimes. In some states, first-time offenders may be granted a diversion that keeps them out of the criminal justice system if they accept responsibility for their offenses and honor restitution and other conditions imposed on them. The successful completion of diversion leaves persons with no formal criminal record, although prosecutors have access to records that indicate who has been granted diversions. Judges in many states use mandated sentencing guidelines that impose sentences for specific offenses based on the severity of the offense and individuals' prior criminal records. Judges must justify departures from a recommended sentencing range.

Coping with a Criminal Record

Former offenders find themselves severely handicapped by their criminal records. In addition to losing voting rights and the right to bear arms, those with felony convictions are barred from obtaining many occupational and professional licenses in most states. Sometimes criminal background checks are required for health care workers who deal directly with patients, and some states have passed laws that revoke the teaching certificates of public school teachers with felony records. Some states have a formal process called "expungement," through which persons who can demonstrate that they have been rehabilitated can have convictions for most crimes removed from their records. Expunged records are not totally destroyed, however. In addition, expunged records can be reopened if further offenses are committed.

—Susan A. Stussy

Suggested Readings

In "Do You Know Who You Are Hiring," *USA Today Magazine* 125 (July, 1997), Edward Niam, Jr., describes the legal problems that can confront employers who hire employees without thoroughly researching their past. If an individual with a serious criminal record were to be hired and then commit a felony, the employer would be liable in tort for negligent hiring practices. In "U.S. Deports Felons but Can't Keep Them Out," *New York Times* (August 11, 1997), Deborah Sontag reports on the efforts of the INS to exclude deported criminal aliens from the United States. Kathleen Vail's "Privacy Rights Versus Safety" in *American School Board Journal* 184 (April, 1997) reports on recent trends to open juvenile records of serious offenders to school superintendents and other educators. *Building Violence: How America's Rush to Incarcerate Creates More Violence,* edited by John P. May and Khalid R. Pitts (Thousand Oaks, Calif.: Sage, 2000), has a chapter on the stigma of criminal history records in the labor market.

See also Age of majority; Arrest; Bail system; Criminal justice system; Felonies; Misdemeanors; Probation, adult; Probation, juvenile; Prosecutors; Sentencing; Three-strikes laws; Trial transcripts.

CROSS-EXAMINATION

*That part of a legal proceedings in which a witness called to testify
in behalf of one party is questioned by the counsel for the opposing
party*

When parties to legal proceedings call their own witnesses to testify, the questions asked of them are known as the direct examination of witnesses. At the conclusion of direct examinations,
opposing parties are allowed to question the same witnesses; this
questioning is known as cross-examination of witnesses. In most
cases, interactions between questioners and witnesses during direct examination are cordial, with the witnesses testifying to matters that support the questioners' cases. However, during cross-
examination, relationships between questioners and witnesses
often become adversarial. However, cross-examinations do not
routinely involve heated exchanges between questioners and witnesses. More often, cross-examinations are methodical exercises
in establishing key points, rather than the fiery confrontations between attorneys and witnesses frequently depicted in dramatized
courtroom settings.

Cross-examinations commonly pursue two aims: to elicit from
witnesses testimony supporting the questioners' cases and to
challenge hostile witnesses' credibility. Even hostile witnesses
occasionally admit—though perhaps reluctantly—at least some
facts that help support the opposing parties' cases. A successful cross-examination presses for such admissions. In addition,
cross-examiners frequently attempt to discredit harmful testimony obtained on direct examination. Attorneys conducting cross-
examinations can choose from among a variety of possible strategies.

An attorney may, for example, question a witness's perception
of an event for which the witness has provided testimony. Perhaps the witness was too far removed from the scene to make an
accurate observation, or perhaps it was dark or the witness's eye-
glasses were left at home. Inquiries into matters such as these may
suggest that the witness's ability to perceive an event was im-
paired. The cross-examiner may challenge, moreover, a witness's
recollection of an event and demonstrate that the recollection is
faulty in certain respects. It may also be that a witness is a close

---

COMMON CHALLENGES TO THE CREDIBILITY OF WITNESSES

- The witness's perception of an event is faulty
- The witness's memory is faulty
- The witness is biased
- The witness has a criminal record
- The witness's testimony is inconsistent with prior statements or depositions
- The witness's testimony is inconsistent with other evidence
- The witness's testimony is inconsistent with common sense

---

friend of the opposing party. In such a case, the cross-examiner would probably disclose this relationship to suggest that the witness is biased. Or perhaps a witness has previously been convicted of embezzling funds from an employer, in which case the cross-examiner might question the witness about the conviction to suggest that the witness is generally untrustworthy. Finally, cross-examination may seek to demonstrate that a witness's testimony on direct examination is inconsistent with other information. The testimony may be shown to be inconsistent with a prior statement made by the witness—for example, a statement made to the police or in a deposition. Moreover, the cross-examiner may seek to demonstrate that the witness's story is inconsistent with other facts established in a case, or that it is simply inconsistent with common sense.

—*Timothy L. Hall*

See also Adversary system; Affidavits; Court reporters; Evidence, rules of; Testimony; Trial transcripts; Trials; Witnesses; Witnesses, confrontation of; Witnesses, expert.

CRUEL AND UNUSUAL PUNISHMENT

Punishment of a particularly degrading, torturous, or barbaric nature, or punishment so disproportionate to the crime or offense as to shock the moral sense of a community; prohibition of cruel and unusual punishments has become a general barometer of a society's civil evolution

In the Eighth Amendment to the U.S. Constitution, the prohibition against cruel and unusual punishment is joined to the prohibition against excessive bails and fines. To the founders of the United States, these practices represented uses of the state's criminal justice machinery that ranged from inappropriate to inhuman. Both sets of practices had sordid histories in England, and the founders believed that the prohibition against both needed to be written into the Constitution in general terms so that the determination of what constitutes a cruel or unusual punishment or excessive bail could be made by each generation in the context of the changing circumstances of life and the evolving norms of civilized societies.

Development

The prohibitions against both cruel and unusual punishment and excessive bail and fines have their roots in English history as far back as the Magna Carta. Curiously, most of the battles between king and countrymen over these matters focused not on cruel and unusual punishments but on the right-to-bail issue. The decisive battles ensued during the seventeenth century, when—as America was being settled on the opposite side of the Atlantic—a 1627 ruling by English judges upholding the king's right to imprison anyone without bail before trial led to a battle between the Crown and Parliament. The latter decisively won with the inclusion in the 1689 British Bill of Rights of a provision outlawing "excessive bail."

One hundred years later the "excessive bail" clause of the British Bill of Rights was linked with the prohibition of cruel and unusual punishments and included, otherwise essentially unaltered, in the Eighth Amendment of the United States Bill of Rights. There was a small degree of controversy over its inclusion.

When the Congress considered the Bill of Rights in 1789, two members objected to the Eighth Amendment because of the subjective and indefinite nature of the terms being employed with respect to both fines and bails ("excessive") and punishments ("cruel," "unusual"). One of these members of Congress also objected more generally to the "cruel and unusual" provision, explaining to his colleagues that "it is sometimes necessary to hang a man, villains often deserve whipping, and perhaps having their ears cut off." Most of those present, however, not only held reasonably definite notions of what constituted cruel and unusual punishments but also were willing to proscribe such punishments even if they were likely to be more effective in dissuading villainy than less cruel, alternative measures.

Throughout the nineteenth century, the Supreme Court limited its interpretation of the cruel and unusual clause essentially to the historic punishments obviously intended to be banned by the framers of the Constitution—for example, burning at the stake, crucifixion, use of the thumbscrew, drawing and quartering, and the breaking of a body on the rack. Not until the landmark 1910 case *Weems v. United States* (1910) was the provision given the liberal construction of having an "expansive and vital character" which alters with the changing sensitivities of modern societies. Since that time, most of the significant cases revolving around the cruel and unusual clause have involved either proportionality issues centering on the form of punishment compared with the nature of the crime or issues pertaining to the constitutionality of capital punishment and its means of implementation.

The argument that the Eighth Amendment can be violated by penalties which "shock" the sense of justice in their severity or by a sentence whose length is "greatly disproportioned to the offenses charged" was first voiced by Justice Stephen J. Field in his dissenting opinion in the 1892 case *O'Neil v. Vermont* (1892). Eighteen years later, the disproportionate test was applied for the first time by a majority in *Weems v. United States*, a case involving a Philippine law prescribing twelve to twenty years of hard labor imprisonment for knowingly entering a false statement in a public record. Subsequently, the proportionality test has been applied in cases involving such matters as court-martial proceedings leading to the revocation of citizenship for desertion in the armed forces in time of war (*Trop v. Dulles*, 1958); the infliction of punishment for being a drug addict (*Robinson v. California*, 1962); and the imposition of life imprisonment without parole for minor, nonviolent crimes (*Solem v. Helm*, 1983).

Capital Punishment

The issue of capital punishment first significantly came before the Supreme Court in 1879 in the case of *Wilkerson v. Utah*, in which the Court upheld execution by firing squad over the objection that it was cruel and unusual punishment. Likewise, the Supreme Court tacitly upheld the constitutionality of capital punishment itself eleven years later when it sustained, in *In re Kemmler* (1890), the use of the electric chair for carrying out executions. At the time, capital punishment was not a controversial issue in American society. Public hangings were still routine, and both the *Kemmler* and *Wilkerson* cases were unanimous decisions. Four generations later, however, the issue of whether capital punishment itself is a cruel and unusual punishment became one of the principal issues confronting—and to a degree dividing—the Supreme Court.

In *Witherspoon v. Illinois*, decided in 1968, the Supreme Court gave its first indication that the death penalty might be in trouble as a part of the United States' criminal justice machinery. *Witherspoon* did not involve the Eighth Amendment. Rather it was a "fair trial" case arising under the Sixth Amendment, in which the Supreme Court invalidated the death sentence imposed on the accused by a "hanging" jury (one from which opponents of the death penalty had been excluded). Noting the divided nature of public opinion on the death sentence throughout the United States, the Supreme Court decided that the jury in the case "fell woefully short of that impartiality to which the petitioner was entitled under the Sixth and Fourteenth Amendments."

The *Witherspoon* ruling emboldened the opponents of capital punishment to mount a judicial assault on the death penalty under the cruel and unusual test of the Eighth Amendment. Their timing proved to be bad, though, for *Witherspoon* was one of the last important, rights-of-the-criminally-accused cases decided during the Warren Court era. By the time the cases challenging the constitutionality of capital punishment under the Eighth Amendment began to reach the Supreme Court, President Richard Nixon had not only replaced a retiring Earl Warren with Chief Justice Warren Burger but also appointed a majority of the nine justices on the Supreme Court with an eye to tilting it in a more conservative, law-and-order direction. Thus, in several 1970's cases involving the constitutionality of capital punishment, the Supreme Court affirmed that, per se, capital punishment is not a cruel or unusual punishment for certain categories of crimes. At the same time it also ruled, in a series of split decisions, that the administration of capital punishment must conform to specific and strict guidelines to ensure that it is not imposed by juries in such a capricious, arbitrary, and/or "freakish" manner as to become cruel or unusual. In *Furman v. Georgia* in 1972, the Court essentially threw out capital punishment as it was then being administered in the United States; four years later, in *Gregg v. Georgia*, it approved the first state statute written after *Furman* that satisfied the Supreme Court's requirements for the constitutional imposition of capital punishment, including a review process designed to compare "each death sentence with the sentences imposed on similarly situated defendants to ensure that the sentence of death in a particular case is not disproportionate" (*Gregg v. Georgia*, 1976). Other judicially mandated requirements involved limiting the discretion of juries in imposing the death sentence and making the right to appeal automatic in capital punishment cases. Still later cases further elaborated the rules for imposing the death sentence in terms of such matters as the relevance in sentencing proceedings of information pertaining to the character of the crime and the character and record of the criminally accused. Mandatory death sentences have routinely been struck down as unconstitutional (*Woodson v. North Carolina, Roberts v. Louisiana*, 1976).

Excessive Bail and Fines

Although the Supreme Court has never specifically addressed the issue of what constitutes an "excessive fine" within the meaning of the Eighth Amendment, except to indicate that the clause applies only to fines levied in criminal proceedings (*Browning Ferris Industries v. Kelco Disposal*, 1989), an evolutionary approach has characterized the judiciary's consideration of the Eighth Amendment's excessive bail clause.

For nearly two hundred years, the prevailing view was that bail existed only to prevent flight and that there is a reasonable amount of bail for any category of crime to ensure that the criminally accused will appear at his or her trial. The right to bail was seen as a basic constitutional right by the Founders, to whom the debtors prisons of Britain and the Crown's willingness to incarcerate political enemies without trial were comparatively recent history. Hence, although it was generally agreed that what constituted "excessive bail" must be determined on a case-by-case basis, the Supreme Court generally adhered to the view that at no point may bail be set at an amount which has either the intent or effect of depriving the accused of the full opportunity to prepare for his or her defense (*Stack v. Boyle*, 1951). Like the cruel and unusual clause, this protection did not necessarily apply to all legal proceedings. Deportation proceedings against alien communists, for example, were exempted from the bail requirement in 1952 (*Carlson v. Landon*), as were juvenile court proceedings some thirty years later (*Shall v. Martin*, 1984). In criminal proceedings, though, the right to bail was basic. Without it, the Supreme Court explained in *Stack v. Boyle*, the accused would be hampered from preparing a defense, punishment could be inflicted without conviction, and "the presumption of innocence, secured only after centuries of struggle, would lose its meaning."

In 1987, however, in the watershed case of *United States v. Salerno*, the Supreme Court created two significant exceptions to this rule. The pretrial detention of "arrestees charged with serious felonies" was to be permitted when the accused are deemed either to pose a threat to the safety of the community if released or likely to flee regardless of the amount of bail posted because of the gravity of the charges against them. Most states have subsequently rewritten their bail statutes to deny bail in certain classes of crime—for example, in cases involving multiple counts of first-degree murder.

The Still-Expanding Eighth Amendment

Like the evolving meanings attached to the concept of equality, which each new generation has had to define for itself since the inception of the Republic, the definitions attached to excessive fines and especially those given to cruel and unusual punishments have been one of the measures by which Americans—as well as citizens in other democracies—have assessed their level of civility. As Chief Justice Earl Warren wrote in *Trop v. Dulles*, the content of the Eighth Amendment "must draw its meaning from the evolving standards of decency that mark the progress of a maturing society." By this test, the citizens of the United States traveled a great distance in the half century following World War II.

As late as 1947, in *Louisiana ex rel. Francis v. Resweber*, the Supreme Court was unwilling to rule that the execution of an individual twice for the same crime (Louisiana's electric chair having failed to discharge a lethal dose of electricity on the first occasion) was a cruel or unusual punishment within the meaning of the Constitution. As late as the 1950's, the whipping post was still being employed as punishment for a variety of petty offenses by the state of Delaware. "The penology of a state," Justice Felix Frankfurter wrote for the majority in *Resweber*, "is not to be tested by the scope of the Eighth Amendment," even though the Supreme Court had at least implicitly assumed that the Eighth Amendment limited state action when it reviewed the early cases involving the constitutionality of capital punishment by firing squad and electrocution.

By the 1990's, not only had the provisions of the Eighth Amendment been made implicitly applicable to the states through incorporation into the due process clause of the Fourteenth Amendment in *Robinson v. California*, but also the prohibition against cruel and unusual punishments had been extended from courtroom sentences to the nature of the confinement in prison cells (which must meet certain minimally decent standards) and to the treatment of prisoners serving sentences. These developments marked substantial departures from existing precedents. As late as 1977, a 5-4 majority on the Supreme Court had upheld the use of "reasonable corporal punishment" in schools in *Ingraham v. Wright*, at least in part by adhering to the traditional view that the cruel and unusual punishments clause only applies to the penalties given to those convicted in state or federal courts. The other side of the coin has traditionally been that the clause does not limit the penalties inflicted on people by the government in such other arenas as school systems, deportation proceedings (*Harisiades v. Shaughnessy*, 1952), the treatment of those in jail awaiting trial (*Bell v. Wolfish*, 1979), and hearings involving committal to mental institutions (*Youngberg v. Romeo*, 1982). By the 1990's, however, federal appellate courts were routinely reviewing the treatment of prisoners before and after trial on the basis of the 8-1 ruling in *Hutto v. Finney* (1978) to the effect that "confinement in prison . . . is a form of punishment subject to scrutiny under the Eighth Amendment standards."

Even more revealingly, by the late twentieth century, litigation involving the cruel and unusual clause had begun to revolve

around topics which in the recent past would have been regarded
as esoteric but scarcely cruel and unusual. Appeals under the
Eighth Amendment have thus been made in cases involving such
issues as mandatory life sentences without parole for those convicted of possessing more than 650 grams of cocaine (*Harmelin v.
Michigan*, 1991), the sentencing of defendants suffering from acquired immunodeficiency syndrome (AIDS), "unreasonable" ex-
posure to second-hand environmental tobacco smoke in prison
(*Helling v. McKinney*, 1993), society's obligation to protect from
physical harm those being involuntarily retained in custody, including those in mental hospitals and orphanages, the prosecution of pregnant addicts, the arrest of the homeless, and death
sentences for juvenile offenders.

The same expansive philosophy can be seen in cases involving
the excessive fines portion of the Eighth Amendment. Although
the Supreme Court continues to adhere to the position that the
size of a fine does not make it excessive no matter how great the
fine may be and that the Eighth Amendment's injunction against
excessive fines applies only to criminal cases, in a civil case arising in Oregon in the 1990's the Supreme Court did adopt an "excessive" test involving the size of a punitive damages award.

Perhaps because of the broadening construction given to the
Eighth Amendment as a restraint on state action, cases involving
this amendment became among the most controversial of those
arising from the Bill of Rights during the late twentieth century.
Many states, for example, have proscribed corporal punishment in
their school systems, even though the Supreme Court has refused
to invalidate it under the Eighth Amendment. Likewise, cases involving the proportionality test have been highly controversial,
especially when tied to capital punishment cases. Sometimes the
Supreme Court's rulings have even provoked a short-term national outrage, as in 1977, when a narrow majority in *Coker v. Georgia* ruled that the death penalty for the crime of raping an adult
woman, in the absence of such aggravating circumstances as the
commission of another crime, constituted a "grossly dispropor-
tional, excessive penalty" which violated the Eighth Amendment.

The United States has not necessarily moved in tandem with
the remainder of the world in its perception of the rules of ordered
decency in the domain of cruel and unusual punishments. In con-
doning the continued use of capital punishment, the Supreme
Court has left the United States nearly alone among developed

democratic states, virtually all of which eliminated capital punishment from their criminal justice systems during the latter half of the twentieth century.

Although the federal judiciary's decisions designed to correct the substandard nature of prison conditions in the United States have often exposed it to domestic criticism for "coddling criminals," several European states have persistently refused to extradite criminals to the United States because of what they perceive to be the unsafe and intolerable nature of American penitentiaries, and European courts of justice have routinely sustained such action. On the other hand, if the definition of cruel and unusual punishments in the United States has not yet become as exacting as that of the European Court of Human Rights, it remains an expanding one, far removed not only from the rack and iron-maiden meanings attached to it by the Founders but also from the proportionality and physical discomfort tests by which the amendment was being interpreted as late as the 1960's.

—*Joseph R. Rudolph, Jr.*

Suggested Readings

For a comprehensive overview of the subject, see Joseph A. Melusky and Keith A. Pesto's *Cruel and Unusual Punishment: Rights and Liberties Under the Law* (Santa Barbara, Calif.: ABC-CLIO, 2003). Good sections on the evolving meaning of cruel and unusual punishment can be found in David J. Bodenhamer and James W. Ely, Jr., eds., *The Bill of Rights in Modern America: After 200 Years* (Bloomington: Indiana University Press, 1993), and Jethro K. Lieberman, *The Evolving Constitution: How the Supreme Court Has Ruled on Issues from Abortion to Zoning* (New York: Random House, 1992). Among the many older, more detailed examinations of the amendment, see Larry Charles Berkson, *The Concept of Cruel and Unusual Punishment* (Lexington, Mass.: Lexington Books, 1975), and, on capital punishment, Frank Carrington, *Neither Cruel nor Unusual* (New Rochelle, N.Y.: Arlington House, 1978). Joan Biskupic and Elder Witt's *The Supreme Court and Individual Rights* (Washington, D.C.: Congressional Quarterly, 1997), Carl J. Franklin's *Constitutional Law for the Criminal Justice Professional* (Boca Raton, Fla.: CRC Press, 1999), and Lynn S. Branham's *The Law of Sentencing, Corrections, and Prisoners' Rights in a Nutshell* (St. Paul, Minn.: West Publishing, 2002) all include chapters on cruel and unusual punishment.

See also Bail system; Bill of Rights, U.S.; Bills of attainder; Capital punishment; Constitution, U.S.; Convictions; Eighth Amendment; *Ex post facto* laws; Sentencing; Verdicts.

DAMAGES

Money awards intended to compensate for losses or injuries due to other parties' breaches of contract or negligence; recovery of such damages is the remedy sought in most civil litigation

The concept of damages differs from that of injury. Damages refer to a sum of money awarded to injured persons that is intended to compensate them for injuries or to punish the party responsible for the injuries, while injury refers to the harm to one person which is caused by another. Damages intended to compensate for a loss are called compensatory, or actual, damages, while damages intended to punish the wrongdoer are called punitive, or exemplary, damages. Such injuries, which need not be physical, can result from a breach of contract or a tort (a civil wrong done by one party against another).

Compensatory Damages

Compensatory damages are intended to restore the injured party to the level of well-being enjoyed prior to the injury or breach of contract. This has ancient origins. The compensation to the owner of a slave killed in biblical times was set at thirty pieces of silver. Thus, owners received some recompense for the loss of their property.

Damages resulting from breach of contract may be determined according to one of several principles. Expectation damages are compensation that restores injured parties to the position in which they would have been had the contract been performed (including profits). Reliance damages are compensation that restores injured parties to the position in which they would have been had the contract never been entered into. This includes expenditures made or liabilities incurred while relying on the performance of the contract. For example, in the case of *Hawkins v. McGee* (1929) Hawkins, a young man with a somewhat deformed hand, underwent an operation in which his hand was to be made perfect. Instead, he emerged from surgery with a seriously deformed hand. His expectation damages were the amount of money that compensated him for the difference between having a perfect hand and a seriously deformed hand. His reliance damages were the amount that compensated him for the difference between a somewhat deformed hand and a seriously deformed hand. Thus, expectation damages exceed reliance damages, since persons enter into contracts only if they expect the result to be an improvement over their precontract condition.

Another concept of contract damages is restitution damages, an award intended to deny the breaching party any unjust enrichment resulting from the breach. For example, if a buyer contracts to buy a rare painting for $20,000 and the seller sells it to another person for $27,000, the original contract has been breached. The court may award restitution damages of $7,000 to the disappointed buyer.

In many contracts the possibility of a breach due to particular contingencies is foreseen and damages are specified within the contract. Such damages are known as liquidated damages. Since these damages are agreed upon by both parties in advance and in good faith, they are generally enforced unless the liquidated damages are held to be unreasonably large.

Certain compensatory damages arising from torts are prescribed by statute and are therefore called statutory damages. Most states have wrongful death statutes and statutes limiting tort claims against civil governments.

Punitive and Special Damages

Punitive damages existed in ancient times, probably before the invention of money, as exemplified in the Code of Hammurabi (eighteenth century B.C.E.) and the Bible's *lex talionis:* "an eye for an eye, a tooth for a tooth, a life for a life," which indicated that the damages to be paid for blinding another was to be blinded oneself. There is no recompense to the victim; rather, the purpose was to punish the responsible party for causing a physical injury. Further, the severity of the punishment was an incentive to exercise care not to injure another. This is still the purpose of punitive damages, but in a modern, money-based economy the punishment is a monetary award payable to the victim.

Punitive damages are often awarded when it has been proved that the defendant has acted maliciously, fraudulently, wantonly, or willfully. Certain punitive damages are prescribed by statute. The best-known example of this is the Clayton Anti-Trust Act (1914), which prescribes treble damages for certain antitrust violations that substantially lessen competition.

Compensatory damages are described as "general" if they are the immediate, direct, and proximate result of an injury or breach or as "special" if they are the natural but not inevitable result. Such damages arise because of the particular circumstances of the injury. Thus, if spilled grease leads a person to slip, fall, and sustain a torn shoulder, but the victim lacked the full use of the remaining arm and both legs due to polio, the result might be total disability. This total disability would be a natural but not inevitable result of the injury and would give rise to special damages. Damages that are not the result of an injury but are the result of some consequence of the injury are called consequential damages. In contract law special damages are those not originally contemplated by the parties. If these damages are reasonably foreseeable and flow directly and immediately from the breach of contract, then they are recoverable.

There are other important distinctions among different classifications of damages. Future damages may be probable, in which case they are called "prospective damages," or they may be uncertain or improbable, in which case they are called "speculative damages." Pecuniary damages are those which can be calculated in monetary terms. The scope of pecuniary damages is constantly being expanded by new techniques employed by economists acting as expert witnesses.

Mitigation of Damages
Although a person who commits a tort is liable for full compensation of the victim, the latter generally has a duty to lessen, or mitigate, the damages. For example, a person with a lifetime employment contract who is nevertheless fired can initiate a wrongful termination action against the former employer. Damages will equal the present value of future contract wages and benefits. However, the former employee has a duty to seek other work, the earnings from which will be subtracted from damages. If the victim does not attempt to mitigate damages, the damages may be

reduced by an amount estimated to be equal to the potential of mitigation.

Although mitigation is generally subtracted from damages, there is an exception: If a victim receives compensation from a third party, such as health or life insurance proceeds from an insurance company or monetary aid from a relative, this amount is not subtracted. To do so would be to reward the wrongdoer for the victim's foresight and caution. This is known as the collateral source rule.

Calculating Damages

In contract law, reliance and expectation damages may be calculated according to a variety of measures: substitute price, lost surplus, opportunity cost, out-of-pocket cost, and diminished value. The substitute price measure awards the victim of a breach of contract the cost of replacing the contracted goods or services with substitutes. If a perfect substitute exists and there is a market price for this substitute, the computation is trivial. If only a near-substitute exists, some calculation is necessary. Surplus, the difference between the value the victim expected to gain from the contract and the value given up, will be lost if the contract is breached. Such a measure of damages can be extremely large. For example, if an inexpensive item is defective, a company, upon selling it, may incur the loss of large profits.

The opportunity-cost measure awards the victim the surplus that would have been realized had the victim chosen the next best opportunity and signed the best alternative contract instead of the actual, breached contract. The out-of-pocket measure of damages takes damages to be equal to the difference between costs incurred by the victim in reliance upon the contract and the value, if any, produced as a result of those costs. In a similar manner, the diminished value measure awards the victim the difference between the value promised and the value actually received. This measure is applied when the contract is imperfectly or partially fulfilled. A related concept is *quantum meruit*, "as much as deserved," which is applied to implied contracts: The value of goods furnished or services rendered may be recovered when they have been accepted and used by another party.

Tort Awards

In tort litigation, in which the victim is a company, lost profits may generally be recovered if there has been physical damage, although some states permit recovery without physical damage. In cases of fraud, an intentional tort, the benefit-of-the-bargain rule calls for the victim to be awarded the difference between the value had the misrepresentation been true and the actual value. In the case of *Woodmont Inc. v. Daniels* the owner of a parcel of land fraudulently represented the land as being free of rock. The contractor, encountering a ledge of rock, had to resort to blasting to finish the job. The contractor was able to recover damages that in-

---

ELEMENTS OF DAMAGE AWARDS

Physical injuries
- Loss of earning capacity (past and future)
- Expenses for medical care physicians, hospitals, therapists, nurses, supportive equipment, medications
- Physical pain and suffering
- Mental pain and suffering
- Disfigurement
- Loss of the ability to enjoy life
- Curtailment of life expectancy

Mental distress
- Loss of earning capacity (past and future)
- Medical care by psychologists and psychiatrists, hospitals, medications, harm to relationships, loss of the ability to enjoy life, fear of future injury

Loss of Consortium
- Spousal loss of affection, support, and sexual relationship
- Children's or sibling's loss of affection

Death Cases
- Family members' losses (wrongful death), such as financial contributions of decedent to family, services, society, support, sorrow (certain states), hedonic damages (loss of life's pleasures)
- Decedent's losses (survival action), such as future earning capacity (less personal maintenance), funeral expenses, medical expenses, pain and suffering, hedonic damages (loss of life's pleasures)

cluded lost profits, not just actual costs. Thus, this rule allows recovery for lost profits. Some states, however, follow the out-of-pocket loss rule, which allows recovery only for costs incurred.

When the victim of a tort is an individual, damages may be recovered for out-of-pocket costs; lost earnings, including salary and noncash benefits; the value of lost household services; and pain and suffering. All of these may be for past or future losses. In addition, in personal injury cases persons may lose the ability to function socially, emotionally, occupationally, or in everyday life. These damages, called hedonic damages, or lost enjoyment of life, have been quantified by economists and have been accepted in many jurisdictions. Other jurisdictions have considered such damages as a part of "pain and suffering," or "mental anguish."

In every case, all damages must be expressed in terms of present value. That is, future damages must be discounted to a sum which, with interest, would equal the future damages at the time at which they would occur. Thus, if one million dollars in future damages would occur two years from now, and the current interest rate is 5 percent, the present value of these damages would be only $907,029.48. This amount, deposited for two years at 5 percent interest, would be worth one million dollars in two years. Similarly, past losses must be compensated with interest. In addition, the Supreme Court, in *Jones & Laughlin Steel Corp. v. Pfeifer* (1983) established that damages must be corrected for inflation. In cases involving punitive damages, awards by juries have generally followed no rule, resulting in extremely high damages in some cases and very low damages in others.

—*John Andrulis*

Suggested Readings

Three works that deal with pretrial discovery are Guozhang Huang's *Introducing Discovery into Civil Law* (Durham, N.C.: Carolina Academic Press, 2003), James E. Hogan and Gregory S. Weber's *California Civil Discovery* (San Francisco: Bancroft Whitney, 1972, 1997) and Edith C. Schaffer's *Discovery* in Bancroft-Whitney's series *California Civil Practice* (San Francisco: Bancroft Whitney, 1992). Treatments of judicial procedural matters that discuss witnesses include Paul Bergman and Sara J. Berman-Barnett's *Represent Yourself in Court: How to Prepare and Try a Winning Case* (2d ed. Berkeley Calif.: Nolo Press, 1998) and Paul Bergman's *Trial Advocacy in a Nutshell* (3d ed. St. Paul, Minn. West

Publishing, 1995). *Bender's Forms of Discovery* (New York: Matthew-Bender; regularly updated) is a ten-volume treatise with sample questions for numerous kinds of cases, including product liability, employment discrimination, slip-and-fall, automobile accident, and breach of contract cases. This and similar lawyer "practice guides" are often available in the reference sections of public libraries. Ann E. Woodley's *Litigating in Federal Court: A Guide to the Rules* (Durham, N.C.: Carolina Academic Press, 1999) has a chapter that focuses on discovery.

See also Acquittal; Breach of contract; Commercial litigation; Compensatory damages; Contracts; Forfeiture, civil and criminal; Garnishment; Judgment proof; Punitive damages; Restitution; Sentencing; Torts; Witnesses, expert.

DEATH ROW ATTORNEYS

Lawyers who typically volunteer for the highly specialized task of representing clients sentenced to death; such attorneys are generally opponents of the death penalty

Although the U.S. Constitution requires state governments to provide attorneys to those who cannot afford to hire their own, this requirement only applies to original trials. Since the vast majority of condemned prisoners cannot afford to hire attorneys, many are not represented by legal professionals after sentencing. Those attorneys who regularly defend death row inmates are volunteers, who often consider themselves crusaders against the death penalty in general.

Since the U.S. Supreme Court decided to allow states to reenact capital punishment statutes in 1976, most states have done so. By 1996 thirty-eight states allowed the death penalty for some crimes. By that year, there were about three thousand prisoners on death row.

The appeals process is long and complicated. The average case lasts eight years and costs $2 to $3 million dollars, and some convicts have remained on death row for as long as twenty years.

Fewer than 3 percent of those who are sentenced to death are actually executed.

After persons are convicted and sentenced, they have an automatic right to appeal to the state supreme court. If this appeal is unsuccessful, there may be an appeal to a federal circuit court. Any decision by either court can be followed by a request for review by the U.S. Supreme Court. Such a request, however, must be made on constitutional grounds. Death row attorneys may take one or more of three courses of action in appealing cases. First, they may try to challenge the original conviction, seeking to have a higher court reverse the decision. Second, they may not contest the guilt of their clients but instead try to alter the sentence on the grounds of mitigating circumstances. Third, they may attempt to challenge the state capital punishment statute on constitutional grounds.

Since so few persons convicted of murders are wealthy, their attorneys are unlikely to be paid sufficiently for their work. If convicted persons have made headlines because of the nature of their cases, their attorneys may gain some publicity. However, such publicity is likely to be negative, as few people think favorably of lawyers who defend convicted murderers.

Death row attorneys are often perceived as making a political statement. A number of books have been written by such attorneys, books that often attack the death penalty on one or more grounds. The costs of a capital trial are enormous. Death row inmates may be inadequately defended at their appeals. It is often pointed out that the prisoners on death row typically are poor or members of minority groups. Finally, there are cases in which it is discovered that prisoners are innocent after they have been executed.

—*Marc Goldstein*

See also Appeal; Attorney types; Capital punishment; Criminal justice system; Cruel and unusual punishment; Defense attorneys; *Habeas corpus*; Indigent criminal defendants; Judicial review.

DECLARATORY JUDGMENTS

Actions undertaken to determine the rights of parties to contracts; such actions are available before or after breaches of contract and serve to resolve controversies over the terms of contracts

All states have statutes allowing declaratory judgments. Under these statutes, a party to a contract may bring an action for declaratory judgment, asking the court to determine the rights and obligations of either party under the contract. A declaratory judgment action may be brought before breach of the contract, so that legal rights and duties are determined (and damages, if any, minimized) before a breach has completely destroyed the relationship between the parties.

In order to obtain a declaratory judgment, the plaintiff generally must plead and prove that (1) a written contract exists (although a minority of states allow an oral contract to support a declaratory judgment); (2) the declaratory judgment will resolve the entire dispute; (3) no other relief is available; (4) there is an actual controversy; (5) there is no other action pending that involves this contractual duty; and (6) the matter can be resolved as a matter of law. A declaratory judgment is a final judgment and can involve the award of damages, injunctive relief, and any other supplemental relief available from the court.

See also Breach of contract; Commercial litigation; Consent decree; Contracts; Litigation.

DEFENDANT SELF-REPRESENTATION

Siutations in which laypersons represent themselves in court; such persons are often designated by the Latin term "pro se," for "himself"

Attorneys rarely represent themselves. Laymen, however, often find reason to represent themselves. One reason is the cost of hiring an attorney, which can be high even in simple cases. Another is vanity.

Judges and lawyers tend not to care for *pro se* activity. Cases are not likely to go as smoothly when one side does not have a clear understanding of the law and of all the nuances and oral shorthand that can occur in a trial. Judges do not like being in a position of either having to explain to the *pro se* what is going on—putting the judge in the position of representing the *pro se*—or else watching the *pro se* be outclassed on legal points. A judge has the power, with proper legal justification, to prevent a person from engaging in self-representation. The judge is more likely to use that power in criminal than in civil cases and in high-stakes than in low-stakes cases.

A person acting as *pro se* should research the case, starting with the statutes involved. Most, if not all, counties and states and a good many universities have law libraries in which such research is possible (although some universities bar nonstudents from their libraries). The state *Digest*, the precedents, and the rules that must be followed in court and in the activities leading up to the trial, such as rules about complaints, answers, interrogatories, depositions, revelation of papers, and summary judgments, should be studied, as should the rules of evidence to the extent that time permits. The rules of evidence are complex and often require rulings by the judge. The *pro se* should enter court prepared, with witnesses, questions about what each witness is to be asked during direct and cross-examination, papers, and photographs. Originals are preferred, but true copies are sometimes allowed.

If the *pro se* testifies, he or she should not ask questions but should give a narrative, while stopping and waiting for the judge's ruling if the other side objects. If an objection is forthcoming, the *pro se* may wish to argue the objection. The *pro se* should stand when the judge enters, leaves, speaks to, or answers the *pro se* but should remain seated when on the witness stand. The *pro se* stays at the council table to conduct direct and cross-examinations. The bailiff transports any papers or exhibits that need transporting. A good *pro se* is polite. There are a number of preliminaries to a trial. The *pro se* should be prepared for them.

—*Dwight Jensen*

See also Attorney types; Attorneys, court-appointed; Competency; Defendants; Defense attorneys; Pleas; Trials.

DEFENDANTS

Persons against whom criminal charges are filed or persons, businesses, or government agencies against which civil lawsuits are initiated

The defendant is a person or other legal entity, such as a business or government agency, facing legal action in either a criminal or civil case. A person suspected of violating criminal laws becomes a defendant when the prosecutor officially files charges. At that moment the legal process begins to move forward to determine whether the person is guilty and, if guilty, what punishment will be imposed. In a civil cases, persons, businesses, or government agencies become defendants when someone files a lawsuit against them. The lawsuit is filed by an individual or organization that believes it has been injured by the defendant in a manner remediable under the law. Civil lawsuits may concern disputes about property ownership, personal injuries, contracts, and a broad range of other noncriminal matters.

There are important differences between defendants in criminal and civil cases. Criminal defendants are entitled to specific constitutional rights, such as the right to be represented by an attorney and to have a free attorney provided if they cannot afford to pay for one. By contrast, defendants in civil cases have no constitutional right to representation, even if they are poor. Civil defendants must hire their own attorneys. Criminal defendants enjoy a privilege against compelled self-incrimination so that they cannot be forced to provide testimony against themselves. Civil defendants have no such protection and can be summoned to provide testimony under questioning by opposing attorneys. Criminal defendants are protected by the presumption of innocence and prosecutors must prove their guilt beyond a reasonable doubt in order to gain a conviction. Civil defendants can be found liable if the opposing party establishes their legal liability by a mere preponderance of the evidence.

People who are defendants bear a heavy burden financially and psychologically. Even if a criminal charge or lawsuit has no legitimate basis, the defendant must mount a vigorous defense. Unless a person is an indigent criminal defendant, significant expenses are incurred in paying for attorneys and other court costs. If the defendant prevails by gaining acquittal or a successful civil verdict, there is no reimbursement of expenses simply because erroneous criminal charges or civil law complaints were filed.

Psychologically, the risk of an unfavorable outcome hangs over the heads of defendants. The legal process is imperfect. Mistakes are sometimes made. Thus, even defendants who feel very confident that they are not guilty or civilly liable cannot necessarily trust that the court will decide in their favor. The risk of a criminal conviction or substantial financial liability becomes an understandable preoccupation for defendants and thereby detracts from the quality of their lives and interactions with friends and family. Even defendants who mount a successful defense are likely to feel punished by the long and expensive process of defending themselves against legal charges.

—*Christopher E. Smith*

See also Acquittal; Attorneys, court-appointed; Bail system; Confessions; Convictions; Defendant self-representation; Effective counsel; Indigent criminal defendants; *Nolo contendere* pleas; Plea bargaining; Pleas; Presumption of innocence; Public defenders; Suspects.

DEFENSE ATTORNEYS

Private attorneys who are engaged to represent criminal defendants and are paid by the clients

Private defense attorneys engage in the representation of persons charged with crimes in local, state, federal, or tribal courts. Unlike public defenders, private defense attorneys are engaged and paid by their clients, rather than by the state.

Criminal defense lawyers must be members of the bar in good standing in the jurisdiction in which they practice. A law student wishing to become a criminal defense lawyer will usually take (in addition to the courses in criminal law generally required in law school) specialized courses preparing them for criminal trial work, including advanced criminal law, trial practice, criminal procedure, and negotiation. Many defense lawyers begin their career as prosecutors in the local district attorney's office and go into private practice after receiving some criminal trial experience.

The defense lawyer's task is to represent the client zealously, regardless of any personal feelings about the defendant or the crime. If the client has not yet been charged, the defense attorney's job is to advise the client on communicating with the grand jury, to accompany the client to meetings with police and prosecutors, and to advise the client as to evidence. Once the client is arrested, the defense attorney will represent the client at bail hearings and arraignment. The defense attorney will often try to "build a Chinese wall" around the client, denying the police and prosecution access to the client and regulating the prosecution's access to evidence to the extent possible. The defense attorney is entitled to any information the prosecution has on the crime and defendant prior to trial, and the defense attorney will often use a private investigator to evaluate this information and discover new information. At trial, the criminal defense lawyer will seek to exclude damaging evidence, or at least minimize its impact, and will present evidence to introduce a "reasonable doubt" in the jury's mind as to guilt. If a defendant is convicted, a criminal defense attorney may participate in filing an appeal, but a different attorney will usually represent the defendant on appeal.

While criminal defense lawyers often take cases to trial, they also spend considerable time negotiating plea bargains for their clients. A plea bargain is an agreement between the prosecutor's office and the defendant for the latter to plead guilty to a particular charge in exchange for a predetermined sentence. A defense lawyer must be prepared to offer a plea bargain to a prosecutor, evaluate any offer of a plea bargain by the prosecuting attorney, make sure that the client understands any offer, and help the client decide either to take the offer or to go to trial. It is, however, ultimately the client's responsibility (not the lawyer's) to decide whether to make or accept a plea bargain offer.

See also Arraignment; Attorney-client relationship; Attorney types; Attorneys, court-appointed; Death row attorneys; Defendant self-representation; Defendants; Indigent criminal defendants; Plea bargaining; Public defenders.

DEPOSITIONS

Oral testimony of witnesses made under oath prior to trials

Prior to the latter half of the twentieth century trials were often a matter of ambush, in which one party did not know what witnesses might be called by an opposing party and what these witnesses might say. Courts and lawyers ultimately concluded that trial by ambush did not always serve the best interests of justice. Accordingly, both federal and state courts eventually adopted procedures calculated to let opposing parties discover in advance of trial what evidence each side was likely to present. These procedures are collectively referred to as pretrial discovery. A crucial component of these procedures is the deposition.

A deposition is an opportunity for a party—or a party's attorney—to ask questions of another party or witness prior to trial to discover what the party or witness might say in court. The person who testifies at a deposition—called the deposition witness—does so under oath, although a judge rarely presides over the procedure. Instead, a court reporter swears the witness in and records both the questions posed to the witness and the witness's answers. The record of the deposition is called a deposition transcript. Normally an attorney for one of the parties asks the questions at the deposition, although parties who represent themselves without an attorney might also ask questions. The process

of asking questions of a deposition witness is referred to colloquially as "taking a deposition."

It costs money to take a deposition. All the attorneys present at
a deposition earn some sort of fee for their presence. In addition,
the court reporter charges a fee, which is normally based on the
number of transcript pages. The party taking the deposition normally pays this fee. In minor cases or when minor witnesses are
deposed, the deposition might last less than an hour and cost only
a few hundred dollars. In major cases, depositions may last for
days or even weeks and cost tens of thousands of dollars.

At depositions, parties discover what witnesses will say if they
are later called to testify at a trial. This helps parties prepare for
trial. More important, however, it helps parties decide what kind
of settlement is appropriate in a case. Most lawsuits never reach
the trial stage. The parties agree to settle their dispute in advance
of trial in more than 90 percent of all cases. In deciding how much
to settle for and under what conditions, parties rely heavily on the
facts discovered during pretrial discovery, especially during depositions. Depositions allow parties to evaluate the strengths and
weaknesses of the witnesses and to gauge their settlement strategies accordingly. In cases that do not settle, attorneys use deposition transcripts during trial to attack the credibility of witnesses
who say one thing at a deposition and another at trial.

—*Timothy L. Hall*

See also Affidavits; Court reporters; Discovery; Lawsuits; Witnesses.

DETECTIVES, POLICE

Sworn police officers with specific, highly specialized investiga-
tive duties who are normally assigned to units specializing in
criminal investigations

The origin of the concept of police detective is generally considered to be tied to Henry Fielding and his Bow Street Runners in
England in 1750. The concept spread throughout Europe and
eventually to the United States. By 1789, the United States govern-

ment had established a special investigative unit known as the Revenue Cutters to thwart smuggling. By the mid 1850's, the concept of assigning specialized investigative (detective) units to municipal police departments was growing in popularity. In most medium and large police departments, investigating the more serious crimes is normally a joint responsibility between officers assigned to patrol activities and those assigned to a detective (or investigations) division. Patrol officers normally handle the preliminary phase of any investigation, and the detectives (investigators) handle the more detailed follow-up phase of the investigative process. Essential qualities of the police detective include objectivity, a thorough knowledge of the criminal justice system and the fundamental laws upon which it is based, the proper method of case preparation, a high degree of self-discipline, and expert knowledge of legally acceptable methods of collecting and preserving evidence.

See also Arrest; Evidence, rules of; Federal Bureau of Investigation; Informants; Law enforcement; Police; Suspects.

DIPLOMATIC IMMUNITY

Special legal protection provided to diplomatic officers against local prosecution

Embassy personnel, who represent their governments in foreign countries, generally abide by local laws. However, when relations between countries become difficult, a host country might charge diplomatic personnel with crimes. Accordingly, the custom in international law is that diplomats abroad are immune from arrest and prosecution for civil and criminal violations of local laws, whether for public or private acts.

Diplomatic immunity is enjoyed by all embassy personnel, including clerical and administrative staff and even such service personnel as chauffeurs, cooks, guards, and maids.

If a foreign embassy employee is charged with a crime or even subpoenaed, the affected government can file a diplomatic pro-

Persona Non Grata

Literally, this means a person who is unacceptable. In diplomatic parlance a public official of one country who is unwelcome in another country is *persona non grata*. When a country labels someone *persona non grata*, that person must leave the country as soon as possible, as all diplomatic privileges have been revoked.

test with the host government. If the host government ignores the protest, a lawyer can defend the diplomat using ample international legal precedent.

Diplomatic immunity is not a license to disobey the law. To deal with flagrant violations of local law, the host country may either ask the foreign country to waive the accused person's diplomatic immunity, a request that is frequently granted, or declare the accused person *persona non grata*, so that the accused may be expelled from the host country.

—*Michael Haas*

See also Arrest; Civil law; Immigration, legal and illegal; Immunity from prosecution; Legal immunity.

DIRECTED VERDICTS

Verdicts entered into by trial judges when the parties with the burden of proof fail to meet their burden

In civil actions a directed verdict or, as in federal practice, judgment as a matter of law may be granted either on the court's own initiative or on the motion of a party. When the party with the burden of proof fails to meet that burden, the trial judge may order the entry of a verdict against that party without allowing the jury to consider the evidence. Upon the entry of a motion for a directed verdict, all reasonable doubts and inferences should be resolved in favor of the party against whom the verdict is asked to be directed. The court must assume as true those facts that the jury may properly find under the evidence.

A party who moves for a directed verdict at the close of the evidence offered by an opponent still has the right after denial of the motion to offer evidence as if the motion had not been made. A motion for a directed verdict that is not granted does not waive a defendant's right to trial by jury even though all parties to the action have moved for directed verdicts. If the motion is denied and the jury eventually enters a judgment that is unfavorable to the moving party, that party may move, depending on the jurisdiction, within five to thirty days for judgment notwithstanding the verdict or, in federal practice, within ten days after the entry of a judgment. Judgment notwithstanding the verdict is a judgment rendered in favor of one party notwithstanding the finding of a verdict in favor of the other party.

In the event of a state criminal trial, essentially all jurisdictions have abolished motions for a directed verdict and instead use motions for a judgment of acquittal or a finding of not guilty. A court, upon the motion of a defendant or its own motion, can order the entry of a judgment of acquittal if the state's evidence is insufficient to sustain a conviction. The court may reserve decision on a motion for judgment of acquittal, proceed with the trial, submit the case to the jury, and decide the motion either before the jury returns a verdict, after it returns a verdict of guilty, or after it is discharged without returning a verdict.

A motion for a judgment of acquittal can be made even after the jury has returned a conviction against the defendant and been discharged. Depending on the jurisdiction, such a motion must be entered within five to thirty days after the jury returned the conviction. The handling of directed verdicts and judgments of acquittal are essentially the same in federal criminal cases as in state criminal trials, but in federal cases a motion for judgment of acquittal made after the return of a conviction must be entered within seven days.

—*Dana P. McDermott*

See also Acquittal; Burden of proof; Civil actions; Convictions; Juries; Jurisdiction; Jury nullification; Reasonable doubt; Verdicts.

DISCOVERY

Process in civil lawsuits and some criminal prosecutions that allows each side to question witnesses, obtain documents and gather information from the other side to help discover facts and prepare for trial

Under modern rules of practice in state and federal courts, discovery allows the parties in civil (and some criminal) cases to require their opponents to provide information relating to the dispute. The theory behind discovery is that it is beneficial to all concerned in legal disputes if each side knows all of the relevant facts rather than being surprised at trial. The old days of clever gamesmanship have given way to an open exchange of information.

Depositions and Interrogatories

Two well-established discovery devices used to elicit information from the opposing side are depositions and written interrogatories. A deposition is a legal proceeding held outside court, usually in an attorney's office or conference room, at which a witness is asked questions under oath. The attorney's questions, the witnesses answers, and anything else said on the record are taken down by a stenographer and typed up in a booklet that the witness has an opportunity to read, correct, and sign. However, if the transcript is corrected, the opposing party may later comment on the correction at a hearing or trial, suggesting that a witness has deliberately changed his or her testimony. Increasingly, depositions have been videotaped, so that a jury may later observe the demeanor of the witness, which can be far more illuminating than the dry words on a page.

During the course of a deposition the attorney representing the witness may object to particular questions. However, since no judge is present at a deposition, the objections are made for the record and are later ruled upon if the testimony is offered in evidence. Generally, unless the objection asserts a privilege, such as attorney-client privilege or the right to privacy, the witness answers the question, which may or may not be admissible depending on the subsequent ruling of the court. Depositions are used to get information and also to pin witnesses down so that they cannot change their stories later. Even though depositions take place out of court and in an informal setting, witnesses take the same oath as in a court of law and must tell the truth, the whole truth, and nothing but the truth.

Transcripts of depositions are generally used in three ways. Excerpts can be quoted in legal motions prior to trial. For example, if a party makes a crucial admission at a deposition, the other side may move to dismiss the case, citing the transcript of the deposition and arguing that no trial is necessary given the fatal admission. The second way a deposition transcript is used is for "impeachment" at trial. If a witness's testimony at trial differs from that at a deposition, the opposing attorney can present the transcript to "impeach" the witness by demonstrating the discrepancy between the old and the new testimony. Finally, entire portions of a deposition may be read to the jury, especially when a witness is dead or unavailable.

Both sides in a civil case may serve written questions, known as "interrogatories," on the other side. The side receiving the interrogatories must generally respond to them in writing within thirty days. The response can either be an answer or an objection stating that the interrogatories are "irrelevant," "overly burdensome," or "privileged." It is the duty of the responding party to provide a full and complete answer containing all of the information known to that party and any of his or her agents, such as employees, accountants, or attorneys.

Some states have adopted form interrogatories, which are not subject to objections and are available on printed forms or computer discs. In addition, lawyers may draft special interrogatories that are tailored to the specific issues in a case. Some states have limited the number of special interrogatories in order to prevent abuse, but even then additional special interrogatories may be asked if the attorney serves a sworn statement explaining the need for additional questions. Interrogatories are used in much the same way as depositions. Carefully drafted interrogatories can be a very efficient way to gather information without the expense of a stenographer.

Document Requests and Requests for Admissions

Two other methods of pretrial discovery are document requests and requests for admissions. Both sides in a civil case may obtain copies of specific documents in the possession of the other party. In some states a party must file a motion with the court seeking permission to obtain documents upon a showing of good cause. In most states and in all federal courts documents may be obtained without prior court approval merely by serving a written request to which the other party must usually respond within thirty days. In some states, the production of documents must be preceded by a written response from the party that has been asked to supply them. This written response indicates any objections and whether any documents will be produced. As with interrogatories, document requests can be a very cost-effective means of preparing a case by permitting the parties to a case to examine key documents, such as letters, reports, invoices, computerized data, photographs, test results, and internal memos. Many cases have been won by parties that have carefully followed the paper trail.

Both sides in a civil case may serve a written request for admissions on the other side. These requests serve two primary purposes. First, a party may ask the other side to admit the genuineness of a particular document so that it can be admitted into evidence without any further testimony regarding its authenticity. Second, a party may ask the other side to admit a particular fact so that at trial or in a legal motion no further evidence need be presented to establish that fact. For example, a female employee suing for sexual discrimination may ask her employer to admit that for the last five years no woman has been hired in a particular job category. If the employer admits this, that fact can be presented at trial without the plaintiff's having to present voluminous personnel records covering all of the employees over the past five years. If a party denies a particular fact, the other party may later seek an award of attorneys fees for the time and expense of having to prove that fact at trial. By use of a carefully drafted set of request for admissions, a party can significantly streamline the evidence necessary to prove the case and may be able to shift a considerable portion of the legal expenses to the other side.

If a party fails to fully and adequately respond to any form of discovery, the moving party may file a motion with the court seeking a court order requiring further responses. If either the failure to provide discovery or the motion to compel is filed without substantial justification, the prevailing party may seek an award of reasonable attorneys fees and costs. Used properly and in good faith, discovery can make litigation more efficient and aid in arriving at the truth.

—*Stephen F. Rohde*

Suggested Readings

Three works that deal with pretrial discovery are Guozhang Huang's *Introducing Discovery into Civil Law* (Durham, N.C.: Carolina Academic Press, 2003), James E. Hogan and Gregory S. Weber's *California Civil Discovery* (San Francisco: Bancroft-Whitney, 1972, 1997) and Edith C. Schaffer's *Discovery* in Bancroft-Whitney's series *California Civil Practice* (San Francisco: Bancroft Whitney, 1992). Treatments of judicial procedural matters that discuss witnesses include Paul Bergman and Sara J. Berman-Barnett's *Represent Yourself in Court: How to Prepare and Try a Winning Case* (2d ed. Berkeley Calif.: Nolo Press, 1998) and Paul Bergman's *Trial Advocacy in a Nutshell* (3d ed. St. Paul, Minn. West Publishing, 1995). *Bender's Forms of Discovery* (New York: Matthew-Bender; regularly updated) is a ten-volume treatise with sample questions for numerous kinds of cases, including product liability, employment discrimination, slip-and-fall, automobile accident, and breach of contract cases. This and similar lawyer "practice guides" are often available in the reference sections of public libraries. Ann E. Woodley's *Litigating in Federal Court: A Guide to the Rules* (Durham, N.C.: Carolina Academic Press, 1999) has a chapter that focuses on discovery.

See also Adversary system; Burden of proof; Chain of custody; Civil actions; Depositions; Evidence, rules of; Lawsuits; Preliminary hearings; Subpoena power.

DISMISSAL

Termination of a legal case by a court before a formal verdict has been reached; dismissed cases may or may not be allowed to be tried again, depending on the reasons for termination

Dismissal occurs when a court disposes of a case before trial begins or before it has been completed. Dismissal may exist with prejudice or without prejudice.

Dismissal with prejudice prevents the same civil suit or the same criminal charge from being brought against the defendant in the future. It is generally limited to situations in which the

---

REASONS FOR DISMISSAL OF A CASE

In civil cases:
- The plaintiff causes unnecessary delays
- The plaintiff fails to comply with court orders to produce evidence
- The plaintiff wishes to withdraw the suit
- The plaintiff and the defendant reach an agreement

In criminal cases:
- The government causes unnecessary delays
- The government has insufficient evidence to support the charges
- The government wishes to withdraw the charges

---

party bringing the suit, known as the plaintiff, or the government entity bringing the charges has caused unnecessary delays or clearly lacks evidence for its case.

Dismissal without prejudice allows the same case to be tried in the future. It generally occurs at the request of the plaintiff or the government when unavoidable circumstances, such as the sudden unavailability of witnesses, make it necessary to delay the case for an unspecified amount of time. It may also occur when the plaintiff and the defendant agree on a settlement without a trial.

—Rose Secrest

See also Acquittal; Cause of action; Civil actions; Double jeopardy; Speedy trial requirement; Summary judgments; Trials; Verdicts.

DISTRICT ATTORNEYS

Government officials who institute criminal proceedings on behalf of local jurisdictions and are responsible for for the conduct of criminal prosecutions

Unlike much of American law, which originated in England (where private prosecution was the rule), the idea of the public district attorney originated in Dutch-speaking areas of the American colonies. The tradition of private prosecution of criminals continued, however, until the mid-nineteenth century.

The terms "state's attorney" and "district attorney" are often used interchangeably, but there is a difference. A district attorney may be an officer of a municipality, a district, or a state. A state's attorney represents only a state. Both "state's attorney" and "district attorney," however, are synonymous with "prosecuting attorney."

A district attorney for a particular federal district is known as a United States attorney. Special prosecutors, or United States attorneys, may be appointed to investigate possible criminal activities of the executive branch of the federal government.

A district attorney is elected or appointed as the legal representative of a particular area with the primary responsibility of instituting proceedings against the violators of laws. The district attorney must be an attorney, usually with a specified minimum number of years in practice. The legislative body of the particular district may prescribe certain other requirements for the office, such as place of residence and minimum age.

The jurisdiction that the district attorney represents may provide assistant district attorneys to assist in the conduct of cases. Many new lawyers gain valuable litigation experience by serving as assistant district attorneys. In addition, the courts may appoint extra prosecuting attorneys, as needed, to help in times of particularly heavy caseloads.

Duties of the District Attorney

Once a person is indicted by a grand jury, the district attorney is responsible for seeing that due diligence—complete attention to the matter at hand, investigation, and prosecution—is exercised. This includes the study of evidence provided by an inquest, evidence gathered by the police in their investigation of a crime, and statements made by witnesses and others.

A district attorney bases the decision on whether to prosecute a crime on a number of criteria. There must be enough evidence to overcome the higher burden of proof which exists in criminal, as opposed to civil, proceedings. The accused comes into court innocent; the prosecution must prove clear and convincing guilt. Because a decision to prosecute is subjective, one defendant may be dismissed while another indicted for the same crime is tried. The decision is made based on the chances of securing a conviction. While a defendant may feel singled out for prosecution, if there exists a genuine basis for the prosecution, due process has been observed.

If the district attorney believes that a case may not be strong enough to ensure conviction, the prosecution may offer the defendant a plea bargain. A plea bargain guarantees conviction on at least a lesser charge and avoids the risk that the accused would be acquitted by a jury. A plea bargain also avoids the expense of time, money, and manpower on a case that may be difficult to win, and it secures a certain conviction.

Responsibility and Liability

The district attorney bears responsibility for how a particular prosecution is conducted, even though the actual courtroom work may be done by assistants. Because of heavy caseloads and administrative duties, a district attorney may personally conduct only a few trials—often those that are "high profile." The district attorney may not attempt to control a grand jury by announcing ahead of time which crimes will or will not be prosecuted, nor can any criminal charges pending before a grand jury be dismissed.

In general, district attorneys cannot be held liable for damages when they are acting within the scope of official duties, but they may be liable for statutory misconduct, official misconduct, neglect of duty, or exceeding the official scope of their duties. District attorneys may be removed by impeachment for official misconduct, failure to disclose evidence that might be favorable to the accused, or failure to observe due process (see *Brady v. Maryland*, 1963).

—*Elizabeth Algren Shaw*

Suggested Readings

For a good overview of the office of district attorney, consult a legal encyclopedia such as *The Guide to American Law* (St. Paul, Minn.: West Publishing, 1983-1985), or a basic dictionary such as Henry Campbell Black, *Black's Law Dictionary* (rev. 4th ed. St. Paul, Minn.: West Publishing, 1968). Also valuable are general legal guides such as Melvin M. Belli, Sr., and Allen P. Wilkinson, *Everybody's Guide to the Law* (San Diego, Calif.: Harcourt Brace Jovanovich, 1986), and Lewis Mayers, *The American Legal System* (New York: Harper & Row, 1964). Michael Parrish's *For the People: Inside the Los Angeles District Attorney's Office, 1850-2000* (Santa Monica, Calif.: Angel City Press, 2001) in an inside look at the operations of a district attorney's office in the second largest city in the United States. *The Prosecutors: A Year in the Life of a District At-*

torney's Office, by Gary Delsohn (New York: E. P. Dutton, 2003), is a journalistic account of the work of the assistant district attorneys of Sacramento, California.

See also Attorney types; Attorneys, United States; Attorneys general, state; Grand juries; Legislative counsel; Prosecutors.

DIVERSITY JURISDICTION

Authority of the federal courts to resolve disputes between citizens of different states or between citizens and aliens when the total amount of damages in controversy exceeds seventy-five thousand dollars

Article III, section 2, of the U.S. Constitution grants authority to the federal courts to resolve disputes among citizens of different states. In the Judiciary Act of 1789, Congress provided that the federal courts had jurisdiction over cases between citizens of different states or between a citizen and an alien. Although the Constitution imposes no requirement as to a minimum amount of damages that must be involved in order to invoke diversity jurisdiction, Congress imposed a requirement that the amount in controversy, exclusive of interest and costs, must exceed a stated sum of damages. The requisite amount has increased over time and was set at seventy-five thousand dollars in the 1990's.

All cases brought under diversity jurisdiction can also be brought in a state court in which one of the litigants is situated. However, the framers of the Constitution created diversity jurisdiction out of a concern that state courts would be prejudiced against litigants from out of state. They believed that federal courts would serve as neutral forums in which citizens of one state would not be favored over those from another state. As Chief Justice John Marshall explained in *Bank of the United States v. Deveaux* (1809), "However true the fact may be, that the tribunals of the states will administer justice as impartially as those of the nation, to parties of every description, it is not less true that the Constitution itself either entertains apprehensions on this subject, or views with such indulgence the possible fears and apprehensions of suitors."

The Supreme Court has clarified the two requirements for diversity jurisdiction. The Court has strictly interpreted the requirement that the case involve citizens from different states, holding in the case of *Strawbridge v. Curtiss* (1806) that there has to be "complete diversity" so that all the plaintiffs must be citizens of different states than all the defendants. In addition, the Court has held that the citizenship of an individual is determined by the state of his or her domicile at the time the case is filed, while a corporation is considered to be a citizen of its state of incorporation and the state where it has its principal place of business. In determining the required jurisdictional amount, the Court held in *St. Paul Mercury Indemnity Co. v. Red Cab Co.* (1938) that the sum claimed by the plaintiff controls whether the requirement is met, as long as it made in good faith.

—Kurt M. Saunders

Suggested Readings

James, Fleming, Jr., Geoffrey C. Hazard, Jr., and John Leubsdorf. *Civil Procedure*. 4th ed. Boston: Little, Brown, 1992.

Woodley, Ann E. *Litigating in Federal Court: A Guide to the Rules*. Durham, N.C.: Carolina Academic Press, 1999.

Wright, Charles A. *Law of Federal Courts*. St. Paul, Minn.: West Publishing, 1994.

See also Constitution, U.S.; Court types; Federal judicial system; Jurisdiction; Multiple jurisdiction offenses; State courts.

DOUBLE JEOPARDY

Guarantee articulated in the Fifth Amendment to the U.S. Constitution protecting persons acquitted or convicted of offenses from being prosecuted a second time for the exact same offenses

The second clause of the Fifth Amendment, part of the Bill of Rights, states "nor shall any person be subject for the same offense to be twice put in jeopardy of life or limb." For the first part of the United States' existence, federal criminal cases were not appealed to the Supreme Court, so it had no federal double jeopardy cases.

Under Chief Justice William H. Rehnquist, the Supreme Court has considered a large number of difficult double jeopardy cases. (Supreme Court Historical Society)

In addition, in *Barron v. Baltimore* (1833), the Court said that the provisions of the Bill of Rights limited the power of only the federal government and were inapplicable to the states. Consequently, there were no state court double jeopardy cases for the Court to review. Not until *Benton v. Maryland* (1969) did the Court conclude that the double jeopardy clause was applicable to the states, relying on the selective incorporation doctrine of the due process clause of the Fourteenth Amendment. Since that time, so many, and sometimes contradictory, double jeopardy cases came before the Court that Chief Justice William H. Rehnquist referred to this area of the law as a Sargasso Sea—one in which even a skillful navigator could become entangled and lost.

Basic Protection

Jeopardy—the immediate threat of conviction and punishment—attaches in a criminal case when a jury is sworn in or, if there is no jury, when a judge begins to hear evidence. Whether jeopardy has attached is important because events occurring before that time, such as dismissal of the charges, will not preclude a subsequent prosecution; a dismissal of the charges after jeopardy has attached would preclude their being brought again.

A defendant who has been acquitted cannot be reprosecuted for that offense. Even with a relatively weak case, a prosecutor who could try the case multiple times might be able to perfect the presentation of witnesses and evidence so that eventually a jury would agree to convict. The Court found that such a result would be fundamentally unfair and would violate double jeopardy in *Ashe v. Swenson* (1970). After an acquittal, no matter how strong the state's evidence may have been, the defendant may not be forced to undergo the stress and expense of another prosecution for that crime, regardless of whether the verdict in the second case is a conviction or an acquittal.

Similarly, the Court ruled that a person cannot be tried again after having previously been convicted of the same offense in *Brown v. Ohio* (1977). However, in *United States v. Ball* (1896), the Court found that a necessary exception to this rule does allow the reprosecution of an individual whose conviction was reversed on appeal. There are many reasons why a conviction might be reversed, such as the improper admission of prejudicial evidence or inaccurate instructions to the jury. In these situations, after the reversal of the first conviction, the case could be retried without using the inadmissible evidence and with proper instructions to the jury, and the retrial would not be double jeopardy.

Exceptions

The doctrine protects against only successive criminal prosecutions or punishments; it does not prohibit a criminal prosecution after a civil action or a civil action after a criminal action. For example, property used in the commission of certain crimes, such as houses, cars, and other vehicles used in the manufacture and distribution of illegal drugs, is subject to forfeiture to the government. Such forfeiture actions usually are deemed to be civil rather than criminal punishments. Therefore, in *United States v. Ursery* (1996), the Court ruled that a person's having to forfeit his or her house and car to the government because they were used in a drug transaction is not the imposition of double jeopardy, al-

---

DOUBLE JEOPARDY AND CIVIL AND CRIMINAL PUNISHMENT

A fraudulent course of action may be punished by the government with criminal and civil fines. The U.S. Supreme Court in *United States v. Hudson* (1997) held that the federal government had the discretion to impose both civil fines and criminal punishment for the same conduct without violating the Fifth Amendment's prohibition against double jeopardy. The Court permitted the government to prosecute individuals for fraudulent loans who had already been civilly fined by the Office of the Comptroller of the Currency for illegal loans. The Court unanimously found no double jeopardy, because the civil fines were not functionally equivalent to punishment.

though the individual had previously been criminally convicted and sentenced for the same drug transaction.

Similarly, those who have served the entire sentence for conviction of a sexual offense, such as rape or child molestation, may subsequently be adjudicated as sexually violent predators and ordered confined and treated until it is safe for them to be released. Because the subsequent adjudication is deemed civil and not criminal, the Court, in *Kansas v. Hendricks* (1997), found there is no double jeopardy, even if such sexual offenders might end up being confined for the rest of their lives.

The dual sovereignty doctrine is another major exception to the protection against double jeopardy. The basic guarantee is that the same sovereign, or government, will not prosecute or punish an individual twice for the same offense. There is no double jeopardy violation, however, if different sovereigns prosecute an individual for the same offense. For these purposes, the federal government of the United States and the government of a given state, such as California, are deemed to be separate sovereigns.

Cities and counties derive their governmental authority from that of the state in which they are located, so that neither a city nor a county is considered a separate sovereign from the state. Consequently, prosecutions for the same offense in, for example, Chicago municipal court and Illinois state courts would violate double jeopardy. In *Heath v. Alabama* (1985), the Court ruled that because the states are separate sovereigns from one another, prosecutions for the same offense by two separate states do not violate double jeopardy. With common crimes, such as murder or rape, it would be unusual for two states to have sufficient contact with the crime to have jurisdiction to prosecute it, but many conspiracies, especially those involving illegal drugs, have sufficient contacts with several states to confer jurisdiction on more than one. Nonetheless, dual sovereignty prosecutions involving two or more states are relatively rare.

—*William Shepard McAninch*

Suggested Readings

Lafave, Wayne, and Jerold Israel. *Criminal Procedure*. St. Paul: West Publishing, 1985.

McAninch, William. "Unfolding the Law of Double Jeopardy." *South Carolina Law Review* 44 (1993): 411.

Miller, Lenord. *Double Jeopardy and the Federal System*. Chicago: University of Chicago Press, 1968.

Thomas, George C. *Double Jeopardy: The History, the Law*. New York: New York University, 1998.

See also Acquittal; Bill of Rights, U.S.; Convictions; Fifth Amendment; Jury nullification; Lesser included offense; Mistrials; Trials; Verdicts.

DUE PROCESS OF LAW

Fair and orderly treatment in both criminal and civil law; procedural due process concerns fair and established procedures, while substantive due process concerns protecting the substance of liberty and property

The Fifth and Fourteenth Amendments to the U.S. Constitution both contain due process clauses; together they forbid federal and state governments from depriving a person of "life, liberty, or property without due process of law." The U.S. Supreme Court has refused to give a single, comprehensive definition of due process; rather, the Court has relied on the case-by-case approach of deciding specific issues as they appear. State rules for due process vary considerably from one state to another.

Origins
Developing from the English common law, the concept of due process was originally limited to judicial proceedings. Chapter 29 of the Magna Carta of 1215 stipulated that the state could not punish a "free man" except by "the law of the land," and a parliamentary statute of 1354 used the term "due process of law" to mean the same thing, a usage established by the Petition of Right of 1628. American colonial documents tended to use the two terms interchangeably.

During the ratification of the American Constitution, four states urged an amendment based on chapter 29 of the Magna Carta, with New York using the term "due process of law." James Madison followed this recommendation by including the due process clause in the Fifth Amendment. Unfortunately, there were no discussions at the time to illuminate the meaning of the clause. In *Murray's Lessee v. Hoboken Land & Improvement Co.* (1856), the Supreme Court interpreted the clause to include the procedures of the Constitution as well as the settled proceedings of English law at the time the Constitution was written (as they were adapted to American conditions).

Fourteenth Amendment Incorporation

The first nine amendments originally did not apply to the states, but some of the framers of the Fourteenth Amendment argued that the new amendment, which did apply to the states, would incorporate the Bill of Rights and make them binding on the states as well as on the federal government. After the *Slaughterhouse Cases* (1873) made this impossible to do through the privileges and immunities clause, the Supreme Court gradually began to use the due process clause as the means of incorporation. During the twentieth century, most of the Bill of Rights was applied to state governments.

The first incorporation case occurred in 1897, when the Court interpreted the due process clause to require states to honor the Fifth Amendment requirement for "just compensation" in the taking of private property. Twenty-eight years later, in *Gitlow v. New York* (1925), the Court ruled that the due process clause included the free expression components of the First Amendment. After *Wolf v. Colorado* (1949), states were required to follow the Fourth Amendment prohibition against "unreasonable searches and seizures," and in *Mapp v. Ohio* (1961), the Court applied this exclusionary rule to the states.

The major incorporation issue of the Sixth Amendment was whether states had the obligation to provide a lawyer for indigent defendants. In the case of the "Scottsboro boys" (*Powell v. Alabama*, 1932), the Supreme Court announced that the concept of due process included the right to counsel when uneducated defendants in a capital case had no chance to present a meaningful defense. In the landmark case of *Gideon v. Wainwright* (1963), the Court announced the right to counsel in all felony cases, and nine years later the Court required states to provide counsel in all cases involving a jail sentence. By this time, the only unincorporated provisions of the Bill of Rights were the Second and Third Amendments, the right to indictment by a grand jury, the right to a jury trial in a civil suit, and the prohibition against excessive fines and bail.

As the Court applied most of the Bill of Rights to the states, justices disagreed about the meaning of the due process clause of the Fourteenth Amendment. Justice Hugo L. Black argued that the clause referred only to the actual provisions of the Constitution, while Justice Felix Frankfurter gave the clause the subjective meaning of fundamental fairness. The majority of the Court, however, followed Justice Benjamin Nathan Cardozo's view that the clause referred to rights in the Constitution which are fundamental and "implicit in the concept of ordered liberty."

Procedural Due Process
Many of the first eight amendments are concerned with issues of civil and criminal procedure. In addition to explicit provisions in the Constitution, there are many ways that a law may violate procedural due process. It is well established, for example, that due process means that statutes can be found invalid because of vagueness. This principle requires that laws be sufficiently clear so that people of common intelligence will not have to guess about possible meanings and that the police will not be given excessive discretion about when they can arrest and charge a person.

One of the major issues of procedural due process is the proper burden of proof for various kinds of cases. In criminal trials, the defendant enjoys the presumption of innocence, and the government must prove guilt beyond a reasonable doubt. For most civil proceedings, in contrast, the standard is the preponderance of evidence, meaning that the side with the most evidence wins. In some proceedings, due process is satisfied by the intermediate standard of "clear and convincing evidence." In different kinds of proceedings, moreover, there are different rules for procedural matters such as the use of evidence, the choice of a jury, the need for a unanimous jury, and so on.

Since the 1970's, the Supreme Court has generally ruled that the due process clauses require government agents to provide a notice and a hearing whenever a person is deprived of liberty or property. The nature of the hearing, however, depends upon circumstances and the extent of deprivation. In the case of *Goldberg v. Kelly* (1970), the Court declared that there must be a trial-type hearing before the termination of welfare benefits. In contrast, when students are suspended from the public schools for disciplinary reasons, the courts usually accept a notice combined with an informal hearing.

Substantive Due Process

The doctrine of substantive due process means that the government may not arbitrarily deprive a person of liberty or property and that all such deprivations must be justified by a satisfactory state interest. The Supreme Court in *Scott v. Sandford* (1857) first used the doctrine in ruling that the Fifth Amendment protected the property rights of slaveowners.

From 1897 to 1937, the Supreme Court interpreted the due process clause of the Fourteenth Amendment as giving substantive protection to economic liberty, especially the "freedom of contract." In cases such as *Lochner v. New York* (1905), the Court overturned numerous economic regulations, including laws for minimum wages and maximum hours. This so-called *Lochner* era continued until *West Coast Hotel v. Parrish* announced the "judicial revolution of 1937." During the *Lochner* years, the court occasionally used substantive due process to protect noneconomic liberties, as in the incorporation of the First Amendment and in *Pierce v. Society of Sisters* (1925), which defended parental rights in the choice of schools.

Although the Court after 1937 no longer used substantive due process to give special protection to economic liberties, it extended the doctrine to protect a variety of other liberty interests. Two watershed cases were *Griswold v. Connecticut* (1965), which ruled anticontraceptive laws to be unconstitutional, and *Roe v. Wade* (1973), which recognized a woman's right to choose to have an abortion. The Court has found it difficult to be consistent in cases involving substantive due process. While the Court in *Cruzan v. Director, Missouri Department of Health* (1990) recognized a constitutional right to refuse medical treatment, it refused to recognize a constitutional right to engage in homosexual practices in *Bowers v. Hardwick* (1986).

In practice, it is often difficult to separate the substantive aspects from the procedural aspects of due process of law. Both refer to a normative legal process which is not arbitrary or oppressive, a process which seeks an accommodation between individual rights and legitimate state interests.

—*Thomas T. Lewis*

Suggested Readings

Useful introductions include John V. Orth, *Due Process of Law: A Brief History* (Lawrence, Kan.: University Press of Kansas, 2003);

Edward Corwin and J. W. Peltason, *Corwin & Peltason's Understanding the Constitution* (San Diego: Harcourt Brace Jovanovich, 1991); and Joel Gora, *Due Process* (Skokie, Ill.: National Textbook, 1977). For history, see A. E. Dick Howard, *The Road from Runnymede: Magna Carta and Constitutionalism in America* (Charlottesville: University of Virginia Press, 1968). For incorporation, see Richard Cortner, *The Supreme Court and the Second Bill of Rights: The Fourteenth Amendment and the Nationalization of Civil Liberties* (Madison: University of Wisconsin Press, 1981). For issues of criminal due process, see Charles Whitebread and Christopher Slobogin, *Criminal Procedure* (3d ed. Westbury, N.Y.: Foundation Press, 1993). Substantive due process is discussed in Henry Abraham and Barbara Perry, *Freedom and the Court* (6th ed. New York: Oxford University Press, 1994), and Gerald Gunther, *Constitutional Law* (12th ed. Westbury, N.Y.: Foundation Press, 1991). For philosophical essays, see J. Roland Pennock and John Chapman, eds., *Due Process* (New York: New York University Press, 1977). More general works that explore due process include *The Lanahan Readings in Civil Rights and Civil Liberties*, edited by David M. O'Brien (Baltimore: Lanahan Publishers, 1999); Howard Ball, *The Supreme Court in the Intimate Lives of Americans: Birth, Sex, Marriage, Childbearing, and Death* (New York: New York University Press, 2002); and Joan Biskupic and Elder Witt, *The Supreme Court and Individual Rights* (Washington, D.C.: Congressional Quarterly, 1997).

See also Bill of Rights, U.S.; Burden of proof; Civil rights and liberties; Constitution, U.S.; Criminal procedure; Fifth Amendment; Long-arm statutes; Night courts; Obstruction of justice.

EFFECTIVE COUNSEL

Constitutional right of all persons charged with committing crimes to have lawyers who are qualified and competent to represent them

Everyone charged with a crime in the United States is entitled under the U.S. Constitution to have a lawyer represent them, because having a lawyer has been held essential to ensuring a fair trial. The presence of lawyers on both sides of a case improves the fairness of a trial, enabling the adversary system to function as

well as possible so that guilty persons can be identified and innocent persons set free. But because the presence of a lawyer only
improves the fairness of a trial if the lawyer is qualified and competent, the U.S. Constitution has been held to guarantee not just
the assistance of a lawyer but also the assistance of a competent
lawyer, whose loyalty to the client is undivided and whose efforts
on the client's behalf are not unduly restricted. This representation is termed "effective" assistance of counsel, and representation which does not meet this standard is described as "ineffective." If persons are convicted of a crime and their lawyers were
constitutionally ineffective, these persons may have their convictions set aside and be eligible to receive new trials.

The Constitutional Right to Effective Counsel

The American model of criminal justice is based on the adversary system. This system requires attorneys on opposing sides
who vigorously present their views of the law and the evidence.
When one side is represented by lawyers who fail to present their
parties' arguments, the adversary system may not function properly in reaching the truth. Such lawyers are said to be "ineffective," and the persons they represented are deprived of their constitutional right to effective assistance of counsel.

The guarantee of effective assistance of counsel applies only in
criminal cases, because it is only in criminal, as opposed to civil,
cases that persons have a right to be represented by lawyers. Regardless of whether criminal defendants can afford to hire (or "retain") their own lawyers or whether they cannot afford to do so and
must have lawyers appointed for them by the court, the right to be
represented has been held to be a guarantee of competent counsel.

How Counsel Can Be Ineffective

Lawyers can fail to provide effective assistance in any of three
general ways. First, they can be ineffective because of a conflict of
interest—something that prevents them from fully and zealously
representing the interests of their clients. Second, lawyers can be
ineffective if a judge restricts their ability to be effective—by preventing them from fully and zealously advocating on behalf of
their clients. Third, lawyers can be ineffective through lack of
competence to handle particular cases or types of cases.

Lawyers are ethically obligated to fully and zealously advocate
first and foremost for the interests of their clients. Sometimes law-

yers can have conflicting interests—for example, by representing more than one client in a case. If lawyers must choose between advancing the interests of one client or another, the client whose interests were not made the first priority may have received ineffective assistance of counsel. Besides making lawyers ineffective, conflicts of interest may also violate ethical rules and can be a basis for sanctions or penalties against such lawyers. Conflicts may result in lawyers' negligent performance of professional responsibilities and can be a basis for a civil action by clients against their lawyers for malpractice. Courts also have made lawyers ineffective—for example, by preventing them from making closing arguments in bench trials (nonjury trials decided by judges alone) or by appointing lawyers shortly before trial and forcing them to proceed with their defense despite inadequate preparation. These practices have been found to render lawyers' assistance in such circumstances ineffective.

Effective Counsel and Successful Counsel

Although conflicts of interest and court restrictions on lawyers' work can make lawyers' assistance ineffective, the most controversial area of ineffective assistance has dealt with incompetent or unqualified counsel. Incompetence can lead to mistakes, such as inadequate investigation of a case, failure to call certain witnesses, or inadequate presentation of evidence. Not all mistakes, however, render lawyers ineffective.

The U.S. Supreme Court has held that the Constitution guarantees defendants the right to have a lawyer who is competent but not necessarily successful. The Constitution guarantees only a fair trial, and if lawyers make trials fair—despite losing—they are considered constitutionally effective. For the purpose of establishing effectiveness, the Court has ruled that lawyers make trials fair by meeting the general level of professional performance of other lawyers. Lawyers need not do what the best lawyers or those with the most resources would do if they were handling the same case.

In the 1984 case of *Strickland v. Washington* the U.S. Supreme Court created the standard by which lawyers' effectiveness was to be measured. The Court made it harder to bring successful claims against lawyers by requiring proof of "prejudice." Prejudice is the legal term for harm resulting from lawyers' mistakes or inaction. To find a lawyer ineffective, the Court required more than proof that the lawyer's performance was worse than that of most lawyers. It further required that this poor performance "prejudiced" or harmed the defendant, specifically by making it more likely that the defendant would be convicted.

Ensuring Effective Assistance of Counsel

A challenge to lawyers' effectiveness usually comes only after cases have been concluded and only when they result in convictions. Determining whether a lawyer was competent requires another proceeding, such as another trial, at which testimony and evidence are presented about the lawyer's work on the case. In such proceedings, lawyers often become principal witnesses. These proceeding are civil rather than criminal cases, even though they concern what happened in criminal trials. They can be held in either federal or state courts if the conviction originally occurred in state court (as most convictions do) and can result in the issuance of a writ of *habeas corpus* (a writ permitting prisoners to challenge wrongful convictions) if the reviewing court finds that lawyers' assistance was ineffective. A 1995 U.S. Department of Justice study of approximately half of all petitions for writs of *habeas corpus* in federal courts found that the largest percentage of such petitions, 25 percent, involved claims for ineffective assistance of counsel. Very few claims of ineffective assistance, however, are successful.

—*David M. Siegel*

Suggested Readings

Codes establishing rules of ethics for lawyers are contained in the American Bar Association's *Model Rules of Professional Conduct and Code of Judicial Conduct* (Chicago: American Bar Association, 1992) and the *Code of Professional Responsibility and Judicial Conduct* (Chicago: American Bar Association, 1977). A statistical study of the types of petitions brought in federal court seeking writs of *habeas corpus*, including those based on claims of ineffective assistance, is the U.S. Department of Justice's *Federal Habeas Corpus Review Challenging State Court Criminal Convictions*, by Roger A. Hanson and Henry W. K. Daley (Washington, D.C.: Bureau of Justice Statistics, September, 1995). Ethical issues relating to the attorney-client relationships are examined in *Ethical Standards in the Public Sector: A Guide for Government Lawyers, Clients, and Public Officials*, edited by Patricia E. Salkin (Chicago: Section of State and Local Government Law, American Bar Association, 1999).

See also Adversary system; Attorney-client relationship; Attorneys, court-appointed; Civil rights and liberties; Competency; Constitution, U.S.; Defendant self-representation; Defendants; Defense attorneys; *Habeas corpus*; Model Rules of Professional Conduct; Unethical conduct of attorneys.

EIGHTH AMENDMENT

Amendment to the U.S. Constitution that forbids requiring excessive bail, imposing excessive fines, and inflicting cruel and unusual punishments

The Eighth Amendment is derived almost verbatim from the English Bill of Rights (1689). Adopted in 1791 as part of the U.S. Bill of Rights, the amendment was intended to prohibit the abuse of federal government power, but the precise meaning of the amendment is unclear and requires interpretation by the Supreme Court.

The first two clauses of the Eighth Amendment (prohibiting excessive bail and fines) have not been applied to the states. Although the Court has never established an absolute right to bail, it has reviewed whether bail has been set higher than necessary to ensure that a defendant appears for trial.

The Court has taken a flexible interpretation of the cruel and unusual punishment clause, stating in *Trop v. Dulles* (1958) that punishments should be evaluated in light of the "evolving standards of decency" of a maturing society. The clause was formally applied to the states in *Robinson v. California* (1962). Barbaric punishments are prohibited, but the Court has refused to hold that the death penalty itself is cruel and unusual punishment. Punishments disproportionate to the crime, the treatment of prisoners, and conditions of confinement, may also violate the Eighth Amendment.

—*John Fliter*

See also Bail system; Bill of Rights, U.S.; Bills of attainder; Capital punishment; Cruel and unusual punishment.

Equal protection of the law

Principle established by the Fourteenth Amendment to the U.S. Constitution that guarantees equal protection under the law to all residents of the United States

The right to equal protection of the law is one of the constitutional rights that was established with the passage of the Fourteenth Amendment in 1868. Declaring all persons born in the United States to be U.S. citizens, the Fourteenth Amendment made it illegal for states to "deprive any person of life, liberty, or property, without due process of law" (the due process clause) and for a state to "deny to any person within its jurisdiction the equal protection of the laws" (the equal protection clause).

The basic idea of the equal protection clause is that the law should not treat one person differently from another on the basis of an irrelevant consideration pertaining to their membership in a particular group. While race, ethnic identity, gender, national origin, religious affiliation, and other characteristics often form the basis for classifying people into groups, these classifications, when written into the law, often lead to reinforcing the power of the majority at the expense of the civil rights of the minority. Thus, the equal protection clause suggests that in order for state law to be just in providing equal protection to all its residents, a state should not use such classifications in its laws unless their legal relevancy can clearly be shown.

The major effect of the equal protection clause has been to improve the situation of racial minorities and women in the United States. In the second half of the twentieth century the clause has been used to overturn a number of laws based on racial or gender classifications. For example, in one of the first and most famous U.S. Supreme Court decisions relying on the equal protection clause, *Brown v. Board of Education* (1954), the Court ruled that segregation in public education was a violation of the U.S. Constitution. In this context, the Court argued, there was no legally relevant point to classifying students according to their race. By applying the equal protection clause, the Court showed that segregation was, in effect, state-backed discrimination against a racial minority. Segregation created a situation of inequality by depriving African American students of their right to educa-

Supporters of the Equal Rights Amendment—a failed attempt to give men and women full legal equality—march in Washington, D.C., in 1977 to celebrate the fifty-seventh anniversary of women's suffrage. (Library of Congress)

tional opportunities on a par with those available to white students.

One of the standards used by the courts to determine if a particular classification has a legally relevant purpose is called the standard of "strict scrutiny." If a state law depends on the "inherently suspect" categories of race, nationality, or alienage, the state must show, should the law be tested in court, that it has a "compelling interest" in using the suspect classification. If a law depends on the category of gender or other categories that are not inherently suspect, the state must show that it has a "rational basis" in using the classification. In both cases, the burden falls on the states to prove that the law is consistent with the equal protection clause of the Fourteenth Amendment.

—*Diane P. Michelfelder*

See also Bill of Rights, U.S.; Capital punishment; Civil rights and liberties; Constitution, U.S.; Criminal procedure; Due process of law; Speedy trial requirement.

EQUITABLE REMEDIES

Remedies granted by courts using their equity jurisdiction as opposed to their legal jurisdiction; courts can expand the usual remedies available to compensate for wrongs; equity courts can fashion such remedies as they see fit in the name of substantial justice

Equitable remedies are those remedies originally granted by an equity court, as distinguished from a court of law. In the English common-law tradition, a court of law could give a plaintiff money, land, or some other property if the plaintiff won a lawsuit. These remedies were often inadequate, however, and did not give people substantial justice. As a result, the courts of equity were developed to expand the relief available. The number of equitable remedies expanded over time; the more traditional ones include injunction, specific performance, reformation, contribution, and estoppel.

An injunction is a legal writ issued by a court of equity directing someone to do or refrain from doing an act that threatens injury to someone else. It is issued only if the legal remedy is inadequate to prevent or pay for the damage threatened. Because injunctions limit the freedom of the person enjoined and often themselves cause damage or inconvenience, a court will grant an injunction only if the harm threatened outweighs the harm that may be caused by the injunction.

Specific performance is an order directed to parties to a contract, compelling them to perform their obligations under the contract. It is most often granted when the subject matter of the contract involves unique goods or land. In such cases, money damages are not sufficient to compensate the injured party; for example, the money cannot be used to purchase an identical item when there is no identical item.

Reformation is an equitable remedy granted when a written instrument does not express the real agreement of the parties. A court will reform or rewrite the instrument to protect an innocent party. Deeds, contracts, and other instruments will be reformed where there has been fraud, error, mistake, or inadvertence. Normally, however, reformation will not be granted if a person had the opportunity to read a contract but failed to do so.

Contribution is the sharing of loss among several people. Two or more people may be liable on the same contract or may have committed a tort together. If one of these people has paid the whole debt or suffered the entire liability, the other parties must reimburse him or her for a proportionate share.

Estoppel is used in contract and similar contexts to prevent a person from denying certain facts. For example, one person may promise something to another. Though there is no legally enforceable contract to verify the promise, the second person may take action based on the promise. If the first person reneges on the promise, insisting that there was no contract, and the second person is harmed as a result, the first person can be estopped on the basis of equity.

Trust law has given rise to many equity issues. A constructive trust is imposed by a court when a person is wrongfully in possession of property belonging to someone else. The person in possession is said to hold the property in trust for the true owner.

See also Civil law; Consent decree; Contracts; Injunctions.

EVIDENCE, RULES OF

Rules governing the facts presented to support legal positions or allegations; these rules establish the weight to be given to facts in court cases and provide reasons for excluding certain from presentation

Evidence to support a position is an important part of the legal system. Originally, the rules governing evidence were not codified but grew out of the common laws of a jurisdiction and traditions regarding what evidence was acceptable to assure reliability. This loose set of rules and traditions was refined through the years and found acceptance in most courts, but it became increasingly obvious that some codification was necessary.

In 1975, the U.S. Supreme Court adopted the Federal Rules of Evidence under a special authorization of Congress. The rules became effective July 1, 1975, and shortly thereafter, basic precepts similar to the federal rules were adopted in all states. Although the federal rules focus on what may be excluded as evidence, these exclusions indicate what may be included as well. The rules provide a framework for a routine and orderly presentation of evidence so that the truth may emerge.

Evidence must be something that tends to prove or disprove an allegation. Evidence is judged on its admissibility, its addition to the burden of proof, its relevancy and weight, and its sufficiency of facts. These principles determine what may be offered as proof and how much credibility it has. Admissible evidence in a criminal matter may include eyewitness testimony, documents, or properly identified weapons.

In accordance with the "exclusionary rule," a judge may exclude certain evidence if it is believed to have been gathered in violation of statutes. The question of whether constitutional rights were violated in the gathering of evidence is raised on appeal only, and the appellate court may order a new trial to be held without the questionable evidence. Two Supreme Court cases were particularly important in establishing the exclusionary rule: *Weeks v. United States* (1914) applied to federal trials, and *Mapp v. Ohio* (1961) to state trials.

If no objection is made to the admissibility of evidence, then all later claims to its inadmissibility are waived. Objections to evidence should be specific; blanket objections, such as incompetence or irrelevance, are considered outdated.

Admissible Evidence

To be admissible and of worth to the matter in court, evidence must have probative value, tending to prove some point in the case. It must be relevant, bolstering the probative value.

In most instances, evidence may not be hearsay, facts that are not directly stated but are reported by a third party. In such cases the original speaker is not available for cross-examination, which is deemed a serious disadvantage to the party trying to refute the hearsay evidence. There are exceptions. Hearsay evidence may be admissible if it is an out-of-court statement made by a litigant, if it consists of business records kept in the normal course of business and the custodian of the records testifies to their authenticity, or if the hearsay can be termed *res gestae*, words closely connected to an occurrence or spoken in the excitement of the moment. In the latter case, the assumption is that the spontaneity of a comment testifies to its truthfulness.

TYPES OF EVIDENCE NORMALLY CONSIDERED INADMISSIBLE IN COURT

- Hearsay evidence—that is, an out-of-court statement offered to prove the truth of the matter asserted in the statement
- Lay opinions concerning matters of which witnesses have no first-hand knowledge
- Privileged communications such as those between a husband and wife or between an attorney and a client
- Irrelevant evidence
- Evidence more likely to inflame the jury's prejudices than to establish a relevant issue
- Testimony describing a document when the document itself could be admitted as evidence
- Evidence that a criminal defendant has committed prior crimes as a way of proving the commission of a crime in the present case
- Evidence illegally obtained by the police
- Oral testimony introduced to contradict the terms of a written agreement
- Involuntary confessions

Excluded from evidence are conversations that are termed "privileged." These include conversations between attorney and client, doctor and patient, member of the clergy and congregant, and husband and wife.

Witnesses are also evidence and may be of two types. The nonexpert or factual witness testifies only to what is personally known. The expert witness has special knowledge that may lead to a clearer understanding of the facts.

The "best evidence" rule calls for the most reliable available proof of the fact. A contract that proves the facts presented by one of the litigants is best evidence, the highest degree of proof available. Direct evidence is proof without the need for other facts leading to it.

Rules for Use of Evidence

The amount of evidence needed depends on the legal standard of proof (the degree of persuasiveness needed) and the burden of proof (the responsibility to establish the existence of a fact) that have been established for a particular matter.

The court itself helps in the presentation of evidence by allowing certain shortcuts, notably inference presumption, and judicial notice. Inference is a logical and reasonable conclusion from the facts presented: From a piece of foreign matter in a canned product, for example, one may infer carelessness in the canning process. Presumption is a conclusion directed by law: A person may be presumed dead, for example, if not heard from in seven years. Judicial notice is the act of the court recognizing a fact without its being put in evidence: Expert testimony is not needed to prove that the earth is round.

Under certain circumstances the court may accept a motion to strike evidence already presented and accepted. The evidence may have been proper when received but was later shown to be objectionable. When the evidence was admitted, agreement may have been made as to a later ruling on its admissibility. The admitted evidence may have been always subject to a motion to strike. A witness may have made a statement without a question being asked or a statement that was voluntary. An answer may not have been responsive to the question asked.

In a civil suit, written admissions may be accepted as evidence. These are out-of-court written statements conceding facts that are relevant to the adversary's case. Admissions permit a trial to move more quickly without the presentation of evidence to prove facts that are already known by all parties.

—Elizabeth Algren Shaw

Suggested Readings

Two comprehensive studies of the use of evidence in trials are *The International Criminal Court: Elements of Crimes and Rules of Procedure and Evidence,* edited by Roy S. Lee et al. (Ardsley, N.Y.: Transnational Publishers, 2001), and Roger C. Park, David P. Leonard, and Steven H. Goldberg's *Evidence Law: A Student's Guide to the Law of Evidence as Applied to American Trials* (St. Paul, Minn.: West Publishing, 1998). Legal dictionaries provide exhaustive descriptions of the many types of evidence. Two of the easiest to read are Steven H. Gifis, *Law Dictionary* (2d ed. Woodbury, N.Y.: Barron's Educational Series, 1984), and *Reader's Digest Family Legal Guide* (Pleasantville, N.Y.: Reader's Digest Association, 1981). For a frequently amusing account of personal experiences in court, including skirmishes over evidence, see Charles Rembar, *The Law of the Land* (New York: Simon & Schuster, 1980). More in-depth studies of evidence include Edmund M. Morgan, *Basic Problems of Evidence* (Philadelphia: American Bar Association, 1961), and John Henry Wigmore, *Evidence in Trials at Common Law* (rev. by John T. Naughton. Boston: Little, Brown, 1961). More specialized studies of evidence include David Thoreson Lykken's *A Tremor in the Blood: Uses and Abuses of the Lie Detector* (New York: Plenum Trade, 1998) and *Expert Witnessing: Explaining and Understanding Science*, edited by Carl Meyer (Boca Raton, Fla.: CRC Press, 1999).

See also Adversary system; Burden of proof; Chain of custody; Confessions; Cross-examination; Discovery; Informants; Inquests; Medical examiners; Standards of proof; Testimony; Trial transcripts; Trials; Unethical conduct of attorneys; Witnesses, expert.

Ex post facto LAWS

Laws enacted "after the fact" of some actions or occurrences that retrospectively alter the legal consequences of the actions or occurrences

Ex post facto laws rewrite legal history to change retroactively the legal significance of a past event. The most obvious example of an *ex post facto* law would be one that subjected an individual to criminal punishment for an act performed before the law's enactment which was innocent at the time of performance. *Ex post facto* laws violate elementary notions of fairness and justice. According to William Blackstone, the great eighteenth century legal commentator, individuals have no cause to abstain from engaging in actions which are innocent at the time performed and only later classified as criminal. To punish individuals on the basis of such retroactive determinations is, he insisted, "cruel and unjust."

Article I of the United States Constitution prohibits *ex post facto* laws, both those enacted by the federal government and those adopted by state governments. Many state constitutions also contain prohibitions against such laws. The Supreme Court, however, early interpreted the Constitution's prohibition against *ex post facto* laws as applying only to criminal or penal laws. The Court adopted this construction of the clause in 1798 in *Calder v. Bull* and has continued to maintain this view. Accordingly, civil statutes may be given retroactive effect without violating the prohibition against *ex post facto* law. Federal or state governments, for example, may generally pass statutes taxing income earned or limiting rights acquired before the statutes' enactment.

The Constitution's *ex post facto* clause embraces three kinds of prohibitions. First, it bars government from punishing as a crime an act which was innocent at the time it was committed. Second, it prohibits government from retroactively increasing the seriousness of the punishment for an act already defined as a crime. Finally, it restrains federal and state governments from eliminating criminal defenses that existed at the time the allegedly criminal act was performed. The *ex post facto* clause does not, however, completely foreclose retroactive legislation relating to criminal law or procedure. Government may, for example, retroactively vary the type of punishment imposed for a crime. It may substitute the electric chair for the hangman's noose without violating the prohibition against *ex post facto* laws. Government may also reduce the degree of punishment meted out for a particular crime. Finally, state and federal governments are free to punish individuals for continuing to engage in conduct that was once not subject to the criminal sanction but was subsequently made illegal. Thus, a person could not be punished for violating Prohibition laws for purchasing liquor before such laws went into effect but could be punished for continuing to possess liquor after possession had been outlawed.

See also Bills of attainder; Constitution, U.S.; Criminal justice system; Cruel and unusual punishment.

EXCLUSIONARY RULE

Judicially created doctrine proscribing the admissibility at trial of evidence obtained illegally through violation of a defendant's constitutional rights

The exclusionary rule, as applied to Fourth Amendment search and seizure provisions, originated with the Supreme Court's 1914 decision in *Weeks v. United States*. Although no emergency conditions existed, police officers had twice conducted nonconsensual, warrantless searches of Freemont Weeks's home, obtaining letters and documents that were later used as evidence against him over his objections at trial. Weeks was ultimately convicted, and the Supreme Court addressed his appeal.

In a unanimous opinion, the Court noted that the Framers of the Constitution intended through the passage of the Bill of Rights to protect the American people from the general warrants that had been issued under the authority of the British government in colonial times. The Court declared that the courts, which are charged with the support of the Constitution, should not sanction the tendency of those who enforce the criminal laws of the country to obtain conviction by means of unlawful seizures. The Court concluded that if letters and private documents can be seized illegally and used in evidence against a citizen accused of an offense, the protection of the Fourth Amendment against unreasonable searches and seizures is of no value.

This newly minted rule was strengthened by *Silverthorne Lumber Co. v. United States* (1920), and *Agnello v. United States* (1925), which made clear that illegally acquired evidence could not be used by the government, regardless of the nature of the evidence. However, the mandatory exclusion of illegally obtained evidence pertained only to federal law enforcement and trials. Although the Court eventually agreed in *Wolf v. Colorado* (1949) that the due process clause of the Fourteenth Amendment prohibited illegal state governmental searches and seizures, it initially maintained that the states did not necessarily have to use the exclusionary rule as a method of enforcing that right. The states were allowed to come up with other safeguards to protect the constitutional rights of their citizens.

Silver Platter Doctrine

The incorporation of the prohibitions of the Fourth Amendment into the due process clause of the Fourteenth Amendment did not secure compliance by state law enforcement officers. In fact, because no real means of regulating unlawful state law enforcement behavior existed, state law enforcement agents cooperated with federal agents by providing them with illegally seized evidence, which was admissible in federal court because it was not obtained by federal agents. This practice became known as the "silver platter doctrine" because federal agents were being served up evidence much like food on a platter.

The silver platter doctrine was denounced by the Court in *Elkins v. United States* (1960), which disallowed the admission of evidence obtained by state officers during a search that, if conducted by federal officers, would have violated a defendant's Fourth Amendment rights. The Court decided that it hardly mattered to victims of illegal searches whether their rights had been abridged by federal agents or by state officers, and that if the fruits of an illegal search conducted by state officers could no longer be admitted in federal trials, no incentive would exist for federal and state agents to cooperate in such abhorrent schemes.

Partially because of state law enforcement officers' disregard for the Fourth Amendment's proscriptions, in *Mapp v. Ohio* (1961), the Court reconsidered its stance on extending the exclusionary rule to state action.

Mapp v. Ohio

In 1957 Cleveland, Ohio, police officers went to Dollree Mapp's home with the goal of finding and questioning a bombing suspect. When the officers requested entry, Mapp refused to let them in without a search warrant. The officers returned a few hours later and forcibly entered Mapp's house. A struggle ensued; officers handcuffed Mapp and carried her upstairs, then searched her entire house, including the basement. They found obscene materials during their search, and she was charged and convicted of possessing them. During her trial, no warrant was introduced into evidence. The Ohio supreme court upheld Mapp's conviction, although it acknowledged that the methods used to obtain the evidence offended a sense of justice.

In the *Mapp* majority opinion, the Court deplored the futility of protecting Fourth Amendment rights through remedies such as civil or criminal sanctions. It noted the failure of these remedies and the consequent constitutional abuses and suggested nothing could destroy a government more quickly than its failure to observe its own laws. The Court declared that if the Fourteenth Amendment did not bar improperly seized evidence, the Constitution would consist of nothing more than empty words. In addition, more than half of the states had already adopted the exclusionary rule through either statutory or case law. Therefore, the Court ruled that the exclusionary rule applied to the states as well as the federal government. This avoided the incongruity between state and federal use of illegally seized evidence. Through *Mapp*, the Court altered state criminal trial procedures and investigatory procedures by requiring local officials to follow constitutional standards of search and seizure or suffer exclusion of evidence at trial.

Rationale for the Rule

Some legal experts theorize that the exclusionary rule is a natural outgrowth of the Constitution. The government cannot provide individual rights without protecting them, and the exclusionary rule provides this function. Therefore, the rule is an implicit part of the substantive guarantees of the Fourth Amendment prohibition against unreasonable search and seizure, the Fifth Amendment right against self-incrimination, the Sixth Amendment right to counsel, and the Fifth and Fourteenth Amendment rights to due process. The exclusionary rule also involves the concept of maintaining judicial integrity. The introduction into evidence of illegally gathered materials must be proscribed to maintain judicial integrity and deter police misconduct.

The most common reason invoked for assertion of the exclusionary rule is that it effectively deters constitutional violations and that this deterrent effect is crucial to the vitality of the constitutional amendments. Beginning with *United States v. Calandra* (1974), the Court viewed the rule as primarily a judicial creation designed to deter police misconduct. Therefore, the Court felt free to balance the costs of excluding evidence against the benefits of the rule's effect as a deterrent and produced an ever-expanding list of judicially acknowledged exceptions to the exclusionary rule.

Exceptions to the Rule

After 1961, when the Court held that the states must apply the exclusionary rule to state investigatory and trial procedures, the rule came under increasing attack by those who argued that it exacts too great a price from society by allowing guilty people to either go free or to receive reduced sentences.

The Court, reflecting societal division over the exclusionary rule, fashioned a number of exceptions to it. For example, in *Calandra*, the Court refused to allow a grand jury witness the privilege of invoking the exclusionary rule in refusing to answer questions that were based on illegally seized evidence, as any deterrent effect that might be achieved through application of the rule was too uncertain. For the same reason, the Court also held that illegally seized evidence may be admitted at trial in civil cases (*United States v. Janis*, 1976) and when it would "inevitably" have been discovered through other legal means (*Nix v. Williams*, 1984) as well as used to impeach a witness's credibility (*United States v. Havens*, 1978) and against third persons (*United States v. Paynor*, 1980).

However, what most eroded the exclusionary rule was the good faith exception, first approved for criminal cases by the Court in *United States v. Leon* (1984). The good faith exception permitted the use of illegally acquired evidence if the officers who seized it did so in good faith. In *Leon*, the Court found no reason to apply the exclusionary rule to a situation in which an officer relied on a search warrant issued by a neutral magistrate that later was found not to be supported by probable cause. The Court reasoned that in such a case, the exclusion of evidence would have no deterrent effect on police officers and would exact too great a price from society. In *Illinois v. Krull* (1987), the Court ruled that the exclusionary rule did not bar the admissibility of evidence seized in good faith reliance on a statute, subsequently found to be unconstitutional, which authorized warrantless administrative searches.

In 1995 the Court again extended the good faith exception when it held in *Arizona v. Evans* that the exclusionary rule does not require suppression of evidence seized in violation of the Fourth Amendment because of inaccurate information based on a court employee's clerical errors. In *Evans*, a police officer made an arrest following a routine traffic stop when his patrol car computer erroneously indicated there was an outstanding misdemeanor warrant for Evans's arrest. When the issue of suppression reached the Court, it again applied the rationale of *Leon*. There was neither any evidence that court employees were inclined to ignore or subvert the Fourth Amendment nor any basis for believing that application of the rule would have an effect on the future behavior of court employees. Therefore, the Court decided that it would not serve the purposes of justice to apply the exclusionary rule in *Evans*.

—*Rebecca Davis*

Suggested Readings

Joel Samaha discusses the history of the exclusionary rule, rationales that justify it, and its social costs and deterrent effects in *Criminal Procedure* (4th ed., St. Paul, Minn.: West Publishing, 1999). For basic information regarding the exclusionary rule and its exceptions, see Louis Fisher's *Constitutional Rights: Civil Rights and Civil Liberties* (2d ed., New York: McGraw-Hill, 1995), Lee Epstein and Thomas G. Walker's *Constitutional Law for a Changing America: Rights, Liberties, and Justice* (3d ed., Washington, D.C.: Congressional Quarterly, 1998), Craig Ducat and Harold Chases's *Constitutional Interpretation: Rights of the Individual* (6th ed., St. Paul, Minn.: West Publishing, 1996), and Joan Biskupic's *The Supreme Court and Individual Rights* (3d ed., Washington, D.C.: Congressional Quarterly, 1997). William T. Pizzi, *Trials Without Truth: Why Our System of Criminal Trials Has Become an Expensive Failure and What We Need to Do to Rebuild It* (New York: New York University Press, 1999), includes a critical examination of the exclusionary rule.

See also Bill of Rights, U.S.; Confessions; Evidence, rules of; Witnesses, confrontation of.

EXECUTION OF JUDGMENT

Official moment, after a verdict of a jury or a decision by the court, that a judgment is entered and becomes effective

The court's entry of a judgment is key to enforcing the judgment. A judgment is a legally binding determination in a lawsuit. In a civil suit, the order is typically a judgment that one party must pay the other party a sum of money. The act of seizing property from a debtor is called execution. In many states the process to enforce a judgment for the payment of money is a writ of execution. The judgment debtor is the party who owes money. The judgment creditor is owed money. Many states permit the judgment creditor to obtain discovery of the debtor's assets. In many states a judgment creditor may enforce a judgment through liens on the judgment debtor's property.

In many states, the process to enforce a judgment is a writ of execution. A wage garnishment orders the judgment debtor's employer to remit part of the debtor's wages until the judgment is satisfied. In many states, the prevailing party may obtain a certified copy of a judgment from the clerk of the court. The judgment may be recorded as a lien on the debtor's real estate property. A few states provide that the wages of a head of household may not be garnished. In many states a sheriff or a sheriff's designee has the power to execute a writ of execution on the debtor's personal or real property. The sheriff may charge a fee for this service. In many states, the clerk may issue a writ of garnishment after a judgment is entered. The writ of garnishment has the effect of attaching all personal property, money, wages, or salary. Once a money judgment is paid, it is said to be satisfied. Judgments are stayed pending appeals.

The code of criminal procedure in many states specifies how criminal fines are executed. Once an execution is returned by the court, the fine and costs must be satisfied by the defendant. If an appeal is taken and the defendant is admitted to bail, a sentence of imprisonment may be stayed. In many jurisdictions the defendant is discharged after serving the jail time required by a judgment. Many states require the sheriff to return the copy of the judgment and sentence and state how it was executed. In states that have the death penalty the criminal code specifies the method of execution. In Texas convicts are executed with a lethal injection sufficient to cause death and the execution is supervised by the director of the Texas Department of Criminal Justice.

An order of support may be issued by a court in domestic relations cases. The court has the power to modify or terminate child-support orders. Support orders may be enforced in most states by an income attachment. A court may order a judgment for past child-support payments if they are not made in a timely fashion.

—*Michael L. Rustad*

See also Appeal; Attachment; Criminal procedure; Due process of law; Garnishment; Probable cause; Search warrant requirement; Verdicts.

Executors

Persons named in wills to administer the estates of decedents' under the supervision of probate courts

If a person dies leaving a will, that document usually appoints one or more persons, often family members or close friends, to administer the dead person's estate. If one dies intestate—that is, without leaving a will—the probate court appoints an administrator. The executor or administrator in either case is ultimately responsible for ensuring that the financial obligations of the deceased person are met and that the remaining assets are distributed according to the wishes of the deceased as stated in a valid last will and testament or, if the person dies intestate, according to the inheritance policies of the state in which the will is probated.

Executors named in a decedent's will often have agreed in advance to serve in that capacity. When their services are required, their first responsibility is to find the official signed and witnessed copy of the will. Often this document is in a safe deposit box in a bank or on file with the decedent's attorney, although some people entrust it to a family member or to the person or persons named to administer the estate.

The decedent may also leave a letter for the executor with less formal instructions than those contained in the will, such as the type of funeral the decedent prefers, the disposition of the remains, and other matters pertaining to final arrangements. It may be the responsibility of executors to arrange the funeral as specified by the decedent or, in the absence of specific instructions, in collaboration with those closest to the decedent. Specific instructions may be overridden by executors and family members if they require unreasonable or extremely burdensome expenditures or violate state or local ordinances.

If the deceased person has left the names and addresses of those who should be informed of the death, notification must be carried out as quickly as possible, but certainly before the funeral takes place. Executors usually inform relevant newspapers and professional organizations of the death, acting either directly or through the funeral director. If the deceased person has left instructions for organ donation, executors must carry out these instructions with considerable dispatch. Delay can vitiate such bequests.

The first bills the estate pays are usually for the funeral. In most states the last will and testament must be filed with the probate court shortly after one dies. Executors, who are responsible for setting up a checking account in the name of the estate shortly after the death, must keep careful records of all expenditures that require withdrawals from this account. Executors may receive compensation, the amount of which, in some states, is a percentage of an estate's total value and, in others, a fee deemed reasonable by the probate court.

—R. Baird Shuman

See also Age of majority; Attorneys as fiduciaries; Family law practice; Probate.

FAMILY LAW PRACTICE

*Specialization within the legal profession dealing with legal issues
that affect the makeup, functioning and well-being of families and
their members*

The law intersects family life at many junctures, from the beginning of family relationships through marriage, adoption, divorce, and death. Where there is law, there is often a need for lawyers. The average American is most likely to encounter the legal system as a participant in a family law case. However, because they are afraid of the high cost of legal advice, many Americans enter the family court system without a lawyer. Lawyers are crucial participants in the law of the family. As they assist family members in navigating the law, family lawyers take on a number of roles. Sometimes they act as aggressive advocates when family law matters become divisive and contested. More often, they act as counselors and mediators. All in all, family lawyers assist their clients on a broad spectrum of subjects, involving matters such as child custody, child abuse, child support, children's rights, juvenile delinquency, the annulment of marriages, spousal support (alimony), prenuptial agreements, cohabitation agreements, spousal abuse, legal separation, and the division of marital or community property.

The Difficult Role of the Family Lawyer

Family lawyers provide unique legal services. Other lawyers may assist warring corporations in battle against one another or aid participants in a business transaction in negotiating a deal with relative strangers. Family lawyers, however, must navigate relationships that may be filled with anger, violence, or suffering and are uniquely enduring in many cases. For example, even after a divorce couples may have obligations to care for their children. The skills that might serve a lawyer in nasty corporate litigation may not best serve family law clients. Moreover, the family lawyer often faces unique conflicts. For example, the lawyer who represents a father seeking divorce cannot be completely blind to the consequences of the father's actions for the children of a marriage.

Normally, lawyers are expected to provide relatively single-minded advocacy on behalf of their clients. The family lawyer, on the other hand, cannot escape concern for family members such as children who may not technically be the lawyer's clients. Family lawyers are thus often in the unique position of having to do what is best for their clients while advising them as to what is best for their children. At times clients' beliefs about what is best for themselves are incompatible with what is actually best for their children. Such a situation creates personal and professional issues that lawyers must resolve.

Lawyers and judges who work in the area of family law are very important to the future welfare of children, because these professionals are often the only ones in family court proceedings who make decisions from an objective, not a personal, point of view. In fact, many aspects of family law involve the well-being, maintenance, support, and custody of minor children. There are also family law issues that involve the rights and responsibilities of parents in relationship to their minor children. These issues come to the fore in cases involving adoption, child custody, child support, termination of parental rights, appointment of guardians, and children's rights.

Cases involving minors require that lawyers know not only the legislation and case law in the states in which they practice but also that of other states. Statutes and judicial interpretations may differ from one state to another. As parents may live in one state and their children or prospective adoptive children in another, the family practice lawyer is responsible for knowing all the laws in all the jurisdictions involved in a case. Lawyers must understand not only the state laws that affect the minors involved in their cases but also pertinent federal law. Federal statutes can affect such procedures as the awarding

---

MATTERS COMMONLY HANDLED BY FAMILY LAW SPECIALISTS

- Adoption
- Annulments
- Child abduction
- Child abuse
- Child custody
- Child support
- Children's rights
- Cohabitation agreements
- Common-law marriages
- Division of marital property
- Divorce
- Domestic violence
- Guardianships
- Legal separations
- Prenuptial agreements
- Spousal maintenance (alimony)

and collecting of child support and the prosecution and sentencing of parents who abduct their minor children.

Financial Issues

Most cases handled by family law specialists involve finances. Even those cases that primarily involve domestic partnerships or child welfare have financial aspects. In divorce cases a lawyer must advise clients about a fair and legal division of property and debt. Part of a fair and legal division is determined by whether clients reside in a community property state (in which property is owned jointly by a husband and wife) or a marital property state (in which property is distributed equitably upon termination of the marriage). Another aspect affecting the division of property and debts involves which party will obtain physical custody of the minor children. Also, the division of property and debts may be affected by whether one marital partner has significantly more income than the other. A family law specialist must be able to weigh all of these factors and offer advice on what sort of property settlements are equitable, legal, and fair in a divorce.

When dealing with issues of spousal maintenance and child support, the lawyer must be able to use appropriate formulas and accepted legal custom to advise clients on what is both legal and fair. In general, spousal maintenance (alimony) payments were not common in the last two decades of the twentieth century. However, in certain situations they may be appropriate. Such maintenance may include payments to a spouse who gave up a career to support the other spouse's career and thus lost significant earnings and career advancement. They may also include payments to a spouse who spent many years as a homemaker and may need maintenance payments for a certain period in order to pursue training and education before becoming employed. Sometimes courts order that alimony be paid to spouses whose standard of living would be greatly reduced in the absence of such payments. In family law cases lawyers must be able to advise their clients about what is fair in the field of spousal maintenance, what is customary, and what a judge is likely to order. To be able to offer this sort of advice the family law specialist must have a great deal of financial acumen.

Child support is another area requiring that lawyers be knowledgeable about family finances. Lawyers must be able to apply approved formulas and guides to determine appropriate payments for child support. How much a parent will have to pay to support a child depends on the parent's income and on whether the parent has custody of the child. Parents with large incomes must pay more in child support than do parents with smaller incomes, because they pay roughly the same percentage of their incomes. Noncustodial parents generally have to provide a greater percentage of their incomes for child support than do custodial parents. Family law specialists must be able to give their clients specific, up-to-date information on these matters.

The drafting of prenuptial agreements is another type of service involving financial planning. If a couple wants to draw up a prenuptial agreement, it is often because there is a great disparity between their assets or incomes. In such cases the purpose of a prenuptial agreement is to protect the assets or income of one of the prospective marriage partners. Also, one or both of the partners may have had children with a previous partner. Thus, the purpose of a premarital agreement may be to protect the children. Family law specialists must know how the laws of the state in question deal with prenuptial agreements. Specialists must also ascertain whether the partners have willingly entered into the agreement and whether they each understand its ramifications, because any future challenges to the agreement will hinge on those conditions.

Ethical Obligations of Family Lawyers

Lawyers in every jurisdiction, including family lawyers, must comply with ethical rules governing their practice. In fact, some ethical obligations of lawyers apply to common family law issues. For example, lawyers generally may not represent clients when doing so would involve a conflict of interest. A conflict of interest prevents a lawyer from serving adequately the needs of a client because of a competing obligation or loyalty. In many jurisdictions, this general conflict of interest requirement means that a single lawyer may not represent both spouses in obtaining a divorce. In contested divorces, each spouse will generally hire a lawyer to represent his or her interests. In more amicable divorces, couples often need an attorney simply to help them implement the agreement they have already reached and to make their divorce final. Even in friendly divorces, however, many jurisdictions forbid one lawyer from representing both husband and wife. This often means that a couple will agree that only one of them will actually be represented by a single attorney.

Another important ethical limit on the practice of family law has to do with the fees that family lawyers collect. Contingency fees, for example, are common in some kinds of representations. A contingency fee is one in which a lawyer's recovery of a fee from a client depends wholly or partially on the lawyer's success in representing a client. A lawyer may represent someone who has been injured because of another's negligent action and stipulate that the lawyer fee will amount to 30 percent or 40 percent of any settlement obtained from the opposing party. In divorce and child custody cases, however, lawyers generally may not accept such a fee. Thus, clients are expected to pay either an hourly rate for a lawyer's services or perhaps a flat fee in straightforward and uncontested cases. For a divorcing spouse without financial assets, the inability to offer a lawyer a contingency fee arrangement or to pay a hefty hourly charge might severely limit the spouse's ability to obtain a good lawyer. At least in some jurisdictions family law courts seek to counter this problem by allowing a divorcing spouse without substantial assets to petition the court to have the opposing spouse pay the legal fees of the first spouse.

Family Law as a Career

Although handling family law cases is certainly a challenge, many lawyers find it a very rewarding challenge. Rewards lie in the fact that the family law practitioner is able to exhibit mastery in many fields, not just in the legal field. The specialist must be an expert in child development, psychology, financial and estate planning, and accounting. In the United States in the last decades of the twentieth century nearly 50 percent of marriages ended in divorce. Thus, there was a real need for lawyers who understood the intricacies of family law. Not only do family lawyers derive satisfaction from their knowledge and expertise but they also derive satisfaction from knowing that in helping individuals to adjust to changes in their lives and in securing the best provisions for the welfare of their children they have made real contributions to a better social order.

There are, however, drawbacks to being a family law specialist. Such specialists often deal with people who are experiencing the strongest emotions: fear, denial, anger, grief, self-doubt, remorse, loneliness, and even feelings of abandonment. It is only natural that many clients direct their emotions toward their lawyers. In a survey of 253 lawyers by the American Bar Association (ABA) in the late 1990's, 60 percent indicated that they had been threatened by clients of opposing attorneys and 17 percent indicated that their own clients had threatened them. The ABA reported that family law specialists receive more threats than any other types of lawyers and that about 25 percent of lawyers employ special precautions against violence, such as panic buttons and security systems.

Another drawback to the family law specialty is that overall family law specialists do not receive as much compensation as lawyers who represent corporations or even individuals and groups in malpractice cases. However, because of high divorce rates it is very likely that family law specialists will continue to have large numbers of clients and that they will be able to make a comfortable living from their work.

Challenges Facing the Family Law Specialty

The family law specialty faced several challenges in the late twentieth century, many of which were created by social movements and trends. Until the 1980's it was generally assumed that mothers were the best persons to serve as the custodians of young children. However, both the feminist and the fathers' rights movements have challenged this assumption for different reasons. Feminists have argued at times that it is not fair either to mothers or their children to assume that mothers should take primary responsibility for the physical and custodial care of children. On the other hand, fathers' rights activists have said that it is not fair for judges to always assume that it is in the best interests of children to place them in the physical custody of their mothers. Thus, family law specialists who want to do what is best for their clients and their children have been caught in the middle. Arrangements such as joint custody and coparenting are partly a result of efforts by the legal profession to meet the needs of parents and children.

The divorce rate has contributed to the growth of family law practices. Family law specialists have attempted to lower the divorce rate by suggesting marital counseling when appropriate. They have also tried to help their clients to achieve more satisfactory divorces by offering mediation and arbitration to settle cases rather than settlements through court hearings. All aspects of divorce challenge family lawyers. They are challenged to help stem the divorce rate by offering their clients alternatives, and they are challenged to help their clients achieve more amicable divorces through the use of mediators and arbitrators, which will ultimately result in a better situation for both clients and their children.

Overall, family law specialists face the challenge of setting up a family law system in all jurisdictions that handles issues of family law in an administrative rather than an adversarial fashion. Settling family law matters administratively is more satisfying for the parties involved than court hearings, and the administrative process helps eliminate the possibility that disgruntled spouses will use the divorce courtroom as a place to compete for property and children in an adversarial manner rather than as a place to cooperate to do what is best for the children.

—*Annita Marie Ward*

Suggested Readings

The many comprehensive works on family law include *Family Law in Perspective*, by Walter Wadlington and Raymond C. O'Brien (New York: Foundation Press, 2001); *Family Law in the Twentieth Century: A History*, by Stephen Cretney (New York: Oxford University Press, 2003); *Family Law in the United States: Changing Perspectives*, by Patricia McGee Crotty (New York: Peter Lang, 1999); *An Introduction to Family Law*, by Gillian Douglas (New York: Oxford University Press, 2001); *An Invitation to Family Law: Principles, Process, and Perspectives*, by Carl E. Schneider and Margaret F. Brinig (St. Paul, Minn.: West Publishing, 2000); and *Family Law in Action: A Reader*, edited by Margaret F. Brinig, Carl E. Schneider, Lee E. Teitelbaum (Cincinnati: Anderson, 1999). Another reference book that addresses all aspects of family law is *Nolo's Pocket Guide to Family Law*, edited by Robert Leonard and Stephen R. Elias (4th ed. Berkeley, Calif.: Nolo Press, 1996). Divorce is the topic of J. Herbie Defazio's *Beneath the Fault Line: The Popular and Legal Culture of Divorce in Twentieth Century America* (Charlottesville: University Press of Virginia, 1997). Webster Watnik's *Child Custody Made Simple: Understanding the Law of Child Custody and Child Support* (Claremont, Calif.: Single Parent Press, 1997) helps the reader to understand the family court system. The issue of family violence is explored in Robert T. Ammerman and Michael Herson's *Assessment of Family Violence: A Clinical and Legal Sourcebook* (New York: John Wiley and Sons, 1992). A useful guide for lay people is Theodore E. Hughes and David Klein, *A Family Guide to Wills, Funerals, and Probate: How to Protect Yourself and Your Survivors* (New York: Facts on File/Checkmark Books, 2001). For an international perspective, see *Cross Currents: Family Law and Policy in the United States and England*, edited by Sanford N. Katz, John Eekelaar, and Mavis Maclean (New York: Oxford University Press, 2000).

See also Age of majority; Annulment; Attorney types; Court types; Executors; Jurisdiction; Juvenile criminal proceedings; Legal guardians; Parole; Probation, juvenile.

FEDERAL BUREAU OF INVESTIGATION

Primary federal law-enforcement agency, whose special agents are charged with investigating violations of more than 260 federal laws

The Federal Bureau of Investigation (FBI) is the investigative arm of the United States Department of Justice. It was founded in 1908 as the Bureau of Investigation and renamed the Federal Bureau of Investigation in 1935. Its charge is to investigate violations of federal laws that do not fall within the purview of other government agencies. Such exceptions, for example, are found in the investigation of counterfeiting operations, which are the responsibility of the Department of the Treasury, or offenses involving the U.S. mail, the responsibility of the chief postal inspector.

As it is presently organized, the FBI, under the leadership of a director, maintains fifty-six field offices in the United States and Puerto Rico. It also staffs more than a forty liaison posts in foreign countries. Of the approximately twenty-eight thousand people it employs, about 11,400 are special agents and more than sixteen thousand are non-agent personnel ranging from clerks, custodians, and secretaries to computer programmers, laboratory scientists, and physicians. The special agents constitute the central investigative core of the agency.

Functions

The FBI has two broad functions. First, it is the federal agency designated to conduct general investigations of federal crimes. Its second general function is to investigate breaches in national security.

Of the federal crimes the FBI investigates, the following most frequently come before it: kidnappings; extortion; bank robbery; the interstate transportation of stolen property; interstate traffic for such illegal acts as racketeering or prostitution; violations of election laws; actions that ignore or threaten the civil rights of United States citizens; crimes on Indian reservations, on the high seas, or on aircraft; threats on the life of the president of the United States or other federal officials; and theft of government property.

The breaches of national security the agency investigates include such areas as espionage, treason, sabotage, and the violation of federal acts designed to protect national security, such as the Atomic Energy Act of 1946. The first group of legal infractions occupies the majority of the agents, although when breaches in national security occur, many agents will sometimes be moved from investigations of infractions in the first group to investigations of the somewhat more sensitive and far-reaching infractions that have to do with national security, which remains a top FBI priority.

Staffing

Although the director of the FBI is appointed by the president of the United States with the approval of the Senate, special agents are drawn from a pool of men and women who have taken and passed a detailed and searching written examination. In order to qualify to take the special agents' examination, candidates must be United States citizens between twenty-three and thirty-five years old. They are required to meet at least one of the following criteria: (1) hold a law degree from an accredited institution; (2) hold a degree in accounting, economics, finance, business, electrical engineering, metallurgy, or the physical sciences from an accredited undergraduate institution; (3) be a college graduate fluent in a foreign language appropriate to the needs of the bureau; (4) have three years of other approved, specialized experience; (5) hold a graduate degree and have two years of full-time work experience; (6) hold a graduate degree in physics, chemistry, geology, biology, pharmacy, pharmacology, toxicology, mathematics, or some branch of engineering; (7) hold a graduate degree in business, public administration, computer science, or the analysis and development of business and financial information systems; (8) have a college degree and three years of experience in biology, engineering, geology, pharmacy, or toxicology; (9) hold a college degree and have three years of experience as a systems or programming analyst who has dealt with business and financial systems.

Essentially, the bureau seeks to hire as special agents people who are capable of logical and analytical thought, who can deal with the scientific aspects of the increasingly sophisticated laboratory work that forensics involves, and who can communicate clearly in English and, when necessary, in specific foreign languages. Not every special agent will possess all of these abilities, but within the organization, large numbers possess some of them.

It is required that candidates be of "good moral character." Because their work is often physically demanding, they must also be in top physical condition. Once selected, potential agents undergo four months of training divided between the FBI Academy, which is located on the U.S. Marine Corps Base at Quantico, Virginia, and FBI Headquarters in Washington, D.C. During this training period, they are schooled particularly in rules of evidence, fingerprinting techniques, investigative procedures, and the kinds of laboratory work upon which the success of their investigations will often depend.

Potential agents are trained in the use of a variety of firearms, including machine guns and other automatic and semiautomatic weapons. They also learn defense techniques to protect themselves in their sometimes dangerous field work.

As their training nears completion, they are assigned to an experienced special agent, working closely with that agent through the remainder of the initial training period. The agents' training continues, however, as long as they are with the FBI through refresher courses, short courses in specialized techniques, and other courses that are readily available for additional training to every agent throughout his or her career.

FBI Directors

The director of the Federal Bureau of Investigation is appointed for a term not to exceed ten years. The most renowned director, J. Edgar Hoover, appointed in 1924, served until his death in 1972. His directorship became so autocratic and inimical to the best interests of the country that upon his death, the ten-year limit was established. Hoover was replaced by a Richard Nixon appointee, L. Patrick Gray III, who served from 1972 until his forced resignation in 1973 when he admitted felonious behavior related to the Watergate investigation.

Nixon appointed Clarence Kelley, who served from 1973 until 1978, to replace Gray. William Webster was appointed to the post when Kelley retired and was replaced at the end of his term by William Sessions. Bill Clinton appointed Louis J. Freeh as director upon Sessions's retirement in 1993. After Freeh's resignation in the summer of 2001, President George W. Bush appointed Robert S. Mueller III director of the FBI.

Beginnings of the FBI

The FBI came into being on July 1, 1908, by questionable means. Charles Joseph Bonaparte, grandnephew of Napoleon I of France, served as the attorney general of the United States from 1906 until 1908. In 1907, he urged Congress to allow a small, permanent detective force to be attached to the Department of Justice.

At that time, the department had no discrete investigative wing and, when it required investigative services, had to borrow agents from the Secret Service, which fell under the jurisdiction of the Treasury Department. This made it difficult for the Justice Department to maintain confidentiality in some highly sensitive investigations. Also, agents on loan were those the Secret Service could spare, seldom their most effective agents. Bonaparte feared that some of these agents, being paid by the job and hoping to stay on at Justice, might go out and create crimes, then solve them for the recognition they would receive, acting as *agents provocateurs* more than as solid investigators.

Bonaparte's request, turned down by Congress in 1907, was resubmitted in 1908. A Congress eager to adjourn and miffed at rumors that Theodore Roosevelt had been using the Secret Service to monitor the lives of some of its more flamboyant members, again denied the request. Many members of Congress feared the establishment of a secret police in the United States, considering it inimical to the ideals of the Founders. Other members, beholden to big business for campaign contributions, were concerned that such an investigative force would accelerate the antitrust activity already being pursued by Roosevelt's administration.

This Congress, completely at loggerheads with Bonaparte, not only denied his request but also added a rider to the Sundry Appropriations Act that prohibited the FBI from continuing its practice of borrowing agents from the Secret Service. Unwilling to accept defeat, Bonaparte, on June 30, 1908, the last day of the fiscal year, used discretionary funds to hire nine men from the Treasury Department as an elite investigative force. They were supplemented by examiners and accountants who brought the full force of investigators to twenty-three.

Bonaparte's elite group, at this point, did not have a name, but when George Wickersham succeeded Bonaparte as attorney general, he dubbed the group the Bureau of Investigation, a name that lasted until 1935, when an expanded bureau was officially named the Federal Bureau of Investigation. The bureau grew during the World War I period, when national security was in the forefront of American minds.

Ascent of J. Edgar Hoover

The FBI is widely identified with J. Edgar Hoover, its director for forty-seven years. Hoover, a native of Washington, D.C., was provincial, complex, and paranoid. He was a hard worker and a master at handling detail and classifying information, skills he learned during his brief employment in 1913 at the Library of Congress.

Soon after Attorney General Harlan Stone appointed Hoover director of the FBI in 1924, the young lawyer made draconian cuts in personnel, weeding out the weaker agents and muddling through with a reduced investigative force. Hoover also engaged throughout his career in cost-cutting, sometimes requesting a smaller appropriation than he had been granted in the preceding year. This frugality brought attention to him as a competent manager, but harried congressmen often overlooked the fact that the director frequently returned with requests for supplemental funds to deal with crises, many of his own making.

As director of the FBI, Hoover collected voluminous incriminating files on practically every prominent American, including every president under whom he served. He threatened to reveal the contents of these files against those who opposed him, which perhaps accounts for his incredibly long tenure as director. He consistently used his files for his personal advantage and permitted many politicians at the highest levels of government to do so.

Upon Hoover's death in 1972, the secretary who had served him for his total tenure as director destroyed the most secret of his files. Steps were taken quickly to enact legislation, in effect since his death, to limit the FBI director's term of office.

Under Hoover's leadership, the bureau grew to nearly sixty field offices with an additional 526 resident offices serving the fifty states and Puerto Rico. Hoover's assaults on organized crime were highly effective, although his tactics often were both unethical and illegal. In an average year, the FBI won more than thirteen thousand convictions, an impressive 97 percent of the cases it brought to trial.

The FBI and the Law

As the FBI is constituted, it has no role in making law but is concerned with investigating and prosecuting violations of federal law. Theoretically, the bureau must abide by established laws and must not violate the civil or constitutional rights of any citizen.

Under Hoover's directorship, however, the law was often violated, particularly in such matters as wire-tapping and surveillance. While Hoover was director, the bureau admitted no women to training as special agents, nor were blacks, Hispanics, or other ethnic minorities welcome. Although efforts were made to correct these violations of law when the directorship fell into the hands of later directors, documented cases of racial and sexual discrimination against female and/or minority special agents have increasingly required official arbitration and legal redress.

A month after Hoover's death, news of the Watergate break-in became public. Richard Nixon's appointee as director, L. Patrick Gray, who attempted to enact some reforms, including admitting female candidates for the special agents' examination, ultimately admitted that he had destroyed incriminating documents relating to Watergate. He resigned under pressure a year after he was appointed.

Gray's resignation sparked a congressional investigation of the agency that revealed the FBI had conducted unauthorized personal investigations for at least four presidents, two of whom—Franklin Roosevelt and Lyndon Johnson—used the FBI to gather material about the personal lives of some of their critics and political opponents. It was also revealed that J. Edgar Hoover had used FBI employees to do extensive maintenance work on his residence and that he consistently commandeered FBI vehicles for his personal use. The FBI paid for many of Hoover's vacation trips, unconvincingly disguised as professional trips, with his aide and frequent companion Clyde Tolson.

Of all the revelations of Hoover's numerous personal vendettas, the one that is in many ways most shocking resulted in his illegally gathering wire-tap information against Martin Luther King, Jr., and sending King's wife an incriminating tape relating to her husband. He was also behind the sending of a note to King suggesting that the renowned civil rights activist should commit suicide.

The Post-Watergate FBI

Gray's resignation was a blow that the FBI, already suffering from a tarnished image, did not need. Under subsequent directors, however, more meticulous controls and a broader view of FBI functions have helped to restore public confidence in the bureau.

As drug interdiction and the need to control violence have become central public concerns, the FBI has engaged in preventive work with local law enforcement agents and community leaders. Its Safe Streets Program is aimed at fighting violent crime and at directing youth away from crime and gang activity. Among its more successful programs during 1992 were Adopt-A-School, Junior G-Men, a mentor program, and a community outreach afternoon program designed to serve latchkey youngsters.

Among the cooperative services in which the modern FBI engages are courses of instruction offered at both the FBI Academy and at other sites throughout the nation and the world for the training of local, state, and international law enforcement personnel. These courses are offered free of charge to qualified law enforcement officers.

Since 1976, the FBI has offered a National Executive Institute, an eighteen-day program at the FBI Academy in Quantico designed specifically for the chief executives of the largest law enforcement agencies in the United States. So successful has this program been that in 1981, the Law Enforcement Executive Development Seminar was established to offer similar opportunities to chief law enforcement executives of middle-sized communities. Faculty at the FBI Academy are also available as consultants to police departments throughout the nation.

The bureau administers the Violent Criminal Apprehension Program (VICAP), a sophisticated, state-of-the-art national data center that collects, collates, and analyzes every element of the investigation of violent crimes. This is in some ways a space-age equivalent of the FBI's "Ten Most Wanted" program, which still exists and which, through the years, has been responsible for the apprehension of thousands of dangerous felons.

In conjunction with the Secret Service, the FBI in 1992 conducted its first court-authorized surveillance of data transmissions related to break-ins of computers owned by the Martin Marietta Electronic Information and Missile Group and various telephone companies, violations with substantial implications for national security.

FBI drug investigations during 1992 resulted in 4,361 indictments, 3,419 arrests, and 2,957 convictions, with some cases still pending. In that year, three hundred special agents of the FBI were reassigned from counterintelligence to augment the work of a thousand special agents already assigned to work on violent crime. By the end of the year, seventy-one FBI task forces were at work in forty-five major cities. In California alone, fifty new agents joined antiviolence investigative teams in July, 1992. This infusion of trained personnel resulted in the arrests of 10,777 felons by year's end.

FBI Laboratories
The FBI operates the only full-service national forensic laboratory in the United States. Established in 1932, it has become the best equipped and most sophisticated such facility in the world. It is available to law enforcement agencies nationwide and throughout the world. One of its services is DRUGFIRE, a computerized forensic clearinghouse for drug-related investigations.

Impact of the FBI
In a free society, an agency such as the FBI must be strenuously monitored and controlled. When Bonaparte made his initial request for the establishment of an investigative agency, Congressman J. Swagar Sherley of Kentucky reminded his congressional colleagues that he knew of no government that had perished because it did not have a secret police force but that he could think of many that had been destroyed because they had one. His admonition is one that has been heeded increasingly by both houses of

Congress since the leadership of J. Edgar Hoover grew increasingly to have a stranglehold on many Americans.

As violence grows, as the drug culture continues to affect American life adversely, and as international terrorism becomes an increasing threat to a free society, Americans can easily acknowledge the need for a strong FBI. Such an agency, however, must live within the laws it is charged with enforcing and must be subject to the kinds of checks and balances that are the linchpins of any free society.

In the wake of the terrorist attacks on the Pentagon and New York City's World Trade Center on September 11, 2001, the FBI took a prominent role in counterterrorism work, beginning with its work in identifying the perpetrators of the attacks. FBI investigations also disrupted alleged terrorist cells in Buffalo, New York; Detroit, Michigan; and Portland, Oregon; and led to the arrests of more than two hundred person accused of supporting terrorist activities. In addition, the FBI worked with the U.S. Treasury Department to freeze hundreds of millions of dollars in assets of organizations believed to have links with terrorists. These and other counterterrorism efforts were, however, subject to criticism by some observers, who believed that new federal laws and law enforcement priorities designed to combat terrorism actually threatened the civil liberties of Americans.

—R. Baird Shuman

Suggested Readings

A good starting point for basic information is *The FBI: A Comprehensive Reference Guide,* by Athan G. Theoharis et al. (Phoenix, Ariz.: Oryx Press, 1999). One of the most fascinating books relating to the FBI is Curt Gentry's *J. Edgar Hoover: The Man and the Secrets* (New York: W. W. Norton, 1991), a well-documented exposé of the long-time director's abuse of his office. See also Ronald Kessler's *The Bureau: The Secret History of the FBI* (New York: St. Martin's Press, 2002). Fred L. Israel's *The FBI* (New York: Chelsea House, 1986), part of Chelsea House's Know Your Government series, although directed at a secondary school audience, is concise, accurate, and candid. Among the more interesting studies of the bureau, most of them exposés, are James Bamford's *The Puzzle Palace: A Report on America's Most Secret Agency* (Boston: Houghton Mifflin, 1982), Nelson Blackstock's *Cointelpro: The FBI's Secret War on Political Freedom* (New York: Vintage, 1976), Fred J. Cook's

The FBI Nobody Knows (New York: Macmillan, 1964), John T. Elliff's *The Reform of FBI Intelligence Operations* (Princeton, N.J.: Princeton University Press, 1979), Harry and Bonaro Overstreet's *The FBI in Our Open Society* (New York: W. W. Norton, 1969), Richard Gid Powers's *G-Men: Hoover's FBI in American Popular Culture* (Carbondale: Southern Illinois University Press, 1983), Andrew Tully's *Inside the FBI* (New York: McGraw-Hill, 1980), and Sanford J. Ungar's *FBI* (Boston: Atlantic Monthly Press, 1976). The *Annual Report of the Attorney General of the United States* provides current information annually about the bureau, which also distributes useful pamphlets about its activities such as *The FBI Mission: To Uphold the Law* (Washington, D.C.: U.S. Government Printing Office, 1989).

See also Attorney general of the United States; Attorneys, United States; Detectives, police; Federal judicial system; Law enforcement; Marshals Service, U.S.; Police; State police.

FEDERAL JUDICIAL SYSTEM

Three-level system that hears federal cases, appeals from state supreme courts, and constitutional questions

The United States has both state and federal courts. Municipal courts are subordinate to the states in which they reside. The federal courts exist independent of the states. They draw their authority from the U.S. Constitution, which established the Supreme Court. The Constitution charges the U.S. Congress with establishing all the lower ("inferior") federal courts. The result has been a federal judicial system comprising over one hundred federal courts of three types: district courts, appellate courts, and the Supreme Court.

U.S. District Courts

The lowest federal courts are the district courts. Each state has at least one U.S. district court, and larger states have as many as four. There are ninety-six U.S. district courts in all. Although these courts are an important part of the U.S. legal system, only about 5 percent of all the country's legal cases are heard in federal district court. Most of the rest are heard in state and municipal courts.

District courts serve as the federal system's primary trial courts, where most federal cases originate. The federal trial court system also includes tax courts, bankruptcy courts, and territorial courts. Cases are usually decided by a judge, although jury trials are occasionally held in district courts. District court decisions must be consistent with U.S. Supreme Court rulings.

District court judges are appointed by the president of the United States with the consent of the U.S. Senate. Most district courts have several judges, although most cases are heard by individual judges. There are some five hundred district court judges in the entire system.

U.S. Courts of Appeals

Although most district court decisions are not in fact appealed, the losing party may do so as a matter of right. Such appeals are made to a U.S. court of appeals. Some decisions by federal regulatory agencies may also be appealed to the U.S. appellate courts, as may decisions by U.S. tax courts.

There are twelve federal Courts of Appeals in the United States. Eleven of these "circuits" serve groups of three to nine states, and the twelfth serves the District of Columbia. Each appellate court has between four and twenty-six judges, who are appointed by the president of the United States with the consent of the U.S. Senate. As other federal courts, federal appeals courts must abide by the doctrine of *stare decisis*—that is, their decisions must be consistent with precedent. Appellate courts are also bound to respect decisions made by the U.S. Supreme Court.

Unlike lower courts, U.S. courts of appeals do not use juries and do not consider new evidence. Indeed, they do not "retry" cases at all. Instead, they determine whether the trial court's decision was consistent with applicable law, including the Constitution. If such a determination is made, the original verdict is upheld (or "affirmed"). If the appellate court determines that the trial court's decision was made in error, the case could be sent back ("remanded") for a retrial by the original court.

Most federal appellate cases are heard by three-judge panels, although all the judges of an appellate court may sit together *en banc* (on the bench) to hear particularly difficult or controversial cases. A party may petition to have an especially controversial decision by an appellate court appealed to the U.S. Supreme Court. However, there is no guaranteed right to a Supreme Court hearing. Because the Supreme Court can hear only a small number of cases, it refuses to consider most appeals.

U.S. Supreme Court

The Supreme Court is the highest court in the United States. Its nine justices are appointed by the president of the United States with the consent of the Senate. The Supreme Court serves as the final court of appeal for federal cases and also hears appeals of decisions rendered by the state supreme courts when federal law is involved. The Supreme Court is given original jurisdiction in cases concerning foreign diplomats and when states sue one another. These account for a very small portion of the Court's cases, which are primarily appellate cases.

In addition to serving as the country's highest appellate court, the Supreme Court also serves a critical role in maintaining the government's separation of powers. Through judicial review the Court can declare laws to be unconstitutional. It can also decide that executive actions violate the Constitution. In addition, the Court can resolve disputes between the executive and legislative branches.

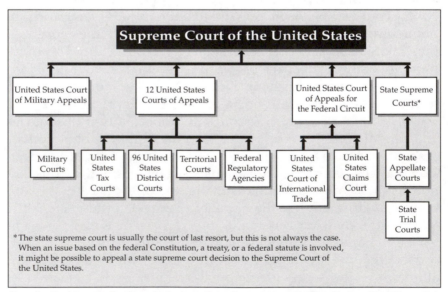

Source: Barbara A. Bardes et al. *American Government Politics Today: The Essentials* (St. Paul, MN: West Publishing, 1994).

Special Courts

In addition to the three main types of federal courts, several additional courts address more specialized cases. These include the U.S. Claims Court, which hears claims against the U.S. government, and the U.S. Court of International Trade, which hears appeals of rulings from the U.S. Customs Office. These courts' decisions can be appealed to the U.S. Court of Appeals for the Federal Circuit and finally to the U.S. Supreme Court. Federal military courts hear court-martial cases, which can be appealed to the U.S. Court of Military Appeals (and finally to the U.S. Supreme Court).

—Steve D. Boilard

Suggested Readings

An authoritative overview of the highest court's role in the federal judicial system is provided in Henry J. Abraham's *The Judiciary: The Supreme Court in the Governmental Process* (10th ed. New York: New York University Press, 1996). See also Abraham's earlier comparative analysis of the federal judicial system, *The Judicial Process: An Introductory Analysis of the Courts of the United States, England, and France* (6th ed. New York: Oxford University Press, 1993). Other up-to-date studies of the judicial system include Ann E. Woodley's *Litigating in Federal Court: A Guide to the Rules* (Durham, N.C.: Carolina Academic Press, 1999), Laurie L. Levenson's *A Student's Guide to the Federal Rules of Criminal Procedure* (St. Paul, Minn.: Thomson/West, 2003), and David A. Dittfurth's *The Concepts and Methods of Federal Civil Procedure* (Durham, N.C.: Carolina Academic Press, 1999). Howard Ball offers an authoritative analysis of the federal judicial system in his *Courts and Politics: The Federal Judicial System* (2d ed. Englewood Cliffs, N.J.: Prentice-Hall, 1987). Robert Carp and Ronald Stidham's *The Federal Courts* (2d ed. Washington, D.C.: Congressional Quarterly Press, 1991) focuses on the lower federal courts. On this subject see also C. K. Rowland and Robert A. Carp's *Politics and Judgment in Federal District Courts* (Lawrence: University Press of Kansas, 1996). Appeals courts are described in Howard Woodford, Jr.'s *Courts of Appeals in the Federal Judicial System* (Princeton, N.J.: Princeton University Press, 1981). A critique of the federal court system is offered by Richard A. Posner's *The Federal Courts: Challenge and Reform* (Cambridge, Mass.: Harvard University Press, 1996).

See also Attorney general of the United States; Attorneys, United States; Constitution, U.S.; Court types; Federal Bureau of Investigation; Judicial appointments and elections; Justice Department, U.S.; Marshals Service, U.S.; Supreme Court, U.S.

FELONIES

Serious criminal offenses—such as murder, rape, kidnapping, arson, embezzlement, or armed robbery—that under federal guidelines are punishable by imprisonment of a year or more or by death

Criminal offenses are often grouped into two major categories, felonies and misdemeanors, which indicate the seriousness of the crime. Misdemeanors are less serious offenses, such as disorderly conduct; felonies are more serious crimes, such as murder, rape, and armed robbery. Federal guidelines define a felony as any crime "punishable by death or by imprisonment for a term exceeding one year." Most states maintain similar definitions, although some states classify crimes according to the place of incarceration for offenders. If incarceration is to be in a state prison, the offense is a felony; if it is punishable by a term in a local jail, it is considered a misdemeanor. (There are further complications in some areas; in Michigan a few misdemeanors are deemed serious enough to warrant time in a state penitentiary.) In some jurisdictions an offense may be considered either a felony or a misdemeanor depending on a number of factors. Larceny (theft), for example, may be classified as a felony (grand larceny) if the value of the item or items stolen is sufficiently high or a misdemeanor (petty larceny) if their value is relatively small.

Most states maintain separate court systems for felonies and misdemeanors. Felonies are tried in county courts, or courts of general jurisdiction. Misdemeanors are handled by local courts with limited jurisdiction. By far, most criminal cases are handled by local (minor) courts, partly because so many charges are only misdemeanors and partly because felony charges are sometimes reduced to misdemeanor charges before a trial begins. Because the charges and punishments meted out to convicted felony offenders are significantly more serious, the handling of felony cases by the courts is much more complex than the handling of misdemeanors. Felony cases involve pretrial, trial, and post-trial proceedings, and they can take a year or more.

In 1963, in the landmark case *Gideon v. Wainwright*, the U.S. Supreme Court held that defendants charged with serious crimes must be provided with a state-appointed attorney if they cannot afford to hire their own attorney. At first this requirement was applied only to felony cases, but in *Argersinger v. Hamlin* (1972) the Court extended the protection to people accused of misdemeanors if the misdemeanor charge could result in imprisonment.

The exact origin of the term "felony" is unknown, but many scholars trace it to the Latin words *felonia* and *fallere*, meaning "to deceive." In England, a felony originally was a breach of the feudal bond resulting in either the temporary or permanent forfeiture of the guilty party's assets. Gradually the definition expanded. In the twelfth century, Henry II attempted to codify the laws of the realm, and he established forfeiture as one of the penalties for murder, theft, forgery, arson, and other similar criminal acts. Soon all crimes punishable in England by forfeiture of property (eventually abolished in 1870), physical mutilation, burning, or death were considered felonies. In 1967, England replaced the former distinctions with the categories arrestable and nonarrestable offenses, but the felony/misdemeanor distinction remains important in the United States.

See also Criminal justice system; Criminal records; Misdemeanors; Perjury; Principals (criminal); Three-strikes laws; Torts.

Fifth Amendment

Amendment to the U.S. Constitution containing protections that include the right not to testify against oneself in order to avoid self-incrimination

Part of the Bill of Rights, the Fifth Amendment protects individuals in criminal cases from arbitrary conduct by the federal government. Through the due process clause of the Fourteenth Amendment, individuals in criminal cases are also protected from arbitrary conduct by state governments. Most state constitutions contain provisions similar to the Fifth Amendment. The Amendment consists of five major protections: The government must formally charge persons with a crime before putting them on trial "to answer" for it; the government cannot try an accused person twice for the same crime—commonly called double jeopardy; accused persons do not have to testify against themselves; government cannot take persons' lives, liberty, or property without due process of law; and property owners shall receive compensation for any property taken for public use. This amendment requires the government to adhere to lawful and fair procedures when it deals with persons it accuses of crimes or whose property rights must be curtailed for the public good, such as might be required when building a public road across private land.

The portion of the Fifth Amendment most commonly cited is the right of silence. Since the government cannot compel people to incriminate themselves, the U.S. Supreme Court has held that all persons who are arrested must be told that they do not have to answer questions from the time they are taken into custody through their trials. This Fifth Amendment protection is part of the Miranda rights that all accused persons enjoy. Persons testifying in a criminal trial who "take the Fifth" do not answer questions put to them by the attorneys.

The Fifth Amendment protection against self-incrimination has been expanded in some areas even in the absence of specific language codifying such expansion. At the same time, courts have not accepted all possible inferences from the rather broad language of the amendment. Practice and precedent have extended the Fifth Amendment's protections to persons not accused of crimes in cases in which their testimony might lead to criminal prosecution against them. For example, courts have not accepted the claim that persons operating illegal businesses have a Fifth Amendment right not to file income tax returns, even though submitting such returns might lead to their criminal prosecution.

The guarantee of due process protects individuals from arbitrary actions by government. Before the government can act against an individual, the individual must be informed of the intended action and be given an opportunity to respond to it.

Governmental actions impinging on property have activated the Fifth Amendment. Government sometimes creates new property when it bestows benefits upon people. Subsequent governmental actions limiting those benefits can be challenged on Fifth Amendment grounds. Governmental actions that affect the value of property or impose new restrictions upon its use can also involve the Fifth Amendment. Environmental legislation that restrict construction have been challenged by property owners who consider such laws an unconstitutional seizure of private property.

—Edward R. Crowther

See also Bill of Rights, U.S.; Confessions; Constitution, U.S.; Double jeopardy; Due process of law; Grand juries; Immunity from prosecution; Indictments; Legal immunity; Miranda rights; Mistrials; Pleas; Self-incrimination, privilege against; Testimony.

FORECLOSURE

Legal proceeding undertaken against a debtor in order to compel the sale of property

Foreclosure terminates a debtor's ownership interest in property that is secured by a mortgage or a deed of trust. Foreclosure proceedings may be instituted not only as a result of a debtor's failure to repay a debt, but also for failure to satisfy the terms of a loan agreement or other loan documents. In states in which mortgages are given to secure debts, a mortgagee (that is, the beneficiary of the mortgage) brings foreclosure proceedings against the debtor in default under the mortgage. In states in which deeds of trust are given to secure debts, the trustee under the deed of trust institutes foreclosure proceedings at the request and on behalf of the lender.

Two principal methods by which mortgages and deeds of trust are foreclosed are judicial foreclosure and the exercise of a "power of sale." The exercise of a power of sale may be utilized when a mortgage or deed of trust contains language authorizing a lender or lender's trustee to sell the mortgaged property. Such a foreclosure sale may be held as a public auction. Otherwise, property may be foreclosed by order of a judge. In some states these two methods may be utilized concurrently. Ultimately, a lender hopes to recover some or all of the outstanding debt from the proceeds of a foreclosure sale or a civil action. In addition to foreclosures of mortgages, certain governmental authorities may institute foreclosure proceedings in order to secure the payment of taxes. These tax foreclosures may be similar to foreclosures instituted by lenders.

The particulars of foreclosure proceedings depend on the method by which a debt is foreclosed and on the laws of the state in which the foreclosure occurs. Generally, the court or an appointee of the court establishes the amount of outstanding debt and the location, time, and date of any foreclosure sale. When the property is occupied by tenants, the court may appoint a receiver to collect rents during the course of the foreclosure proceedings. Procedures for notification of foreclosure vary from state to state. Notice to individual debtors may involve service by the local sheriff or notification by certified mail. Public notice may also be required, and such notice may involve posting court orders or notices at the property or in some public place (for example, the county courthouse). Notification may also be served by the publication of information on the foreclosure in a local newspaper.

Foreclosure of mortgaged property is only one of several remedies available to a lender when a debtor is in default under a loan. A lender may elect to modify the terms of a loan—for example, by lowering monthly payments while increasing the overall amount or term of the loan. A lender may also sue the debtor for the full amount of the loan, with or without instituting foreclosure of the mortgaged property. In some states a lender may agree to a deed in lieu of foreclosure. In such a case, a debtor conveys all title and interest in mortgaged property to a lender without going through the foreclosure process, usually in exchange for the lender's agreement not to sue the debtor for any remaining debt.

—*Erin Gwen Palmer*

See also Bankruptcy; Forfeiture, civil and criminal; Garnishment.

FORFEITURE, CIVIL AND CRIMINAL

Government appropriation of goods owned by convicted criminals that have been obtained illegally—a procedure used frequently to punish drug dealers

Forfeiture occurs when the criminal justice system seizes property and goods that have been stolen, used in the commission of a crime, or purchased using money obtained illegally. Forfeiture can be enacted through either civil or criminal law. If done through the criminal law, forfeiture takes the form of sanction (or punishment) by the court. This type of punishment can be used as an alternative to prison or in conjunction with a prison sentence. Forfeiture is a common element in the sentencing of drug dealers and distributors, whose possessions are almost entirely obtained through illegal drug sales. In some jurisdictions, property obtained through forfeiture is auctioned to the public or used by the police department itself. Typical items seized by police include vehicles, homes, and other personal property such as stereo equipment and televisions. When items are seized under civil law, a finding of guilt in the criminal court is not necessary.

See also Bills of attainder; Criminal procedure; Damages; Felonies; Foreclosure; Garnishment.

FRIVOLOUS LAWSUITS

Lawsuits and tactics that have no real basis in law and only abuse the legal system

Parties sometimes file frivolous lawsuits, suits that have no hope of winning, simply as a way of intimidating or harassing other parties who are forced to defend themselves. Frivolous positions and tactics are sometimes used by prisoners who may, for example, claim violation of rights because the prison serves smooth peanut butter rather than crunchy. Corporations sometimes engage in frivolous positions when they threaten to sue people of moderate income for large sums of money when all such people have done is fight the location of a factory near their homes. If such tactics went unchecked, court systems could become clogged, greatly increasing the length of time it would take for the resolution of genuine legal disputes.

The problem has been to impose sanctions on the use of frivolous tactics without discouraging innovation in the law. Rule 11 of the Federal Rules of Civil Procedure and state rules modeled from it have prohibited frivolous positions and tactics and have allowed courts to impose sanctions on lawyers and clients who use them. Lawyers may overcome a charge that their position is frivolous by showing that they have researched the matter and found support for their position in judicial opinions, even dissenting opinions, or in law review articles. In this way, vigorous and innovative advocacy is protected.

—*Patricia A. Behlar*

See also *Habeas corpus*; Indigent criminal defendants; Lawsuits; Model Rules of Professional Conduct.

GAG ORDERS

Pejorative term used by the electronic and print media for what law courts call "restrictive orders"

A gag order is a less-than-flattering term used by journalists to describe a restrictive order set down by a court. The court order directs the news media not to publish or speak of information that it has learned about a court case. This is a punitive form of government control of the free press.

The power of the government to approve what can or cannot be published—under a threat of punishment—has a long and foreboding history. Governmental attempts to use prior restraint orders have taken place, with predictable regularity, when turmoil occurs. The U.S. Supreme Court does not prohibit "gag orders" in all circumstances, ruling that they are permissible only when publication would establish a clear and present danger to a defendant's right to a fair trial. Trial judges, recognizing that gag orders against the press are unconstitutional, instead bar both the press and the public from pretrial and trial hearings.

Gag orders can also be imposed on witnesses who are subpoenaed to testify in court. The restrictions on jurors present a different problem. Judges can instruct members of a jury not to discuss aspects of a case with anyone during the course of a trial.

—*Earl R. Andresen*

See also Judges; Speedy trial requirement; Trial publicity; Trials; Witnesses.

GARNISHMENT

Court-ordered procedure by which a person's earnings are withheld by an employer for payments of debts

Garnishment is one of several ways in which the law allows creditors to obtain payment for debts. Wages and bank accounts are the most common targets of garnishments. However, before a creditor may receive garnished money from a debtor, the creditor must have obtained a legal judgment against the debtor. The debtor's employer or other organization that holds the money will be served with questions and a summons stipulating when and where such answers must be filed. The creditor must also send the debtor a garnishment notice, which tells the debtor that he or she may ask for a hearing to dispute the garnishment or wage deduction. The clerk of the court informs the debtor and the employer or organization holding the debtor's money when and where such a hearing will be held.

If there is no dispute or the dispute is settled in favor of the creditor, the creditor's attorney will issue a release of satisfaction. Upon receiving this document, the debtor's employer or the organization holding the money will forward the stated amount to the creditor or the creditor's lawyer. If the amounts received by the creditor are not sufficient to pay the debt, the creditor may commence additional garnishments or proceedings for wage deduction orders. Creditors should be aware that some states do not allow garnishment of wages, while other states place limits on the amount of money that may be taken from a debtor's paycheck.

Title III of the Consumer Credit Protection Act of 1968 protects an employee from being suspended or discharged because of wage deduction proceedings or from being fired if pay is garnished for one debt. The law does not prohibit discharge if the employee's earnings have been garnished for a second or subsequent debts. Title III also limits the amount of the employee's earnings that may be garnished. The amount is based on an employee's disposable earnings, which is what is left after legally required deductions have been made for federal, state, and local taxes, social security, and other governmental taxes. The law protects everyone receiving wages, salaries, commissions, bonuses, or income from a pension or retirement program, but tips are not considered earnings for the purposes of Title III. The law does not regulate situations in which workers voluntarily agree that their employers may turn over some specified amount of their earnings to a creditor.

In court orders for child support or alimony, the garnishment law allows an employer to withhold up to 50 percent of a worker's disposable earnings if the worker supports another spouse or child and up to 60 percent if the worker does not support another spouse or child. An additional 5 percent may be garnished for support payments that are more than twelve weeks in arrears.

—*Alvin K. Benson*

See also Attachment; Bankruptcy; Damages; Execution of judgment; Foreclosure; Forfeiture, civil and criminal.

GOOD TIME

Time subtracted from a prison sentence for good behavior while in prison

Good time (or "time off for good behavior") is defined as a number of days subtracted from a prison sentence. It is based on the notion that inmates should have some motivation for good behavior while serving their sentences. All felony prison sentences in the United States provide for release prior to service of the full sentence by reason of some form of good time if there is no parole The control of good time can have a considerable impact on institutional discipline. Based on existing regulations and case law, an inmate's good time can be forfeited for misconduct or criminal behavior while in prison. Court decisions, however, have mandated that good time cannot be taken from an inmate without due process.

Three factors should be noted with regard to good time. First, as a general rule, good time is based on the length of the sentence. The longer the sentence, the more good time awarded per month of the sentence. Second, the amount of good time awarded per month varies considerably from government to government. Third, the way good time is calculated varies considerably from government to government. Some governments subtract good time from the total sentence, whereas others subtract it from other points in the sentence such as the minimum parole eligibility date.

See also Criminal justice system; House arrest; Parole; Probation, adult; Sentencing.

GRAND JURIES

Legal bodies formally charged with determining if there is suffi-cient evidence in criminal investigations to proceed to trial

Grand juries, unlike trial juries, do not determine the guilt or innocence of the accused but assess whether the government has enough evidence to advance to a criminal trial (grand juries do not operate in civil proceedings). In this way the grand jury is intended, in the words of the Supreme Court, to "serve as a buffer or referee between the government and the people who are charged with crimes."

The grand jury was imported to the American context as part of English law and was originally meant to protect the colonies against capricious actions of royalist courts. Grand juries were explicitly recognized in the U.S. Constitution's Fifth Amendment, which specifies that "No person shall be held to answer for a capital, or otherwise infamous crime, unless on a presentment or indictment of a Grand Jury" while laying out a limited number of exceptions for those engaged in military or militia service.

Operation and Composition

Grand jury proceedings, which occur as part of the criminal process at both the state and federal level, usually begin when a "bill of indictment," a written accusation of a crime, is submitted to the jury by a prosecutor. The grand jury then examines the government's case, conducting hearings in which witnesses are called and evidence presented. Again, in contrast with trial proceedings, these hearings are conducted in secret, the public is excluded from attendance, and the accused has no right to present evidence, although the jury may grant this right. Grand juries operate without the direct supervision of a judge—who still exercises some oversight outside the jury chamber—and proceedings are usually dominated by the prosecution, in part because defense attorneys are generally excluded from participation. While grand juries are normally formed to assess evidence presented by prosecutors, at times they are constituted as independent investigative bodies, the basic function of which is to determine whether there is enough evidence of a crime to proceed to trial.

Federal grand juries have twenty-three members, while state grand juries vary in size from five to twenty-three members. If a legally specified number of jurors from this group believes that the evidence is sufficient to continue prosecution, the grand jury issues an indictment, also known as a "true bill," to the court with jurisdiction over the case. If a true bill is not returned, the case is dismissed and a "no bill" or "ignoramus" rendered. At the federal level twelve jurors are needed to return an indictment or ignoramus, and in the states the number varies depending on the juries' overall size. In any event, unanimity is not required; by some estimates grand juries issue indictments 95 percent of the time.

Grand jury members are usually selected at random from voting rolls, although the process varies somewhat at the state level. Grand jurors generally serve for three to eighteen months, although the terms of service can run shorter or longer. Thus, a single grand jury typically reviews a large number of cases.

Powers of the Grand Jury

Witnesses who appear before grand juries possess few procedural rights. Prosecutors are not required to consider or present evidence that might demonstrate the innocence of the accused. In *Williams v. United States* (1992) the U.S. Supreme Court ruled that federal prosecutors need not present evidence favorable to the defense in seeking indictments. Moreover, while the accused may know the names of those testifying before the grand jury, they have no right to confront and cross-examine them. Some evidence inadmissible before trial juries is acceptable in the context of a grand jury inquiry, including hearsay. Those appearing before a grand jury have no right to representation by counsel, although they may request to consult with an attorney outside the grand jury chamber. Some states permit attorneys to be brought into the jury room.

The courts have consistently upheld the broad powers and prerogatives of the grand jury, including the secrecy of its proceedings and its power to compel witnesses to appear, testify, and provide evidence. However, in *Kastigar v. United States* (1972) the U.S. Supreme Court found that grand juries' power to subpoena witnesses and compel testimony must be balanced against constitutional protections against self-incrimination found in the Fifth Amendment to the U.S. Constitution. The Court ruled that compelled testimony and any information or evidence directly derived therefrom cannot be used in subsequent criminal proceedings against the testifying individual—who might still be prosecuted through evidence obtained independently from the grand jury. The Court has consistently avoided insisting that the grand jury is constitutionally required at the state level, making the grand jury provisions of the Fifth Amendment one of the few portions of the Bill of Rights that have not been applied to the states. In *Hurtado v. California* (1884) the Court held that the grand jury protections of the Fifth Amendment need not be extended to the states.

Informations and Presentments

While numerous states authorize the grand jury system, many others use an alternate process known as an "information" to determine whether the prosecution's case should proceed to trial. In an information, a prosecutor provides a written accusation of a crime to the court with the initial authority to hear the case.

Usually the prosecution's accusation is initially inspected by a magistrate to ensure its propriety.

On occasion, grand juries go beyond simply determining the sufficiency of the evidence before them by offering "presentments." While not quite indictments, presentments draw attention to alleged illegal or corrupt activities. In 1974, for example, a grand jury presentment identified President Richard M. Nixon as an "unindicted coconspirator" for his role in the Watergate scandal.

Grand juries are used in most federal felony prosecutions, although the information is employed in noncapital criminal cases at the district court level and in some civil cases. The state use of grand juries varies widely, with some states employing them optionally and others relegating them to certain classes of investigations, such as in the event of corruption charges against public officials. Grand juries are no longer employed in England; their importance in the U.S. legal system is unique.

The grand jury has been the object of frequent criticism, both from those who find it a cumbersome element of the legal system and from those who consider it a menace to criminal rights and civil liberties in general. The former critics often point to the information as a preferable, more efficient procedure for advancing the course of a criminal investigation. Those who object that grand juries have great potential for abuse argue that prosecutors' untrammeled authority within the grand jury chamber allows them to intimidate witnesses and cajole jurors, so that the indictment becomes more of a foregone conclusion than an actual check against improper investigations. Defenders of the existing grand jury insist that it serves a critical function in ensuring that the charges against a suspect stem from well-considered evidence rather than from malice, haste, or expedience.

—*Bruce G. Peabody*

Suggested Readings

For discussions of grand juries in the context of criminal procedure generally see Rolando V. del Carmen's *Criminal Procedure* (3d ed. Belmont, Calif.: Wadsworth, 1995), Carl J. Franklin's *Constitutional Law for the Criminal Justice Professional* (Boca Raton, Fla.: CRC Press, 1999), and Henry J. Abraham's *The Judicial Process* (6th ed. New York: Oxford University Press, 1993). The latter includes a concise account of the historical roots of the grand jury, which is the focus of R. D. Younger's *The People's Panel: The Grand Jury in the United States, 1634-1941* (Providence, R.I.: Brown University, 1963).

See also Bill of Rights, U.S.; Criminal justice system; Criminal procedure; District attorneys; Fifth Amendment; Indictments; Inquests; Juries; Jury duty; Preliminary hearings; Presumption of innocence; Suspects; Testimony; Trials.

GRIEVANCE COMMITTEES FOR ATTORNEY DISCIPLINE

Committees that investigate and prosecute complaints of misconduct by members of state bar associations

Lawyers have a professional obligation to conduct themselves in accordance with the highest ethical standards. They are officers of the court and their conduct is governed by the Code of Professional Responsibility. Attorney grievance committees have the authority to investigate claims and complaints against lawyers and to prosecute complaints of professional misconduct. In most jurisdictions these committees have the power to admonish, reprimand, suspend, or disbar lawyers who violate ethical standards. In most states the highest state court has authority over the conduct of lawyers. The court or its designee appoints grievance committees to investigate grievances stemming from the attorney-client relationship. Many states have professional staffs to assist grievance committee's investigating grievances.

The authority to regulate and discipline New York lawyers is vested in the Appellate Divisions of the New York State Supreme Court. New York, for example, has eight grievance committees throughout the state. Each committee has the power to investigate written complaints of professional misconduct concerning lawyers within their regions. New York's Lawyers' Fund for Client Protection provides reimbursement for clients who have lost money as a result of their lawyers' dishonest actions. The fund is financed by all lawyers licensed in New York State. Grievance

Committees may recommend disbarment, suspension, or lesser sanctions depending on the severity of the offense, aggravating circumstances, or mitigating circumstances. Grievance committees in other states have a similar structure, with committees consisting of both attorneys and full-time professional staffs.

—*Michael L. Rustad*

See also American Bar Association; Attorneys; Bar associations; Model Rules of Professional Conduct; Unethical conduct of attorneys.

Habeas corpus

Right of prisoners to have the constitutionality of their imprisonment reviewed by a federal court

Habeas corpus, literally "you have the body," originated as a common-law writ in England. In the United States, the writ of *habeas corpus* was guaranteed in Article I of the U.S. Constitution. Federal statutes enacted in 1789 and 1867 empowered federal courts to hear *habeas* cases for federal and state prisoners.

Habeas corpus, often called a collateral attack, is a limited right. Its basic purpose is to ensure that a person's constitutional right to liberty is not being violated. It is available only to people who are in custody and who have already exhausted the direct appeals of their conviction. It is technically a civil action rather than criminal, and the prisoner's actual guilt or innocence is not the issue. Instead, the prisoner must prove that something about his or her incarceration violates the U.S. Constitution. Most frequently, the prisoner will claim constitutional errors occurred during the original trial (for example, that the jury was improperly chosen) or that there is something unconstitutional about the sentence given (for example, that it is cruel and unusual punishment). Prisoners who succeed with their *habeas* claims are not typically set free but instead are given a new trial or new sentence. Significantly, even if the prisoner was convicted and incarcerated by a state, *habeas corpus* proceedings may be brought in federal court.

The Warren Court

Although the right to *habeas corpus* is as old as the Constitution, the rules relating to the scope of *habeas* review were primarily set by the Supreme Court during the second half of the twentieth century. During the years when Earl Warren was chief justice of the Supreme Court (1953-1969), the Court took an expansive view of the right. A majority of the justices believed that this was necessary because of the extreme importance of the right to liberty. Broad reviews of trial courts' decisions would protect the right to liberty and ensure that correct decisions were reached.

An example of the Warren Court's approach to *habeas* is the case of *Fay v. Noia* (1963), in which the Court upheld Noia's *habeas* challenge of his felony murder conviction. Noia's conviction had been based entirely on a confession that had been coerced in violation of his Fifth Amendment rights. Justice William J. Brennan, Jr., writing for the majority, stated that *habeas* was the "ultimate remedy" in the struggle for personal liberty.

Not all jurists and legal scholars agreed with the Warren Court's approach to *habeas* law. In fact, during the tenures of Chief Justices Warren E. Burger and William H. Rehnquist, a majority of the justices adopted a considerably narrower view of the scope of *habeas corpus* relief. The primary reason was their concern over the number of *habeas* cases federal courts were compelled to hear. In addition to burdening the courts, this interfered with the finality of decisions, encouraged frivolous claims, and contributed to the drawing out of legal proceedings. In death penalty cases, for example, *habeas* challenges could delay executions for decades. Furthermore, these justices believed, federalism required that federal courts give great respect to state courts' decisions.

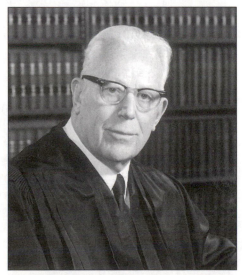

Under Chief Justice Earl Warren, the U.S. Supreme Court took an expanded view of the principle of habeas corpus. (Supreme Court Historical Society)

A Changing View

One of the most significant post-Warren *habeas* decisions was *Stone v. Powell* (1976). Defendants in two different cases challenged their convictions on the grounds that the trial courts had admitted evidence that was the product of unconstitutional searches and seizures. The Court held that prisoners cannot raise Fourth Amendment issues in *habeas* cases if they had a fair chance to litigate those issues in the state courts.

The Court further limited *habeas* rights in *Teague v. Lane* (1989), a case that dealt with the retroactivity of court decisions. If a federal court announces a new rule of criminal procedure after a prisoner's conviction is final, that prisoner may not take advantage of that rule in subsequent *habeas* claims. The reason given for this decision was the interest in preserving the finality of decisions; without such a rule, it was argued, established convictions would be perpetually subject to review as the law evolved.

In 1993 in *Herrera v. Collins*, the Court again endorsed a restricted view of the right to *habeas corpus*. Herrera had been sentenced to death for murdering a police officer. Several years after he had exhausted his direct appeals and after he had filed several unsuccessful *habeas* petitions, he brought a new *habeas* claim in federal court, claiming that new evidence had appeared that would prove his actual innocence of the crime. The Court held that he was not entitled to *habeas* relief based solely on a claim of actual innocence; because he could point out no procedural errors at his original trial, his death sentence was affirmed.

By the end of the twentieth century, the Court's conservative approach to *habeas corpus* was well established. This approach was supported by Congress, which in 1996 passed the Antiterrorism and Effective Death Penalty Act. Among other things, the act required that *habeas* claims be brought no more than one year after a claimant had exhausted his or her state appeals and generally limited prisoners to a single *habeas* petition.

—*Phyllis B. Gerstenfeld*

Suggested Readings

Del Carmen, Rolando V., Mary Parker, and Frances P. Reddington. *Briefs of Leading Cases in Juvenile Justice*. Cincinnati: Anderson, 1998.

Freedman, Eric M. *Habeas Corpus: Rethinking the Great Writ of Liberty.* New York: New York University Press, 2001.

Samaha, Joel. *Criminal Procedure.* 3d ed. St. Paul, Minn.: West Publishing, 1996.

Stahlkopf, Deborah. "A Dark Day for *Habeas Corpus*: Successive Petitions under the Antiterrorism and Effective Death Penalty Act of 1996." *Arizona Law Review* 40 (1998): 1115.

Wood, Horace G. *A Treatise on the Legal Remedies of Mandamus and Prohibition: Habeas Corpus, Certiorari, and Quo Warranto.* 3d ed. Revised and enlarged by Charles F. Bridge. Littleton, Colo.: Fred B. Rothman, 1997.

See also Appeal; Arrest; Capital punishment; Constitution, U.S.; Convictions; Courts-martial; Effective counsel; Indictments; Martial law; Presumption of innocence; State courts.

HARMLESS ERRORS

Errors that are trivial in nature and do not prejudice the substantial rights of the parties declaring them and do not affect the outcome of legal actions; parties cannot obtain new trials or have verdicts set aside or otherwise disturb judgments based on harmless errors

The issue of harmless error arises when a party to a lawsuit has taken his or her case to trial and is not satisfied with the outcome. The party may declare that an error or errors took place at some stage of the lawsuit, thereby necessitating a new trial or reversal of the verdict on appeal. In order for the party to obtain a new trial or reversal of the verdict, the party must show that the error prejudiced his or her substantial rights and that the error affected the outcome of the case. If the error did not affect the substantial rights of the party or change the outcome of the case, the error is said to be harmless, and a new trial or reversal of the verdict will not be warranted.

One of the most common grounds for alleging error is in the admission or exclusion of evidence. In these cases courts generally look to the whole case to determine whether the erroneous admission or exclusion of the evidence prejudiced the party and would have changed the outcome of the case.

See also Appellate practice; Lawsuits; Mistrials; Objection; Reversible errors; Trials.

HEARINGS

Preliminary examinations in courts to resolve legal issues that may not warrant full trials

Trials normally resolve major questions, such as who has injured whom, who has caused what damages, or whether a person charged with a crime is guilty or innocent. However, before presiding over these kinds of major questions, courts must routinely decide a variety of minor questions, such as whether a particular venue is the proper location in which to try a case, whether a trial should be moved to another place, or whether one party should be forced to turn over to the other certain confidential business information prior to trial. These sorts of preliminary questions must be resolved, and courts frequently use hearings to give parties an opportunity to admit evidence and make arguments that may be useful in determining the questions.

A hearing is in some ways a kind of minitrial. No jury is present, however. The court decides the question at issue and may allow attorneys to call witnesses to testify under oath or to make arguments pertinent to the case. As in a trial, attorneys are permitted in a hearing to cross-examine opposing witnesses. Often court reporters transcribe the proceedings so that parties aggrieved at a judge's decision on some point will be able to show an appellate court exactly what happened at the hearing. The judge presiding over a hearing may pronounce a decision immediately upon the conclusion of the proceedings. Sometimes, however, the court takes the matter under advisement, meaning that it reflects further upon the matter before reaching a decision.

—*Timothy L. Hall*

See also Change of venue; Injunctions; Inquests; Preliminary hearings; Restraining orders, temporary; Trials.

HOUSE ARREST

Punishment requiring convicted offenders to remain in their homes at all times, except to attend school or work; a type of punishment that is an alternative sanction that diverts offenders from secure incarceration and helps to reduce jail and prison populations

House arrest requires convicted offenders to remain in their homes. Most offenders are allowed to leave their homes to attend school or to go to their places of employment, but they must return to their homes immediately following school or work. The most lenient type of house arrest simply requires that the offender adhere to a specified curfew. More serious offenders may be monitored using an electronic device which straps around the ankle and allows free movement by offenders within their homes. Probation officers can then check on their probationers with a simple telephone call, which notifies them if the offender has left the home. House arrest is known as an alternative sanction, or an alternative to incarceration. When offenders are diverted from secure incarceration into an alternative such as house arrest, jail overcrowding problems are diminished. Some critics, however, have accused house arrest of being an attempt at "net widening" which increases control of the criminal justice system over offenders.

See also Arrest; Criminal justice system; Good time; Incapacitation; Parole; Personal recognizance; Probation, adult; Sentencing.

IGNORANCE OF THE LAW

Invalid excuse for committing an offense

The maxim that "ignorance of the law excuses not" was a Roman law principle assimilated into the common law. Modern Anglo-American common law restates this ancient maxim as "ignorance of the law is no excuse" or "everyone is presumed to know the law." The common-law justification of the rule was to encourage citizens to learn the law. Failure to comprehend the legal effect of making an admission provides no excuse for a defendant. As one court put it, "Ignorance of the law excuses no one." The modern trend of the law is a steady erosion of the ignorance of the law doctrine.

The common-law position was based on the fact that most common-law crimes were *malum in se,* or inherently evil. The "ignorance of the law" maxim is less compelling for complex statutes that criminalize conduct that is not inherently evil. Many activities in the modern regulatory state are wrong simply because a legislature defines them as wrong. Regulatory offenses are often referred to as *malum prohibitum,* or public welfare crimes. The "ignorance of the law" defense has a continuing vitality for many public welfare offenses. Nevertheless, persons may be prosecuted for violation of a water pollution statute even if they profess to having been ignorant that the activity is illegal.

Criminal defendants may be prosecuted for receiving stolen goods even if they did not know that such receipt is illegal. The fact that the U.S. Congress used the adverb "knowingly" to authorize punishment of those not having a permit for firearms does not lead to the conclusion that there is an exception to the ignorance of the law defense. Similarly, ignorance is no defense in other substantive fields of the law. Employers are not excused for failing to maintain a safe workplace simply because they were unaware of occupational safety laws. Ignorance of the law does not excuse public officials from requirements imposed upon them by sunshine, or open government, laws.

The ignorance of the law doctrine is inapplicable to offenses that are defined with a state-of-mind requirement. However, the U.S. Congress or a state may define knowledge of the law as an element of an offense. In such statutes, a willful violation requires some mental state more culpable than mere intent to perform a forbidden act. Courts often rule that the word "willfully" requires knowledge of the law, which is an exception to the presumed knowledge principle. Likewise, mistake of fact or the law may be an excuse or defense if it negates the mental state that is the element of a crime.

The willfulness required for criminal contempt is the knowledge that one is violating a court order, not the knowledge that the violation of the order is a crime. A mistake of fact is a misapprehension of fact which, if true, would have justified the act or omission. Mistake of law or ignorance of the law is a defense when a defendant's willfulness or knowledge is an element of the defense. Another exception to the no-excuse doctrine occurs when a defendant has relied on an interpretation of law given by a public official. Courts are more receptive to the mistake of law defense if the statute is complex or ambiguously worded. If there is a complex business, environmental, or other complex statute, courts sometimes permit ignorance of the law to excuse a violation. The policy justification for this exception to the general rule is the danger of convicting individuals involved in apparently innocent activity.

—Michael L. Rustad

See also Common law; Defendants; Statutes.

IMMIGRATION, LEGAL AND ILLEGAL

Major source of population growth in the United States that affects national and regional economic health, ethnic and cultural diversity, utilization of governmental services, and other domestic conditions

For much of the twentieth century, the United States has absorbed more legal immigrants than the other countries of the world combined. In addition to legal immigration, each year several hundred thousand persons enter the country to reside illegally. In the 1990's, about one in four foreigners settling in the United States did so in violation of immigration laws. Immigration affects American society in fundamental ways, but the costs, benefits, and moral obligations surrounding immigration are matters of dispute. The debate over immigration is fraught with conflicting statistics and conflicting values and centers on three primary topics: humanitarianism, economics, and nationhood.

Humanitarianism

A large part of the rationale for accepting immigrants into the United States stems from humanitarian concerns. In theory, U.S.

policies seek to assist people of other nations who experience political oppression, discrimination, famine, civil war, or any number of other tribulations. In this context, allowing individuals to try to escape the worst of their problems by immigrating to the United States can be seen as a form of international aid.

The United States, like most other Western democratic countries, offers asylum to refugees of political repression. The United States distinguishes between political refugees fleeing persecution and economic refugees seeking a better standard of living. The system, however, is subject to inefficiency and abuse. Ascertaining whether a person is a political or economic refugee is a difficult and time-consuming task. Typically, there is a large backlog of asylum cases awaiting official action, and while the government is processing a case, the applicant may become "lost" within the general population. Such cases constitute one source of illegal immigration. Government efforts to locate and repatriate these illegal refugees are often ineffective. Moreover, many such enforcement actions raise justice issues of their own. Some groups in the United States have dedicated themselves to shielding illegal immigrants from immigration authorities and laws. Such efforts reached a peak in the 1980's, when a number of churches and even cities declared themselves "sanctuaries" for aliens who did not have official refugee status.

American public sentiment for political refugees has fluctuated widely over time. The anticommunist and anti-Soviet feelings prevalent during the Cold War made dissidents and defectors from Eastern Europe and the Soviet Union especially welcome. Unusually brutal governmental crackdowns, such as those by the Chinese government at Tiananmen Square in 1989, raise public sympathy for political refugees, particularly for activists fighting for democracy. Poignant examples of human tragedy, such as ethnic cleansing in Bosnia and the warehousing of orphans in postcommunist Romania, can spur Americans to adopt foreign children and to sponsor the immigration of adults and families. Some international crises, such as the fall of South Vietnam in the mid-1970's, dramatically increase the number of political refugees coming to the United States. These large waves of refugees can fatigue American public support for immigration. Further, incidents of international terrorism inflicted upon Americans—such as the September 11, 2001, attacks on the Pentagon and the World Trade Center—can reduce public acceptance of foreign immigrants (particularly when they belong to groups associated with terrorism, rightly or wrongly, in the public consciousness).

Economics

Persons without any claim of experiencing political repression can also apply to immigrate to the United States. Many are motivated by economic and societal opportunities. Traditionally, immigration of this sort has contributed significantly to the growth of the U.S. population and economy. A rapid influx of immigrants, however, may overwhelm the country's ability to assimilate them, burdening social services and housing stocks, absorbing employment opportunities, and heightening racial and ethnic tensions. The net economic effects of the presence of immigrants is a matter of debate. Proponents claim that immigrants tend to pay more in taxes than they receive in social services, that they perform jobs American citizens prefer not to take, and that they tend to have a strong work ethic. Yet to the extent that immigrants have lower levels of education and lower wage demands—both are particularly true of illegal immigrants—their presence may skew the economy toward more service-oriented, labor-intensive jobs. The presence of a surplus of cheap labor may reduce incentives to invest in greater mechanization. Some critics charge that large numbers of immigrants make finding employment more difficult for poor Americans, particularly for poor members of minority groups.

To regulate those effects, the federal government controls immigration through eligibility requirements and numerical limits. Deciding who will and will not be permitted to immigrate raises obvious justice issues. Until the mid-1960's, government established immigration quotas on the basis of nationality, at times excluding some national and racial groups entirely. Since the mid-1960's, permission to immigrate to the United States has been awarded largely by lottery.

Persons who are unable to secure legal resident status may resort to illegal means for entering the country. In response, the U.S. government has taken steps to block illegal border crossings. In 1924, the U.S. Border Patrol was established to police the country's borders. The Mexican border is more heavily policed than the Canadian and has been fortified with surveillance devices and metal fencing. These measures have led some critics to identify the U.S.-Mexico border with the infamous Berlin Wall, although

Work Performed by Immigration Lawyers

Immigration lawyers, who work with immigrants and with businesses employing or desiring to hire immigrants:

- Analyze the facts in the case of someone desiring to immigrate
- Explain all benefits for which immigrants may be eligible
- Recommend the best way to obtain legal immigrant status
- Complete and file appropriate applications
- Keep up with new laws affecting their clients
- Speak for clients in discussions with the Immigration and Naturalization Service (INS)
- Represent clients in court
- File necessary appeals and waivers

Adapted from: American Immigration and Lawyers Association, "A Guide to Consumer Protection and Authorized Representation," Washington, D.C.: AILA, 1998.

others argue that the imprisonment of people within a country and the exclusion of people from a country concern different questions of morality.

U.S. efforts to limit immigration involve economic and market forces in a number of ways. The perceived promise of economic opportunity in the United States, coupled with immigration restrictions, has given rise to human smuggling operations, particularly in Mexico. In the early 1990's, about half the aliens illegally entering the United States were assisted in some way by smugglers. In addition to taking police measures, the U.S. government has tried to stem illegal immigration by reducing the incentives for it. The 1994 North American Free Trade Agreement (NAFTA) was touted in part for its projected role in improving economic opportunities in Mexico, thus reducing the incentive to emigrate. At the same time, governmental benefits to illegal aliens were restricted, partly in the hope that such limitations will make the prospect of living illegally in the United States less attractive. Federal welfare payments, food stamps, unemployment compensation, and other federal benefits are available to legal, but not to illegal, immigrants; however, primary education and medical services cannot be withheld from illegal aliens. In ruling on such issues, the U.S. Supreme Court has held that the equal protection clause of the Fourteenth Amendment does not depend on citizenship status.

Border states have been especially sensitive to the economic and social costs of illegal immigration. These states often bear the brunt of service provision, infrastructure maintenance, law enforcement, and other social costs of illegal immigration. In 1994, California voters passed Proposition 187, a referendum that sought to deny state benefits, including health care, welfare, and education, to illegal aliens. (The referendum was immediately challenged as unconstitutional.) Some states have sued the federal government for the costs of supporting illegal aliens, asserting that the federal government was negligent in not stopping such aliens at the country's borders. Border states have also challenged federal census figures, arguing that the allocation of federal benefits (including apportionment of congressional seats) should account for illegal aliens.

Race, Ethnicity, and Nationhood

Although the humanitarian motives that ostensibly underlie many U.S. immigration laws seldom are defined in terms of race and ethnicity, the federal government frequently has controlled immigration on the basis of national origin. Beginning in the 1920's, the United States established immigration quotas defined by national origin. Immigrants from European countries historically have been favored.

Immigration patterns have shifted dramatically over time, however, and not always as a result of changes to U.S. immigration policy. In the 1950's, most immigrants came from Europe and Canada. By the 1970's, partly as a result of international events, the majority of immigrants were coming from Asia, Central America, and the Caribbean. The effects of different immigration patterns are compounded by higher birthrates among some immigrant groups; such effects are further accentuated by the disproportionate number of young adults among persons immigrating to the United States.

Consideration of immigration in terms of race and nationality raises the question of how the American people should be defined as a nation. The United States' sense of nationhood stems more from shared morals, values, and norms than from ethnic, racial, or even cultural characteristics. Yet the traditional conception of the United States as a "melting pot" of various ethnic and racial groups was challenged in the 1980's and 1990's by critics who claimed that such a concept unfairly pressures immigrants and racial minorities to conform to a largely white, middle-class culture. In its place, such critics offered a "salad bowl" metaphor of the United States, envisioning the various cultures of America's citizens as retained in a diverse mosaic. In this view, assimilation, including perhaps even the mastery of English language, is unnecessary and perhaps undesirable. Nevertheless, immigrant groups themselves overwhelmingly desire to adopt American mores and culture, believe that people who come to the United States should learn to speak English, and sense that the country suffers from excessive immigration.

Immigration policies thus cut to the heart of the United States' sense of nationhood. By defining who can live in the country, who can receive services, and what is required to become a citizen, the government defines what it means to be an American. These policies also describe the nation's sense of its moral obligations to foreign persons in need, and the enforcement of these policies helps to direct the future makeup of the American population.

Policies

American immigration policy has shifted widely over time. Although much of the country's early growth was fed by immigration, the United States has periodically restricted immigration in general or the entry of certain groups in particular. An example of the latter is the Chinese Exclusion Act of 1882, which was repealed in 1943. The first broad immigration control laws were established in the 1920's with the National Origins Act, which attempted to limit the inflow of immigrants and to fix the ethnic proportions of the U.S. population via national quotas.

World War II, the Holocaust, and the political dislocations that followed the war prompted the United States to revise its immigration laws. After a series of ad hoc alterations, in 1952 the Immigration and Nationality Act codified the disparate immigration laws and ended immigration and naturalization prohibitions by race. The Hart-Celler Act of 1965 expanded the 1952 law, ending national origin quotas entirely. In addition, this act established the reuniting of families as a goal of U.S. immigration policy. In a further move away from group- and nationality-based admissions policies, the Refugee Act of 1980 required that decisions to admit refugees be made on a case-by-case basis.

By the 1980's, the growing number of illegal immigrants had once again pushed immigration reform into the public spotlight.

The Immigration Reform and Control Act (IRCA) of 1986, an attempt to balance the interests of anti-immigrant and immigrant-rights groups, took two approaches to the problem. To reduce illegal immigration, the act imposed sanctions on employers hiring illegal aliens and strengthened the country's border enforcement. At the same time, the IRCA granted amnesty to illegal aliens who had resided in the country since at least 1982. Further modifications to immigration and refugee laws and policies continued throughout the 1980's and early 1990's, prompted partly by the end of the Cold War and the increase in civil wars around the world. In 1990, for example, the Immigration Act raised immigration quotas by 40 percent, their highest level since 1914.

—Steve D. Boilard

Suggested Readings

Numerous books on immigration focusing on various legal aspects of the subject are readily available. A representative sample includes *Immigrants in Courts*, edited by Joanne I. Moore and Margaret E. Fisher (Seattle: University of Washington Press, 1999); Bill Ong Hing's *Immigration and the Law: A Dictionary* (Santa Barbara, Calif.: ABC-CLIO, 1999); George J. Borjas, *Friends or Strangers: The Impact of Immigrants on the U.S. Economy* (New York: Basic Books, 1990); James D. Cockcroft, *Outlaws in the Promised Land: Mexican Immigrant Workers and America's Future* (New York: Grove Press, 1986); Brent Nelson, *America Balkanized: Immigration's Challenge to Government* (Monterey, Va.: American Immigration Control Foundation, 1994); Julian Simon, *The Economic Consequences of Immigration* (Cambridge, England: Basil Blackwell, 1989); and Virginia Yans-McLaughlin, ed., Immigration Reconsidered: History, Sociology, and Politics (New York: Oxford University Press, 1990). *A Reader on Race, Civil Rights, and American Law: A Multiracial Approach*, edited by Timothy Davis, Kevin R. Johnson, and George A. Martínez (Durham, N.C.: Carolina Academic Press, 2001) includes a chapter on race and immigration law.

See also Amnesty; Attorney general of the United States; Diplomatic immunity; Law enforcement.

IMMUNITY FROM PROSECUTION

Exemption from duty or penalty that is granted to encourage testimony that might not otherwise be given

The Fifth Amendment to the United States Constitution grants persons the right to refuse to incriminate themselves by testimony in a court of law. By the due process clause, the Fourteenth Amendment to the Constitution extends this same protection to individuals who are witnesses or defendants in state courts.

When it is difficult to find witnesses to a crime, and when the best witness is a person who participated in the crime, immunity from prosecution, or "use immunity," may be offered to induce that person to testify against others involved in the crime. The witness may then truthfully testify about the crime and escape prosecution for that crime or, in some cases, for other activities connected to the particular crime.

Once an offer of immunity is accepted, a witness may no longer claim self-incrimination during testimony. If a witness still refuses to testify after accepting immunity, the witness may be charged with contempt of court. A person may voluntarily waive the right against self-incrimination. In such a case, no immunity is offered, and the testimony given by the witness may be used in that proceeding, or in later proceedings, against that witness.

See also Amnesty; Bill of Rights, U.S.; Diplomatic immunity; Fifth Amendment; Informants; Judicial bias; Legal immunity; Testimony.

IMPEACHMENT OF JUDGES

Legal process for removing from office judges who engage in serious misconduct

Impeachment is the process of removing public officials from their posts before their normal terms of duty expire. It is normally reserved for serious misconduct on the part of public officials, including judges. Under the U.S. Constitution, for example, federal officials, including federal judges, may be impeached upon a showing that they have engaged in acts of treason, bribery, or "other high crimes and misdemeanors." In the case of federal impeachments, the House of Representatives may vote to commence impeachment proceedings against federal judges, while the Senate actually conducts impeachment trials and votes on whether to impeach.

Impeachment proceedings against federal officials have occurred most frequently with respect to federal judges, although even these have been relatively rare. The closing years of the twentieth century witnessed the impeachment of three federal judges: Judges Harry Claiborne, Alcee Hastings, and Walter Nixon. Frequently, but not inevitably, judicial impeachment fol-

In 1805, Supreme Court Justice Samuel Chase faced impeachment charges. (H. B. Hall/Collection of the Supreme Court of the United States.)

lows a criminal conviction for some offence. Judge Harry Claiborne was impeached in the 1980's after being convicted of tax
fraud, and Judge Walter Nixon was impeached after his conviction for perjury. Judge Hastings, on the other hand, was acquitted
of criminal charges but was subsequently impeached by the
Senate.

One might imagine that impeachment proceedings would be
unnecessary in cases in which judges have been convicted of
criminal violations. In fact, judges so convicted frequently resign
and thus escape the further indignity of impeachment. However,
such resignations are not inevitable and certainly not always
quickly accomplished. Federal judge Robert Collins was imprisoned in 1991 but continued to draw his annual salary until his resignation in August, 1993. Harry Claiborne, unwilling to consider
resignation, drew his judicial salary for two years while he served
a prison term in the 1980's, until Congress finally impeached him.

Attempts to impeach judges have not been reserved simply for
the rank and file of the judiciary. Even judicial luminaries, such as
Supreme Court justices, have sometimes had to endure the stern
gaze of a Congress willing to consider their impeachment. In
1805, for example, Justice Samuel Chase faced impeachment proceedings against him but ultimately prevailed, causing Thomas
Jefferson to grouse that the prospect of impeachment was "not
even a scarecrow." In the twentieth century, Justice William O.
Douglas had to fend off impeachment charges led by then-House
minority leader Gerald R. Ford. Douglas was ultimately vindi-
cated when the House Judiciary committee refused to recommend impeachment articles to the House.

—*Timothy L. Hall*

See also Federal judicial system; Judges; Judicial appointments
and elections; Judicial bias; Judicial conduct code; Judicial confirmation hearings.

Incapacitation

Aim or rationale of punishment that seeks to control crime by rendering criminals unable, or less able, to commit further crimes, such as by incarcerating offenders

Incapacitation refers to the idea that certain forms of punishment are an effective means of reducing crime if they restrict the abilities and opportunities of criminals to commit crimes. For example, confining offenders in prison removes them from society and renders them unable to commit further crimes against the general public. Execution has the ultimate incapacitating effect. Even parole may help to incapacitate criminals by limiting their movement and thus restricting their opportunities for committing crimes.

The nineteenth century British utilitarian philosopher Jeremy Bentham discussed incapacitation in a treatment of the ends of punishment. Bentham regarded the principal end of punishment as control of conduct, and he used the term "disablement" to refer to the effect of punishment on the offender's "physical power." This was contrasted with reformation, which refers to the use of punishment to control conduct by influencing the offender's will, and with deterrence, whereby punishment sets an example and thus controls the conduct of people besides the offender. Contemporary discussions of the aims and effects of punishment follow Bentham, at least roughly, in distinguishing among reform or rehabilitation, incapacitation, and general deterrence by example or threat of punishment.

Incapacitation is an expected, or at least hoped for, effect of punishment. An incapacitative effect, however, does not occur in two types of situations. The first is the case in which the offender would not have committed any additional crimes even if he or she had not been punished. The second is the situation in which another individual takes the place of the incarcerated criminal, taking advantage of the opportunity that has opened. This often occurs in the case of criminal activity related to gangs, when the arrest and imprisonment of one member may not result in a decrease in crime. Other gang members or new recruits often fill the position vacated by the arrest of a gang member.

Studies have not established that a strict incapacitation approach to crime control is likely to lead to a significant reduction in the rate of crime. Skeptics point to periods during which crime rates have risen despite increased use of imprisonment. Studies have yielded mixed estimates of any incapacitative effect, with some research projecting a slight increase in crime (4 or 5 percent) with a reduction in prison use. Other research has projected a substantial decrease in crime if the prison population were increased. There is some evidence that the effect of incapacitation varies with types of criminal behavior. Some criminologists have recommended a policy of selective incapacitation—for example, of "career criminals" or violent criminals. Some states have enacted laws imposing life sentences on persons convicted three times of violent or serious crimes; these are sometimes colloquially called "three-time loser" laws or "three strikes and you're out" policies.

See also Capital punishment; Cruel and unusual punishment; House arrest; Sentencing; Three-strikes laws.

INDEMNITY

Agreement between two parties by which one promises to reimburse the other for the loss or damage that may be incurred because of the occurrence of a specified event

Many contracts, such as insurance policies, contain indemnification clauses. The principle of indemnity in insurance is to compensate the insured by placing him or her in the same financial position after the loss as before it. For example, property insurance provides for payment for loss or damage that the insured owner may incur from fire or vandalism. Similarly, automobile liability insurance provides compensation to the insured party for damages due to injuries caused to other persons by negligent operation of an insured vehicle. Some life insurance policies contain a double indemnity clause, whereby the insurance company agrees to pay twice the amount of the policy if the insured individual dies from accidental causes.

It is important for persons to make decisions on contracts or insurance policies only after careful review of the wording and the facts surrounding a potential or actual claim. Insurance policies not only indemnify the insured but typically also include a number of exclusions that may appear to fall within the coverage of the basic insuring clause. For example, intentional acts are not generally indemnified, nor are damages to third-party property held for storage.

—*Alvin K. Benson*

See also Compensatory damages; Contracts; Liability, civil and criminal; Punitive damages.

INDICTMENTS

Formal written accusations made by grand juries charging persons with crimes; the first steps in most criminal prosecutions

A bill of indictment is usually drafted by a prosecuting attorney and submitted to a grand jury along with witnesses and other supporting evidence. The people who serve on the grand jury convene to evaluate the prosecutor's evidence; if a majority finds that evidence warrants a trial, the jury then releases a bill of particulars informing the accused of the offense charged.

Grand juries can also conduct their own investigations and make accusations or "presentments" without a bill of indictment. Similarly, prosecutors in some states can make accusations without grand jury review. These non-grand jury charges, which are called "informations," were challenged in the case of *Hurtado v. California* (1884). Because the Fifth Amendment requires grand jury indictment for federal crimes, Hurtado argued, the Fourteenth Amendment's due process clause required states to do the same. The Supreme Court, however, upheld the process of information, finding that states may use various methods of initiating criminal prosecutions, provided that such methods are fair. The result is that the right to grand jury indictment applies only to federal crimes.

See also Arrest; Bill of Rights, U.S.; Criminal procedure; *Habeas corpus*; Inquests; Model Penal Code; *Nolo contendere* pleas; Statutes of limitations.

INDIGENT CRIMINAL DEFENDANTS

Persons foramlly charged with crimes who, due to their poverty, cannot adequately provide for their own defense

Although social scientists have long debated the causes of crime, it is beyond dispute that the impact of the criminal justice system is felt most heavily among the most economically disadvantaged members of society. In city after city, young, unemployed men dominate the criminal dockets. Nearly two out of three incarcerated individuals lack a high school diploma, and less than 8 percent have ever attended college. Controversy concerns whether poverty causes crime or merely funnels deviants into relatively unremunerative and highly risky kinds of criminal activity, where they are more likely to be apprehended. Another theory is that these crime statistics reflect institutional class biases in the criminal justice system, such as the inability of the impoverished defendant to mount an adequate defense. The commitment to equal justice under law is severely tested by a criminal justice system that imposes further disabilities on the most disadvantaged members of the community.

The Supreme Court noted in *Griffin v. Illinois* (1956), "There can be no equal justice where the kind of trial a man gets depends on the amount of money he has." This egalitarian impulse was most completely manifest in right-to-counsel cases and seemed to peak during the late 1950's and 1960's. It was, however, tempered by considerations of federalism and the realization that public aid to all indigent defendants would be expensive and unpopular. In *Powell v. Alabama* (1932), also known as the Scottsboro case, the Court overturned rape convictions of seven itinerant African American youths. The youths were sentenced to death after one-day trials conducted in an atmosphere of racial hostility and at which they had been casually represented by an attorney unfamiliar with Alabama law who volunteered for the case on the morning of the trial. The Court found the trial to be fundamentally unfair. Adequate representation for such vulnerable defendants required the appointment, at public expense, of effective counsel with ample skill and time to prepare a credible defense. However, in *Betts v. Brady* (1942), the Court confined the right to appointed counsel in state prosecutions to cases in which special circumstances, not including mere poverty, rendered the defendant particularly vulnerable.

The Right to Counsel

In *Johnson v. Zerbst* (1938), the Court found that the Sixth Amendment required the appointment of counsel for all federal felony trials, a right not extended to state legal systems until *Gideon v. Wainwright* (1963). *Gideon* well illustrated the issues presented by the indigent defendant. An unemployed drifter with a poor education and a record of petty crimes, Gideon was denied appointed counsel at his trial for breaking and entering a pool hall and stealing change from a cigarette machine. Forced to defend himself, Gideon failed to explore several credible defenses or adequately cross-examine the state's single—and dubious—witness. After the Court overturned his conviction, Gideon was tried a second time. At last represented by an attorney, he was acquitted.

The principle of *Gideon* was extended to other areas of the criminal process but not comprehensively. *Escobedo v. Illinois* (1964) and *Miranda v. Arizona* (1966) extended the right to appointed counsel into the pretrial stages of the criminal process. *Griffin* required states to waive costs for filing appeals, in this case the expensive production of a trial transcript. The right to counsel was also extended to sentencing but only to the initial appeal. In *Ross v. Moffitt* (1974), the Court held that the state need not supply appointed counsel for discretionary appeals to the state supreme court. Presumably, no such right exists for appeals to the U.S. Supreme Court, although the Court has appointed counsel once a case is accepted for review. In *Gagnon v. Scarpelli* (1973), the "special circumstances" rule of *Betts* was revived for probation revocation hearings, requiring the appointment of counsel only for probationers who were unusually disadvantaged beyond their poverty.

Perhaps the clearest example of the Court's lessened favor of the appointment of counsel is *Argersinger v. Hamlin* (1972), in which the Court declined to extend the *Gideon* precedent to all misdemeanor cases. It ruled that the trial court needs to provide assistance of counsel only in cases in which the contemplated punishment is incarceration. Misdemeanor courts are known for their summary procedures, in which the mere presence of counsel often results in dismissal of charges. Because even conscientious judges operate under bureaucratic pressure to keep up with heavy caseloads, *Argersinger* is widely ignored in practice. Most misdemeanor defendants are unlikely to be incarcerated and are anxious to pay their fines and be done with it. For the indigent, however, even a modest fine can have a significant impact on his or her living standard.

Questions of Fairness

An issue yet to be effectively addressed involves the adequacy of counsel for poor defendants, whether appointed or retained. Many defendants are represented by court-appointed public defenders. Despite their talent and good intentions, public defenders tend to operate under the pressure of unrealistic caseloads and inadequate funding. Defendants who, like the "Scottsboro Boys," first encounter their attorney just before trial are not unusual. Without time or resources to conduct a thorough investigation of the case, public defenders are often reduced to arranging a plea bargain. The economics of criminal defense work often place the private attorney in a similar position.

If access to judicial process is fundamental to the fair administration of criminal justice, it would be expected that the Court would facilitate the indigent's access to its own forum. The Court permits petitioners for *certiorari* to file *in forma pauperis*, or as a pauper. The resulting waiver of the Court's modest filing fees may be more symbolic than substantive, since less than 1 percent of such petitions are accepted for review. In the 1990's the numbers of *in forma pauperis* petitioners was the fastest growing segment of the Court's caseload, which came to account for more than half of all petitioners. Many of these are filed by prisoners alleging deficiencies in their convictions. Most are frivolous, although an occasional *in forma pauperis* petition, like that in *Gideon*, results in a significant decision. The Court requires a person filing *in forma pauperis* to provide documentation of his or her impecunious circumstances.

—*John C. Hughes*

Suggested Readings

Casper, Jonathan. *American Criminal Justice: The Defendant's Perspective*. Englewood Cliffs, N.J.: Prentice-Hall, 1972.

Cole, David. *No Equal Justice: Race and Class in the American Criminal Justice System*. New York: New Press, 1999.

Feeley, Malcome. *The Process Is the Punishment: Handling Cases in Lower Criminal Court*. New York: Russell Sage, 1992.

Lewis, Anthony. *Gideon's Trumpet*. New York: Random House, 1989.

Reiman, Jeffrey H. *The Rich Get Richer and the Poor Get Prison: Ideology, Class, and Criminal Justice*. Needham, Mass.: Allyn & Bacon, 1997.

Uviller, H. Richard. *The Tilted Playing Field: Is Criminal Justice Unfair?* New Haven, Conn.: Yale University Press, 1999.

See also Attorneys, court-appointed; Death row attorneys; Defendants; Defense attorneys; Effective counsel; Legal guardians; Public defenders.

INFORMANTS

Persons outside police forces who are used by police to gain insights into the activities of particular persons or groups who may be committing, or planning to commit, crimes

In order to acquire the necessary evidence to file charges against suspects or even simply to gain knowledge of alleged criminal activities, police have historically relied on informants. In nineteenth century Great Britain police forces used informants to gather information on secret political organizations. In the United States in modern times, the Federal Bureau of Investigation (FBI) and other police forces use informants to gather evidence on organized crime, motorcycle gangs, and white supremacist groups.

Police informants are valuable to law enforcement for several reasons. They almost always belong to particular organizations or know specific individuals about whom the police want information. As members of organizations the police are spying on, they have privileged knowledge that is not available to outsiders. Attempts to infiltrate organizations using police officers, even undercover ones, are often difficult, because criminal organizations are secretive and suspicious of outsiders.

There are several reasons why informants cooperate with the police. The main reason is money. They are frequently, but not always, paid for their information. Their egos also play a role. Informants have something the police want, putting them in a privileged position. The compromise factor is another element: To gain the assistance of criminal insiders, the police may use bargaining ploys, such as offering to reduce criminal charges or promising immunity from prosecution. Finally, informants may assist of their own free volition because they are unhappy with the organizations, persons, or activities with which they are involved.

Several important issues are raised by the use of informants. First is the illegal activity in which they may engage in the employ of a police force. Police forces generally try to have their informants avoid engaging in illegal activities, since this weakens their credibility as witnesses. Another issue is informants' role as *agents provocateurs*, persons who incite others under investigation to commit incriminating acts. As *agents provocateurs* they actually encourage the criminal activities about which they are reporting on behalf of the police. Another problem is the vulnerability of relying on members of criminal organizations for accurate information. There is even the danger that informants may deliberately provide the police with inaccurate information in an effort to sabotage an investigation. Police forces deal with this potential problem by proceeding with caution when dealing with such persons and, whenever possible, by using other sources to gather information. Finally, by using informants, the police put these persons' lives in danger. Thus, the police must monitor their safety and attempt to ensure that the relationship is kept hidden from those under investigation.

—*Steve Hewitt*

See also Citizen's arrest; Detectives, police; Evidence, rules of; Federal Bureau of Investigation; Police; Private investigators; Probable cause; Witnesses.

INJUNCTIONS

Court orders requiring parties to do, or to refrain from doing, specified actions

The most common form of lawsuit is one in which one party seeks a monetary recovery from another. Sometimes, however, the aim of a lawsuit is not to obtain money but to obtain an order from a court commanding someone either to do or not to do something. The command that a court gives in such cases is called an injunction.

Injunctions generally take one of three forms: permanent injunctions, preliminary injunctions, or temporary restraining orders. A permanent injunction is the order that a court makes at the conclusion of a trial, after determining that the injunction is justified. Frequently, however, the party seeking an injunction needs more immediate relief. Between the beginning of a lawsuit and its ending a good deal of time normally passes: often between two and four years. For the party seeking an injunction, this may be impossibly long. In such cases, the law provides the possibility of a court order that does not wait until the end of a trial. When a court determines that a party is likely to be successful in proving its need for a permanent injunction, the court may order a preliminary injunction to maintain the status quo until a trial is complete.

Even a preliminary injunction takes time to obtain. A party must file a lawsuit and request the preliminary injunction. Then the court must schedule a hearing at which the parties to the lawsuit offer evidence for or against the preliminary injunction. This delay may be more than a party can bear in some cases. The party who needs an immediate court order can seek a temporary restraining order. This is an order that may be obtained in a matter of days or even hours and is intended to preserve conditions until a court has the chance to rule on an application for a permanent injunction.

Injunctions are common in cases in which one party alleges that another is engaged in some damaging or illegal conduct. A business which believes that a former employee is about to give the business's trade secrets to a competitor might seek an injunction ordering the former employee not to divulge the secrets. A citizens group convinced that a manufacturer is polluting a local river might seek an injunction ordering the manufacturer not to pollute. Women or minorities who believe that a government agency has discriminated against them by refusing to grant them promotions might sue the agency seeking a court order prohibiting the discrimination. A wife, concerned that a former husband might inflict violence upon her or her children might seek an injunction preventing the former spouse from approaching her and her children.

—*Timothy L. Hall*

See also Breach of contract; Civil actions; Consent decree; Equitable remedies; Hearings; Lawsuits; Restraining orders, temporary; Torts.

INQUESTS

Inquiries held by groups of people who have the legal right to make investigations

The word "inquest" comes from Latin meaning to inquire or to search. Inquests are held to obtain various types of information. In the United States and Canada the most common type of inquest is a coroner's inquest, which is used to investigate a death that apparently occurred by unnatural means. Typically, the county coroner selects a jury from the voter registration rolls to investigate an unexplained or suspicious death. The inquest is a criminal proceeding that takes the form of a preliminary investigation, and in the case of a violent death the inquiry not only investigates the physical nature of the death but may also examine evidence involving the moral nature of the crime.

If an autopsy is deemed necessary in order to ascertain the cause of death, the coroner has the right to order this procedure. For the inquest to be valid both the coroner and the jury must view the body. Hence, the body of the deceased must be found before an inquest can proceed. Any witnesses are examined before the inquest jury and the jury reports its findings to the coroner.

The coroner then prepares a record of the inquest's findings that includes the identity of the deceased and the time, place, cause, and manner of death. This report may be used by a grand jury as the basis for a murder indictment.

—Alvin K. Benson

See also District attorneys; Evidence, rules of; Hearings; Preliminary hearings; Witnesses.

JOINT AND SEVERAL LIABILITY

Liability for injuries is the responsibility of more than one person in joint liability and of only one person in several liability

The fundamental premise of the U.S. civil justice system is that any person or entity found liable for personal injury or property damage to another must pay money to compensate for the loss. A primary concern of an injured person is who must pay and how much must be paid. These questions become more complicated when more than one person or entity is found liable to pay for personal injury or property damage to another.

When only one person is found liable to pay compensation for the injury to another person, then that person is severally liable. Several liability means that a person who is liable must pay the entire amount of compensation due the injured party. When more than one person is found liable to pay compensation for an injury to another, then those persons are jointly liable for payment of compensation. The concern of jointly liable persons is how much of the entire amount of compensation due the injured person must each jointly liable person pay. If the jointly liable persons are joint and severally liable, then they are responsible for paying the entire amount of compensation due the injured party. This means that the injured party can seek full payment of compensation from one of many jointly and severally liable persons without regard to any other jointly and severally liable person. In the absence of joint and several liability, a jointly liable person only pays a portion of the total amount of compensation due an injured person.

—*Michael F. Flynn*

See also Civil law; Damages; Liability, civil and criminal; Negligence; Strict liability; Torts.

JUDGES

Public officials who are charged with authoritatively and impartially resolving disputes presented in courts of law

Judges serve a critical role in the criminal justice system, both as the authoritative managers of courtroom proceedings and often as the impartial arbiters of facts, guilt, and sentences. Judges are therefore expected to possess a number of valuable qualities that equip them to meet the high standards and demanding tasks of their office.

Managing the Courtroom

The United States tends to employ what is known as an adversary system in the courtroom, which means that the parties in a legal dispute are expected to present their cases in their own best interests. In such a setting, the judge is not expected to assist either side in making its case or even to seek out evidence and facts. Instead, it is expected that such evidence will be made available by the parties either through deliberately presenting pertinent facts or through cross-examination. The judge's role thus becomes one of enforcing the rules and ensuring that a fair trial take place. Some describe this role as akin to that of a referee enforcing the rules of a game. However, the judge's role typically goes beyond the tasks implied by this analogy.

The complexities of U.S. law, coupled with the sometimes tense emotions and deliberate deceptions in the courtroom, can conspire to make the judge's task of ensuring a fair trial extremely difficult. The judge can be expected to exercise an almost superhuman combination of wisdom, compassion, logic, circumspection, integrity, and objectivity. While they may fall short of this ideal, judges typically are better trained and more disciplined than the general population. Almost all federal and state judges have law degrees and extensive courtroom experience, often as attorneys. Standards for municipal judges are usually less demanding. However, the respect accorded to the profession overall is valuable to judges in maintaining authority in the courtroom.

Deciding Verdicts and Imposing Sentences

In addition to managing courtroom proceedings, judges frequently must pass judgment at the conclusion of a trial. This function is sometimes served partly or wholly by juries. Judges can be called upon to determine guilt or innocence, to pass sentences in criminal trials, and to ascertain damages in civil trials.

In determining guilt or assigning blame, judges often must choose between two well-presented and plausible arguments. Sometimes, however, they are faced with two problematic and poorly presented arguments. Either way, they are frequently forced to make a definitive decision based on conflicting and incomplete information. In doing this, they must draw on a thorough knowledge of the law and a keen understanding of human nature while being familiar with the facts of a case.

Once guilt is determined, sentencing remains a difficult and complex task faced by judges. Most crimes can warrant a range of penalties, depending on the particular circumstances. Judges are expected to weigh such matters as the violence or damage caused by the crime, personal information about the defendant (such as age, criminal record, and evident contrition), and the conclusiveness of the conviction. This last point is especially relevant when a jury, rather than the judge, decides the matter of guilt.

Judges are usually constrained in their sentencing decisions by statutes that limit the types and lengths of sentences. In some cases their sentencing discretion is broad. In others the range of permissible sentences is quite narrow. For example, judges are often bound by mandatory sentencing guidelines for certain crimes. Many of these guidelines were enacted in the 1970's and 1980's by legislative bodies that were frustrated by the wide divergence of sentences for essentially the same crimes handed down by different judges. Some judges have lost their jobs because of their alleged unwillingness to mete out suitably harsh penalties. In the 1980's, for example, several California supreme court justices lost their reelection bids in the wake of public anger that they repeatedly overturned death penalty convictions. In the late 1990's the federal government and many state governments passed "three-strikes" laws, which required that persons convicted of three felonies be sentenced to life imprisonment. Thus, judges are subjected to legal and political constraints in their sentencing duties that can limit judicial independence.

Judicial Independence

Of all the qualities judges must have, impartiality is perhaps the most important. If a judge possesses personal interests linked to the outcome of a trial or if a judge is subject to political pressure, then the entire criminal justice system can be undermined. Different jurisdictions promote judicial independence in a variety of ways: by establishing lifetime (or at least long-term) judicial appointments, by requiring that judges recuse themselves from cases in which they have a personal interest, by paying them generous salaries to reduce their susceptibility to bribes, or by prohibiting them from practicing law while in office.

Federal judges in the United States are appointed by the president of the United States and confirmed by the U.S. Senate. Similarly, judges in many state systems are appointed by the governor and confirmed by the state legislature, although in many other states judges are elected or periodically reaffirmed through a popular vote. In a small number of states judges are nominated by a special nominating commission appointed by a state officer, serve for a fixed "probationary" period, and are then subjected to a popular confirmation vote to earn a full term. In each system of judicial appointment, there is some effort to balance the competing needs of independence and accountability.

The legitimacy of the judiciary relies not only on judicial objectivity and independence but also on the public perception of these qualities. Governments therefore make deliberate efforts to symbolically illustrate judicial independence: Courts and judicial chambers are usually separated from executive and legislative buildings; judges wear somber, ecclesiastical-looking black robes; judicial elections are studiously nonpartisan; and courtrooms are frequently adorned with images of scales, swords, and other symbols of justice.

As either a supplement or alternative to the principle of impartiality, the notion of judicial balance is sometimes put forward as an important factor in ensuring justice. That is, multimember courts (such as supreme courts and many appeals courts) are sometimes made up judges with a range of ideological backgrounds. The idea is that both "liberal" and "conservative" views should be represented on the bench. In the late twentieth century more controversial efforts were undertaken to ensure that the judges of a given jurisdiction reflect the ethnic, racial, and gender diversity of the populations they serve. These and other efforts to achieve balance among judges challenge the notion of justice as an absolute quality to be sought in each judge's actions and decisions.

—Steve D. Boilard

Suggested Readings

David M. O'Brien has collected a number of reflections by judges about the issues they face and their philosophies of jurisprudence. See *Judges on Judging: Views from the Bench* (Chatham, N.J.: Chatham House, 1997). A more analytical treatment of judicial thought and behavior is provided by Susan U. Philips in *Ideology in the Language of Judges: How Judges Practice Law, Politics, and Courtroom Control* (New York: Oxford University Press, 1998). See also Wayne V. McIntosh and Cynthia L. Cates's *Judicial Entrepreneurship: The Role of the Judge in the Marketplace of Ideas* (Westport, Conn.: Greenwood Press, 1997). *Great American Judges: An Encyclopedia*, edited by John R. Vile, with a foreword by Kermit L. Hall (2 vols. Santa Barbara, Calif.: ABC-CLIO, 2003), has biographies of one hundred notable state and federal judges. *"Doing Justice" in the People's Court: Sentencing by Municipal Court Judges*, by Jon'a Meyer and Paul Jesilow (Albany: State University of New York Press, 1997), examines all aspects of the workings of municipal courts and their judges.

See also Adversary system; Advisory opinions; Court types; Criminal justice system; Impeachment of judges; Judicial appointments and elections; Judicial bias; Judicial conduct code; Judicial confirmation hearings; Jury nullification; Sentencing; Three-strikes laws; Trials.

JUDGMENT PROOF

Situation in which a defendant is protected by bankruptcy or other statutes and is consequently beyond the reach of collection efforts

A judgment may be entered in favor of a plaintiff. The plaintiff becomes a judgment creditor and may proceed against the defendant's property or estate. For example, a judgment creditor may file a lien against the defendant's future wages. However, a judgment rendered in favor of a party may be uncollectible because of the defendant's bankruptcy. Section 362 of the U.S. Bankruptcy Code automatically stays all actions that could commence or could have been commenced against the bankrupt debtor. The automatic stay includes judgments.

A judgment creditor may file a request for relief from the stay for cause such as fraud. However, the bankruptcy court may make the defendant judgment-proof by discharging debts, including judgments against him or her. Even if a judgment is not discharged, property of the judgment debtor may be exempted from collection for policy reasons. The U.S. Bankruptcy Code and state statutes exempt property such as automobiles and tools from the claims of creditors. Also, the defendant's home may be exempt and out of the reach of a judgment creditor. The fresh-start policy of bankruptcy law may result in the discharge of an otherwise valid tort—a civil wrong done by one party against another—or contract judgment.

Many corporate defendants in mass product liability cases have filed for protection under the Bankruptcy Code. The effect of a filing is to make tort victims creditors. All reorganizations result in the corporate defendant being judgment-bound for punitive damages. However, corporate defendants may become judgment-proof for various reasons. One issue is whether corporations should be able to make themselves judgment-proof against punitive damages by filing for Chapter 11 reorganization under the federal bankruptcy laws. In the 1980's most asbestos product liability defendants filed for bankruptcy in the wake of multimillion dollar punitive damage awards. Most firms ended up paying a small percentage of compensatory damage judgments. The benefit of declaring bankruptcy was to discharge liability for punitive damages.

—*Michael L. Rustad*

See also Bankruptcy; Damages; Judicial appointments and elections; Punitive damages; Torts.

JUDICIAL APPOINTMENTS AND ELECTIONS

Methods by which judges are chosen

In his book *Democracy in America* (1835) the French political scientist and historian Alexis de Tocqueville noted that "scarcely any political question arises in the United States that is not resolved, sooner or later, into a judicial question." Since de Tocqueville's time, the United States has become even more litigious, and it is rare when issues of government policy do not end up before courts and the judges who staff them. Consequently, legal scholars and the average citizen alike are interested in who these judges are, what their attitudes on the issues before them are, and, most importantly, whether the methods of their selection affect who sits on the bench and the substance of their decisions. Frequently, the methods of selecting judges indicate a trade-off between the desire for judicial independence, on one hand, and judicial accountability to the voters, on the other.

Federal Judicial Selection

The United States has a federal judicial system designed to enforce federal laws and a state judicial system in each of the fifty states to enforce state laws. At the state level each state is free to establish the method of judicial selection that it deems most desirable. The method for selecting federal judges, however, is determined by Article II of the U.S. Constitution, and the selection of all federal judges (for district courts, courts of appeals, and the U.S. Supreme Court) follows the same formal process. This process clearly weighs judicial independence more heavily than judicial accountability, although the latter is not completely lacking at the federal level.

Formally, all federal judges are nominated by the president of the United States and confirmed by a simple majority in the U.S.

Senate. According to Article III of the Constitution, federal judges serve during "good behavior"—that is, they enjoy life tenure unless they are impeached and convicted by the U.S. Congress for having committed "Treason, Bribery, or other high Crimes and Misdemeanors," in the words of Article II. No legal requirements, such as age requirements, are placed on persons wishing to become federal judges.

In reality, federal judicial selection is somewhat complicated. At the U.S. District Court level, presidents typically follow the process of senatorial courtesy—that is, they confer with the U.S. senator of their party from the state in which there is a judicial vacancy and nominate the senator's chosen candidate. Because a court of appeals circuit encompasses several states, presidents have a freer hand in choosing judges for courts of appeals, although they frequently rely on the advice of senators within the circuit in question. In nominating justices for the U.S. Supreme Court presidents have the greatest discretion of all in selecting whomever they wish. Nevertheless, their nominees must be confirmed by the U.S. Senate. In nominating justices, presidents select judges whose political philosophies resemble their own and who most often belong to the same political parties.

Other actors in the judicial selection process are the U.S. attorney general, the Federal Bureau of Investigation (FBI), and the American Bar Association (ABA). Typically, the president puts the attorney general in charge of screening candidates and has the FBI conduct a background check for potential problems that may render candidates unsuitable for judgeships. Since the time of President Dwight D. Eisenhower (1953-1961) the ABA's Standing Committee on the Federal Judiciary has also been allowed to review nominees in order to evaluate their professional credentials.

Thus, the process of choosing federal judges is a highly political one in which presidents and senators attempt to staff the courts with those whose political philosophies and methods of legal interpretation are similar to their own. In addition, life tenure provides federal judges with substantial judicial independence to make decisions they deem correct, even though these decisions may not be popular with voters.

State Judicial Selection

Because the fifty U.S. states are free to select their own state court judges according to methods they deem most desirable, there is no single method of judicial selection. However, the methods of state judicial selection can generally be divided into five categories: appointment by the governor, partisan election, nonpartisan election, the merit system, and election by the legislature.

Gubernatorial appointment, which is utilized in seven states, is the oldest form of state judicial selection, dating to the period of the American Revolution (1775-1783). In most of the states that practice this system another body, such as the state senate, is required to confirm the governor's nominees. Gubernatorial appointment fell out of favor in the states in the early 1800's, because it was thought that the potential for corruption existed when governors appointed unqualified cronies and political hacks to judgeships simply to pay off political debts and reward the party faithful.

In the 1830's gubernatorial appointments came to be replaced by partisan elections, which were seen as a more democratic method for choosing state court judges. In a partisan election system, which is used in eleven states, candidates for judgeships run for election and are identified on the ballot by their political party affiliation. Although this system was initially seen as more democratic than gubernatorial appointments and one that would hold judges accountable, it too fell out of favor in the early 1900's during the Progressive Era. Opponents argued that partisan elections, like gubernatorial appointments, allowed political parties and corrupt political machines to control what should be the nonpartisan administration of justice.

In the early 1900's many states replaced the partisan election of judges with nonpartisan elections. Nonpartisan elections, the method used in eighteen states, also require that judges run for election. However, the candidates are not identified on the ballot with political parties. The Progressives believed that nonpartisan elections would take the "politics" out of state judicial selection and allow for the election of judges based on competence rather than party affiliation.

By the 1940's, however, nonpartisan elections fell into disfavor with many because it was thought unseemly of judges, who were supposed to be neutral magistrates of the law, to debase themselves by becoming mere politicians, currying favor with the voters, running political campaigns, and seeking campaign donations from lawyers and others who might appear before them in court.

Countering what many saw as the evils of elections, many states in the mid-twentieth century began adopting the merit system, or the Missouri Plan. Typically, this system, used in twenty-one states, provides for a judicial nominating commission composed of lawyers appointed by the state bar association, nonlawyers appointed by the governor, and a judge from the state supreme court. The nominating commission accepts applications from those interested in filling a judicial vacancy, reviews and evaluates applicants, and sends a list of three to five acceptable names to the governor. The governor is required to select one name from the list to fill the vacancy. This person then serves for a certain period of time, after which a noncompetitive retention election is held. In such elections, judges run unopposed; the voters are simply asked whether the judges should be retained for another term.

Although designed to take the politics out of judicial selection, the merit system has been criticized because of the political games that go into appointing members to the nominating commission and into the commission's selection of candidates that are placed before the governor. Additionally, some believe that judges selected through the merit system, because they are initially appointed and then reelected in noncompetitive elections, are not sufficiently accountable to the electorate.

The fifth method of judicial selection, election by the legislature, is used in only three states. Under this system state court judges are elected by the state legislature. Studies have shown, however, that the most frequent winners in these legislative elections are, not surprisingly, former members of the legislature who have either retired or been voted out of office.

The number of states using these various methods of judicial selection totals more than fifty, because some states use more than one method depending on whether a vacancy occurs in a trial or appellate court or in a rural or urban area. The methods used by each state depend on whether judicial independence or judicial accountability is more highly valued. Scholars have found that there are regional variations in judicial selections. Gubernatorial appointments are practiced most frequently in the Northeast, partisan elections in the South, nonpartisan elections in the North and Midwest, and merit selections in most states in the West. Regardless of how they select their judges, most states, unlike the federal government, require that periodic assessments take place by mandating fixed terms of office that range from two to fourteen years, although a few states allow judges to serve until retirement.

Effects of Judicial Selection Methods

There is much debate among scholars over whether the methods of judicial selection affect who sits on the bench and whether these methods affect the decisions they make. Studies have shown that the methods by which judges are selected has little impact on their demographic and professional characteristics. That is, in terms of education, previous employment, race, sex, religion, and other measurable factors judges in the United States tend to be remarkably similar to one another, regardless of whether they are elected, appointed, or chosen on the basis of a merit system.

At the same time, other studies have shown that women and minorities have a somewhat greater chance of being selected to the bench in those jurisdictions that use merit or appointive systems than in those in which judges are elected. Likewise, some studies have shown that the practice of judicial elections actually influences some state supreme court justices' decisions in death penalty cases. They may vote to uphold the death penalty on appeal in order to minimize electoral opposition and appease their constituents.

—*Michael W. Bowers*

Suggested Readings

General treatments of judicial selection at the state and federal levels can be found in Lawrence Baum's *American Courts: Process and Policy* (2d ed. Boston: Houghton Mifflin, 1990), Henry R. Glick's *Courts, Politics, and Justice* (3d ed. New York: McGraw-Hill, 1993), Christopher E. Smith's *Courts, Politics, and the Judicial Process* (2d ed. Chicago: Nelson-Hall, 1997), Harry P. Stumpf's *American Judicial Politics* (2d ed. Upper Saddle River, N.J.: Prentice-Hall, 1998), and G. Alan Tarr's *Judicial Process and Judicial Policymaking* (St. Paul, Minn.: West Publishing, 1994). Issues of state judicial selection are covered specifically in Harry P. Stumpf and John H. Culver's *The Politics of State Courts* (New York: Long-man, 1992), while U.S. Supreme Court appointments are thoroughly discussed in Henry J. Abraham's *Justices and Presidents* (3d ed. New York: Oxford University Press, 1992) and David J. Danelski's *A Supreme Court Justice Is Appointed* (New York: Random

House, 1964). Bradley Canon's "The Impact of Formal Selection Processes on the Characteristics of Judges: Reconsidered," in *Law and Society Review* 6 (1972), finds little difference in the characteristics of judges selected by various methods. For an argument that methods of selection affect judges' decisions, see Melinda Gann Hall's "Electoral Politics and Strategic Voting in State Supreme Courts," *Journal of Politics* 54 (1992).

See also American Bar Association; Federal Bureau of Investigation; Impeachment of judges; Judges; Judicial confirmation hearings.

JUDICIAL BIAS

Failure of a judge to exercise absolute impartiality in every aspect of a court trial

The impartiality of judges is their most important professional qualification in the U.S. judicial system. In other legal systems— those, for example, of continental Europe—judges play more active roles in the gathering and presentation of information relating to a case. In the United States, however, judges principally rely on parties and their advocates to present their cases. Judges serve as objective and disinterested arbiters of trials, leaving partisanship and advocacy to the lawyers and parties involved in cases. Thus, it is crucial to their judicial role that judges remain neutral with respect to the competing claims presented to their attention.

Because the impartiality of judges plays such a central role in the U.S. system of justice, rules of judicial conduct attempt to secure this impartiality by regulating judicial conduct both on and off the bench. The rules by which many jurisdictions measure the conduct of judges are the Model Code of Judicial Conduct, adopted by the American Bar Association (ABA) in 1990 and implemented in a number of states. These rules generally prohibit bias and prejudice on the part of judges and conflicts of interest that might undermine their impartiality.

Judicial Bias

The American legal system generally expects that the judges who preside over legal proceedings base their decisions on evidence and argument offered there rather than on information and improper predispositions the judges might have already acquired. The Model Code of Judicial Conduct attempt to secure the necessary judicial impartiality by prohibiting judges from participating in cases in which they have some bias against a party or a lawyer. "A judge shall not," according to the rules, "in the performance of judicial duties, by words or conduct manifest bias or prejudice, including but not limited to bias or prejudice based upon race, sex, religion, national origin, disability, age, sexual orientation or socioeconomic status, and shall not permit staff, court officials and others subject to the judge's direction and control to do so." In addition, the rules require that judges disqualify themselves from cases in which they have personal knowledge of disputed issues. This disqualification is intended to prevent judges from relying on their own personal knowledge of important facts rather than on the facts actually offered by parties or lawyers.

The Model Code of Judicial Conduct concern themselves not only with the danger of actual bias on the part of judges but also with the danger that the public might perceive judges to be biased. In general, this focus on both realities and appearances is in keeping with the declaration of the rules that judges should avoid "impropriety and the appearance of impropriety." Public confidence in the judicial process is diminished both when judges act improperly and when they merely appear to act improperly. Thus, to prevent the appearance of bias, the rules explicitly prohibit judges from being members of organizations that practice improper discrimination on the basis of race, sex, religion, or national origin. Even if judges do not share in the discriminatory attitudes of these groups, public knowledge of a judge's membership in such a group might reasonably cast doubt on the judge's impartiality.

Judicial Conflicts of Interest

Bias threatens judicial impartiality by substituting stereotypical views of particular classes of people for a reasoned consideration of evidence and argument. A related threat to judicial impartiality arises when a judge's personal interest in a case slants the judge's perspective and impairs his or her ability to view evi-

EXAMPLES OF JUDICIAL BIAS, APPEARANCE OF IMPROPRIETY, AND DISQUALIFICATION

- Allowing family, social, political, or other relationships to influence a judge's judicial conduct or decision
- Implying or allowing others to imply that they have special influence with the judge
- Holding membership in organizations that practice improper discrimination on the basis of race, sex, religion, or national origin
- Treating persons involved in court proceedings impatiently and discourteously
- Demonstrating bias or prejudice based on race, sex, religion, national origin, disability, age, sexual orientation, or socioeconomic status
- Allowing, except in extraordinary circumstances, one side of a lawsuit to communicate with the judge without the knowledge of the other side
- Making comments about matters pending before the judge that would affect the outcome or impair the fairness of judicial proceedings
- Disclosing information obtained in the judicial role for nonjudicial purposes
- Failing to report to bar authorities information suggesting that a lawyer has violated ethical rules in such a way as to raise substantial question about the lawyer's honesty, trustworthiness, or general fitness to practice law
- Failing to disqualify himself or herself in proceedings in which the judge's impartiality might be reasonably questioned
- Serving as judge in cases in which he or she has a personal bias or prejudice against a party or lawyer in the case
- Engaging in frequent financial or business transactions with persons likely to appear before the court over which the judge presides
- Accepting improper gifts
- Practicing law while serving an appointment as a judge
- Engaging in political activities while serving an appointment as a judge, except those in which a judge, subject to popular election, campaigns for himself or herself

Source: American Bar Association's 1990 Code of Judicial Conduct.

dence and arguments objectively. This clash between a judge's personal interests and the interests of the judicial system in the fair and impartial administration of justice is generally referred to as a conflict of interest. A conflict of this sort is not the unique affliction of judges but one against which all persons in positions of trust must guard, including attorneys and public officials. Conflicts of interest might be thought of as a kind of bias, since they cause a judge's perception of a case to be slanted in favor of the side aligned with the judge's personal interests.

Sometimes a judicial conflict of interest arises out of a judge's special relationship with one of the participants in a case. For example, a judge whose child is a party in a case might unfairly favor the child in decisions relating to the case. A judge whose husband is acting as a lawyer in a case might unfairly favor her husband's arguments. To avoid this kind of relational conflict, the Model Code of Judicial Conduct prohibit judges from presiding over cases in which spouses or close relatives are parties or lawyers. Moreover, the rules state in more general terms that judges shall not allow family relationships to influence their judicial conduct or judgment.

Another variety of conflict arises when a judge or someone closely related to the judge has a personal financial stake in a matter before the judge. For example, a judge who is a stockholder in a local bank might well find it difficult to preside impartially over a case in which someone claims to have been injured by the bank and seeks a substantial monetary award from the bank to compensate for this injury. A victory for the injured party in the case might threaten the judge's own financial interest, since the value of the judge's stock might be diminished by a judgment against the bank. Similarly, if the judge's spouse is a lawyer in a law firm sued for legal malpractice, the judge will be unable to preside fairly over the legal malpractice suit, since it threatens to harm the financial interests of the judge's spouse. To protect against these forms of conflict, the Model Code of Judicial Conduct specify that judges shall disqualify themselves from presiding over cases in which they, their spouses, or their close relatives have more than a minimal financial stake.

Disqualification of Judges

Judges who recognize a personal bias or conflict of interest that might jeopardize their impartiality in particular cases are expected, under the Model Code of Judicial Conduct, to disqualify themselves from participation in these cases. Judges who disqualify themselves under these conditions are sometimes said to have recused themselves. Sometimes the parties or the lawyers in a case might file a motion with the court requesting that the judge disqualify himself or herself.

Judges who fail to disqualify themselves when it would be appropriate that they do so may prompt two kinds of corrective action. In the first place, judges who violate relevant rules of judicial ethics, such as those stated in the Model Code of Judicial Conduct, can be reprimanded or otherwise punished for such violations. Many states, for example, have specially appointed commissions that supervise the conduct of judges. These commissions, subject generally to the supervision of the highest court of the state, may investigate and punish violations of judicial ethics. The failure of judges to disqualify themselves under the appropriate circumstances might subject them to discipline. In the second place, parties who believe that judges have failed to disqualify themselves when appropriate may complain to a higher court. For example, a party who loses a case, believing that a judge's unfairness was responsible for the loss, might appeal the loss to a higher court. The higher court, under this circumstance, would typically consider evidence of a judge's bias or conflict of interest. If convinced that the judge should have declined to preside over a case, the higher court might overturn the decision in the case and order a new trial.

—*Timothy L. Hall*

Suggested Readings

A good starting point for this subject is Linda G. Mills's *A Penchant for Prejudice: Unraveling Bias in Judicial Decision Making* (Ann Arbor: University of Michigan Press, 1999). Max Boot's *Out of Order: Arrogance, Corruption, and Incompetence on the Bench* (New York: Basic Books, 1998) includes a useful, if controversial, discussion of judicial ethics. For a more sweeping consideration of ethics in a variety of governmental, business, and professional contexts, readers should consult Peter W. Morgan and Glenn H. Reynolds's *The Appearance of Impropriety: How Ethics Wars Have Undermined American Government, Business, and Society* (New York: Free Press, 1997). *Judicial Conduct and Ethics*, by Jeffrey M. Shaman, Steven Lubet, and James J. Alfini (2d ed. Charlottesville,

Va.: Michie, 1995), and *Judicial Disqualification: Recusal and Disqualification of Judges*, by Richard E. Flamm (Boston: Little, Brown, 1996), contain detailed discussions of the rules on judicial ethics. The primary source of rules governing judicial conduct is the 1990 *Model Code of Judicial Conduct*, published by the American Bar Association's Standing Committee on Ethics and Professional Responsibility (Chicago: American Bar Association, 1990). Charles R. Ashman's *The Finest Judges Money Can Buy, and Other Forms of Judicial Pollution* (Los Angeles: Nash Publishing, 1973) discusses a variety of types of judicial corruption. For an international comparison of judicial corruption see *Judicial Misconduct: A Cross-National Comparison*, by Mary L. Volcansek with Maria Elisabetta de Franciscis and Jacqueline Lucienne Lafon (Gainesville: University Press of Florida, 1996). Also useful is *Ethical Standards in the Public Sector: A Guide for Government Lawyers, Clients, and Public Officials*, edited by Patricia E. Salkin (Chicago: Section of State and Local Government Law, American Bar Association, 1999).

See also Adversary system; Impeachment of judges; Judges; Judicial conduct code.

JUDICIAL CLERKS

Recent law-school graduates employed by state and federal judges to assist in the performance of court-related duties

Judicial clerks, typically called "law clerks" or simply "clerks," are recent law-school graduates hired by judges to serve as legal assistants. A clerk's responsibilities are defined by the supervising judge and might include such tasks as verifying case citations, reviewing petitions for appeals, researching legal issues, and drafting written opinions. Clerkships normally last one or two years, although career clerks exist, as some judges prefer greater stability. Methods of selection vary widely, ranging from open competitions to recommendations from law school professors. Appointments, especially in appellate courts, tend to go to the top graduates of the country's leading law schools.

Horace Gray, who served as a justice on the U.S. Supreme Court from 1882 to 1902, is credited with having started the practice of hiring judicial clerks while he was still a state judge. (Library of Congress)

The first clerkship can be traced to 1875, when Horace Gray, a Massachusetts judge, employed a Harvard law graduate recommended by his brother, a professor at the university. At his own expense, Gray hired a replacement each year. Gray continued this practice when he was appointed to the U.S. Supreme Court in 1882. A few years later, Congress provided funds to Supreme Court justices so that they could hire paid assistants. Over the next fifty years, clerkships expanded significantly at both the state and federal levels. By the 1990's all federal judges and appellate state judges employed the services of at least one clerk, with many supervising two or more. A number of state trial judges also have clerks.

Clerks generally work under the direct supervision of individual judges. Some judges define narrow roles for clerks, such as checking the accuracy of legal citations or researching a point of law. Other judges envision a broader role for clerks, asking them to evaluate legal arguments presented in cases or to draft written opinions. Additionally, appellate court judges direct clerks to screen discretionary petitions for court review. U.S. Supreme Court justices assign clerks to the "cert pool" to review thousands of *certiorari* petitions each year. Writs of *certiorari* are orders from higher courts to lower courts to deliver the entire record of legal cases for review. Requests are distributed randomly to individual clerks and they prepare formal memoranda recommending cases for acceptance.

Two different types of clerks are found in some courts. There are the more traditional clerks, sometimes called "elbow" clerks who serve side by side with individual judges. In addition, there are "staff attorneys" working for the entire court. In courts with both types of clerks, staff attorneys generally engage in activities before cases are heard while elbow clerks assist judges after cases are presented.

The use of clerks has been criticized because of the influence they may exert on the judicial process, from selecting cases for review to shaping how cases are decided. Critics argue that judges are appointed to make these determinations and that clerks are not prepared to handle such responsibilities, because they lack the real-world experiences possessed by judges. Supporters counter that clerks help judges in moving an ever-increasing volume of cases through the legal system while ensuring that justice is still appropriately administered.

—*William A. Taggart*

See also *Certiorari*, writ of; Clerks of the court; Federal judicial system; Law schools; Opinions.

JUDICIAL CONDUCT CODE

Ethical rules adopted in most jurisdictions to govern the conduct of judges

Since the early twentieth century the American Bar Association (ABA) has attempted to develop guidelines for judicial conduct. The ABA adopted the Canons of Judicial Ethics in 1924 and the Model Code of Judicial Conduct in 1972. The ABA substantially amended this code in 1990, and a significant number of states have adopted this amended code to regulate the conduct of judges in their jurisdictions.

The Model Code of Judicial Conduct seeks to preserve the integrity and independence of judges by prohibiting them from being influenced by family, social, political, or other relationships in the conduct of their official business. In some cases the code requires that judges disqualify themselves from participation in cases in which their impartiality might reasonably be questioned.

In addition, the code prohibits conduct that might otherwise be classified as private or personal when such conduct risks undermining the integrity of the judiciary. For example, judges are prohibited from belonging to organizations that practice inappropriate discrimination on the basis of race, sex, religion, or national origin. In general, the code requires that judges conduct their nonjudicial affairs in such a way as to minimize conflicts with their judicial obligations.

—*Timothy L. Hall*

See also American Bar Association; Annotated codes; Bar associations; Impeachment of judges; Judicial bias; Model Penal Code; Unethical conduct of attorneys.

JUDICIAL CONFIRMATION HEARINGS

Hearings by legislative bodies that are held in the process of appointing judges

Confirmation hearings can occur at the federal or state level. At the federal level, federal judges who have life tenure under Article III of the U.S. Constitution must be nominated (proposed for appointment) by the president of the United States. Nominees must be presented to the U.S. Senate for its "advice and consent"— in other words, its approval of nominees by majority vote. Legislative approval of a nomination is sometimes referred to as "confirmation." In some states judges are appointed by the governor and subject to approval by one house of the state legislature.

When the U.S. Senate receives a judicial nomination, it refers it to the Senate Judiciary Committee for initial consideration. After this committee has investigated the nominee's professional qualifications and character, it ordinarily holds a public hearing at which the nominee generally testifies. Nominees typically do not state their views on specific cases that they may have to decide as judges. To the extent that they are questioned about their "judicial philosophy" (their general approach to legal issues), questions are usually based on nominees' previous writings. Sometimes interest groups who favor or oppose nominations also testify. After the hearing, the committee votes on whether to recommend that the Senate confirm the nomination.

Except for nominations for seats on the Supreme Court, most judicial nominations are relatively uncontroversial and thus do not lead to extensive hearings.

—*Bernard W. Bell*

See also Constitution, U.S.; Impeachment of judges; Judges; Judicial appointments and elections.

JUDICIAL REVIEW

Power of the courts to review and declare unconstitutional the actions of the executive and legislative branches of government as well as the decisions of lower courts

Judicial review is a preeminent means of enforcing the rule of the law in political systems operating under a written constitution; the process of judicial review has led to the federal judiciary assuming major policy-making authority in the United States.

Although it has tangential roots in the lawmaking roles of the courts of medieval England, the process of judicial review—that is, of courts ruling on the constitutionality of statutory law, executive action, and the decisions of lower courts—may be regarded as one of the United States' contributions to the art of government. In the United States it has led to the federal judiciary assuming a major role in the evolving interpretation of the Constitution. Since World War II, the same device has spread widely to other democracies as a means of guaranteeing individual rights and the rule of law.

Development

One of the distinguishing characteristics of the Anglo-American legal system is that it is a common-law system composed not only of statutory law but also of bench (or judge-made) law. The system began with the emergence of the common-law and equity courts of medieval England. The former applied existing customs to the cases confronting its judges; the latter formed new rules to cover cases for which no relevant custom prevailed or where a rigid application of existing norms would create hardship or injury. In both instances the rulings of the courts became a part of the law of the realm, and it is in these courts that the power of the judiciary to make as well as apply the law has its origins.

It was not until the drafting of the U.S. Constitution at Philadelphia in 1787, however, that the process of entrusting the judiciary with the official task of reviewing the constitutionality of the actions of other branches of government, levels of government, and lower levels of the judiciary formally began. Two inventions at Philadelphia necessitated that development. First, in seeking a government based on a more permanent law than the statutory acts of momentary majorities as well as a system in which all would be subject to the same laws, the Framers of the Constitution created the first political system founded on a single, written set of political rules declared "the supreme law of the land" (Article V of the Constitution). This higher law required an interpreter-enforcer, and in adopting Baron de Montesquieu's political model of three separate branches and powers of government (the law-making, law-enforcing, and law-adjudicating branches), the founders entrusted that task to the federal courts. Likewise, in adopting a system of dual (federal and state) levels of government, in which the powers of the federal government were enumerated and the states retained essentially what was left over, the constitutional system invited legal conflicts over jurisdictional issues. These had to be umpired, and the constitutional vehicle for umpiring them was also to be the judiciary.

Investing the Supreme Court with this authority provoked little controversy from the 1787-1789 period of constitution making through the first decade of the new Republic. In writing "Federalist Number 78" to urge the citizens of New York to ratify the pending Constitution, Alexander Hamilton linked the preservation of constitutionally limited government directly to the practice of judicial review by "the medium of courts of justice, whose duty it must be to declare all acts contrary to the manifest tenor of the Constitution void." The argument produced scarcely a ripple of contention, especially compared with the wrath which the Supreme Court incurred for not ruling unconstitutional the much-hated Alien and Sedition Acts enacted by Congress during the 1796-1801 presidency of John Adams.

Nor was there any serious criticism of the Supreme Court in 1796 when, in *Hylton v. United States*, it assumed that it had the power to declare an act of Congress unconstitutional in agreeing to review the constitutionality of the carriage tax enacted by the Congress. Even in *Marbury v. Madison* (1803), the heated reaction to the decision was far less because Chief Justice John Marshall declared an act of Congress unconstitutional than because he took the occasion to scold the Jeffersonians for wrongful actions even as he ruled that the Supreme Court lacked the ability to right that wrong (because the Judiciary Act was unconstitutional). Still, it was not until the decision in *Marbury* that the exercise of judicial review resulted in the invalidation of an act of Congress. Consequently, Marshall's decision in that case is properly revered as a precedent-setting moment in the development of both American constitutional law and the American political process.

Judicial Review and the American Political Process

In subsequent cases, the Supreme Court extended the power of federal courts to nullify as unconstitutional the decisions of state courts (*Martin v. Hunter's Lessee*, 1816), state laws (*McCulloch v. Maryland*, 1819), and presidential action (for example, President Harry Truman's 1951 attempt to seize steel mills during the Korean War, disallowed by the Supreme Court in *Youngstown Sheet & Tube Co. v. Sawyer*, 1952). Indeed, the willingness of federal courts to exercise judicial review vis-à-vis state legislation and state court opinions was essential to the survival of federalism in the United States. Legal chaos would have resulted without the federal courts judiciously applying the supremacy clause to sustain the unfettered execution of the laws of Congress. Yet the willingness of the Supreme Court to assert the independence of the judiciary over the will of popularly elected majorities in Congress and popular presidents, also established by John Marshall in *Marbury v. Madison*, has been equally important to the development of the rule of law and separation of powers democracy in the United States.

Judicial review involves more than nullifying acts of government for contravening the Constitution. It embraces the power to interpret the Constitution to ascertain the validity of acts of government. In reviewing the authority of the federal government, the Supreme Court has historically taken a permissive approach. In so doing, the federal judiciary has been a major instrument for expanding the powers of the federal government and enabling government in the United States to function for more than two hundred years under a document written in the eighteenth century and intentionally made difficult to change by the formal amendment process.

There are four broad categories of power that the federal government is constitutionally recognized to possess: those expressly delegated to Congress and enumerated in Article I; those which may be reasonably implied from the delegated powers and represent appropriate means to their achievement; those inherent powers, such as the right to acquire land by conquest, which give the United States the same powers in foreign affairs as other countries; and the residual (or emergency) powers to do what is necessary to survive in the face of foreign or domestic crises. Of these, only the enumerated powers were explicitly conferred upon the federal government under the Constitution. The others have been "discovered" in the Constitution by the Supreme Court in such seminal cases as *McCulloch v. Maryland*. Moreover, the enumerated powers have been steadily given a much wider construction than was attached to them in 1789.

The expansion of the powers of the central government has not been at the expense of individual rights and liberties. The Supreme Court's interpretation of the provisions of the Bill of Rights and the Fourteenth Amendment has profoundly expanded the freedom of American citizens vis-à-vis all levels of government, profoundly influencing the nature of American politics and society in the process. The selective incorporation of most of the provisions found in the Bill of Rights into the due process clause of the Fourteenth Amendment, for example, resulted in an overhaul of the United States' system of justice during the 1949-1966 period framed by *Wolf v. Colorado* and *Miranda v. Arizona*. This period bestowed on Americans, regardless of their state of residence, the right to freedom from unreasonable searches and seizures, to confront their accusers, to a fair trial by jury in criminal cases, and to have an attorney not only in criminal trials but also in pretrial interrogation proceedings. Likewise, the emphasis given to the rights of citizens under the "equal protection of the law" clause of the Fourteenth Amendment contributed greatly during the second half of the twentieth century to the emergence of a more integrated, empowered, and egalitarian society in the United States.

Restraints on Judicial Review

The ability of the federal courts to hear such controversial cases as those involving women seeking the right to terminate unwanted pregnancies, and decisions such as that of *Roe v. Wade* (1973) recognizing a woman's constitutional right to do so, has led critics of the Supreme Court to attack it as acting above the law. This indictment is misconceived. Although it is true that once the Supreme Court rules on the meaning of the Constitution, its

When a hostile majority on the Supreme Court threatened to undermine his New Deal programs during the mid-1930's, President Franklin D. Roosevelt proposed to alter the balance of power by "packing" the Court with six new justices, who would ensure the survival of his programs. (National Archives)

decision becomes the supreme law of the land and is only alterable by constitutional amendment or by the Supreme Court reversing itself in a later case, the federal judiciary does not lie outside the constitutional system of checks and balance. To the contrary, the president and Congress have three powerful tools at their disposal to influence the process of judicial review.

First, the size of the Supreme Court is fixed by the Congress, not the Constitution. Although the sitting justices hold their positions for life (barring impeachment), additional justices could theoretically be added to turn a 6-3 majority on the Supreme Court into a 6-9 minority, as President Franklin Roosevelt contemplated doing in 1936 when the Supreme Court proved initially hostile to his New Deal legislation.

Congress can also deny the judiciary the right to review certain types of cases, for the appellate jurisdiction of the federal judiciary is derived from acts of Congress, not the Constitution. If these steps are too direct and intrusive to find support in public opinion, critics of an active judiciary have long been able to delay the process of judicial review by slowing the process of filling vacancies on the lower federal courts and thus increasing the workload on the remaining judges.

These restraints, combined with the inherently controversial nature of many of the cases which the federal courts receive regarding safeguarding the rights of unpopular individuals, have prompted the federal courts to restrain themselves in their exercise of judicial review. Well aware that judicial review is a policy-making power and that nonelective bodies engage in it at their potential peril in a democratic political system, over the years the Supreme Court has developed an elaborate set of rules of judicial self-restraint for itself and the lower federal courts. Federal courts, for example, stay out of essentially political (and especially partisan) conflicts. Similarly, cases are heard only when there is an actual controversy (no advisory opinions are given), and the litigants must have a substantial interest in order to have legal standing. Above all, laws normally are presumed valid and are interpreted, as much as possible, in ways that uphold them. Issues of constitutional validity are considered only when there is no other basis upon which to decide a case.

—Joseph R. Rudolph, Jr.

Suggested Readings

Useful general studies include *Judicial Review and Judicial Power in the Supreme Court*, edited by Kermit L. Hall (New York: Garland, 2000); Keith E. Whittington, *Constitutional Interpretation: Textual Meaning, Original Intent, and Judicial Review* (Lawrence: University Press of Kansas, 1999); Robert Justin Lipkin. *Constitutional Revolutions: Pragmatism and the Role of Judicial Review in American Constitutionalism* (Durham, N.C.: Duke University Press, 2000); *Judicial Review and Judicial Power in the Supreme Court*, edited by Kermit L. Hall (New York: Garland, 2000); and Louis Michael Seidman, *Our Unsettled Constitution: A New Defense of Constitutionalism and Judicial Review* (New Haven, Conn.: Yale University Press, 2001). On the general need for judicial review, see Alexander Hamilton's essay No. 78 in any edition of the *The Federalist Papers*, which Hamilton wrote along with John Jay and James Madison after the Constitution was drafted. Among the many outstanding books on judicial review and constitutional law in the United States, see Edward S. Corwin's classic, *Court over Constitution: A Study of Judicial Review as an Instrument of Popular Government* (Princeton, N.J.: Princeton University Press, 1938); Henry J. Abraham, *The Judicial Process* (6th ed. New York: Oxford University Press, 1993); Michael J. Gerhardt and Thomas D. Rowe, Jr., *Constitutional Theory: Arguments and Perspectives* (Charlottesville, Va.: Michie, 1993); and Sylvia Snowiss, *Judicial Review and the Law of the Constitution* (New Haven, Conn.: Yale University Press, 1990). Henry Julian Abraham's *The Judicial Process: An Introductory Analysis of the Courts of the United States, England, and France* (New York: Oxford University Press, 1998) is a broad survey of court systems with discussion of judicial review.

See also Advisory opinions; Appeal; Appellate practice; Constitution, U.S.; Death row attorneys; Judges; Jury nullification; Supreme Court, U.S.

JURIES

Bodies of persons assembled to give impartial verdicts in civil or legal trials, basing their decisions on evidence presented by both sides of disputes

In the United States the right of a defendant to a trial by jury is guaranteed under the U.S. Constitution. Generally speaking, criminal defendants have the right to a trial by jury. A criminal defendant who pleads not guilty cannot waive the right to a jury trial except in limited cases, which vary from state to state. If the penalty includes a long prison sentence or capital punishment, the waiver is not available. A criminal defendant effectively waives the right to a jury by pleading guilty. In federal court, civil litigants are guaranteed the right to a jury trial under the Seventh Amendment to the Constitution, provided that the amount contested is over twenty dollars.

In the state court system each state has the authority to decide whether civil litigants are entitled to a jury trial. In many states the jury may also determine punishment in both criminal and civil trials. A jury composed of laypersons not connected in any way with the dispute before them provides a layer of protection for the litigants and at the same time protects the judicial system from allegations of unfairness or bias toward particular litigants. This protection is especially important in criminal trials, in which the defendant is prosecuted by a city, state, or federal agency. Given the large numbers of jury trials, the amount of criticism to which they are subjected is relatively small, although high-profile cases involving famous people or large amounts of money are often closely scrutinized by both the legal community and the popular press, television, and radio.

The jury has existed for about eight hundred years in Anglo-American jurisprudence. While the early development of the jury is cloudy, it is generally agreed that the jury as it is now known emerged a few years after a papal edict in 1215 deprived of religious sanction one form of trial by ordeal reserved for the clergy. Thereupon, other medieval trial systems—those brought to England's shores by the invading Normans in 1066—including trial by battle, compurgation, and the remaining forms of trial by ordeal, fell into disuse, and the jury form emerged to fill the void.

While there are some earlier instances of "juries," it was not until about 1220 that the convicting jury emerged. Serving on early English juries was often risky for jurors, because they could be punished for a verdict that did not comport with the interests of the Crown.

Organization of Juries

A modern jury is generally composed of twelve jurors selected from a pool of citizens who are called for jury service. The twelve-member jury has its roots in very early trial forms, in which compurgators, or witnesses for each side, usually decided disputes in groups or multiples of twelve. Since the 1970's it has been constitutionally permissible for a jury to be composed of only six persons, even in some criminal trials. While a criminal defendant may petition the court for a smaller jury, most jurisdictions still require twelve-person juries in criminal trials to ensure that the prosecution present a case strong enough to convince a greater number of people. Smaller juries are often employed in civil trials mainly to save time and money. However, the debate continues about how the number of persons on the jury affects the decision-making process, with some critics arguing that the larger number provides a greater chance that the jury will represent a cross section of the community and others arguing that dominating cliques may form in larger juries that can adversely influence jury decisions.

Jury Instructions

At the beginning of a trial the judge usually instructs the jury about the trial proceedings and provides an orientation to the general facts of the case. At the end of the trial and before the jury begins its deliberations, the judge must also provide clear instructions to the jury indicating the applicable law. For example, in a homicide case jurors may be asked to determine whether the defendant is guilty of first- or second-degree murder, the legal and practical significance of which is that different charges carry different penalties. Demanding this of the jury requires that the judge clarify the difference between the two standards. Furthermore, judges cannot merely read the statute or code that describes such a distinction, especially when the statute or code is itself unclear.

A mistake made in instructing the jury could be serious enough to warrant a review of that court's verdict. In 1938 California's trial judges became the first in the United States who were required to follow pattern jury instructions, which are composed, compiled, and published by a committee and typically contain general and special instructions for common federal and state cases. By the 1980's a majority of states had adopted pattern instructions. While these instructions are not mandatory in all jurisdictions, some jurisdictions recommend their use. Two common criticisms of the instructions given to juries on the applicable law are that the instructions are given much too late in the trial, thereby forcing jurors to rely on their memory of evidence that may have been presented days or weeks earlier, and that pattern instructions are so broadly written that they are ambiguous. In civil cases judges may also provide juries with a list of questions that the juries must resolve in deciding cases.

Jury Deliberations

If a court's rules do not specify who the jury foreperson is—usually the first person selected for the jury—the jurors elect a foreperson when they begin their deliberations. The foreperson initiates and leads jurors through their deliberative process by introducing issues, prompting discussion, and summarizing the discussion. The foreperson also records the jurors' votes and announces the jury's verdict to the court.

Various jury studies indicate that jurors typically discuss the evidence first and settle questions about the evidence before moving on to the verdict. In fact, a common sight in some jury rooms is a sign encouraging jurors to discuss the evidence before any votes are taken. However, some juries take the opposite approach and begin by voting and then debating the strengths of each side to the dispute. Votes are taken either openly or secretly with each method influencing the nature of the debate that follows. Even such factors as the shape of the jury room table have been found to affect the nature of the discussion, if not the verdict, with some jurors, by virtue of their position at the table, taking on more dominant roles in the deliberative process than others. Criminal trials, with a few exceptions in noncapital offenses, require that the jury reach a unanimous verdict; civil trials generally require only a majority verdict.

Once the jury has reached its verdict, it may be called upon to decide the sentence in a criminal case or the monetary award in a civil case. This is often a difficult task, because the judge's instructions on this phase of the deliberations are stated broadly and often indicate only that the plaintiff should be made "whole." This area of jury decision making often receives sharp criticism because of the large sums of money that are sometimes awarded. In this phase of deliberations jurors consider special damages, which include medical expenses and lost income that resulted from injuries, and general damages, which include the plaintiff's pain and suffering. If the jury believes that the defendant's conduct was particularly irresponsible, the jury may decide to make an example of the defendant by awarding the plaintiff punitive damages in addition to special and general damages.

Jury Polling

The polling of the jury can occur in both civil and criminal trials. Polling must occur immediately after the verdict is announced and before it is recorded. In criminal trials in which the jury cannot reach a unanimous verdict, the judge may poll the jurors by asking them individually whether they believe that further deliberations would be fruitful. Each juror usually responds in writing. Similarly, a criminal defendant found guilty might also request a poll of the jury to ensure that the verdict is indeed unanimous. When it is evident from the poll that the announced verdict is not unanimous after all, the judge may grant a retrial. In civil trials this device is commonly used by attorneys after the verdict to gather information from the jurors that might be helpful to the lawyers in future cases or that might be helpful in deciding whether to appeal a verdict. When polled, jurors state their decision, not their reasons for the decision. Thus, once the trial is over and the jurors have discharged their duty, they may often be approached by the lawyers in the case for more detailed information about how they reacted to the lawyers' handling of the case. However, unlike polling the jury within the confines of the trial, jurors are not compelled to respond to these requests, since they have already discharged their obligations to the court. Lawyers usually need the court's permission to interview jurors in this fashion

Rules of Behavior and Misconduct

Jurors may violate a defendant's right to a fair trial by their own misconduct during a trial. Jurors are not permitted to discuss the trial with other jurors (or with anyone else) until the deliberation phase of the trial. Such conduct leads to the dismissal of the offending juror. Other forms of conduct that could lead to dismissal include sleeping during the trial, being inattentive to the trial proceedings, or reading about the trial in the media while it is in progress. With the dismissal of the juror, the trial may, in some jurisdictions, continue without its full jury complement without violating a defendant's right to a fair trial. To accommodate this potential problem, some courts use a jury of fourteen jurors, with twelve of the fourteen randomly selected at the completion of the trial but before jury deliberation.

—*Paul Bateman*

Suggested Readings

An excellent starting point is Randolph N. Jonakait, *The American Jury System*. New Haven, Conn.: Yale University Press, 2003. For a history of the development of the jury in England and the United States and for a discussion of the constitutional underpinnings of the right to a trial by jury see chapter 1 of James J. Gobert and Walter E. Jordan's *Jury Selection: The Law, Art, and Science of Selecting a Jury* (2d. ed. Colorado Springs: Shepard's/McGraw-Hill, 1990) and *Twelve Good Men and True: The Criminal Trial Jury in England, 1200-1800*, edited by J. S. Cockburn and Thomas A. Green (Princeton, N.J.: Princeton University Press, 1988). For a sampling of jury instructions from the beginning of trial to its conclusion see *Pattern Jury Instructions (Civil Cases), Committee on Pattern Jury Instructions*, District Judges Association, Fifth Circuit (St. Paul, Minn.: West Publishing, 1998). Valerie P. Hans and Neil Vidmar's *Judging the Jury* (New York: Plenum Press, 1986) provides a lively examination of the criticism of jury trials, with examples from some famous twentieth century trials, and a discussion of the development of the American jury as it evolved from the English tradition. John Guinther's *The Jury in America* (New York: Facts on File, 1988) provides a detailed account of jury selection procedures and juror obligations and a discussion of several important research studies related to juries and litigation in the United States. Useful studies of the actual workings of juries include *Punitive Damages: How Juries Decide*, by Cass R. Sunstein et al. (Chicago: University of Chicago Press, 2002), and Stephen D. Easton, *How to Win Jury Trials: Building Credibility with Judges and Jurors* (Philadelphia: American Law Institute-American Bar Association Committee on Continuing Professional Education, 1998).

See also Change of venue; Convictions; Directed verdicts; Grand juries; Jury nullification; Jury sequestration; Trial publicity; Trials; Verdicts.

JURISDICTION

Authority of a specific court to decide a legal dispute and its power to enforce its judgments

No court can exercise its authority unless it has jurisdiction over both the parties and the dispute in question. Jurisdiction over the parties is referred to as personal jurisdiction, while jurisdiction over the dispute is referred to as subject matter jurisdiction.

Personal Jurisdiction

Individuals can be civilly sued in counties in which they reside or in which they do business. For example, a person who lives in Los Angeles County can be sued in courts that are situated in that county. However, persons who live in Suffolk County, New York, cannot be sued in Los Angeles County unless they do business in that county.

The concept of doing business has expanded over time. Originally, persons did business only in the county where their offices, factories, or other physical facilities were located. Given advances in communications, however, including the Internet, persons increasingly engage in business in counties and states far from their principal place of business. Consequently, persons can be sued in any county or state into which they send goods or from which they solicit business, provided that overall circumstances make such lawsuits fair and reasonable. In other words, if only a few orders are placed in a distant state, it would be unfair and unreasonable for the courts of that state to exercise jurisdiction over a nonresident. However, if a significant amount of goods are sold and delivered into a distant state, it is more foreseeable and therefore more fair and reasonable for the nonresident to have to answer in the courts of that state for legal claims arising out of debts or injuries caused by those goods.

For example, if a company with an office and factory in Illinois produces ladders and sells 10 percent of its output in Mississippi, the company can generally be sued in Mississippi by someone in that state who is injured because of a defective ladder. The Mississippi court would have personal jurisdiction over the ladder company because that company is deemed to be doing business in that state, even though it has no office or factory there.

There are other grounds for a court to exercise personal jurisdiction, including presence, consent, ownership, and use or possession of property. In some cases, if a defendant is physically present in a state and is served with legal notice, the court may exercise personal jurisdiction even if the individual does not live or do business there.

Often contracts between companies or individuals in different states specify that any lawsuits arising out of such contracts must be filed in one of those states. For example, if a novelist who lives in Montana signs a contract with a publisher in New York specifying that any dispute arising out of the contract shall be filed in New York, any lawsuit between the novelist and the publisher must be filed in New York unless the contract is invalid or unenforceable for some reason. The novelist has consented to personal jurisdiction in New York.

If real estate or personal property is located in a particular state, the courts of that state have jurisdiction over disputes specifically arising out of that property. Technically, this is referred to as *in rem* jurisdiction. For example, if someone living in Arizona and someone else living in New Jersey together own a piece of vacant land in Maryland, either party could file a lawsuit in Maryland regarding a dispute over that real estate, regardless of the fact that neither party lives in Maryland or does business there other than owning the property. If one party is properly served with notice of the lawsuit and fails to appear or have a lawyer appear in the case, the court may issue a valid judgment affecting the land that is fully binding upon the party who has ignored the lawsuit.

Likewise, if a dispute arises in Tennessee over a truckload of peanuts that originated in Georgia headed for Nebraska, the courts of Tennessee would exercise *in rem* jurisdiction over the shipment of peanuts and could render a valid judgment concerning that specific dispute, because the truck was physically located in Tennessee.

Subject Matter Jurisdiction

For a court to have jurisdiction in a case, it must have subject matter jurisdiction over the dispute itself. This is sometimes referred to as competency. Subject matter jurisdiction involves the amount of money involved in the controversy and the nature of the legal dispute.

Most state courts have two or three levels based on the amount of money in dispute. For example, small-claims courts may have jurisdiction over disputes up to $5,000, municipal courts have jurisdiction over disputes up to $25,000, and superior courts have jurisdiction over disputes greater than $25,000. Federal courts have jurisdiction over claims between citizens of different states if the amount in controversy is at least $100,000.

Certain courts have jurisdiction over particular types of disputes. For example, in most states probate courts have jurisdiction over wills and estates, while family law courts have jurisdiction over divorces and child-custody disputes. Thus, the probate court has no jurisdiction to hear and decide a divorce case, and a family law court has no jurisdiction to adjudicate a disputed will.

Federal courts have exclusive jurisdiction over claims arising under certain federal laws. For example, federal courts have exclusive jurisdiction over copyright, trademark, and patent infringement suits.

Challenging Jurisdiction

A party who believes that a court has no jurisdiction in a matter has a choice to decide when to challenge jurisdiction. A defendant may ignore the suit and then challenge jurisdiction if and when a judgment is entered and the plaintiff seeks to enforce it in the defendant's home state. On the other hand, the defendant may attack jurisdiction at the very outset of a lawsuit. The defendant in the former case runs the risk of losing the opportunity to contest the merits of the claim if jurisdiction is later upheld. The latter approach usually involves greater legal expense, because the defendant must retain legal counsel in a distant state to file a motion challenging jurisdiction.

Even though a court may have valid personal and subject matter jurisdiction over a particular dispute, one of the parties may ask the court to transfer the case to another jurisdiction on the grounds of *forum non convieniens*, or inconvenient forum. The court, in its sound discretion, could decide that because most of the witnesses and evidence in a case are situated in another state, it is more convenient and less expensive to hold the trial in that state rather than where it was originally filed. Since the interests of the parties are usually evenly balanced and each side prefers that the case be held in the home state, a *forum non convieniens* dispute is usually decided according to what is most fair, reasonable, and convenient to third-party witnesses or, in rare instances, whether the public interest is served by transferring the case.

—*Stephen F. Rohde*

Suggested Readings

Two works that deal with the question of jurisdiction are Bernard Ernest Witkin's "Jurisdiction," in *California Procedure* (4th ed. San Francisco: Witkin Legal Institute, 1996), and John M. Haberlin's "Selecting the Forum: Jurisdiction and Venue," in *Bancroft-Whitney's California Civil Practice: Procedure* (2d ed. San Francisco: Bancroft Whitney, 1992). Henry Abraham offers a clear description of the differences among courts in *The Judicial Process: An Introductory Analysis of the Courts of the United States, England, and France* (7th ed. New York: Oxford University Press, 1998). There are more than two thousand federal and state courts. Listings of the various types of courts are available in *BNA's Directory of State and Federal Courts, Judges, and Clerks* (Washington, D.C.: BNA Books, 1997) and *Want's Federal-State Court Directory 1998: All Fifty States and Canada* (New York: Want Publishing, 1997). Lenore Banks examines from a citizen's viewpoint the daunting task of selecting the correct court in *The Judicial Maze: The Court System in New York State* (Albany, N.Y.: League of Women Voters, 1988). For an international perspective, see *Jurisdiction in International Law*, edited by W. Michael Reisman (Brookfield, Vt.: Ashgate/Dartmouth, 1999).

See also Appeal; Cause of action; Change of venue; Court types; Diversity jurisdiction; Long-arm statutes; Multiple jurisdiction offenses; State courts; Summons.